John Adams, Giles Duncombe, John Q. Adams

Trials per Pais

or, The law of England concerning juries by nisi prius, &c. - With a compleat treatise

of the law of evidence, collected from all the books of reports - Vol. 1

John Adams, Giles Duncombe, John Q. Adams

Trials per Pais

*or, The law of England concerning juries by nisi prius, &c. - With a compleat treatise of the
law of evidence, collected from all the books of reports - Vol. 1*

ISBN/EAN: 9783337844493

Printed in Europe, USA, Canada, Australia, Japan

Cover: Foto ©Suzi / pixelio.de

More available books at **www.hansebooks.com**

Trials per Pais:

OR, THE

LAW of ENGLAND

CONCERNING

Juries by *Niſi Prius, &c.*

With a Compleat TREATISE of

The Law of EVIDENCE,

Collected from all the Books of Reports ; together with Precedents, and Forms of Challenges, Demurrers upon Evidence, Bills of Exception, Pleas *Puis le Darrein Continuance, &c.*

The Eighth Edition, with large Additions.

CONTINUED

Down to this preſent Year ; together with ſuch ſubſequent Reſolutions, as have been given in the Courts of *Weſtminſter-Hall* : The Whole put into a Method moſt uſeful and eaſy to the Practiſer.

With a full and copious Table to the whole.

Very Uſeful and Neceſſary for all Lawyers, Attornies, and other Practiſers, eſpecially at the ASSIZES.

Originally compiled by GILES DUNCOMB, heretofore of the *Inner-Temple*, Eſq; and continued by a Careful Hand.

In TWO VOLUMES.

VOL. I.

LONDON:

Printed by H. WOODFALL and W. STRAHAN, Law Printers to the King's moſt Excellent Majeſty ; for T. WALLER, oppoſite to *Fetter-Lane, Fleet Street.* M.DCC.LXVI.

I Do allow the Printing and Publishing of this B O O K, Entituled, *Trials per Pais :* Or, *The Law of* England *concerning Juries by* Nisi prius.

Fr. Pemberton.

TO THE

PRACTISERS

OF THE LAW.

Gentlemen,

IN the Dedication of Books, such Persons should be chosen whose Studies and Profession agree with the Nature of the Subject. To prove *Conclusions* in one *Science* by the *Heterogene Principles* of another; to make a *Grammarian* Patron to a Piece of the *Mathematicks*; to dedicate a Treatise of *Logick* to a Master of *Musick*; or a Matter of *Practice* to a Man of *Speculation*; would not only be im-

proper

proper, but abfurd. You know that in the whole Practice of the Law, there is nothing of greater Excellency, nor of more frequent Ufe, than Trials by *Juries*. In this, our Common Law (and not without juft Caufe) values itfelf beyond the *Imperial Law*, before the *Canon Law*, or any other *Laws* in the World. And feeing the Hopes and Life of all the Procefs, the Force of the Judgment and the Truth, nay, the Right of the Parties lie in the Trial; for as one elegantly fays, *Qui non probat*, at the Trial, *dicitur veritate & jure carere*; and indeed the Knowledge of all the *Law* tends to this: For without Victory at the Trial, to what Purpofe is the Science of the *Law?* The Judge can give no Sentence, no Decifion without it, and muft give Judgment for that Side the Trial goes; therefore I may well fay, 'tis the chief Part of

the

the Practice of the *Law.* And if so, to whom shall I offer this Treatise, but to you the Practisers?

I need say nothing for small Tracts and Treatises; the infinite Number of them in the *Civil Law* (there being for every Title a distinct Tract) nay the Number of them in our *Law*, sufficiently shew their Use.

Joachimus Forbus Ringelbergius, in his Book *de Ratione Studii,* giving Directions what Books Students ought to carry with them when they change Places, and travel from one to another, tells us that out of the Volumes (by Reason of their Bigness not portable) he used to tear several Leaves, and take them with him in his Journeys; and so he said he had served the Works of *Pliny, Tully, Plato, Demosthenes, &c.* altho'

A 3   he

he had given great Prices for them ; which juftifies the Writing of this Treatife, the fubject Matter thereof being of fuch general Ufe in all Circuits.

When I read the elaborate Books of *Farinacius de Teſtibus*, and the three exquifite and incomparable Volumes of *Maſcardus de Probationibus*, in the *Cæſarian* and *Pontifical Laws*, (which Works were fo valued and efteemed that they were looked upon as new Lights fent from Heaven, by the Profeſſors of thofe *Laws*) I could not but fee the Defect and Want of fuch Books in our Law : For furely they are as neceſſary in the one as in the other. And although I cannot compare my weak Endeavours with thofe Excellent and Methodical Works, theirs being intire, this only *quaſi* an Abridgment, fitted for Ufe, not for Show : Yet until more learned and

judicious

judicious Proficients in our Law fhall undertake the Work, I thought fit to produce mine.

To compare this Sort of Trial by *Jury* with the Trials of other Laws and Countries, and declare how much and wherein it excels them all, after *Fortefcue de laudibus, &c.* and his learned *Commentator*, would be like the Arrogance of Limning after *Appelles*, and requires the Room of a Volume, rather than an Epiftle. And confidering my own Infufficiencies, I fhall praife it more by faying nothing, than all I can : For to fay lefs than a Thing deferves, would be, inftead of an Encomium, a Difparagement. Therefore I fhall content myfelf, only to fay, That Trials in other Laws are by Witneffes only, privately examined ; this, by Witneffes publickly examined and confronted ; and by *Jury* alfo, and fo confequently the

Fact

Fact is settled with the greater Certainty of Truth, upon which the Uprightness of the Judgment depends.

It would be well if there were less Corruption in the returning of *Juries*; but I think 'tis paralell'd, if not exceeded, by that of examining Witnesses privately, on whose Depositions the Trials in other Laws consist: And so there must be no Objection against the Thing. I hope an Expedient may be found out to prevent the Corruption in returning *Juries*, but I believe it never can in the other.

To say this Trial by *Jury* is too popular in a Monarchy, would be a good Objection from a *Frenchman*, but not of any *Englishman*, who lives under the best tempered Monarchy, and the best Sort of Government in the World, to which
this

this Manner of Trial is ſo proper and accommodated, that neither the Wiſdom of our Anceſtors could, nor (I may ſay) can this preſent, nor After-Ages invent a better.

But as the unſkilful *Painter* drew a Curtain before what he could not expreſs with his Pencil, ſo muſt I veil with Silence the Excellencies of this celebrated *Trial*, which I am not able to delineate.

Gentlemen,

To make an Apology for the Stile of a Law-Book, eſpecially of an Epitome, would be a vain Thing ; *Ornari res ipſa negat, contenta doceri* ; neither ſhall I make any Apology for my undertaking this Work : If 'twas better performed, yet *Momus* would be carping ; and if it was worſe, it would

would be good enough for him, who cannot, or will not do it better : Be it what it will, your kind Reception will abundantly satisfy

Your Servant,

G. *Duncombe.*

THE

PREFACE

TO THE

FIRST EDITION.

THE Philofopher could not fee a Man unlefs he heard him fpeak; *Loquere ut videam.* Speech is the Index of the Mind, and the Mind only difcriminates the Man. For although an *Ideot*, who hath but the Shape of a Man, may with Silence fo hide his Folly, that Strangers to his Manners cannot difcern him from a Sophifter: Yet, doubtlefs, Silence is the greateft Enemy to Learning, the Grave wherein Oblivion buries the Parts and Knowledge of the braveft Spirits.

Where-

The PREFACE.

Hiſtor. facil.
Princeps.

Wherefore learned *Saluſt*, from this takes his *Exordium*; *Omnes homines qui ſeſe ſtudent præſtare cæteris animalibus, ſumma ope niti decet, ne vitam ſilentio tranſeant, veluti pecora* : Thoſe Men who would excel Beaſts, ſhould labour that their Lives might not paſs in ſuch Silence as Beaſts do. It ſeems he deemed that Man little ſuperior to a Beaſt, who acted nothing to prolong his Memory : For this he held to be the Duty of every Man, ſaying, *Quo mihi rectius eſſe videtur, ingenii quam virium opibus gloriam quærere ; & quoniam vita ipſa, qua fruimur, brevis eſt, memoriam noſtri quam maxime longam efficere* : In my Opinion, it is far better to acquire Glory by the Riches of Wit, than Strength ; and becauſe our Lives are ſhort of themſelves, we ſhould endeavour by Ingenuity to eternize their Memory.

Nulla dies
ſine linea.

And to effect this *Nulla dies abeat, quin linea ducta ſuperſit* : No Day ſhould paſs over our Heads, wherein we ſhould not act ſome memorable exploit : Men ſhould not live like *Snails*, never ſtirring out of their Houſes ; but be active (I mean not Buſy-Bodies in other Mens Matters, but) in their own Callings, of which the wiſe *Cato* tells us, *Every Man ſhould give a reaſonable Account :* And if we believe the famous

mous *Seneca, Nihil est turpius quam grandis natu senex, qui nullum habet vitæ suæ argumentum, quo diu se vixisse dicat præter ætatem :* Nothing is more unworthy than an old Man, who has nothing to shew for his Antiquity but a grey Beard; whose Soul served only as Salt to keep his Body sweet; and is no sooner Dead, than forgotten, long before he is half rotten : Yet who is so apt to deride the Endeavours of other Men, as this ancient *Ignoramus,* whose Wrinkles in his Face, worn-out Looks, and many Years, sway more with the vulgar People, than all the Arguments of Law or Reason? Had *Seneca* been such a silent *Momus,* the World would never have been blest with his so learned Works. And doubtless Writing Books is needful in no Science more than in the Law. For without Books, how would the Lawyers do for Arguments at the Bar, or Resolutions at their Chambers; whence the Oracle, Sir *Edward Coke,* pronounces this, *Omnes debere Jurisprudentiæ libris componendis animum adjicere :* That all Men ought to addict themselves to the composing Books of Law; some to the Reporting of the Judgments and Resolutions of the Judges, who are *Lex Loquens*; and some to the collecting of those Cases and Resolutions, methodizing and fitting them for some particular Purpose, as *Littleton, Staundford,*

The PREFACE.

Staundford, Fitzherbert, Crompton, Perkins, Finch, &c. And indeed, moſt of the Law Books extant, if not all, (ſetting aſide the Reports) are nothing elſe but Collections out of others. This I ſpeak, not in Derogation of them in the leaſt; for as 'tis equally, if not more laborious, ſo 'tis full as glorious, judiciouſly to cull authentick Caſes out of the Volumes of the Law, (where ſo many are no Law) and rightfully place them in a particular Treatiſe, as 'tis to report the Judgments and Reſolutions from the Mouth of the Court; for the Reporter is but the Court's Secretary, and *Coke's Inſtitutes* merit as much as his Reports; and *Aſh's* Tables, *Fitzherbert* and *Brook's* Abridgments are as uſeful as the Year-Books themſelves, of which Kind of Collections, one elegantly thus breaks out, *Quo quidem beneficio, haud ſcio, an aliud aut legum Candidatis magis gratum, aut Reipublicæ magis commodum, aut divini honoris illuſtrationi magis idoneum, vel cogitando quidem conſequi quiſquam poterit.* Than which Benefit I know not whether any Man can ever imagine another, either to Lawyers more grateful, or to the Commonwealth more profitable, or for the Illuſtration of Divine Honour more fit. For with the leaſt Labour, a ſmall Price, and little Time, they preſent you with thoſe Reſolutions and Judgments
which

which lie fcatter'd in the voluminous Books of the Law; which would otherwife coft much Time, Pains and Charges to find out. The Thoughts of which Publick Good firft gave Life to thefe Endeavours of mine: Not that any one fhould in the leaft imagine, that I am fo guilty of vain Oftentation, as to believe that my Parts or Abilities can perform any Thing in this Kind like other Men: No, *Ipfe mihi nunquam Judice me placui.* I could never yet pleafe myfelf with my own Labours, much lefs are they worthy to pleafe others; *haud equidem tali me dignor Honore.* However, when I confider, that no Man hath yet written particularly concerning this Subject, and of what general Ufe it is; I doubt not but that this Treatife will receive a favourable Conftruction from moft Men, and a plaufible Acceptation from others.

The Ufe of it is in a Manner Epidemical; fince moft Mens Lives and Eftates are fubject to that Trial *per Pais* here demonftrated; but in particular the Practifers at Law (efpecially *Circuit-Advocates, Attornies, Solicitors, Clerks,* &c.) and all *Jurors* (for whofe Direction it is of fingular Ufe) are chiefly concerned herein. But I will not hang a Bufh out, to invite and prepoffefs your Judgments, *Vincat Utilitas.* The Profit which every ingenious Reader

The Ufe of the Book.

4   fhall

shall gather out of it, will speak more for it than the best Eulogical Preface.

And for my own Part, I profess my self to be *Philomathes*, but not *Polymathes*. And notwithstanding the hard-favoured Objections which some Men cast upon it, I really think the Study of the Law to be the most pleasant Study in the World. And he which delighteth in the Study of any other Art or Science, must consequently be delighted with this. For the Knowledge of the Law, as *Doderidge* saith, is most truly stiled, *Rerum Divinarum humanarumque scientia*, and worthily imputed to be the *Science of Sciences*, for therein lies hid the Knowledge of every other Learned Science.

So that he which gives himself to the Study of Divinity, may here fill himself with holy and pious Principles of Divine Laws: For, *Lex est sanctio sancta, jubens honesta, & prohibens contraria; sanctum etenim oportet esse quod sanctum definitum:* The Law is a holy Sanction or Decree, commanding Things that be honest, and forbidding the Contraries: Now the Thing must needs be holy, which by Definition is determined to be holy. So that in this Respect, saith *Fortescuc*, Men may well call Lawyers *Sacerdotes*, that is, Givers

or

or Teachers of Holy Things. For the Laws being Holy, it follows that the Minifters and Setters forth of them muft be Givers of Holy Things; and fo by Interpretation doth *Sacerdos* fignify; and doubtlefs, he which duly confiders thofe Rules of *Theology*, which lie fcattered throughout the whole Body of the Law, muft needs conclude our Laws to be Commentaries upon the Old and New Teftament; and do fo much bear the Image *Legis Divinæ*, that they may well be attributed to the Moft High.

The Rules of *Grammar*, *Philofophy Natural*, *Political*, *Oeconomick* and *Moral*; as alfo the Grounds of *Logic*, and of other Arts and Sciences, fo much abound in our Books, that the very Reading of the Law will make a Man *Mafter* of thofe Sciences. And fince *Rhetorick* is *Ars ornate dicendi*, and confifteth of thofe two Parts *Elocution* and *Pronunciation*, How can we read in our Law Books thofe learned Arguments, elegant Speeches and Judgments, pronounced with fuch Eloquence and Elegance of Words and Matter, and not conclude, That Rhetorick is the Glory and Grace of a Lawyer? Though fome (not gifted that Way) would perfwade us that the Law hath little Relation to it.

If ·

The PREFACE.

If any Man be delighted in hiſtory, let him read the Books of Law, which are nothing elſe but Annals and Chronicles of Things done and acted from Year to Year, in which every Caſe preſents you with a *petit* Hiſtory; and if Variety of Matter doth moſt delight the Reader, doubtleſs, the reading of thoſe Caſes, (which differ like Men's Faces) tho' like the Stars in Number, is the moſt pleaſant Reading in the World.

I thought to have expatiated myſelf in this Eulogical Commendation of the Study of the Law; but when I conſider the Glory of the Thing itſelf, I think it but in vain to light the Sun with Candles; and as no Arguments will perſwade one to love againſt Nature; ſo he, whom the Excellency of the Law itſelf cannot invite to ſtudy it, will never be forced to it with the Fiſt of Logic, or other perſwaſion: Wherefore 'tis now Time to expoſe myſelf to the Cenſure of the Reader, who always judges according to his Capacity or Affection; for which Cauſe, if I were to chuſe my Readers, I could wiſh with *Caius Lucilius, Quod ea quæ ſcribo, neque ab indoctiſſimis, neque a doctiſſimis legi, quod alteri nihil intelligerent, alteri plus fortaſſe, quam ipſe de ſe:* That this Trea-

tiſe

tife might not be read of the moft learned, nor of thofe who are not learned at
all, becaufe thefe underftand nothing, and
the others more perhaps than myfelf.

However, I put this Requeft to all, *Ut* Bracton, Lib.
fi quid fuperfluum, vel perperam pofitum in 1. f. 1.
hoc opere intervenerit, illud corrigant &
emendent, vel conniventibus oculis pertran-
feant: Cum omnia habere in memoria, &
in nullo peccare, divinum fit potius quam
humanum: That if any Thing be fuper-
fluous, and placed amifs in this Work, that
they will either correct and amend it, or
without Carping connive at it; fince to
remember to do all Things right, and nothing amifs, is rather the Part of God than
Man: Wherefore, let him which never
offended, caft the firft Stone.

A Summary of the Contents of each Chapter in this BOOK.

CHAP.

The CONTENTS.

CHAP. IX.

CHAP. X.

CHAP. XI.

CHAP. XII.

CHAP.

The CONTENTS.

CHAP. XIII.

CHAP. XIV.

V O L. II.

CHAP. XV.

CHAP. XVI.

Trials

Trials per Pais.

CHAP. I.

The Derivation of the Word Jury. *The Definition, Antiquity and Excellency of Juries.*

JURY (Jurata) cometh of the *French* Word *Jurer, i. e. Jurare*; and fignifieth in Law, thofe twelve Men who are fworn *Judges* in *Matters of Fact*, evidenced by Witneffes, and debated before them: I call them *Judges*, becaufe, as 'tis the Property of the *Court, jus dicere*; fo it is in the Power of the *Jury* to determine the *Fact*, upon an Evidence *Pro* and *Con.* according to thofe common *Adages, Ad quæftionem Juris refpondent Judices; Ad quæftionem Facti refpondent Juratores:* And as the *Judgment* of the Court ought to be guided by the *Law*, fo is the *Verdict* of the *Jury* by the Evidence. They of the *Jury* are called *Juratores, Jurors, a jurando*, as in ancient Laws *Sacramentales, a Sacramento præftando.*

I need not here divide, and fhew the Differences of *Juries*, nor the feveral Sorts, they being fo well known, *viz.* The *Grand Jury*, or *Great Inqueft*, and *Petty Jury*, or *Jury of*

Vide cap. 12. Juries.

Vide cap. 15.

The Antiquity and Excellency of Juries.

Life and Death, in Criminal Caufes; and in Civil Caufes the *Affize Jury*; *Inqueft of Office*, by fome called *Inqueft of Jury*, and *Inqueft of Office*. Something concerning each of thefe, will incidently be fpoken of in what follows. As to the Excellency of *Juries*, it appears from their Antiquity.

Sir *Henry Spelman*, *verb.* (*Inquæftio*) fays, Trial by *Juries* was ufed in *England*, *Normanis nondum ingreffis, Leg. Ed. Confeff. ca.* 38. *Poftea inquififfet Juftitia*, i. e. (*Juftitiarius*) *per Lagamannos*, i. e. (*legales homines*) *& per meliores homines de Burgo*, *vel de Villa*, *vel de Hundredo*, *ubi manfiffet Emptòr*, *&c.*

For as to the Trial by twelve Men, though Mr. *Daniel* and *Polydore Virgil* deny it to be older than the Conqueft, and the latter fays, there is no Religion in it, but in the Number; yet he ftands fairly corrected by that excellent and learned Antiquary, Mr. *Camdèn*, *p.* 153. who fays, *Whereas* Polydore Virgil *writeth*, *That* William *the Conqueror firft brought in the Trial by twelve Men*, *there is nothing more untrue*; *for it is moft certain and apparent by the Laws of* Ethelred, *that it was in Ufe many Years before*, &c. And whereas *Lamb. verb.* (*Centuria*) fays, *In fingulis Centuriis Comitia funto*, *atque liberæ Conditionis viri duodeni*, *ætate fuperiores*, *una cum Præpofito Sacra tenentes jurento*, *fe adeo virum aliquem innocentem haud damnaturos*, *fontemve abfoluturos*, he refers to the Laws of *Ethelred*, *chap.* 4. cited by the learned *Spelman*, *verb.* (*Jurata.*)

And to the fame doth my Lord *Coke* refer *Com. fuper Lit.* 155. and Preface to his third and eighth Report. And as to the Religion in the Number of twelve, my Lord *Coke* gives

Inftances

Inftances *ubi fupra*, and Sir *Henry Spelman*, in *verb.* (*Jurata*) *fupra*, makes Addition thereto.

So that I may truely fay, Trials by *Juries* have been ufed in this Nation Time out of Mind, and were contemporary and coeval with the firft Civil Government thereof, and Adminiftration of Juftice; for amongft the firft Inhabitants, the *Britains*, the *Freeholders* were ufed in all Trials.

And Trial by *Juries* was (as you fee practifed by the *Saxons*) continued by the *Normans*, and confirmed by *Magna Charta*; and was ever fo efteemed and prized in this Ifland, that no Conqueft, no Change of Government ever prevailed to alter it.

'Tis true, Trials by *Juries* before the Time of *H.* 2. were not fo frequent, becaufe *Sadæ* or *Purgationes, Ordalia*, Trials by hot Iron, hot Water, cold Water, Duels, and other fuperftitious Ways were then in Ufe; but Trials by *Juries* were here in the *Saxons* Time, and were found here, and not brought in by *William the Conqueror* from *Normandy*; nay, rather fettled by *Edward the Confeffor* in *Normandy*, where he a long Time was, and taught many Laws, as you may fee in the Book of the Cuftoms of *Normandy*.

Glanvil, lib. 2. cap. 7. fays, *Ex æquitate autem maxima prodita eft legalis ifta inftitutio,* fpeaking of thefe Trials in Oppofition to Duels, *&c.*

Their general Ufe (being the only Triers of The Ufe of *Chofes in fait*, almoft in all Courts through-Juries. out *England*) fpeaks them a *publick Good.* To be tried by one's Peers is the greateft Privilege a Subject can wifh for; and fo excellent is the Conftitution of the Government of this Kingdom, that no Subject shall be tried but by his Peers. The Lords by theirs, the Commons by theirs; which is the Fortress and Bulwark of their Lives, Liberties and Estates: And if the Good of the Subject be the Good of the King, as most certainly it is, then those are Enemies to the Good of the King and State, who attempt to alter or invade this fundamental Principle, in the Administration of the Justice of this Realm, by which the King's Prerogative has flourished, and the just Liberties of the People have been secured so many Ages.

And what Answer shall I make to the Princes, *vehementer admiror,* (*videlicet,* Wherefore are not *Juries* used in other *Countries,* if they are so good?) but that of *Fortescue* the Learned, who best could tell, *scil.* That other *Countries* can scarce produce one *Jury* so well accomplish'd with *Wealth* and *Ingeny,* as one *County,* nay, one *Hundred* can in *England.*

Fortescue, cap. 29.

But not to dwell in the *Porch,* I will address myself to the *Gravity* of the *Law,* where you must not so much expect the *Flash* of *Rhetorick* as the *Light* of *Reason*; no, the *Law* knows best how to express herself in her own *Terms*; wherefore all other *Sciences* must learn, with Reverence, to keep their Distance, and (as the Golden *Finch* sings) be glad to have their *Sparks* raked up in her *Ashes.*

Things, not Words, most regarded in the Law.

Finch, c. 3.

And since an *Issue* is *previous,* and the Matter of a Trial, I shall first give you the Description thereof, and then touch upon the several Trials allowed by the Law, for the Discussion of the Truth.

CHAP.

C H A P. II.

Of an Iſſue, and divers Sorts of Trials thereof; and when a Trial ſhall be by a Jury, and when not; when by Certificate, when by the Spiritual Law, when by Battel, and when by an Almanack; when Iſſue ſhall be firſt tried per Pais; *what ſhall be tried by the Court; and what by Examination of the Attorney, Sheriff,* &c.

ISSUE, *(Exitus)* ſaith *Coke,* is a ſingle, certain and material Point, iſſuing out of the Allegations and Pleas of the *Plaintiff* and *Defendant,* conſiſting regularly upon an Affirmative and Negative, to be tried by twelve Men: And it is two-fold, *ſcil.* either ſpecial, as where the ſpecial Matter is pleaded; or general, as in Treſpaſs, *Not Guilty:* In Aſſize, *Nul tort, Nul diſſeiſin,* &c. And as an Iſſue natural cometh of two ſeveral Perſons, ſo an Iſſue legal iſſueth out of two ſeveral Allegations of adverſe Parties.

Iſſues are join'd upon an Affirmative and Negative, and being taken generally it refers to the Count and not to the Writ; and when all is confeſs'd and avoided, it cannot be taken upon the Time.

Special Iſſues are to be taken in one material Point, which may be beſt underſtood and tried.

No Iſſue can be taken after a Judgment *quod eat inde ſine die;* it may be well taken upon a

1 Inſt. f. 126.
Omnia unum aliquem ſortiuntur exitum, vel per patriam, vel per Judices terminandum.
Finch Epiſtle.

B 3   *Pre-*

Prefcription, but not upon a *Poffeffion only. Vin. Trial* 58.

Two Negatives fhall not be fuffer'd, nor *two Affirmatives* unlefs the Iffue cannot otherwife be tried; but where a Negative goes before and an Affirmative follows, the Iffue is perfect *et e con.*

It cannot be taken upon a *Negative pregnant* which implies other fufficient Matter, but upon that which is fingle and fimple.

An Iffue join'd upon an *abfque hoc, &c.* ought to have an Affirmative after it, and fome Iffues are good upon Matter affirm'd and denied, tho' not exprefs'd in precife Words; nor is an Affirmative and a Negative always requifite to the forming of an Iffue, as in the Cafe of *Partes finis nihil habuerunt.*

General Iffues are always in the *Negative*, and contrived in fuch Words as not to deny the whole Fact in the Count.

Special Iffues are, where Matter Special is alledged in defence, and both Parties thereupon join Iffue, or in Demurrer. *Vin. ubi fupra* 63.

Where the Defence confifts in Matter of *Law*, the Defendant *may* plead Specially, but where it is purely of *Fact* he *muft* plead the general Iffue; and where a Man hath not any Colour, the general Iffue is to be taken.

Some Negative Pleas are Iffues of themfelves, whereto neither Plaintiff or Defendant can reply, otherwife than by a *Similiter*, and a Demurrer is an Iffue in Law to be tried by the Court, and Iffues ought to be joined upon what is moft material in the Pleadings, and he who pleads the firft Negative concludes the Iffue; but if the Defendant plead in the Negative to the *Writ*, the Plaintiff fhall reply in the Affirmative and conclude the Iffue. *ibm.* 68.

And to give you likewife his Definition of Trials, 1 Inft. *Trial*, it is to find out, by due Examination, 124. b. the Truth of the Point in Iffue, or Queftion between the Parties, whereupon Judgment may be given: And as the Queftion between the *Note*, That Parties is two-fold, fo is the Trial thereof; for upon a De-either it is *quæftio juris*, (and that fhall be tried murrer to by the *Judges*, either upon a Demurrer, Spe-fue to Part, cial Verdict or Exception: For, *Cuilibet in fua* though it is *arte perito eft credendum, & quod quifque no-* the beft Way *verit, in hoc fe exerceat,*) or it is *quæftio facti* : And to give Judg-the Trial of the Fact is in divers Sorts; Firft, *quæftio juris* chiefly, and moft commonly, by a *Jury* of firft, yet the twelve Men, (of which Kind of Trial my De-Court may try fign is principally to treat in this Book.) the *quæftio facti* firft, at their Difcretion. 1 *Inft.* 72, 125. *Latch* 4. *Rol.* Tit. *Trials,* 626, 723.

For by twelve Men are Matters of Fact (for Proceedings the moft part) tried with us in *England,* in in Civil Caufes both Criminal and Civil; in Caufes Civil, Caufes. after both Parties have faid what they can one againft another in Pleading; if there arife a Queftion about any Matter of Fact, it is refer-red to twelve indifferent Men, to be impanel-led by the Sheriff; and as they bring in their *Verdict,* fo Judgment paffeth. And this the Judge is to declare as the Law is upon the Fact found: For the Judge faith, the *Jury* finds thus, and then the Law is thus, and fo we judge. For the Law arifes upon the Fact.

For Criminal Caufes the Courfe is thus: At Proceedings the *King's Bench* for *Middlefex,* and at the great in Criminal and general *Affizes,* and at the general *Seffions of* Caufes.

the Peace, there is one *Jury*, called the *Grand Jury*, which confifts commonly of twenty-four fubftantial Men, out of one or more Hundreds within the County, returned by the *Sheriff*, and they are to confider of all Bills of Indictment prefented to them, which they either approve of, by writing from Bill, or difapprove, by writing upon them not found; and thofe which they approve of, are to be tried by another *Jury* called the *Petit Jury*. Or the *Grand Jury* may charge any Perfon, upon their own *Prefentment*, which will be of the Force of an Indictment; and the Party charged may traverfe the Offence, and bring it to be tried by a *Petit Jury*.

Some leffer Matters in thefe Courts are proceeded upon without *Jury*, and fome Things are removed by *Certiorari* into higher Courts, and then muft be tried there; and that Thing, to which there is a Traverfe put in, muft be tried and ended by a *Petit Jury*, which (for the moft part) in all Civil and Criminal Caufes are but twelve Men, which ought to be Free Men, not Villains or Aliens, and lawful Men not outlawed, and alfo Men of Worth and Honefty.

But becaufe it is neceffary to be known, that there are many Ways allowed by the Common Law to try Matters of Fact, befides this by *Juries*, I will here repeat fome of them: And for this, firft hear the *Oracle*, who tells you, that he had read of fix Kinds of *Certificates* allowed for *Trials* by the Common Law.

1 Inft. 74.

Trials by Cert'ficate:

1. The doing of Service by him that holdeth by *Efcuage* in *Scotland*, was to be tried by the *King's Marfhal* of the Army, *Per fon Certificate*

tificate en escript south son seal que serra mis a Justices, saith *Littleton.*

2. If it be alledged in Avoidance of an Outlawry, that the Defendant was in Prison at *Bourdeaux,* in the Service of the *Mayor* of *Bourdeaux,* it shall be tried by the Certificate of the Mayor of *Bourdeaux.* *Note*; This was when *Bourdeaux* was Parcel of the Dominions of the King of *England. Rol.* Tit. *Trial, f.* 583.

3. For Matters within the Realm, the Custom of *London* shall be certified by the Mayor and *Aldermen,* by the Mouth of the *Recorder.* *Vide apres* 14.

4. By the *Certificate* of the *Sheriff,* upon a Writ to him directed, in Case of Privilege, if one be a Citizen or Foreigner.

5. Trial of Records by *Certificate* of the *Judges,* in whose Custody they are by Law. All these be in Temporal Causes.

6. In Causes Ecclesiastical, as Loyalty of Marriage, general Bastardy, Excommengement, Profession: These and the like, are regularly to be tried by the *Certificate* of the *Ordinary.* *Vide apres* 13.

If the *Defendant* claim his Privilege as a Scholar of the University of *Oxon,* of such a College or Hall: This shall not be tried by *Certificate,* but *per Pais. Rol.* Tit. *Trial,* 583. *N.* 1.

Concerning *Certificates* of Spiritual Persons, *vide Rol. ibid* 591, 592.

7. A Record shall be tried by the Record Records. itself, and not *per Pais.* (a) But Matter of Fact

(a) A Matter of Record before the Justices shall not be put in Trial per Pais, whether it be so as the Record proves, or not; but it shall be tried by the Record itself. *Vin. Abr.* Tit. *Trial,* 9 pl. 1.

con-

concerning a *Record* is triable by a Jury; as whether a Plaint, &c. was levied according to the Custom; and *non prosecutus est ullum breve*, is triable by the Country. *Hob.* 244. *Hutt.* 20. So if a Statute hath two Seals, or but one, 1 *Leon.* 229. 2 *Cro.* 375. 1 *Inst.* 125. *b.* So in a *Per quæ servitia*, if the Tenant *says, that he did not hold of the Conusor the Day of the Note levied,* this shall be tried *per Pais.* *Vin. Abr.* Tit. *Trial* 9. *pl.* 3. cites 11 *H.* 4. 72. *b.* In Escape upon a *Cepi* returned, *Ne unques in son gard* shall be tried *per Record*; but upon a *Capias* not returned, the Prisal shall be tried *per Pais.* So shall an Action brought by *Covin,* for the *Covin* is not of Record. In *Scire Facias* by the King, to have Execution of a Judgment in *Quære Impedit,* if the Defendant pleads, that after the Recovery the King presented thereto, and so Judgment executed; and the Issue is, Whether the King present by Cause of the Judgment, or by Cause of a Voidance after the Death of *J. S.* who was presented by a Stranger after the Voidance upon which the King had Judgment; this shall be tried *per Pais,* and not by Record, though it was said, that it is of Record in Chancery for what Cause the King presented. *Vin. Abr.* Tit. *Trial* 10. *pl.* 11. And for this Reason, in pleading of *Letters Patent* the Place need not be alledged where the *Letters Patent* were made, because the *Defendant* cannot plead *Nul tiel Record,* but must plead *Non concessit,* and then the Jury shall come from the Place where the Lands lie. *Vide l.* 6. *f.* 15. 1 *Inst.* 117, 260. *Plo. Com.* 231. But upon a *Non est factum* pleaded to a *Deed,* there must be a Place alledged where the *Deed* was made, because (though the *Deed,* as to the

Matter

(margin: Mixt with Fact.)

(margin: Deed.)

Matter of Law, be triable by the Court, yet) the Sealing and Delivery thereof, and other Matters of Fact, muſt be tried by the Jury; ſo that in this Caſe of a *Deed*, there is a Trial *per Pais*, and by the Court.   1 *Inſt. f.* 35. *Vide apres* 15.

The Iſſue upon an Indictment, or Acquittal thereupon, it ſhall be tried by the Record. *Vin. Abr.* Tit. *Trial* 9. *fol.* 2. cites 20 *H.* 6. 10. *b.* If the Iſſue be *upon an Allowance of a Protection in banco*, it ſhall be tried by the Record. *Vin. Abr.* Tit. *Trial* 9. *pl.* 4. cites 20 *H.* 6. 10. *b.* In Debt againſt the Warden of the Fleet for an eſcape, if the iſſue was where he was impriſoned upon the Execution, or for other Cauſe, it ſhall be tried by the Record. *Ibid. p.* 6. If a Man juſtifies an Impriſonment, becauſe he is a Juſtice of the Peace; this Matter ſhall be tried by the Record, and not *per Pais. Vin. Abr.* 10. *pl.* 9. In debt upon an eſcape againſt the Mayor of the Staple for ſuffering *J. S.* in Execution on a Statute Staple, to go at large, if Defendant ſays that he was not in Priſon upon the Execution, but upon a Plaint there; this Iſſue ſhall be tried *per Pais*; becauſe the Defendant is to certify the Record, if he ſhall be tried by it, which is not reaſonable in his own Cauſe; for peradventure he will certify it falſly. If the Iſſue be whether a ſuppoſed Statute Merchant be true or forged, it ſhall be tried by the Record where it was acknowledged, if the Mayor who took it be alive, though he be out of the Office now; for it is a Matter of Record. 17 *E.* 3. 39. *b.* So if the Mayor be dead; for it continues a Record triable. *Contra* 17 *E.* 3. 49. *b. Vin. Abr.* Tit.

Trial

What Iſſues ſhall be tried *per Record.*

Trial 10. Whether a Place be within the Ligeance of the King of *England* or in *Scotland*. A *Fine sur Release* rendering his Body in Discharge of his Bail, shall be tried by the *Record*. *Rol.* Tit. *Trial*, 574. The Time of inrolling *Letters Patent* shall be tried *per Pais*. *Co. Lib.* 4. 71. 9 *H.* 7. 2.

Office rasing a Record.   *Seisin* of an Office in any Court, or rasing a Record in any Court, by the *Filazers* and *Attorneys* of the Court.

Peers. **The Lords may command a Jury to be impanelled to try Misdemeanors.**   8. A *Peer* of the *Realm*, *i. e.* a *Lord* of the Parliament, shall upon an Indictment of Treason or Felony, Misprision of Treason, and Misprision of Felony, be tried by his *Peers*, without Oath. 1 *H.* 4. 2. But in Appeal at the Suit of the Party, he shall be tried *per probos & legales homines Juratores.* 10 *E.* 4. 6. *&c.* because that is not the King's Suit, but the Party's. *Vide lib.* 9. 31. *Le case del Abbot de Strata Marcella.* And in a *Præmunire*, his Trial shall be *per Pais.* *Bulst.* 1 *Part*, 198. Dutchesses, Countesses or Baronesses, although married, shall be tried as *Peers* of the *Realm* are; but so shall not Bishops and Abbots. *Stam.* 153. 20 *H.* 6. 9. 2 *Inst.* 48, 49, 50, 156. *b.* 294. 2 *Inst.* 30. But Bishops shall be tried by the *Peers* in Parliament.

12 Rep. 93. **Lamb. Inst. f. 520.** **3 Inst. 30.**

9. Always when *Reasonableness* is in question, it shall be determined by the *Court* in which the Action dependeth; so shall the Exposition of Statutes, and the Maxims and *General Customs* of the Realm, but it is otherwise of particular Customs, for they shall be tried *per Pais. Vin. Trial*, 22.

Nothing the Judges of Record do, as *Judges*, shall be tried by the Country. *Idem* 23.

The

The Cuftoms and Ufages of every Court Cuftoms of fhall be tried by the Judges of the fame Court, Courts, &c. if they are pleaded in the fame Court, *ibid.* tried by the Judges. and many other Things are tried by the Judges; as the Reafonablenefs of a Fine of an Offender, or upon Surrender of a Copyhold Eftate; and fo it is of Cuftoms, Services, and alfo of the Time that a Tenant at Will fhall have to carry away his Goods; and thefe Cafes come under the Rule which makes *Matter of Law to be tried by the Judges. Vide* 1 *Inft. f.* 59. *b.* And in fome Cafes Matter of Fact fhall be tried by the Judges; as if the Plaintiff appear by *Attorney* in Court, and then the Defendant pleads that the Plaintiff is dead; if one appears, and faith he is the Plaintiff, whether he is or not, fhall be tried by the *Judges; lib.* 9. 30. So the Nonage of an Infant, generally by Infpec- Infpection. tion of the Court. But in many Cafes, In- V. Bulft. fancy fhall be tried *per Pais,* as if an Infant par. 131. appear by Attorney, in *Error,* this fhall be Rol. Tit. tried *per Pais, lib.* 9. 31. and fo it is in an Trials, 571. *Æftate probanda.*

Maihem: In an Appeal of *Maihem,* the Court Maihem. may adjudge this upon the View, at the Prayer of the Defendant.

Maihem may be tried again by the Court, by Infpection for Increafe of Damages upon the Infpection of Surgeons, if the Court be in Doubt, and the Adjudication made upon fuch View is peremptory and conclufive to each Party; but then thefe Things are to be confidered; *Firft,* It muft be a *Maihem,* and not a bare Wounding. *Secondly,* The *Maihem* muft be afcertained in the Declaration. fo as that it may appear that the *Maihem* infpected, and the *Maihem* in the Declaration be all one; as was refolved, *Mich.*

Mich. 21 *Car.* 2. *B. R.* in the Case of *Badwel* and *Burford* ; the principal Case of which was, That the Defendant whipp'd the Plaintiff's Horse, which made him throw her, and another Horse trod on her, and maim'd her Hand; and adjudged no Increase of Damages in that Case, being a consequential, and not a direct *Maihem.* *V. Rol. Trial,* 578.

Trial by In-
spection be-
cause of Re-
cord.

Nonage in a *Writ of Error* to reverse a Judgment, or a Fine of the Tenant by Resceit of one vouched *come deins age, & issint praie le parol a demurrer,* Nonage *sur aid praier en Appeal, Audita Querela,* to avoid a *Statute, Recognizance, Accompt* ; and in all Actions where 'tis prayed that the *parol demurroit,* Nonage shall be tried *per Inspection.* But in Accompt against one of full Age, if he plead Nonage when he was Bailiff, this cannot be tried by Inspection. *Rol.* Tit. *Trials,* 572. How this Trial by Inspection shall be, *vide Rol. ibid.* at large.

In all Cases where the Matter may be tried by Inspection, Examination or Discretion of the *Justices,* if they doubt the Matter, they may refuse to try this, and compel the Parties to a Trial *per Pais,* or other Proofs. 21 *H.* 7. 40. *per touts Justices.*

The Court may examine the Infant upon a *Voier dire,* whether he be within age, and may examine the Godfather and Godmother. In all Cases where the Matter may be tried by Examination or Discretion of the Justices, they may if in Doubt refuse it, and compel the Party to put it in Trial of the Country ; as in Infancy the Court may refuse to try by Inspection, and compel the Party to try it *per Pais.*

In Error by an Infant to reverſe *a Fine*, after Inſpection and found *within Age*, the Judgment may be reverſed after his full Age.   But if an Infant ſuffer a *Common Recovery* by Guardian as Tenant to the Præcipe, and within Age brings Error to reverſe it; yet the Infancy, admitting it is erroneous, ſhall not be tried by *Inſpection*, as in the Caſe of a Fine.   Though in the Caſe of *Raby* and *Robinſon*, *Keb.* 892. on a Recovery ſuffered by an Infant as Vouchee, it was ſaid by *Twiſden*, and allowed by *Keeling*, as an excellent Difference, as beſt to prevent Delay, that the Trial may be by *Pais*, or Inſpection. *Vin.* Title *Trial* 7, 8.

The Court is Judge of the Infancy, and not the Jury, where the Infant hath been inſpected by the Court, and the Infancy recorded; as in the Caſe of *Fletcher* and *Vidian* in *Styles* 472. And in the Caſe of *Couſins*; 1 *Vent.* 69. in Error to reverſe a Fine for Infancy, the Party being in Court was inſpected, and upon Affidavits and a Copy of the Pariſh Regiſter of the Party's Age, the Inſpection was recorded by the Court who declared the Iſſue of Infancy might be tried at any Time after full Age. *Vin. ſup.*

10. There are many Trials allowed by the Common Law, by Witneſſes only, without a Jury; as of the Life and Death of the Huſband, in *Dower*; ſo the *Proof* of a *Summons*, or the *Challenge* of a *Juror*, muſt be tried by Witneſſes; and regularly, the Proof ought to be by two or three Witneſſes. 1 *Inſt.* 6. And divers other Things muſt be tried by Examination of the Parties and Witneſſes; as the Trial by *Wager of Law*, &c. *Finch* 423.

Trials by Witneſſes and Proofs.

V. 4 Inſt. 278.

Nonage

Glanvil, lib. 13. cap. 15. Nonage was anciently tried by the Verdict of eight Men, but now by Inſpection ; and full Age by twelve Men.

Appeal. In an Appeal by a *Feme* of the Death of her Huſband, if the Defendant ſay that the *Baron* is alive in another County ; or generally, that he is alive, this ſhall be tried by *Proofs*, 41 *Aſſize* 5. *Vide Rol.* Tit. *Trial*, 577. what ſhall be tried by *Proofs* in an *Aſſize*, and what not.

Annuity. In a Writ of Annuity, if the Defendant ſay the Party is dead in *Britain*, this ſhall be tried by *Proofs*. 25 *E.* 3. 70.

Dukes, &c. 11. *Duke* or no *Duke*, *Earl* or no *Earl*, *Baron* or no *Baron*, ſhall be tried by the King's Writ, *lib.* 5. 35. *lib.* 6. 53. But *Dutcheſs* or no *Dutcheſs*, &c. by Marriage, ſhall be tried *per Pais*, becauſe the Marriage is Matter of Fact.

League. 12. In a Plea *del alien nee*, the *League* between the *King* and the Sovereign of the *Alien*, ſhall be tried by the Record of the *Chancery*, becauſe every *League* is of Record. *Lib.* 9, 32.

Manor. 13. If a *Manor* be *Ancient Demeſne* or not, it ſhall be tried by the Book of *Domeſday*, which is in the *Exchequer*. But whether certain Acres be Parcel of ſuch a Manner or no, it ſhall be tried by the country. *Ibid.*

Courts not of Record. 14. The Proceedings of a Court which is not of *Record* (as the County-Court, the Hundred-Court, the Court-Baron, &c.) ſhall be tried by the Country, and not by the *Rolls* of the Court, becauſe they are no Record. *Ibid. Co. Lit.* 117. *b.*

By Charters and Records. 15. The Privileges and Liberties of Courts of Record, Cities and Boroughs, muſt be tried by their Charters and Records.

16. When

16. Whether the *Ordinary* committed *Admini-* Wills and Adminiftra-tions.
stration to the Plaintiff, or whether the Tefta-
ment was proved before the *Ordinary*, or whether fuch a Will be the Will of the Party, or
whether he died Inteftate or not? In all thefe
Cafes the Trial fhall be *per Pais*; becaufe *Probate* of Wills, and conftituting Adminiftrators,
did not belong to *Ecclefiaftical Judges originally*,
but were given to them of late. But Trial
thereof is left to the Common Law, and was
not given to them. *Lib.* 9, 32, 40.

An Executor brings an Action of Debt; the
Defendant pleads that the Teftator never made
him Executor; if the Plaintiff gives in Evidence the *Probate* of the Will, the Defendant
fhall only give Evidence in *Difaffirmance* of the
Plaintiff's Probate, which is Matter of Fact;
but as to Matter of Law, the Court gives Credit thereto; as where another Will was made,
for there the Parties might have appealed; but
if the Seal be counterfeit, or the *Probate* forged,
it is triable *per Jury. Adj. Pafch.* 20 *Car.* 2. 1 Lev. 235.
B. R. *Noel* and *Wells. Vide Wentworth's Executor* 69.

The Trial of all Criminal Matters is by the Criminal Matters.
Country, and the Party accufed cannot be de-
nied it, unlefs it be his own Fault; as where
he is mute, and will not put himfelf upon his
Country in due Time; for then without farther Trial Judgment *de Pain fort & dure* is
paffed by the *Judges* upon him. *Staundf. pl.
Coron.* 150.

16. In an Action upon the Cafe for calling Plo. Com. 267.
one *Baftard*, the Defendant juftified that the Special Ba-
Plaintiff was a *Baftard*; and it was awarded, ftardy.
that this fhould be tried *per Pais*, and not by

the *Ordinary. Hob.* 179. And ſo Plea that the Plaintiff was born at ſuch a Place before Marriage, this is *ſpecial Baſtardy,* and ſhall be tried *per Pais. Plow.* 14. *Dyer* 89. *vide hic cap.* 22.

Cuſtoms of
London. 17. When an Iſſue is taken, whether a *Cuſtom* or no *Cuſtom* in *London,* if the Mayor, Commonalty and Citizens be Parties, or intereſted in the Action, this Cuſtom ſhall be tried by a *Jury,* and not by the Certificate of the *Mayor* and *Aldermen,* by the *Recorder. Hob.* 85. *Day* and *Savadge*'s Caſe. *Devant* 3. *Style* 137. *Moor* 871. *Vide apres* Tit. *Viſne. Roll.* Tit. *Trial,* 579, 580.

The Cuſtom of *London* ſhall be certified by the *Mayor* and *Aldermen,* by the Mouth of the *Recorder. Co. Lit.* 74.

In an Information upon the Statute 5 *Eliz.* for uſing a Trade to which the Defendant was not bound an Apprentice, if the Defendant plead a Cuſtom of the City, That he who is free of one Trade, may uſe any other; this ſhall be tried by the Mouth of the *Recorder. Roll.* Tit. *Trial,* 579. G. *pl.* 3.

Note this Difference, he that is free of one Manual Trade, cannot uſe another Manual Trade: but it is otherwiſe of thoſe Trades which are not Manual: In ſuch, one that is free of one, may uſe another by the Cuſtom.

Liberties claimed by Cuſtom in *London,* the Cuſtom of making Indentures of Apprenticeſhip void, if not inrolled *(a)* within a Year, the Cuſtom

____

(a) If the Indentures be not inrolled before the Chamberlain within the Year, upon Petition to the Mayor and Aldermen, *&c.* a *Scire facias* ſhall iſſue to the Maſter to ſhew Cauſe why not inrolled; and if it was through the Maſter's

Cuftom to devife Lands, Foreign Attachment,
&c. fhall he tried by the Mouth of the *Recor-*
der. But the Iffue, whether there be a Market
every Day in the Week in *London,* fhall be tried *per Pais,* becaufe the Iffue is not upon the
Cuftom. *Roll.* Tit. *Trials, 580. Vide hic cap.* 8.

18. A Matter of Record being mixt with a
Matter of Fact, fhall be tried *per Pais,* and not
by the Record. *Hob.* 244. *Peter* and *Stafford's*
Cafe.

Matter of
Record mixt
with Matter
of Fact.

19. In Writs of Right and Appeals that
touch Life, Trial may be by *Battel,* or by *Ju-*
ry, at the Defendant's Choice; the *Battel,* in
a Writ of Right, muft be by *Champions* (who
muft be Freemen) but in an Appeal it muft be
in proper Perfon. The *Champions* in a Writ of
Right are not bound to fight longer than until the Stars appear; and if the Champion of
the Tenant can defend himfelf until then, the
Tenant fhall prevail: The *Judges* of the Court
of *Common Pleas* are *Judges* of the *Battel,* in
a Writ of Right; and the *Judges* of the *King's*
Bench, in an Appeal of Felony. It feems they
feldom or never killed one another in this Trial
by *Battel,* for their Weapons are but Battoons,
and he that was vanquifhed, was prefently, upon *Proclamation* made, to acknowledge his Fault
in the Audience of the People, or elfe to cry
Cravant in the Name of Recreantife; and upon this Judgment was to be given; and after
this the *Recreant* fhould *amittere liberam legem,*

Trials by Bat-
tel. Writ of
Right. See
the Manner of
it 1 H. 6. 6.
7. *Bro. Droit*
de recto, pl.
20.

Mafter's Default, the Apprentice may fue out his Indentures; otherwife if through the Fault of the Apprentice;
as if he would not come to prefent himfelf before the
Chamberlain, &c. for it cannot be inrolled unlefs the Infant is in Court and acknowledges it. 2 *Roll. Rep.* 305.
Palm. 361. See 1 *Mod.* 271.

C 2   that

that is, fhould become infamous, *&c.* 2 *Inft.* 247. *Finch* 421. *lib.* 9.' 31. *Mirror of Juftice* 161, 162, *&c.* 1 *Inft.* 294:

Grand Affize. *Glanvil* faith, The Trial by Grand Affize came by the Clemency of the Prince. *Eft autem* (faith he) *Magna Affifa Regale quoddam beneficium, Clementia Principis de confilio Procerum populis indultum.*

For the Trial of Treafon, Murder and Felony, as well upon Appeals as upon Indictments, fee *Staundf. Pleas of the Crown.*

By *Glanvil, cap.* 1. *lib.* 14. it appeareth, the Trial of thefe Crimes by the old Law was this: If there were no direct Proof nor Accufer, or if there was any Accufer or direct Proof, yet if the Party denied the fame, then the Trial was by Wager of Battel, if the Party accufed was not fixty Years old, and of found Limbs; but if he was older or not found, then he was to be **Per judicium** tried *per judicium Dei,* namely, *per calidum fer-* **Dei.** *rum vel aquam,* that is, if he was a Freeholder, he was to run bare-foot and bare-leg'd over a Row of hot Iron Bars; and if he paffed three Times without Stop or Fall, he was acquitted. And if he was a meaner Perfon, called *Rufticus,* he was to run through Veffels filled with fcalding Water.

Recovery by 20. In a Writ of *Difceit,* upon a Recovery **Default.** by Default, the Trial fhall be, if the Judgment was given upon the *Petit Cape,* by the *Summo-* **Summoners,** *ners,* if upon the *Grand Cape,* by the *Summo-* **Pernors,** **Veiors.** *ners, Pernors* or *Veiors,* and not *per Pais*; So if a *Recovery* by Default in a real Action be pleaded, **Nient Com-** to which the other faid, *Nient comprife,* this **prife.** fhall not be tried *per Pais,* but by the *Summoners* and *Veiors. Lib.* 9. 32. See *Viner, Trial,* 28, 29.

En

En Affise if the Issue be, whether the Land was extended in an *Elegit, &c.* this shall be tried by the Extendors joined with the Assize. 31 *Aff.* 6. *vide Rol.* Tit. *Trial,* 581, 582.

Of Trials *per l'Escheator, per Examination,* *vide ib.*　　Escheator, Sheriff.

In an Appeal, if the Exigent be awarded, and the Party pray a Writ to enquire of the Goods and Chattels, and to seize them, this may be awarded to the Escheator, or Sheriff, at the Election of the Court. 41 *Aff.* 13. *vide hic cap.* 24, 27.

21. In Debt upon a simple Contract, Detinue, *&c.* the Trial may be by *Wager of Law* or *per Pais,* at the Defendant's Election. But when the Defendant wageth his Law, he ought to bring with him Eleven of his Neighbours, who will avow upon their Oath, that in their Consciences he said true, so as he himself must be sworn *de fidelitate,* and the Eleven *de credulitate, ib. Finch* 423. and 1 *Inst.* 295. you may read excellent Learning concerning this Trial.　　Wager of Law.

22. If *Profession* be denied, it shall be tried by the Court Christian, but if the Time of the *Profession* be in Issue, this shall be tried by the Country, *lib.* 4. 71. So though an Inrolment, or other Matter of Record, cannot be tried *per Pais,* yet the Time when the Inrolment was made, may be tried *per Pais;* so whether the Party appeared in such a *Court,* or on such a Day, *&c.* shall be tried *per Pais. Cro.* 3 *Part,* 131. So whether one was Sheriff such a Day or not, *Cro.* 1 *Part,* 421. *Admission, Institution, Plenarty* and *Ability of the Person* shall be tried by the Bishop: But Induction shall be tried by the Country, and so shall Avoidance by Resignation. *Dyer* 229. *Moor* 61. And void or not void, shall be tried *per Pais,* 1 *Inst.* 344. and *Plenarty* if the　　Profession. Inrolment. Appearance. Sheriff. Admission, Plenarty, *&c.*

Clerk be dead. *Mirror of Justice* 324. *lib.* 6. 49. The Cause of Refusal of a Clerk by the Bishop shall be tried by the *Metropolitan*, if the Clerk be living; but *per Pais*, if he be dead. *l.* 5. 58.

Per Spiritual Law.
Vi.. hic cap. 16.

Ability shall be tried by the *Ordinary*, if the Clerk be alive; but if dead, then *per Pais*: Institution, Resignation, full or not full, Profession, unless alledged in a Stranger, Prior removeable at Will or perpetual, general Bastardy, the Right of Espousals, Divorce, &c. shall be tried by the *Bishops*: But in many Cases, these Matters being mixed with other Circumstances, shall be tried *per Pais*.

Per Pais.
For although Institution, Resignation, &c. are Spiritual, yet Avoidance, Induction, &c. are notorious to the Country.

As if the Church be void by Resignation, or void or not void, Induction, Institution and Induction together, because the Common Law shall be preferred, Prior or not Prior.

Nota; Marriage of a Wife in Possession shall be tried *per Pais*, but not the Right of Marriage, as *ne unques accouple in loyal Matrimony*, this Right must be tried by the Bishop's Certificate. *Leon.* fol. 53.

Bastardy alledged in a Stranger to the Writ, or in one dead, or Abatement of the Writ, whether a Feme be a Feme Covert in Possession, &c. in Trespass by Baron and Feme, *Nient son feme* shall be tried *per Pais*. And see in *Rol.* Tit. *Trial*, 584, &c. many Cases where Bastardy, Marriage, &c. shall be tried *per Ley* Spiritual, or *per Pais*. The Time, &c. of Consecration of a Bishop, and of other Spiritual Matters, shall be tried *per Pais*. By what Spiritual Person the Trial shall be, and for what Case, *vide ib*. *Leigh* and *Hammer's* Case.

Ideot.

23. An *Ideot* found so from his Nativity by Office, may come in Person in the *Chancery*, before

fore the *Chancellor*, and pray that before him and such Justices or Sages of the Law, which he shall call to him, (who are called the Counsel of the King) he may be examined whether he be an *Ideot* or no; or by his Friends he may sue a Writ out of *Chancery*, returnable there, to bring him into the *Chancery*, *ibid. coram nobis & concilio nostro examinand'*. *Lib.* 9, 31.

24. If it be in Question, Whether the *She-* ^{Sheriff.} *riff* made such a Return or not, it shall be tried by the *Sheriff*: If whether the *Under-Sheriff* made such a Return or not, it shall be tried by ^{Return.} the *Under-Sheriff*: If the Question be, Whether such a one be *Sheriff* or not? he is made by Letters Patent of Record, and therefore it shall be tried by the Record. *Ib. Cro.* 1 *Part*, 421.

25. If an *Approver* say, That he commenced ^{Dures.} his *Appeal* before the *Coroner per dures*, this shall be tried by the *Record* of the *Coroner*; and if it be found that he did it without *dures*, he shall be hanged. *Broke, Corone*, 74.

26. The Trial, Whether a *Statute* shewed ^{Statute.} before, be the true *Statute* or not, shall be by the Examination of the *Mayor* and *Clerk* of the *Statutes*, which took the *Statute*, and not *per Pais, ib.* Whether a *Statute* hath two Seals or not, shall be tried *per Pais*. *Leon.* 228, 229.

27. In Assize, the Tenant said, That the ^{Escheator.} Lands were taken into the King's Hands, this shall be tried by the Examination of the *Escheator*. *Rol. Trial*, 582. *L.* 1.

28. If one in Avoidance of an *Outlawry*, al- ^{Certificate.} ledge that he was in Prison at *Bourdeaux, ultra mare, in servitio Majoris de Bourdeaux*, this shall be tried by the *Mayor's* Certificate; and in such like Cases, other Trials shall be by the *Certifi-*

cate

cate of the *Marſhal of the Hoſt*, and by the *Cap-*

Meſſenger.   *tain of Calais*, and alſo by Meſſenger, of a Thing done beyond Sea. *Ib.* 583. *N.* 3.

If the Defendant claim Privilege as Member of a College in the Univerſity, and Iſſue be thereupon joined, it ſhall be tried *per Pais*, and not by Certificate of the Vice-Chancellor of the Univerſity or Principal of the College. *Vin. Trial*, 38.

The Stat. 1 *Eliz. c.* 1. " Ordains, That " every Biſhop ſhall tender the Oaths to each " of the Clergy in his Dioceſe, and ſhall certify " the Refuſal into *B. R.*" 'Tis upon this Certificate the Refuſer ſhall be there indicted, though the Certificate be by the Biſhop's Chancellor. *Ibid.* 53.

Petit Cape.   29. At the *Petit Cape*, the Tenant ſaid, That he was impriſoned three Days before the Default, and three Days after; this ſhall be tried by the Examination of the Attorney. *Nient Attach. per* 15 *Jours in Aſſize* ſhall not be tried

Bailiff.   *per Pais*, but by Examination of the Bailiff. *Ib.*

Almanack.   30. It ſeems an *Almanack* is ſo infallible, that it hath countervailed the Verdict of a *Jury*. For in Error of a Judgment given in *Lynne*, the Error aſſigned was, That the Judgment was given at a Court held there on the 16th Day of *February*, 26 *Eliz.* and that this Day was *Sunday*, and it was ſo found by Examination of the *Almanacks* of that Year: Upon which it was ruled, that this Examination was a ſufficient Trial, and that a Trial *per Pais* was not neceſſary, although it were an Error in *Fact*; and ſo the Judgment was reverſed. *Cro.* 3 *Part, fol.* 227. 1 *Leon.* 242. the ſame Caſe, and there

it

it is faid, that it was twice fo ruled before. See
Poftea Cb. 15. *p.*

31. In ancient Times there was a Trial in
Criminal Caufes called *Ordalium* ; for upon Not Ordeal.
guilty pleaded, the Defendant might put himfelf upon God and the Country (which is upon
the Verdict of twelve Men, as is the Ufe at this
Day), or elfe upon God only ; and then if he
was a Freeman, he was to be tried by Fire,
that is, he was to *go barefooted over Nine Plow
Shares Fire-hot* ; and if he was not hurt by this,
then he was to be acquitted, otherwife condemned ; and this was called *The Judgment of
God*, becaufe the Defendant had put himfelf
upon God only. But if he was a Slave, then
his Trial was to be by Water, and that divers
Ways, which all appear in *Lambard* Word *Ordalium*. From which Kind of Trial I prefume
we ftill retain this Expreffion of an innocent
Perfon, *That he need not fear Fire or Water* : This
Manner of Trial was firft prohibited by the *Canons*, and afterwards totally abolifhed by Parliament, fo as to be no Trials but by Jury. The
Trial by *Battel* (a) is likewife prohibited by the Battel.
Canons, but not by *Parliament*, as you may read
in the *Ninth Report, fol.* 32.

32. When the Matter alledged extendeth to Which Trial
a Place at the Common Law, and a Place within fhall be firft.

(a) Trial by Battle ftands *repealed by Canons only*,
though fufficiently *abrogated* by difufe. *Vin. Abr.* Tit.
Trial, 33. Yet in P. 34. from *Petty's Conftit.* he tells us,
That from the Conqueft till *Hen.* 7. Trials might be *by
God and his Country*, or the Offender might elect to be
tried by *God alone*, as by Ordeal, which was *repealed* by
Parliament in *Hen.* 7. Time.

a Frana Franchiſe, it ſhall be tried at the Common Law. 1 *Inſt.* 125. 4 *Inſt.* 221.

Trial in one Iſſue binds in another.

In what Caſes a Trial in one Iſſue ſhall bind the ſame Party in another Iſſue, upon the ſame Matter.

In Debt againſt two *per ſeveral Præcipes*, if one plead a Releaſe, and they are at Iſſue upon the Deed, and the other plead the ſame Iſſue, if it be found the Deed of the Plaintiff in the former Iſſue, this ſhall bind him in the ſecond Iſſue. 12 *H.* 4. 8.

In Treſpaſs, if the Defendant plead *Villenage* in the Plaintiff, if this be found againſt the Defendant, this ſhall bind him in the ſame Iſſue, in another Action in the ſame Court, betwixt the ſame Parties. 44 *Aſſ.* 5.

If a Man be found guilty of a Conſpiracy upon an Indictment at the King's Suit, this ſhall not bind in a Writ of Conſpiracy at the Suit of the Party, but he may plead Not guilty. 27 *Aſſ.* 13.

If a Man upon an Indictment of Extortion, confeſs it, and put himſelf in the King's Grace, and makes Fine, &c. this ſhall bind him, and he ſhall not plead Not guilty to the Suit of the Party; for a Confeſſion is ſtronger than a Verdict. 27 *Aſſ.* 57. *per Sharde. Vide Rol.* Tit. *Trial,* 625.

In what Caſes Trial againſt one ſhall be againſt others.

He which is not Party to the Iſſue, nor can have Attaint, or challenge the Inqueſt, ſhall not be bound by the Trial. 11 *H.* 4. 30.

And therefore in treſpaſs againſt two, and one pleads a Releaſe, and the other juſtifies as his Servant; if the Iſſue be found againſt the Maſter, it ſhall not conclude the Servant. 11 *H.* 4. 30. *Rol. Ib.* 625. *K.* 2.

One

One fhall not be compelled to try a Traverfe At what Time
the fame Seffions he makes it ; for a Man fhall the Trial fhall
have Time to make his Defence, and is not fup- be.
pofed to be ready to anfwer fudden Objections ;
and for this Reafon many Judgments upon Indictments have been reverfed. *Rol. Trial,* 625.
L. 1.

Juftices of *Oyer* and *Terminer,* nor Juftices of
Peace, cannot inquire and determine the fame
Day : But Juftices of *Gaol-Delivery* and Juftices
in *Eyre* may. *Ibid.*

Juftices of Peace cannot proceed to the Delivery of a Perfon indicted of Felony before them
the fame Day he is arraigned. 22 *Ed.* 4. *Coron.*
44. Declared by all the Juftices of *England,* to
be obferved as a Law. *Ibid.*

In an Indictment in *B. R.* or in the fame
County ; and removed thither, the Defendant
may be arraigned and tried the fame Day. For
the *King's Bench* is a Court of *Eyre* for all Offences in that County : Otherwife of an Indictment removed out of another County. *Vide Rol.*
Tit. *Trial,* 626. many Cafes *de ceo.*

33. All Matters done out of the Realm of Martial Af-
England, concerning War, Combat, or Deeds fairs.
of Arms, fhall be tried and determined before
the Conftable and Marfhal of *England,* before
whom the Trial is by Witneffes, or by Combat, Witneffes, or
and their Proceeding is according to the Civil Combat.
Law, and not by the Oath of twelve Men. 1
Inft. 261. Wherefore, if the King's Subject be
killed by another of his Subjects in any foreign
Country, the Wife or Heir of the Dead, may
have an Appeal before the Conftable and Marfhal, whofe Sentence is upon the Teftimony of
Witneffes, or Combat. *Ibid.* 74. So if a Man
                                    be

be wounded in *France*, and die thereof in *England*. *Ibid.* 4 *Inſt.* 140.

What Iſſue ſhall be firſt tried.

It is worthy our Obſervation, to take Notice, when there are ſeveral Iſſues, which of them ſhall be firſt tried; and for this you have already heard, That where Iſſue is joined for Part, and a Demurrer for the Reſidue, the Court may direct the Trial of the Iſſue, or judge the Demurrer firſt, at their Pleaſure; though by the Opinion of *Dodderidge*, it is the beſt way to give Judgment upon the Demurrer firſt, becauſe when the Iſſue comes afterwards to be tried, the *Jury* may aſſeſs Damages for the whole.

Latch 4.

Damages.

A *Scire facias* was brought upon a *Recognizance* in *Chançery*, *the Ter-tenants* pleaded ſeveral Pleas, the Plaintiff demurred to one, and took Iſſue on the other, the Record was ſent into *B. R.* to try the Iſſue, and it was tried, and *Verdict pro Plaintiff*, the Demurrer not being argued; and it was adjudged *per B. R.* that Judgment ought to be given on both by that Court. *Jeffreyſon* and *Dawſon*'s Caſe, *Hill.* 21, 22 *Car.* 2. *B. R. Vide* for theſe Things, 1 *Rol. Abr.* 534, 535. *Rol. Rep.* 287. and in the principal Caſe, 4 *Inſt.* 80. was denied to be Law.

2 Keb. 621.

Immaterial Iſſue.

An immaterial Iſſue joined, which will not bring the Matter in Queſtion to be tried, is not helped after Verdict by the Statute of *Jeofails*, but there muſt be a Repleader; becauſe this is a Matter of Subſtance; for if there were no Iſſue, there could be no Verdict, and ſo it is as if nothing had been done in the Cauſe.

Plea to the Writ.

In an Action againſt two, the one pleads in Abatement of the Writ, the other to the Action, the Plea to the Writ ſhall be firſt tried;

for

for if that be found, all the whole Writ shall abate, and make an End of the Business; for the Plaintiff ought not to recover upon a false Writ.   1 *Inst.* 125. *b.*

In a Plea Personal against divers Defendants, Plea to the the one Defendant pleads in Bar to Parcel, or whole first which extendeth only to him that pleadeth it; tried. and the other pleads a Plea which goeth to the whole: The Plea that goeth to the whole (that is) to both Defendants shall be first tried, because the other Defendant shall have Advantage thereof; for in a Personal Action, the Discharge of one is the Discharge of both.

As for Example; If one of the Defendants in Release. Trespass pleads a Release to himself (which in Law extends to both), and the other pleads Not Rol. *Tit.* guilty (which extends but to himself;) or if Trial, 628. one pleads a Plea which excuseth himself only, and the other pleads another Plea which goeth to the whole, the Plea which goeth to the whole shall be first tried; for if that be found, it maketh an end of all: And the other Defendant shall Discharge of take Advantage hereof, because the Discharge of one dischar- one is the Discharge of both.   But in a Plea real geth both. it is otherwise, for every Tenant may lose his Part of the Land; as if a *Præcipe* be brought as Heir to his Father against two, and one pleads a Plea which extendeth but to himself, and the other pleads a Plea which extends to both, as Bastardy in the Demandant, and it is found for him, yet the other Issue shall be tried; for he shall not take Advantage of the Plea of the other, because one Jointenant may lose his Part by his Misplea.   1 *Inst.* 125. *b.*

Brown and *Staundford*, Justices, consulted with Grammarians in Things of Grammar; and *Hulls*
a Ba-

a Bachelor of Law (*tempore H. 6.*) was called into Court to ſhew the Difference between preciſe and cauſative Compulſion. *Vide Plow.* 122, 127, 128.

Paſch. 16 *Car.* 2. B. R. An Action of *Trover, &c.* was brought *de ſex Capitalibus fibulatis, Anglice,* ſix laced Coifs; after Verdict for the Plaintiff, it was moved in Arreſt of Judgment, that the *Latin* Words were both Adjective, and ſo not certain: But it was anſwered, That *Capital* is a Subſtantive, and the *Nomenclator* of *Weſtminſter-School* was produced to warrant it; and it was adjudged for the Plaintiff accordingly; and the Court allowed that Authority before *Rider's Dictionary.*

Chriſtian Name amended. *Henley* and *Burſtal*; In the pleading and joining of the Iſſue, the Defendant's Chriſtian Name was miſtaken; and reſolved by the Court, that it might be amended, it being right before in the Record. 1 *Ventr.* 25.

New Trial directed by the Court of Chancery in Replevin. A Bill was exhibited in *Chancery,* complaining that a Verdict in *Replevin* had been unduly obtain'd; and it was decreed that there ſhould be a new Trial, the Complainant paying the Coſts of the former: This could not have been tried again at Law, becauſe the Verdict in *Replevin* is concluſive. 2 *Vent.* 35.

Juror producing a Court-Roll to his Companions, Cauſe for a new Trial. *Goodman* verſus *Cotherington*; the Jury being charged with an Iſſue, and departed from the Bar, one of them went from his Companions and fetched a Court-Roll, which induced the Jury to find for the Plaintiff; and it was held to be a good Cauſe for a new Trial: But *Twiſden* ſaid, that in Caſe of ſuch a Miſcarriage in *Pais*, no Notice ſhould be taken of it on Affidavits, unleſs it were indorſed on the *Poſtea.* 1 *Siderfin* 235.

Throg-

Throgmorton's Cafe; where an Iſſue is join- A Term's
ed and a Year paſſes, the Plaintiff cannot bring Notice re-
the Cauſe to Trial without giving a Term's No- quired, where
tice. *Per Cur.* If Notice were given the Term been a Year
before, and they did not proceed that Term, at Iſſue.
but the next, then fourteen Days Notice is ſufficient; and if after a Year is lapſed, the Defen- Not ſo where
dant will try the Iſſue by Proviſo, a Term's the Defendant
Notice is not neceſſary, for that the Plaintiff tries it by Pro-
ought to be at all Times ready to try it. 1 *Si-* viſo.
derfin 34.

Sir *Hugh Povey's* Cafe; the Court held, Need not give
That ſince the Defendant, by his Privilege of a Term's No-
Parliament, had delayed the Plaintiff above a tice where
Year after Iſſue joined, the Plaintiff ſhould not the Defendant
be obliged to give him a Term's Notice of Tri- occaſions the
al, any more than where a Defendant ſtays the Privilege, &c.
Proceedings by an Injunction obtained out of
Chancery. Ibid. 92.

A full Term's Notice excluſive is neceſſary,
but Notice of Trial at any Time within the
Year, though afterwards countermanded, is a
ſufficient Proceeding to bring the Plaintiff out
of the Rule.

Where Proceedings had ſtaid twelve Months,
and afterwards a Trial, the Verdict was ſet aſide,
becauſe Notice of Trial was not given before the
Eſſoin Day of the Term preceding the Trial.
This was in *C. B.*

Paſ. 13 *G.* 2. *C. B.* was a Rule made to ex-
plain the Rule for giving a Term's Notice, *and
Ordered,* that in all Cafes where no Proceedings
have been in four Terms excluſive of the laſt
proceding, the Party who deſires to proceed
ſhall give a Term's Notice, and before the Eſſoin Day of the fifth or other ſubſequent Term,
and that a Judge's Summons, if no Order be

I   made

made thereupon, ſhall not be deem'd a Proceeding, but that a Notice of a Trial, though afterwards countermanded, ſhall be deemed a Proceeding.

Notice for a Priſoner left with a Turnkey eight Days before the Trial, ſufficient.

Rex verſus *Baron*; it was held, That Notice of Trial left with a Turnkey of the *Marſhalſea*, eight Days before the Trial, was good Notice, as well in Criminal Caſes as Civil. *Sid.* 231.

Defendant in Indictment of Perjury, may try it by Proviſo.

Where Iſſue is joined upon an Indictment of Perjury, and the Proſecutor does not try it, the Party indicted may try it by Proviſo. 1 *Sid.* 317.

Where a new Trial may be granted, and where not.

Read verſus *Dawſon*; in an Information of Perjury, it was found for the King, and moved upon ſeveral Affidavits to have a new Trial. The Court were of Opinion, That they had not Power to grant a new Trial, without Conſent of the Counſel for the King, although to them there appeared ſufficient Cauſe for a new Trial: But they agreed, That in Debt by an Informer, the Court might grant a new Trial upon Cauſe ſhewn, without Conſent of the Counſel, becauſe there the Party had Intereſt. 1 *Sid.* 49.

Wheeler verſus *Honour*; it was there held, That a new Trial ought not to be granted after a Trial at Bar, but upon great Cauſe; and it was ſaid, There were not above two Inſtances to be met with, where a new Trial had been granted upon a Motion after a Trial at Bar. *Sid.* 58.

Fact mixed with Matter of Record, to be tried *per Pais.*

If Matter of Fact and Matter of Record are ſo intermixed that they cannot be divided, the whole ſhall be tried by the Country. *Sid.* 314.

Avoidance and Plenarty, how to be tried.

Watſon verſus *Baker*; If an Iſſue be, whether a Church be void or not void, this ſhall be tried by

by the Country ; but if the Iſſue be whether
the Church is full or not full, it ſhall be tried
by Certificate: So if the Iſſue be, whether ſuch Covert or
a Feme be Covert or Sole, this ſhall be tried by Sole *per Pais.*
the Country; but if *unque accouple in loyal Ma-* Loyal Matri-
trimony, it ſhall be tried by Certificate. And mony *per* Cer-
the Reaſon of thoſe Caſes is, That void or not tificate.
void, Covert or Sole, are Things notorious to
the Country, and diſtinguiſhable, by them ; but
Plenarty or Loyal Matrimony are not within
their Conuſance, and therefore not triable by
them ; for Plenarty is by Inſtitution, and Loyal The Reaſon;
Matrimony ought to be agreeable to the Laws
eſtabliſhed in that Caſe, of which the Country
are not Judges. *Sid.* 390.

Able or not able in *Quare Impedit*, if the Clerk
refuſed be living, ſhall be tried *by the ordinary*,
for the Clerk is to be examined ; but if the
Clerk be dead, *per Pais*, for he cannot then be
examined.

So, whether the Church be void by Deprivation, it ſhall be tried by the *Ordinary*; but if
the Voidance be alledg'd to be *by Death*, it ſhall
be tried *per Pais*.

Inſtitution ſhall be tried by the Ordinary, for
it is Spiritual; but *Induction* or *Inſtallation*, *per
Pais*: And ſo it is, if the Iſſue be upon Inſtitution and Induction, for the Common Law ſhall
be preferred. *Vin. Trial*, 40.

A *Divorce* ſhall be tried by the Ordinary, and
not *per Pais*; ſo ſhall *general Baſtardy*; but *ſpecial Baſtardy per Pais*.

If Iſſue be join'd *Marriage or no Marriage*, it
ſhall be tried by Certificate of the Biſhop; but
if the Queſtion be, Whether the Party was married *to another or not?* the temporal Court ſhall

judge of the Matter without Certificate. *Ibid.* 47.

Nient letter'd in *Quare Impedit* againſt the Ordinary, ſhall be tried by the Metropolitan, for the Ordinary is intereſted; but if the Metropolitan be dead, and the See void, it ſhall be tried by the Guardians of the Spiritualties. *Ibid.* 49.

The Biſhop of *Durham* has temporal Juriſdiction, and writes to his Clerks to certify Baſtardy, *&c.*

Whether a Biſhop be *conſecrated* or not? ſhall be tried by the Metropolitan, who ſhall certify the *Year and Day* of the Conſecration, from which Day the Temporalties ſhall be delivered to him. *Apud eundem* 53.

Pais.   Of Trials *per Pais* it is not to be doubted (ſaith *Dugdale*) but that the moſt antient Form of Trials in *Civil* Caſes as well as *Criminal* was by a certain Number of Men ſworn, who upon Teſtimony given of the Fact were to judge and determine.

Intent prohibited may be tried *per Pais*; and though the beſt Trial of an Intention is by the Act intended when done; yet this Intent may be tried by other Circumſtances and Evidences of the Fact, beſides the bare doing of the Fact; as in the Caſes of thoſe Acts which *prohibit* the Importation of foreign Coin, or of the taking of Wooll, Gold, Silver, *&c. with intent* to utter or tranſport, the *Intent* join'd with the Act ſhall be tried by ſuch Circumſtances which evidence the Intent, for Intention and Knowledge lie in Averment and Proof; but generally ſpeaking, *Intention* where it is not prohibited is not triable, as that a Man did ſuch a particular Thing *eâ Intentione* to do it, this is not triable;

indeed

indeed, fometimes upon *another Fact* put in Iffue, the Jury fhall try the Intent collaterally, as in Murder. *Vin. Trial,* 69, 70.

The *Boundaries* of a Parifh is triable *per Pais,* and in all Cafes where the Matter to be tried is In the Difcretion of the Juftices, they may fend it to the Country.

Sealing and Delivery of a Deed is triable by Jury; but whether a man be *confiliarius & in lege eruditus* is not triable by Jury. So whether Land be *reputed* parcel of a Manor, this fhall not be tried *per Pais,* for it is too uncertain, and may be fo reputed by fome and not by others, or only for a fhort Time. The *Courfe* of the Court cannot be tried by Jury, for it is Matter of Law; nor can the general Cuftom of *England* in charging a Carrier or Innkeeper for Goods neglected or ftolen; but where an act of parliament makes an Offence, and is filent in the Manner of Trial, it fhall be intended *per Pais. Ibid.* 71.

Gilbert verfus *Martin*; an Action of Covenant was brought in *Hampfhire,* and a Breach affigned for not repairing a Houfe in *Berkfhire,* and Iffue joined upon *non infregit Conventionem.* And a Verdict for the Plaintiff in *Hampfhire*: Mov'd in Arreft of Judgment, that this was a Mif-trial; and of that Opinion was the Court. *Sid.* 157.

Breach of Co-venant af-figned in another County, Mif-trial.

Bulftrode verfus *Hall* and *Stevens*; the View was granted in a Trial at Bar, after the Jury had appeared and heard Part of the Evidence. *Sid.* 148.

View after the Jury appear.

Rex verfus *Davis & al.* An Information for an Affault and Riot was tried at the Affizes for *Devon,* and a Verdict for the Defendants that they were not guilty. And on a Motion

No new Trial after Acquittal.

for a new Trial upon Affidavits of the Fact, and that the Judge's Directions were to find the Aſſault, it was denied; for the court ſaid, there could be no Precedent ſhewn for it in caſe of Acquittal. *Shower* 336.

Trial by two Witneſſes. Where a Trial is not by Jury, but *per Teſtes*, there muſt be two in all Caſes. *Shower* 361.

Rex verſus *Bear, Hill.* 10 *W.* 3. *B. R.* Indictment for Compoſing, Writing, Making and Collecting ſeveral Libels; reſolv'd that the whole Libel need not be ſet forth in the Indictment; but if any Part qualifies the reſt, it may be given in Evidence. *Salkeld* 417.

If a Libel be publickly known, having a written Copy of it is an Evidence of a Publication; but otherwiſe, where it is not known to be publiſhed. *Ibid.*

Death of Defendant before the Commiſſion-Day, not aided by the Statute; but if after Commiſſion-Day, it is aided. *Mich.* 6 *Ann. B. R.* Ejectment laid in *Devonſhire*, to be tried at *Exeter*, the Defendant died the Day before the Aſſizes began at *Exeter*; and upon a trial on full Evidence, Verdict *pro Quer.* and Motion in Arreſt of Judgment. *Et per Cur.* Firſt, the death of either Party before the Aſſizes is not remedied by the Statute; but if the Party dies after the Aſſizes begins, though the Trial be after his Death, that is within the Remedy of the Statute; for the Aſſizes is but one day in law, and this is a Remedial Law, and ſhall be conſtrued favourably. 2. The Court held, That in this Caſe it was in their Diſcretion, whether they would upon Motion arreſt Judgment, or put the Party to a Writ of Error; accordingly they refuſed to arreſt the Judgment, and the party was put to his Writ of Error, that the Point might be put in Iſſue and tried by a Jury. 1 *Salkeld* 8.

Duke's

Duke's Cafe, *Mich.* 9 *W.* 3. *B. R. Duke* Judgment for was upon a Trial at Bar convicted of Perjury, a corporal Pu- and upon the *Capias* he was outlawed ; and up- nifhment can- on the Exigent it was moved, That judgment not be given of the Pillory might be given againft him in his Abfence. his abfence. *Et per Holt* Ch. J. Judgment cannot be given againft any Man in his Ab- fence for a corporal Punifhment ; there is no fuch Precedent.   If a man be outlawed of Fe- lony, Execution was never awarded againft the Felon till brought to the Bar.   A *Capias ad Satisfaciendum Domino Regi pro fine,* is common, but there never was a Writ to take a Man and put him in the Pillory ; and fo faid Sir *Samuel Aftry* upon fearch of Precedents. 1 *Salkeld* 400.

Duke of *Norfolk's* Cafe, *Trin.* 1 *Ann. B. R.* Judgment A Verdict was given in *Eafter* Term, and be- may be after fore Judgment figned the Plaintiff died.   *Et* Plaintiff's Death, pro- *per Holt,* Ch. J. That fhall not hinder the vided it be Judgment being enter'd, provided it be with- within two in two Terms after ; and the Statute of Frauds Terms after and Perjuries only requires the Time of Sign- Verdict. ing fhould be enter'd upon the Roll ; and this is only for the Benefit of Purchafers ; for if Judgment be figned in the Vacation, yet 'tis enter'd as of a Term before, and none but a Purchafer fhall be admitted to fay, it was figned as of any other Time ; and it is the Courfe of the Court, to let all Things be done in the Vacation, as of the Term before. 1 *Sal-keld* 401.

By the 8 & 9 *W.* 3. *cap.* 11. *Intitled an Act* Full Cofts in *for the better preventing frivolous and vexati-* Trefpafs, &c. *cus Suits,* it was enacted, ‘ That where feve- to every De- ‘ ral Perfons fhall be made Defendants to any fendant ac- ‘ Action of Trefpafs, Affault, Falfe Impri- quitted upon Trial.

D 3   ‘ fonment,

' sonment, or *Ejectione firmæ*, and any one or
' more shall upon Trial be acquitted by Ver-
' dict; every Person so acquitted shall recover

Unless the Judge certify. ' his Costs of Suit, unless the judge shall im-
' mediately after the Trial in open Court,
' certify upon the Record that there was a
' reasonable Cause, for making such Person or
' Persons a Defendant or Defendants to such
' Action.

Costs upon a Demurrer. ' And that if any Person shall commence
' in any Court of Record any Action or Suit,
' wherein upon demurrer Judgment shall be
' given against the Plaintiff or Defendant;
' or if at any Time after Judgment given for

Costs on a Writ of Error. ' the Defendant, the Plaintiff shall sue a Writ
' of Error, and the said Judgment shall be af-
' firmed, or the said Writ discontinued, or the
' Plaintiff nonsuit therein, the defendant shall
' have Judgment to recover his Costs against
' such Plaintiff, and Execution by *Capias ad*
' *satisfaciendum, Fieri facias* or *Elegit.*

Costs in Debt for not setting out Tithes. ' That in all Actions of Waste and Debt,
' upon the Statute for not setting forth of
' Tithes, where the Damage found by the
' Jury shall not exceed twenty Nobles; and
' in all Suits upon writs of *Scire facias:*
' And upon Prohibitions, the Plaintiff obtain-
' ing Judgment, or Award of Execution after
' Plea pleaded, or Demurrer joined therein,
' shall likewise recover his Costs of Suit; and
' if the Plaintiff become nonsuit or discontinue,
' or a Verdict pass against him, the Defen-
' dant shall have Costs and Execution for the
' same,

Wilful Tres-pass, full Costs. ' That in all Actions of Trespass commenc'd
' in any Court of Record, where it shall ap-
' pear at the Trial, and be certified by the
' Judge

' Judge on the back of the Record, That the
' Trespass was wilful and malicious, the Plain-
' tiff shall recover not only his Damages, but
' full Costs of Suit.

' Provided nothing herein contained shall al- *Not extended*
' ter the laws in Being, as to Executors and *to executors,*
' Administrators, in such Cases where they are *and Admini-*
' not at present liable to pay Costs of Suit. *strators.*

' That in all Actions to be commenced in *Plaintiff or*
' any Court of Record, if the Plaintiff die af- *Defendant*
' ter any interlocutory Judgment, and before a *dying after*
' final Judgment, the said Action shall not a- *an interlocu-*
' bate, if the said Action might be originally *tory Judg-*
' prosecuted by his Executors or Administra- *ment, and be-*
' tors ; and if the Defendant die after such in- *fore a final*
' terlocutory Judgment, and before a final *Judgment,*
' Judgment, the Action shall not abate, if such *the Action*
' Action might be originally prosecuted against *shall not a-*
' his Executors or Administrators ; and the *bate.*
' Executors or Administrators of such Plaintiff,
' after such interlocutory Judgment, may have
' a *Scire facias* against the Defendant if li-
' ving ; or if dead, against his Executors or
' Administrators, to shew Cause why Dama-
' ges should not be assessed and recovered a-
' gainst him or them ; and if he or they do
' not appear at the Return, and shew suffici-
' ent Cause to arrest the final Judgment, or
' being returned warned, or upon two Writs
' of *Scire facias*, it being returned that the
' Defendant had nothing whereby to be sum-
' moned, or could not be found ; a Writ of
' Inquiry of Damages shall be awarded, which
' being executed and returned, Judgment final
' shall be given for the Plaintiff, his Executors
' or Administrators.

' If

Death of one of the Plaintiffs or defendants, where is more than one, fhall not abate the Action.

' If there be two or more Plaintiffs or Defendants, and one die, if the Caufe of Action furvive to the furviving Plaintiff, or against the furviving Defendant, the Writ or Action fhall not abate; but fuch Death being fuggefted upon the Record, the Action fhall proceed.

Plaintiff in Debt on Bond, &c. for Non-performance of Covenants, to affign as many Breaches as he thinks fit.

' That in all Actions profecuted in any Court of Record, upon any Bond or penal Sum for Non-performance of Covenants, the Plaintiff may affign as many Breaches as he fhall think fit; and the Jury at the Trial fhall and may affefs Damages for fuch of the faid Breaches fo affigned, as the Plaintiff at the Trial fhall prove broken, and the like Judgment fhall be entered on fuch Verdict as hath been ufually done in fuch Actions.

And the Jury may affefs Damages accordingly.

And if Judgment be given for the Plaintiff, upon Demurrer, Confeffion or *nihil dicit*, the Plaintiff upon the Roll may fuggeft as many Breaches as he fhall think fit, upon which fhall iffue a Writ to fummon a Jury to appear at the Affizes of that refpective County, to inquire of the Truth of every one of thofe Breaches, and to affefs Damages accordingly: And the Juftices of Affize fhall make Return thereof to the court from

Defendant paying Damages and Cofts affeffed, Execution to be ftay'd.

whence the fame iffued: In Cafe the Defendant after fuch Judgment entered, and before fuch Execution executed, fhall pay into Court fuch Damages fo affeffed, and Cofts of Suit, a Stay of Execution fhall be entered of Record; or if by reafon of Execution executed, the Plaintiff or his Executors or Adminiftrators fhall be fully paid all fuch Damages, together with his Cofts and reafonable Charges, the Body, Lands, and
' Goods

' Goods of the Defendant shall be forthwith
' discharged, and the Satisfaction entered upon
' Record : Yet shall such Judgment stand and *But the Judg-*
' be as a further Security to answer the Plain- *ment to stand*
' tiff, his Executors, &c. such Damages as *as a Security*
' shall or may be sustained, for farther Breach *against farther*
' of any Covenant in the same Deed or Wri- *Breaches.*
' ting contained, upon which the Plaintiff,
' &c. may have a *Scire Facias* upon the said
' Judgment against the Defendant, his Heir, *Whereupon*
' Ter-tenants, Executors, or Administrators, *the Plaintiff*
' suggesting other Breaches, and to summon *may have a*
' them to shew Cause, why Execution shall not *Scire facias:*
' be awarded upon the said Judgment; upon
' which there shall be the like Proceedings as
' aforesaid : And upon Payment of Damages
' and Costs, Proceedings to be again stay'd,
' and so *toties quoties*, and the Defendant dis-
' charged out of Execution.'

By 4 & 5 *Ann. c.* 16. intitled, *An Act for
the Amendment of the Law, and the better Ad-
vancement of Justice*, it was enacted, ' That *On demurrer*
' upon Demurrer joined in any Court of Re- *no Imperfec-*
' cord, the Judges shall give Judgment as the *tions to be re-*
' Right and Matter in Law shall appear, with- *garded, but*
' out regarding any Imperfection or Defect in *such as are*
' any Writ, Return, Pleading, or Process, ex- *set down as*
' cept those which the Party demurring shall *Causes of*
' set down as Causes of his Demurrer, notwith- *Demurrer.*
' standing such Imperfection or Defect have
' been taken to be Matter of Substance, and
' not aided by 27 *Eliz. c.* 5. so as sufficient
' Matter may appear, upon which the Court
' may give Judgment. And no Exception
' shall be taken for an immaterial Traverse,
' Default of entring Pledges, upon Bill or De-
' claration, or not alledging the bringing into
' Court

' Court any Deed mentioned in the Pleading,
' Letters Testamentary, or of Administration,
' or for Omission of *Vi & armis & contra Pa-*
' *cem*, or either of them, or *bcc parat. est veri-*
' *ficare*, or *parat. est verificare per Recordum,*
' or *prout patet per Recordum* : But the Court
' shall give Judgment without regarding such
' Imperfections or Defects, or other Matter of
' like Nature, except shewed for Cause.

In *Replevin*
several Mat-
ters may be
pleaded with
Leave of the
Court.

' That the Defendant or Tenant, or Plain-
' tiff in *Replevin*, in any Court of Record, with
' Leave may plead as many several Matters as
' are necessary. [*And it is upon the Equity*
of this Clause, that the Courts do now in ge-
neral allow the Defendant in most Actions by
Rule to plead as many several Pleas as he shall
be advised.]

If such Mat-
ter be insuffi-
cient, full
Costs.

' Proviso, If any such Matter on Demurrer
' be judged insufficient, Costs shall be given at
' the Discretion of the Court: Or if a Ver-
' dict be found on any such Issue for the Plain-
' tiff or Demandant, Costs shall be given in like
' Manner ; unless the Judge certify that the
' Defendant, Tenant, or Plaintiff in *Replevin*
' had a probable Cause to plead it.

No dilatory
Plea to be
received.

' That no dilatory Plea shall be received in
' any Court of Record, unless the Truth there-
' of be proved by *Affidavit*, or some probable
' Matter shewn.

Where Pay-
ment may be
pleaded in
Debt.
Condition of
a Bond satif
fied, Payment
may be plead-
ed.

' In Debt on a single Bill, Debt, or *Scire*
' *facias* upon a Judgment, the Defendant may
' plead Payment in Bar. In Debt upon a
' Bond, if the Defendant before Action
' brought, hath paid the principal and Inte-
' rest due by the Defeasance or Condition, he
' may plead Payment in Bar.

" Pending

' Pending an Action on such Bond, Defend- Defendant
' ant may bring in Principal, Interest and discharged on
' Costs in Law and Equity, and then the bringing in
' Court shall give Judgment to discharge the Principal, In-
' Defendant. terest, and
Costs.

Lazier versus *Dyer*, *Mich.* 2 *A. B. R.* If- If there be no
sue being joined and entered as of *Trinity* Proceeding *in*
Term, the Plaintiff rested till the *Trinity* Term *Fact*, within
following, and then gave notice of Trial after four Terms,
the Term; and a *Venire facias* and *Distringas* a Term's No-
was taken out in the Vacation, but tested and tice of Trial.
entered as of the Term. *Per Cur':* This is
not sufficient Notice; for though in Law this
was a Proceeding within the Term; yet in Fact
it was a Proceeding in Vacation, and therefore
there was not a Term's Notice of Trial.
2 *Salk.* 457.

In all Cases in which there have been no
Proceedings for four Terms, exclusive of the
Term in which the last Proceeding was had, the
Party who desires to proceed again, shall give
a Term's Notice to the other of such Proceeding; such Notice to be given before the Essoin
Day of the Fifth or other subsequent Term; a
Judge's Summons, if no Order be made thereupon, shall not be deemed a Proceeding, but
a Notice of Trial, though afterwards countermanded shall. Rule *Easter*, 13 *Geo.* 2. And

Verdict set aside for want of a Term's No-
tice, there having been no Proceedings for a
Year, pursuant to the above Rule. *Mich.* 17
Geo. 2. *Blackmore* v. *Smith.* 2 *Barnes*'s Notes
242.—This does not extend to Motions to *end*
Proceedings. *Ibid.* 244.

Said *per Cur.* That the King shall pay Costs Crown pays
for an Amendment, but shall not pay Costs for Costs for A-
not going on to Trial: But where there is a but not for
Prosecutor, not going on
to Trial.

Proſecutor, he ſhall pay Coſts for Amendments, and for not going on to Trial both. *Hil.* 8 *W.* 3. *The King* v. *Edwards. B. R.* But then there muſt be an *Affidavit* of the Name of him who is the Proſecutor, for that does not appear upon the Indictment: And if the Defendant does not know the Proſecutor, he ought to apply to the Attorney General, who will inform him. *Salk.* 193.

If a Cauſe has continued *four* Terms without Proſecution after Iſſue joined, there muſt be a Term's Notice of Trial, ſuch Notice to be given before the Eſſoin-Day of the Fifth, or other ſubſequent Term. A Judge's Summons, if no Order made, is no Proceeding; but a Notice of Trial though countermanded, is. *Harriſon's Pract. B. R.* 137. *Str.* 211, 1164.

The Court, on Motion for a new Trial, held, that the giving Notice of Trial, at the End of half a Year after Iſſue joined, would prevent the Neceſſity of giving a Term's Notice, till a Year after the laſt Notice, which was given and countermanded. *Str.* 531.

Demurrer to Part, and Iſſue to other Part. *Anonymus, Mich.* 13 *W.* 3. *B. R.* If there be a Demurrer to Part, and an Iſſue upon the other Part, and Judgment be given for the Plaintiff upon the Demurrer, he may enter a *Non Proſ.* as to the Iſſue, and proceed to a Writ of Inquiry on the Demurrer; but without a *Non Proſ.* he cannot have a Writ of Inquiry, becauſe on the Trial of the Iſſue, the ſame Jury will aſcertain the Damages for that Part to which the Demurrer was. *Per Cur'. Salk.* 219.

Where a new Trial will not be granted. *Watſon* verſus *Sutton*; a new Trial will not be granted for Matter omitted to be inſiſted on at a former Trial. *Salk.* 273.

3   *Cur.*

Cur. declared, That it was againſt the Rule No Trial at Bar before Iſſue joined ; of Court to grant a Trial at Bar in any Caſe before Iſſue is joined, and accordingly it was refuſed in this Caſe, becauſe Iſſue was not joined, though both Sides conſented ; for till the Court knows what the Iſſue is, it is below their Dignity to direct it to be tried at Bar, for it may be an Iſſue in which there may be no manner of Difficulty. *Eaſter,* 12 *Geo.* 1. The Caſe of the Borough of *Chriſt-Church* in *B. R. M. S.* Rep. *Eaſter,* 4 *Geo.* 2. *Butler* Executor v. Lord *Montgomery,* S. P. *Ibid.*——No Trial at Bar nor the Term it is prayed. can be the Term it is prayed. *Ibid.*

Trials at Bar are grantable either upon the Value of the Lands or Difficulty of the Title. *M.* 4 *Geo.* 2. *Haycroft* v. *Roſe, MS. Rep.*

For putting off Trials for want of Witneſſes, it is neceſſary to ſwear that the Party is adviſed, and believes the Perſons abſent are material Witneſſes, and that he cannot ſafely proceed to Trial without their Evidence, and alſo to add when they are expected.

C H A P. III.

Of a Venire facias ; *to whom it ſhall be directed ; when to the Sheriff, when to the Coroners, when to Eſliſors, and when to Bailiffs, when well awarded,* &c.

HAVING given you the Epitome of what Trials are allowed by the Common Law, and what ſhall be tried *per Pais,* and what not, we ſhall now apply ourſelves more particularly to the Trial by Juries : And becauſe a *Venire facias*

facias is the Foundation and *Caufa fine qua non* of a Jury, (I mean in Civil Caufes;) for in Criminal, as upon Indictments, the Juftices of Gaol-Delivery give a general Command to the Sheriff, to caufe the Country to come againft their Coming, and take the Panels of the Sheriff, without any Procefs directed to him; yet Procefs may be made againft the Jury, though it is not much ufed. *Staunford Pleas del Corone* **155.** I will firft recite the Writ *in terminis,* the rather becaufe I intend to order my Difcourfe according to the Method of the Writ.

Venire facias.   *Rex, &c. Vic.* B. *Salutem. Praecipimus tibi quod venire facias coram Jufticiariis noftris de Banco apud Weftm. tali die duodecim liberos & legales homines de vicinet. de* C. *quorum quilibet habeat quatuor libras terrae, tenement. vel reddit' per annum ad minus, per quos rei veritas melius fciri poterit; & qui nec* D. E. *nec* F. G. *aliqua affinitate attingunt, ad faciend. quandam Jur. patriae inter partes praedict. de placito, &c. quia tam idem* D. *quam praedict.* F. *inter quos inde contentio eft, pofuer. fe in Jur' illam. Et habeas ibi nomina Jur. illorum & hoc breve. Tefte, &c.*

This is one of thofe *Latin* Letters, (as *Finch* terms them, *f.* 237.) which the King fends with Salutation to the Sheriff; but withal commands him, That he caufe to come twelve free and lawful Men of his County, to refolve the Queftion of the Fact in Difpute between the Parties upon the Iffue; and it is a Judicial Writ, iffuing out of the Record, for Plaintiff or Defendant, after they have put themfelves upon the Country : For upon the Words *Et de hoc ponit fe fuper patriam,* by the Defendant, or

Et

Et hoc petit quod inquiratur per patriam, by the Plaintiff, and Issue joined thereupon, the Court awardeth the *Venire facias,* viz. *Ideo fiat inde Jurat.'*

When Issue is joined in Chancery, that Court awards the *Venire* to be returnable in *B. R.* and there is no other Way to give a Day here in *B. R.* but by such an Award ; and it is always so done. *Vin. Trial,* 295.

Ideo venit inde Jurat. is Error in inferior Courts, for it ought to be *Ideo Præcept. est vic. quod ven. fac',* &c. *Siderfin* 364. and it should be *de visneto de* C. specially. *Keble* 2 Part, 350.

And if they come not at the Day of the Writ returned, then shall go forth against them an *Habeas Corpora* and *Distringas* to bring them in to try the Matter. The which two last Writs are usually made with this Clause, *Nisi prius Justiciarii venerint,* &c. and are returnable after the Time of the Judges coming their Circuit.

And first, you see it is directed *Vicecomiti,* i.e. to one who is *Vicecomes,* and hath the Regimen of the County instead of the Earl of that County, to whom once it did belong ; as we are taught in the *Mirror, cap.* 1. *sect.* 3. *scil.*
' That it appeareth by the Ordinance of ancient
' Kings before the Conquest, that the Earls of
' the Counties had the Custody or Guard of the
' Counties.   And when the Earls left their Cu-
' stody or Guards, then was the Custody of
' Counties committed to Viscounts, who there-
' fore are called *Vicecomites.'*

What great Repose and Trust both the King and Laws put in this great Officer, the Oracle tells you, 1 *Inst.* 168.   That he is Sheriff, that is, *Præfectus Comitatûs,* Governor of the Coun-

Sheriff. 1 Inst. 168.

What Trust in the Sheriff.

ty ;

ty ; for the Words of his Patent be, *Commifimus vobis Cuftodiam Comitatûs noftri de, &c.* And he had a threefold Cuftody, *triplicem Cuftodiam, viz.* Firft, *Vitæ Juftitiæ* ; for no Suit begins, and no Procefs is ferved but by the Sheriff. *And he is to return indifferent Juries for the Trial of Mens Lives, Liberties, Lands, Goods, &c.* Secondly, *Vitæ Legis,* he is after long Suits and chargeable, to make Execution, which is the Life and Soul of the Law. Thirdly, *Vitæ Reipublicæ,* he is *Principalis Confervator Pacis* within the County, which is the Life of the Commonwealth, for *Vita Reipublicæ Pax.*

To whom the *Venire facias* ought to be directed. Yet notwithftanding the Height and Latitude of this great Officer's Power and Truft, the Law adjudges him in many Cafes not capable to do fo much as return a Jury ; for if he be of Kindred by Nature, or of Affinity by Marriage, to any of the Parties, or (that I may fay all in a little) if he be not as indifferent almoft in all Refpects, as he is whom the Law allows to be a Juror, he ought not to meddle **Coroners.** with the returning of the Jury ; but the *Venire facias* fhall be directed to the Coroners (or to fome of them, if the Refidue are not indifferent) who in that Cafe are *hac vice Vicecom.* And if the Coroners are not indifferent, then **Fortefcue, cap. 2. 5.** the *Venire* fhall be directed *ad 2 Electores,* that is, to two whom the Court fhall chufe and deem fit to return the Jury ; and to the Return of thefe *Elifors* or *Eflifors, ab Eligendo,* no **Eflifors.** **Challenge.** Challenge will be admitted, *Bro. Tit. Venire* **Sheriff of London.** *facias,* 14. as to the Array, but to the Polls, **Of *London* or of any Place, where two Perfons make one Sheriff.** 1 *Inft.* 158. If one of the Sheriffs of *London* be a Party, then the *Venire* may be directed to the other Sheriff ; if the Under-Sheriff be a Party, yet the *Venire* may be directed to the Sheriff,

Sheriff, with this Proviso, *Quod Sub-Vic. tuus in nullo se intromittat cum executione istius brevis.* 18 *E.* 4. 3.

Judicial Writs may be directed to the Coroners, as the *Venire facias*, where the Parties are at Issue ; there, upon the Surmise of the Plaintiff, that the Sheriff is his Cousin, and upon Prayer that the *Venire* be directed to the Coroners, for Avoidance of his own Delay that might happen by the Challenge of the Array, the Defendant shall be examined, whether it be true or not ; and if he confesses it, then the *Venire* shall be awarded to the Coroners ; for then it appears to the Court by the Defendant's Confession, that the Sheriff is not indifferent ; but if the Defendant denies it, then the Process shall be awarded to the Sheriff because the Sheriff's Authority and Profit shall not be taken away, without Cause apparent to the Court ; and the Defendant shall never take any Challenge for that Case : But if the Defendant will alledge any such Matter, and pray a *Venire facias* to the Coroners, there the Plaintiff shall not be examined ; neither shall such Allegations be allowed, because Delays are for the Defendant's Advantage, and the Defendant may challenge the Jury for this Cause, and so is at no Prejudice.

And see in *Term. Hill.* 3 *H.* 7. *f.* 5. *placit. ult.* in a *Quare impedit,* where the Defendant shewed how the Sheriff was Cousin to the Plaintiff, and prayed a Writ to the Coroners, but it was denied him upon the same Reason. *Fitz.* Tit. *Suggestion, placit.* 8. Br. *Challenge,* 153.

In the Lord *Brooks*'s Case, *Trin.* 1657. B. R. In Ejectment, the Court was moved that the Lord *Brooks* might be made Ejector, which was granted ; then the Court was informed that the Lessor of the Plaintiff was High She-

Margin notes:

Suggestion.

1 Inst.157. b.

Of whom.

Coroners.

So in Ejectment against four, upon Affinity of the Sheriff to one of the Defendants. Roll. Tit. Trial, 668. Examination.

Not of the Defendant's Suggestion.

The Defendant may not have a *Venire facias* to the Coroners.

riff of the County, and that the Coroner was Under-Sheriff; and it was prayed that *Elisors* might return the *Jury*; but the Court would not grant it at the Prayer of the Defendant, though the Plaintiff offered to agree to it, it being in a Trial by *Nisi prius*; but had it been in a Trial at Bar, they would have granted it. But the regular Course is for the Plaintiff to pray it, or else the Defendant may challenge the Array at the Assizes; for it is a principal Challenge, that the Lessor of the Plaintiff is High Sheriff, or of Kindred to the Sheriff; for which see *Hutt.* 25. *Moor* 470. *Roll. Rep.* 328. And it was so adjudged, *Trin.* 15 *Car.* 2. *B. R. Duncomb* and *Ingleby*, that it is a principal Challenge.

For what Caufes Procefs fhall be direct-ed to the Co-roners.

' In Ejectment, the Plaintiff fuggefted, That he and one of the Coroners were all of the Livery *del Countee Wigorn'*, and prayed a *Venire facias* to the other Coroner; although this is no principal Challenge, and the Defendant might have oppofed the Prayer, yet becaufe he confeffed it, the Award was well to the Coroner. So if the Caufe be, that one of the Coroners be retained of Counfel with the Plaintiff. If the Suggeftion do not comprehend a principal Challenge, but only of Favour, this is not fufficient to award Procefs to the Coroners: But if it be a principal Challenge, as Affinity, &c. if the Defendant confefs it, the Award fhall be to the Coroners; if he will not confefs it, then to the Sheriff; and in fuch Cafe the Defendant fhall never challenge the Array for that Caufe: So if the Plaintiff pray Procefs to the Coroners for Favour in the Sheriff, if the Defendant fay that this is not favourable, he fhall

3   never

never challenge for Favour, unless *de puisne temps.* 2 *Roll. Trial,* 668. *H.*

If the Array be quashed, because made. by the Sheriff's Minister, who was aiding and of Counsel with one of the Parties, yet the Writ shall not be directed to the Coroners, but to the Sheriff, commanding him to make the Panel by another Officer ; as, *ita quod* the Under-Sheriff *ne se intromittat, &c.* 2 *Roll. Trial,* 669. *pl.* 12.

Note; The Sheriff may appoint a general Officer in a Court, and his Return shall be good. *Keble* 1 Part 357.

If the *Tales* be quashed for Affinity in the Sheriff, but not the principal Panel, because it was made before the Affinity, yet all shall be awarded to the Coroners, *scil.* the *Distringas* of the principal Panel, and that they return a new *Tales* ; for there shall be but one Officer ; if the Array be quashed, because made but by one of the Coroners, or for Affinity in one, *&c.* yet the Process shall still go to the Coroners, *ita quod* the said Coroner *ne se intromittat.* 2 *Roll. Trial,* 669. *pl.* 17, *&* 670. *K. pl.* 2.

If Default be in the Sheriff and Coroners, the Court may chuse two *Eslisors* (*a*) ; and if the Parties can say nothing against them, they shall make the Panel. *Ibid.* 670. *L. pl.* 1.

To whom the Process shall be directed for Default in the Sheriff and Coroners.

But the *Distringas* shall not be directed to *Eslisors,* for the Court cannot make Officers to distrain the King's Liege People, but the King may. 8 *H.* 6. 12. *Dubitatur.*

2 Roll. Trial, 670. L. 2.

(*a*) *Eslisors* are Persons appointed by a Court of Law, to whom a Writ of *Venire facias* is directed to impanel a *Jury,* on *Challenge* to the *Sheriff* and *Coroners* ; to return the Writ in their own Names, with a Panel of the Jurors Names. 15 *Ed.* 4. 24. *pl.* 4.

Procefs may be directed to the Juftices of Affife, by Affent of Parties, not without.

When a Panel is made by the *Eflifors*, they fhall afterwards ferve all Procefs that comes upon this, as the Sheriff fhould. 15 *Ed.* 4. 24. 18 *Ed.* 4. 3, 8. *Roll.* Tit. *Trial* 670. For it may be the Sheriff will diftrain only thofe who are his Friends and be partial.

1 Inft. 158. *Venire facias* once directed to the Coroner, fhall not be to the Sheriff afterwards.

When the Procefs is once awarded to the Coroners, for a Default in the Sheriff, if there be a new Sheriff made afterwards, who is indifferent, yet the Procefs fhall not revert, but continue to the Coroners *pendant le Plea.* 14 *H.* 7. 31. *Bro.* Tit. *Venire facias* 17. So the Entry is, *Ita quod Vicecomes fe non intromittat.* 18 *E.* 4. 3. 8 *H.* 6. 12. And though a new Sheriff comes in before it be returned, yet the Coroners fhall proceed to the Execution of it.

Sheriff fhall not return the *Tales*, where he cannot the *Venire facias*.

And therefore, where the Sheriff ought not to return the *Venire*, he cannot return the *Tales.* For in Error in the *Exchequer-Chamber*, of a Judgment in the *Queen's Bench*, the Error affigned was becaufe the *Venire facias* was awarded to the Coroners, for Confanguinity in the Sheriff; and it was returned by Coroners, and afterwards the *Tales* was awarded, and it was returned by the Sheriff, and it was tried, and a Verdict given, and Judgment. And for this Caufe held to be erroneous, and not aided by the Statute of 32 *H.* 8. or 18 *Eliz.* Wherefore the Judgment was reverfed. *Cro. El.* 574. *Bro.* Tit. *Octo Tales,* 9.

I will inftance one Cafe more in the fame Reports, *fol.* 586. becaufe it is very full in the Point. After Iffue in Trefpafs, the Plaintiff for his Expedition furmifed, that he was Servant to the Sheriff, which being confeffed by

I   the

the Defendant, the Process was awarded to the
Coroners; and after Verdict it was moved in
Arrest of Judgment, that the *Tales de circum-* Where the
stantibus was awarded, and returned by the Coroner re-
Sheriff, which was held by the whole Court to turns the *Ve-*
nire facias, he
be good Cause for staying the Judgment; for ought to re-
it is a Mis-trial not aided by any of the Sta- turn the *Tales.*
tutes; for Process being once awarded to the
Coroners, the Sheriff afterwards is not the Officer to return the Jury, no more than any other
Man; and Process ought always to be returned
by him, who is an Officer by Law to return it;
otherwise it is merely void. But afterwards,
upon View of the Record, it appeared that the
Tales was returned by the Coroners, and their
Names annexed thereto; wherefore it was without further Question. But the Court said, If No Name to
their Names had not been annexed to the *Tales,* the Return.
yet it had been well enough; for they be annexed to the first Panel, and it shall be intended that the right Officer returned it; and
the usual Course is, That to such *Tales* there is
not any Officer's Name subscribed, and yet it
is good enough; for it is not within the Statute
of *York,* which appoints, That the Name of
the Sheriff should be subscribed; but it was moved that the Record of the *Postea* is, That the
Tales were returned by the Sheriff; but the
Court held, That it was amendable, and it was
done accordingly, and the Plaintiff had Judgment.

But if the *Venire* be awarded to the Coro- *Venire facias*
ners, for Default in the Sheriff, and they to the Sheriff,
do nothing upon the Writ; then, upon a after one a-
warded to the
Default discovered in the Coroner, *de puisne* Coroners.
temps, the Party may shew this to the Court,
and have a *Venire* awarded to the Sheriff, (if

there

there be an indifferent one made in the mean Time) or elfe to *Eſliſors*, & *ſic è converſo*.

In Error of a Judgment in *Cheſter*, the Parties being at Iſſue, a *Venire* was awarded to the Sheriff, and at the Day of the Return, it was entred *Quod Vicecomes non miſit breve*. And then the Plaintiff prayed a *Venire facias* to the Coroners, for Cozenage betwixt him and the Sheriff, which was awarded accordingly ; and at the Day of Trial the Defendant made Default, and there, upon Judgment, Error was aſſigned, becauſe that after the Plaintiff had admitted the Sheriff to execute the Writ, he could not pray a *Venire facias* to the Coroners, without ſome Cauſe *de puiſne Temps*; *ſed non allocatur*, becauſe there was nothing done upon the firſt Writ. And the Defendant having made Default, it was not material. *Cro.* 3. Part 853.

Venire facias to the Coroners, after one to the Sheriff.

But the Defendant might have demurred to this Prayer; for if the Plaintiff pray a *Venire facias* to the Sheriff, he ſhall not challenge the Array, nor have a *Venire* afterwards to the Coroners, becauſe the Sheriff is his Couſin, or for any other principal Challenge, whereof he might by common Intendment have Conuſance, when he ſo prayed the *Venire facias* ; for upon ſhewing this Cauſe at firſt, he might have prayed Proceſs to the Coroners; but for a principal Challenge, of which, by common Intendment, the Plaintiff could not know at the firſt, as that the Defendant is of Kindred to the Sheriff, &c. he may afterwards challenge the Array when they appear; or if the Sheriff doth nothing upon the Writ, he may pray a new *Venire* to the Coroners. 15 *H.* 7. 9.

No Venire farias to the Coroners, after one to the Sheriff.

If

If the Plaintiff prays a *Venire facias* to the Coroners, becaufe he is of Kindred to the She- riff, if the Defendant will not confefs this, but denies it, this fhall be entred, and the Defen- dant fhall not challenge the Array for this Caufe afterwards. *Br.* Tit. *Venire facias,* 21 and 23.

If the Defen- dant denies the Plaintiff's Suggeftion, he fhall have no Benefit of it by Challenge.

If a *Venire facias* be awarded to the Coro- ners, where it ought to be to the Sheriff, or the *Vifne* cometh out of a wrong Place, yet if it be *ex affenfû partium,* and fo entred of Re- cord, it fhall ftand ; for *omnis confenfus tollit er- rorem.* 1 *Inft.* 126. *lib.* 5. 36. But if it be directed to the Coroners, where it ought to be to the Sheriff, without fuch Confent of Parties, this is an infufficient Trial, not remedied by any Statute, except it be upon an infufficient Suggeftion, and then the Statute of 21 *Jac. c.* 13. helps it.

By Confent, the *Venire fa- cias* may be directed to a wrong Offi- cer.

Mif-trial without fuch Confent.

Upon Suggeftion that the Plaintiff and the Sheriff, and one of the Coroners are of Kin- dred to the Plaintiff or Defendant, or upon any other Suggeftion which contains a principal Challenge, the *Venire facias* may be directed to other Coroners. *Dyer* 367.

Venire facias to fome of the Coroners.

Error of a Judgment in *Northampton,* be- caufe in *Northampton,* the Court being held be- fore the Mayor and two Bailiffs, the *Venire fa- cias* upon the Iffue was awarded to the two Bailiffs to return a Jury, before the Mayor and Bailiffs, *fecundum confuetudinem,* which being re- turned, and Judgment given, the Error af- figned was, becaufe the Bailiffs being Judges of the Court, could not alfo be Officers to whom Procefs fhould be directed, there being no Cu- ftom that can maintain any to be both Officer and Judge. But all the Court (*abfente Hyde*)

Bailiffs.

E 4　　　　conceived

conceived it might be good by Cuftom, and that it is not any Error; for the Judges be not the Bailiffs only, but the Mayor and Bailiffs; and it is a common Courfe in many of the ancient Corporaions, where the Bailiffs are Judges, or the Mayor and they be Judges; yet in refpect of executing Procefs, they be Officers alfo; and one may be Judge and Officer *diverfis refpectibus*; as in Rediffcifin, the Sheriff is Judge and Officer: Whereupon Judgment was affirmed. *Cro.* 1 Part 138.

Judge and Officer to return Writs.

In Trefpafs and Affault laid in the Count, to be at the Palace of *Weftminfter,* it was adjudged, That the *Venire facias* fhall iffue *al Garden del Palace,* and not to the Sheriff of *Middlefex. Bro.* Tit. *Ven. fac.* 31.

Venire facias to the Garden of the Palace of Weftminfter. Roll. Tit. *Trial,* 667.

In Trefpafs againft two, if one plead, and two Iffues are joined upon his Plea, and two other Iffues are alfo joined, and the Court award a *Venire ad triandum tam exitum illum quam prædictum alium exitum inter* the Plaintiff and the other Defendant, *&c.* this is a good Award, although there be feveral Iffues betwixt the Plaintiff and both Defendants, becaufe that this Word *Exitus* may be for all, *reddendo fingula fingulis. Hob.* 91.

Award of Venire facias.

If an Inqueft remain for Default of *Rapers,* and a *Decem Tales* is awarded, and the Defendant faith for his Deliverance, That he is Lord of the *Rape,* where, *&c.* and that all there are within his Diftrefs, and prays a Writ to the next Hundred; the Court may try this by *Triors* prefently, without a Return of the Sheriff; and if it be true, may award to the next Hundred; otherwife, if it be falfe. 3 *H.* 6. 39.

Prochein Hundred.

Rex

Rex verſus *Reed:* Upon an Information of Perjury at the Common Law, one of the Jurors was named *J. S.* in the *Venire,* and *J. S.* junior in the *Diſtringas,* and yet held to be good. 1 *Sid.* 66.

Variance between the *Venire* and *Diſtringas,* and yet good.

In an Action on the Caſe for Deceit; or, in an Action on the Caſe for an Eſcape; the Court will not change the *Venue* from the County where the Plaintiff hath ſuppoſed the Fact to be done. 1 *Sid.* 87.

Where the Court will not alter the *Venue.*

Tubbe verſus *Whiteworth:* In an Action on the Caſe, it was moved in Arreſt of Judgment, That the *Venire facias* was of *Taunton-Dean,* and therefore no good Trial, for *Taunton-Dean* was a large Country, conſiſting of ſeveral Vills; but the Court held it to be good after Verdict, and that it ſhould be intended the Vill, and not all the Country of *Taunton-Dean.* 1 *Sid.* 88.

Venue from a Place containing ſeveral Vills.

In *Kighly* verſus *Bulky,* it was held, That where the Iſſue was local, the *Venire* could not be changed by the Conſent of the Parties. 1 *Sid.* 339.

If the Iſſue be local, not to be changed by Conſent.

Swaine's Caſe: If there be two Cauſes of Action in the Declaration, one in one County, and the other in another County; and *Affidavit* of the Cauſe of Action (if any) in one of them, yet that ſhall not exclude the Plaintiff of his Election; as in *Trover,* if the Defendant becomes poſſeſſed in *Kent,* and he brings the Goods and ſells them in *London,* and the Plaintiff brings his Action in *London;* there, upon the common *Affidavit,* the *Venire* ſhall not be removed from *London;* and in the principal Caſe now moved in *Aſſumpſit,* the Promiſe was agreed to be in *Dorcheſter,* and the Breach in *Middleſex;* and the Plaintiff declared in *Middleſex,*

Cauſe of Action in two Counties, the Plaintiff may chuſe either.

dlesex, and the Court upon *Affidavit* would not change the *Venue* to *Dorchester*.   1 *Sid.* 405.

Venue twice changed.

King versus *Atkins: Action sur Assumpsit* was brought in *London*, and upon the common *Affidavit*, the *Venire* was changed to *Hampshire*; and although it was changed, the Plaintiff in another Term made *Affidavit*, That his Cause of Action arose in *Northamptonshire*, and upon a Rule, that he would not give in Evidence any Matter out of *Northamptonshire*, it was laid there, notwithstanding he had first laid it in *London*.   1 *Sid.* 442.

Where there are two Sheriffs, and one challenged, the *Venire* shall be directed to the other Sheriff, and not to the Coroners.   *Shower* 329. *Comberb.* 191.   1 *Salk.* 144.   *Carthew* 214.

One Sheriff not indifferent, *Venue*, to be directed to the other. *Venire de novo* to issue, where the Parties do not proceed to Trial at the first Assizes after the *Teste* of the *Habeas Corpora* or *Distringas*.

If any Plaintiff, or Demandant, being at Issue, shall bring to the Sheriff any Writ of *Habeas Corpora*, or *Distringas*, with a *Nisi prius* Issue, in order to try such Issue at the Assizes, and such Plaintiff or Demandant shall not proceed to Trial at the first Assizes after the *Teste* of such *Habeas Corpora, &c.* In all such Cases, other than where Views of Jurors shall be directed, the Plaintiff or Demandant, when he shall think fit to try the said Issue at any other Assizes, shall sue forth a new Writ of *Venire*, whereupon the Plaintiff or Demandant may proceed to Trial; and so *toties quoties*, as the Case shall require: So also where the Tenant or Defendant shall bring the Cause to Trial by *Proviso.* 7 *&* 8 *W.* 3. *cap.* 32.

By *Stat.* 3 *G.* 1. *c.* 15. *sect.* 8. It is enacted, ' That if any High Sheriff of any County of ' *England* or *Wales*, shall happen to die before ' the Expiration or Determination of his Year, ' or before he be lawfully superseded, in such
'   ' Case

' Cafe the Under-Sheriff, or Deputy Sheriff by
' him appointed, fhall neverthelefs continue in
' his Office, and fhall execute the fame, and all
' Things belonging thereto, in the Name of
' the faid deceafed Sheriff, until another Sheriff
' be appointed for the faid County, and fworn
' in the Manner as is herein after directed.
' And the faid Under-Sheriff or Deputy-She-
' riff fhall be anfwerable for the Execution of
' the faid Office in all Things, and to all Re-
' fpects, Intents and Purpofes whatfoever, du-
' ring fuch Interval, as the High Sheriff fo de-
' ceafed would by Law have been, if he had
' been living; and the Security given to the
' High Sheriff fo deceafed, by the faid Under
' Sheriff and his Pledges, fhall ftand, remain,
' and be a Security to the King, his Heirs
' and Succeffors, and to all Perfons whatfo-
' ever, for fuch Under Sheriff's due Perform-
' ance of his Office during fuch Interval.'

Note; Since the Jury Act 3 *Geo.* 2.
c. 25. the *Venire facias* muft be *de corpore
comitatus* in Actions upon *penal* Statutes.
2 *Str.* 1085.

CHAP.

CHAP. IV.

What Faults in the Venire Facias *fhall vitiate the Trial, what not. When a* Venire Facias de novo *fhall be awarded; when feveral* Venire Facias's. *When the* Venire Facias *fhall be betwixt the Party and a Stranger to the Iffue; who may have* Venire Facias *by* Provifo, *and when.*

Venire facias, why the Writ fo called.

WE have now fhewed you to what Officer the *Venire facias* fhall be directed; the next Step in the Writ is *Præcipimus tibi quod Venire facias :* Which Words *Venire facias* are the moft effectual Words in the Writ, and therefore they give the Denomination to the whole Writ: And here Opportunity is offered us to fpeak fomething of a *Venire facias* in general. I am not ignorant how our Books fwarm with Cafes, which arife from the Defects in this Procefs, and how that Verdicts have been fet afide, Judgments ftayed and reverfed, for want of fufficient Returns, Mifawarding, Difagreement with the Rolls, Difcontinuance, and many other Faults in this

Statute of *Jeofails,* 21 *Jac.* 1. 13.

Writ. But the Statutes of *Jeofails* (efpecially the Statute 21 *Jac.* 1. *cap.* 13.) have pardoned (as I may fo fay) thefe Enormities: As, *The Awarding his Writ,* Hab. Corpora, *or* Diftringas, *to a wrong Officer, upon any infufficient Suggeftion, or by Reafon the* Vifne *is in fome Part mifawarded, or fued out of more Places or fewer Places than it ought to be, fo as fome Place be right*

*right named : The Misnaming of any of the Jury,
either in Surname, or Addition in any of the said
Writs, or in any Return thereupon, so that upon
Examination it be proved to be the same Man that
was meant to be returned ; or if no Return be upon
any of the said Writs, so as a Panel of the Names
of the Jurors be returned, or annexed to the said
Writ ; or if the Sheriff or Officer's Name, having
the Return thereof, is not set to the Return of any
such Writ, so as upon Examination it be proved
that the said Writ was returned by the Sheriff or
Under Sheriff, or such other Officer :* In all these
Cases the Judgment shall not be stayed nor reversed for these Defects.

But this Act doth not extend to any Writ,
Declaration, or Suit of Appeal of Felony or
Murder, nor to any Indictment or Presentment
of Felony or Murder, or Treason ; nor to any
Process upon any of them ; nor to any Writ,
Bill, Action, or Information upon any popular
or penal Statute ; wherefore, since Informations
and popular Actions are grown so frequent, the
Attornies, &c. herein had best beware of these
Jeofails.

By this Statute many Defects are remedied, Popular Acti-
which are not by the Statutes of 32 *H.* 8. on, &c.
cap. 20. and 18 *Eliz. cap.* 14. yet all are not ;
for this Act only helps the Misnaming of a Juror in Surname, or Addition, and saith nothing
of his Christian Name : Wherefore I conceive
the Law in *Codwell's* Case, in the fifth Report, Christian
as it was then ; which is, that if a Juror be Name mista-
misnamed in his Christian Name on the *Venire,* ken in the
though he be named right in the *Distringas* *Venire facias,*
and *Postea,* yet this is ill, and not amendable ; incurable.
and with this agrees *Goddard's* Case, *Cro.* 2
Part 458.

And

Chriſtian
Name right
in the *Venire
facias,* and
wrong in the
Diſtringas.

And ſince the Court (*Cro. Car. fol.* 203.) doubted thereof, I may well put the Queſtion ; If a Juror be right named upon the *Venire,* and miſnamed in his Chriſtian Name in the *Diſtringas, &c.* whether this is amendable, or not ? Without Diſpute it is not by the Statute of 21 *Jac.* for that only helps the Surname. But with Reverence to the Court's Doubt, I con- ceive clearly, it is holpen by the Statutes of 32 *H.* 8. and 18 *Eliz.* as a Diſcontinuance of Proceſs ; and I may with the more Confidence believe it, becauſe in *Codwell's* Caſe aforeſaid, where, in the Panel of the *Venire,* a Juror was named *Palus Cheale,* and in the *Diſtringas, &c.* he was right named *Paulus Cheale* ; and ſo, be- cauſe he was miſnamed in his Chriſtian Name in the *Venire,* Judgment was arreſted. But it is there adjudged, That if he had been well named upon the *Venire,* and miſnamed on the *Diſtringas* or *Poſtea,* then upon Examination it ſhould be amended. But the Counteſs of *Rut- land's* Caſe, *Lib.* 5. 42. is expreſs in the Point, and ſo is *Cro. Eliz.* 860. *Rol.* 196. *Teppet* in the *Venire,* and *Tipper* in the *Diſtringas,* a- mended. And ſo if the Miſtake be in the Pa- nel *Jurata,* the Sheriff may come into Court and amend it. And ſo if *Samuel* be in the *Ve- nire* and *Diſtringas,* and *Daniel* in the *Nomina Juratorum,* upon Examination, this may be amended. And ſo if the Name be right in the *Venire,* and miſtaken in the Chriſtian Name in the *Diſtringas* or *Poſtea,* it is amendable. *Rol.* 197. And ſo if he be *de A.* in the *Venire* and *Diſtringas,* and *de B.* in the *Nomina Juratorum,* this is amendable.

And it is to be known, that in moſt Caſes where the *Venire facias, Habeas Corpora,* or

Diſtringas

Distringas be defective, they are to be amended; but if the Malady be so fatal in the *Venire*,
that it causes a Mis-trial, (as in the Mistake of
a Juror's Christian Name, or where a Juror
not returned, is sworn, *&c.*) then the Verdict is *Venire facias*
to be set aside, and a *Venire facias de novo* to be *de novo.*
awarded; and so was it to be upon those Mis-
takes, (now amendable by the Statutes) before
the making thereof; and where a Jury giveth One Jury shall
a Verdict, which is accepted and recorded by not try a
the Court, be the Verdict perfect or imperfect, Cause twice.
the Jurors are discharged, and shall never try
the same Issue again upon a new *Nisi prius.*
But if the Verdict be so imperfect, that Judgment cannot be given upon it, then the Court
shall award a *Venire facias de novo*, to try the
Issue by other Jurors. *Lib.* 8. 65. *Bulstr.*
2 Part 32.

If upon an Issue all the Matter be not fully *Venire facias*
inquired, a *Venire facias de novo* shall issue. *de novo.*
18 *E.* 3. 50.

In an *Audita Querela*, If the Parties go to
Issue upon Payment, according to the Defea-
zance of the Statute, and this is found for the
Plaintiff, but the Jury do not assess Damages,
the Court shall award a *Venire facias de novo*,
to assess Damages. 22 *E.* 3. 5. *Vide hic cap.* 6.
and *Roll.* Tit. *Trial*, 593. *pl.* 11.

If the Record of the *Nisi prius* be *unum mo-
dum tritici* for *modium*, and the Plaintiff is nonsuit at the Assize, for this Mistake, if the Record in Court be right, *scil. Modium*, this Nonsuit shall not be recorded, but a *Venire facias de
novo* shall be awarded. So for any other Mistake, as if the Record in Court be in *Grays-
Inn-Lane, &c.* and the *Nisi prius*, which is but
a Transcript, be *Graves-Inn-Lane, &c.* For
this

this is a Nonfuit upon another Record than what is in Court. *Roll. Trial,* 721. *pl.* 5 & 9.

In Battery againft Three, who plead three feveral Pleas, and upon the Writ of *Nifi prius,* two Iffues are found for the Plaintiff, and Damages affeffed; but nothing is found for the third Iffue; this is a Mif-trial, and a *Venire facias de novo* fhall iffue. *Ibid.* 722. *pl.* 13.

Detinue. In Detinue, if the Jury find Damages and Cofts, but no Value, as they ought, this fhall not be fupplied by a Writ of Inquiry of Damages, but a *Venire facias de novo* fhall be granted. And fo of other Defects in finding the full Iffue. *Ibid. pl.* 15.

Venire facias de novo. In a *Quare Impedit,* if the Iffue be found for the Plaintiff, but by Negligence the Jury do not inquire of the four Points, *fcil. de plenitudine, ex cujus Præfentatione, fi tempus femeftre tranfierit,* and the Value of the Church *per Annum;* this fhall be fupplied by a Writ of Inquiry, without a *Venire facias de novo,* becaufe the Court *ex Officio* ought to have charged the Jury with the four Points of Inquiry; and if the Jury had found them, no Attaint lay; for as to this, they were but as an Inqueft of Office. *Ibid. pl.* 16. 10 *Coke* 118. *Dyer* 135.

Annuity. In a Writ of Annuity, if the Iffue be found for the Plaintiff, but the Jury do not affefs Damages or Cofts, this fhall not be fupplied by a Writ of Inquiry, but a *Venire facias de novo* fhall be granted. *Roll. Trial,* 722. *pl.* 17.

Ejectment. In Ejectment againft Baron and Feme, and the Jury find the Wife Not guilty, and find a Special Verdict as to the Hufband, which fpecial Verdict is afterwards adjudged infufficient by the Court, a *Venire facias de novo* fhall be granted for both, as well the Wife as the Hufband,

band, and the Wife may be found guilty, because the Record and Issue is intire, and the
Verdict is insufficient and void *in tout.   Ibid.
pl.* 18.

So if there be several Issues, and the Jury Imperfect
find some well and directly, and in others spe- Verdict.
cial Verdicts, which are imperfect, a *Venire facias de novo* shall be granted for all, and the
Jury may find contrary to their first finding.
Ibid. pl. 19.

In Trespass of Assault and Battery, and taking away of Grain ; and the Defendant, as to
the Battery, justifies in Defence of his Grain ;
upon which the Plaintiff demurs ; and as to
the Grain he pleads Not guilty, which is found
for the Plaintiff, and the Jury do not tax Damages for the Battery depending in Demurrer
as they ought ; in this Case, if the Demurrer
be afterwards adjudged for the Plaintiff, yet
the Damages for this cannot be afterwards supplied and taxed by a Writ of Inquiry of Damages, but a *Venire facias de novo* shall issue to
Trial, because all is comprised in the Original.
Vide apres, cap. 13. and *devant, cap.* 2.   *Ibid.
pl.* 20.

Who shall grant it ?

In a *Scire facias* upon a Recognizance in
Chancery, if the Parties be at Issue, upon which
the Record is commanded into *B. R.* and there
it appears that the *Venire facias* is not well
awarded, the *Venire facias de novo* shall be a-
warded in the *King's Bench,* and not in the
Chancery.   Roll. Tit. *Trial,* 723.

In *Yelverton's* Reports, *fol.* 64. The Case is, *Album breve,*
That a *Venire facias* was made *Vicecomiti,* leav- the County
ing out *Salop,* for which there was a Blank left left out in a
in the Writ.   But *revera* it was returned by *Venire facias,*
the Sheriff of *Salop.*   In Arrest of Judgment it

was alledged, That the *Venire facias* was vitious for this Caufe; but *Gawdy* faid it fhould be amended; and by *Fenner* and *Williams*, it is as no Writ, becaufe it is not directed to any Officer. And then it is aided by the Statute of *Jeofails*; for it might rather be called a Blank than a Writ, becaufe it was directed to no Officer. If there be no Return of the Sheriff indorfed upon the *Venire facias*, it was held not amendable. 35 *Eliz. Lib.* 5. 41. Otherwife of the *Diftringas*, if that be *Album breve*, and no Return, if the *Venire facias* be right. *Roll. Amendment*, 204. *pl.* 2, 3.

Several *Venire facias's.*

In Cafes where there are feveral Defendants, who plead feveral Pleas, the Plaintiff may chufe either to have one *Venire facias* for all, or feveral for every one of the Defendants; but (if you will be ruled by *Standford*) the fureft Way is to have a *Venire facias* againft every one, and then one cannot have Benefit of the other's Challenge; neither fhall the Death of one abate the *Venire facias* againft the other, (this he fpeaks of in Appeals); but if the Court once award a joint *Venire facias*, you cannot have feveral *Venire's* afterwards, though there be nothing done upon the firft; except it be upon Matter *de puifne Temps*, as the Death of one of the Defendants, &c. *Lib.* 8. 66. *Lib.* 11. 5, 6. *Staundf.* 155. *Bro.* Tit. *Venire facias* 2. 35.

One *Venire facias* in feveral Iffues.
Vide Roll.
Tit. Trial, 596, 620, 667.
Hob. 88, 51.

But now it is the ufual Courfe to have but one *Venire facias* upon feveral Iffues, though againft feveral Defendants. *Cro.* 3 Part 866. *Hob.* 36, 64. And fo ufual, that the Court declared, *Cro.* 2 Part 550. That there never fhall be feveral *Venire facias's* to try feveral Iffues in one County; for what need the Plaintiff trouble himfelf and the Country with feveral,

when

when one Jury will serve his Turn ; *Et frustra
fit per plura quod fieri potest per pauciora.* But
otherwise if it be in two Counties. *Cro.*
3 Part 866.

If *A. B. C.* and *D.* be indicted for one Felony or Murder before any Justices, they may
issue one *Venire* or several.

If the Sheriff and another be joint Obligors
in a Bond, and one pleads *non est factum,* and
the other Conditions performed, and Process is
awarded to the Coroners, and the Issues tried by
one *Venire,* yet this is good.

There is a great Difference between a several
and a joint Plea, for where many join, there
goes but one *Venire ;* but where they sever then
there shall be several *Venires;* or if there be but
one, it must be special, and mentioned to be
for the Trial of several Issues. *Vin. Trial,* 300.

After Issue joined by two Defendants, if one *Venire facias*
of them die, and then a *Venire facias* is awarded between the
betwixt the Plaintiff and both the Defendants, Plaintiff and
and so in the *Habeas Corpora* and *Distringas,* yet two Defen-
this shall not vitiate the *Venire facias, &c.* to one is dead.
make Error ; because, though one of the De-
fendants be dead, yet the other being alive, it
is sufficient. And there needs be no Surmise
in Judicial Writs, that one of the Defendants is No Surmise
dead ; it is Time enough to shew it to the in Judicial
Court at the Day in Bank. *Cro.* 1 Part 4, 26. Writs of
But if there be two Defendants, and the *Venire* Death of one
facias be but against one of them, it is Error. of the Parties.
7 *H.* 4. 13. and *Bro.* Tit. *Ven. fac.* 11 *Cro.*
1 Part 426.

If the *Venire facias* bears Date before the *Venire facias*
Action brought, or varies from the Roll, yet dated before
it is aided by the Statutes of *Jeofails. Cro.* 1 the Action
Part 38, 90, 91, 203, 204. *Miscontinuance or* brought.

Discon-

Difcontinuance, or Mifconveying of Procefs, is aided by 32 H. 8. 30. *The Want of any Writ original or judicial, Defaults in their Form, and infufficient Returns thereupon, are aided by* 18 Eliz. 14. Cro. 3 Part 259. But you muft have a Care the *Venire facias* be not faulty in any

Parties Names miftaken in a *Venire facias,* Mif-trial. other Matters of Subftance; for if the Parties Names be miftaken, or the Iffue, as if the Iffue be *ne unque Executor,* and the *Venire facias* be *in placito debiti, &c.* this is a Mif-trial. *Cro.* 2 Part 528. So it is if the *Venire facias* be *in placito tranfgreffionis,* where the Action is *in placito tranfgreffionis & ejeEtionis firmæ.* This Mifawarding of Procefs is not aided by any of the Statutes; and better it were that there had

No *Venire facias* holpen. been no *Venire facias* at all in fuch a Cafe, for then the Statutes would have holpen it. *Cro.* 3 Part 622. *Stat.* 18 *Eliz.* 14.

Return of Procefs. If a *Venire facias* be directed to the Coroners, all the Coroners ought to join in the Return, they being Minifters, not Judges; and fo both the Sheriffs of *London* ought to join, or elfe the Return is not good. *Hob.* 97.

Where the Writ is awarded to the Coroners *ex affenfu partium,* it is good, though the Defendant might otherwife have croffed the Prayer.

Where it is to be awarded to the Coroners, and where it is not a principal Challenge; yet if the Defendant confefs it, it is good; but if it be not confeffed, the Court will not grant it, for the Defendant may have his Challenge if it be favourably made: But if the Plaintiff had faid the Sheriff had been his Relation, or any other principal Challenge, the Procefs fhall go to the Coroners, for the Matter came from the Plaintiff himfelf; whereas in the other Cafe, it cannot be tried but by the Confeffion of the
Party

Party himfelf. If the Defendant had faid, the Sheriff was not favourable but an indifferent Man, there he fhall not challenge for Favour unlefs he fhewed fome Caufe fubfequent.

In Debt the Plaintiff prayed a *Venire* to the Coroners, becaufe the Sheriff was his Mafter. After Verdict for the Plaintiff, this Matter was moved in Arreft of Judgment, as being no principal Challenge ; but the Plaintiff had his Judgment, though he did not conclude to the Favour. *Vin. Trial,* 305.

Procefs fhall not iffue to the Coroners but where Default is in the Sheriff himfelf ; and where the Writ is once awarded to the Coroners for Default in the Sheriff, no fubfequent Procefs fhall be awarded to the Sheriff, though pending the Plea a new and indifferent Sheriff be appointed ; for the entry is general *quod vic. fe non intromittat.*

In *Replevin* the Parties were at Iffue, and the Avowant confeffed himfelf to be Sheriff, and prayed a *Venire* to the Coroners, and had it. *Ibid.* 307.

Upon Confeffion that one of the Coroners was of Affinity to the Party, the Array was quafhed, and new Procefs iffued to the other Coroners, *ita quod the Coroner of Kin fe non intromittat.* Ibid. 308.

Where a *Venire* is awarded to Coroners, and no Challenge be fuggefted upon the Roll to warrant it, this is Caufe to ftay Judgment, and not aided by any Statute ; nor can the Court amend the Direction of Procefs to a wrong Officer. *Ibid.* 309.

Note ; The principal Statutes of *Jeofails* are 8 *H.* 6. *cap.* 12. and *cap.* 15. 32 *H.* 6. *cap.* 30. 18 *Eliz. cap.* 14. 21 *Jac. cap.* 13. and 16 *&*

17 *Car.* 2. 8. intitled, *An Act to prevent Arrests of Judgments, and superseding Executions.* And the three first of these Statutes do not extend to Appeals, nor to Pleas of the Crown, or any Proceedings upon them, for these are excepted, nor to the Amendment of any Exigent, to make any one outlawed. As you may see at large, *Lib.* 8. 162. *Blackmore's* Case.

Note ; If the *Diftringas* be betwixt wrong Parties, as if the Parties Names are mistaken, the Judge of Affize cannot proceed if the Mistake be infifted upon ; although it would have been no Error after Verdict ; held so before Juflice *Windham, Lent Affizes,* 1681. And so I have known it ruled by other Judges, and the Trial refufed. See *Littleton's* Reports 253.

And the four laft of the faid Statutes do neither extend to them, nor to Actions or Informations upon Penal Laws, only in the laft of them, *viz.* 16, 17 *Car.* 2. there is a Limitation in the Negation of the Extent, *scil. Other than concerning Customs, Subsidies of Tonnage and Poundage, to which it doth extend.*

If the *Venire facias* be directed *Vicecomiti London Salutem, &c. Præcipimus tibi,* and not *vobis,* after Verdict this is amendable. 39 *Eliz.* B. R. Adjudged. *Roll. Amendment,* 200. *pl.* 31.

And so it is, if after *& habeas ibi hoc breve, & Nomina Juratorum* be left out. *Ibid.* and 204. *pl.* 7.

But if the Award of the *Venire facias* upon the Roll be right, and the Writ wrong, it may be amended by the Roll, as the Mifprifion of the Clerk. *Ibid.* 201. *pl.* 36.

If the Words *Quorum quilibet habeat* be left out, or *duodecim,* or *qui nulla affinitate attingunt,* or *Vicecomiti* be left out, thefe are amend-

3   **able**

able as Miftakes of the Clerk. *Roll.* 204, 205.
pl. 8, 9, 10. *Amendment.*

By Stat. *5 G. 2. c. 13.* it is enacted, ' That
' where any Verdict hath been or fhall be given
' in any Action, Suit, Bill, Plaint, or De-
' mand in any of his Majefty's Courts of Re-
' cord at *Weftminfter*, or in any other Court of
' Record within *England* or *Wales*, the Judg-
' ment thereupon fhall not be ftaid or reverfed
' for any Defect or Fault either in Form or
' Subftance, in any Bill, Writ Original or Ju-
' dicial, or for any Variance in fuch Writs from
' the Declaration or other Proceedings.

' Provided neverthelefs, that nothing in this
' Act contained fhall extend or be conftrued to
' extend to any Appeal of Felony or Murder;
' or to any Procefs upon any Indictment, Pre-
' fentment or Information, of or for any Of-
' fence or Mifdemeanor whatfoever.

In fome Cafes a *Venire facias* fhall be award- *Venire facias*
ed to make an Inqueft betwixt a Stranger to the between a
Writ and Iffue, and the Party. I will inftance Party and a
but in one, and that is upon the Statute of Stranger.
Weftm. 2. *cap.* 6. If a Tenant being impleaded
to vouch to Warranty, and the Vouchee denieth the Deed, or other Caufe of the Warranty, *&c.* that the Demandant may not hereby
be delayed, he may fue out a *Venire facias* to
try the Iffue between the Tenant and Vouchee.

Inquefts in Pleas of Land fhall be as well ta- Inqueft, at
ken at the Requeft of the Tenant, as of the De- whofe Re-
mandant. 2 *Edw.* 3. *cap.* 16. If the Plaintiff queft.
or Demandant defifteth in profecuting his Acti-
on, and bringeth it not to Trial, then the De- *Venire facias*
fendant or Tenant may fue forth a *Venire facias* by *Provifo.*
with a *Provifo*, which is to no other End but
that the Sheriff fhould fummon but one Jury, if

the Plaintiff alſo ſhould have brought him another Writ to the ſame Purpoſe ; and although (as my Lord *Dyer* ſaith, *fol.* 2 1 5.) the Granting of this *Venire facias, &c.* with a *Proviſo,* depends much upon the Diſcretion of the Court, yet for the greater Part it is not grantable for the Defendant, unleſs when he is Actor as well as the Plaintiff ; or unleſs there be a Default, and *Laches* in the Plaintiff ; therefore there can be no Trial by *Proviſo* againſt the King (unleſs with the Attorney General's Conſent) becauſe no Default or *Laches* can be imputed to the King.

Proof preſently after Iſſue joined.But an Avowant in Replevin may have a *Venire facias* with a *Proviſo,* immediately after Iſſue joined, becauſe he is Actor, and in Nature of the Plaintiff.

Garniſhee.If the Plaintiff in Detinue and the Garniſhee be at Iſſue, and the Plaintiff prays a *Niſi prius* ; and this is granted ; yet the Garniſhee at the ſame Time may have a *Niſi prius* with *Proviſo,* becauſe he is Plaintiff alſo. *Lib.* 6. 46. *Roll.* Tit. *Trial,* 629.

*Tarde.*If the Plaintiff deliver the Writ to the Sheriff *tarde,* ſo late that he cannot ſerve it, the Defendant ſhall have a Writ with *Proviſo. Roll. Trial,* 666. *B. pl.* 1.

But at the ſame Time the Plaintiff may have another Writ, and the Sheriff may return which of them he pleaſes at his Election. *8 H.* 6. 6. *Ibid. pl.* 2.

The *Proviſo* ought to be, *quando duo brevia ſunt in eodem gradu & qualitate.* Ibid. pl. 1.

If the Default be in the Plaintiff after Iſſue in the proſecuting of the *Venire facias,* then the Defendant may have a *Venire facias* with *Proviſo,* but not a *Habeas Corpora* with a *Proviſo,* until the Plaintiff hath made a Default in the

2   ſame

ſame Writ ; for he ought only to have the ſame Proceſs with a *Proviſo,* in which there was a Default of the Plaintiff firſt : And therefore, although the Defendant had a *Venire facias* with a *Proviſo* upon a Default of the Plaintiff, yet he cannot have a *Niſi prius* by *Proviſo,* without another Default of the Plaintiff. *Ibid. pl.* 2.

If the Defendant had a *Habeas Corpora* by *Proviſo,* and the Jury remain for want of Hundredors, yet he cannot have a *Diſtringas Jur.* with a *decem Tales cum proviſo,* until a Default of this Requeſt of a *Tales* is in the Plaintiff. *D.* 15 *El.* 318. 10.

But *Note* the *Nota* (in *Staundford*'s Pleas *del Coron. fol.* 155.) That if by Negligence of the Plaintiff, the Defendant ſues a *Venire facias* with a *Proviſo,* yet the Plaintiff may at his Pleaſure ſtay the Defendant, that he ſhall not proceed in his Proceſs, in praying a *Tales* upon the Defendant's Proceſs, as it appears *T.* 15 *H.* 7. *fol.* 9. And the Defendant ſhall never be received to purſue this Proceſs with a *Proviſo,* ſo long as the Plaintiff purſues, or is ready to purſue, as appears *Mich.* 14 *H.* 7. *fol.* 7. *How the Plaintiff may ſtop the Defendant's Proviſo.*

Mich. 10 *Geo.* 2. *B. R. Dodſon* verſus *Taylor.* The Plaintiff having ſlept over an Aſſizes, the Defendant gave Notice of Trial, and carried the Cauſe down to Trial by *Proviſo* the then laſt Aſſizes at *Kingſton* ; but the Defendant not having entred a Rule for that Purpoſe with the Clerk of the Rules, the Words of which are, *fiat Niſi prius per proviſo ſi querens fecerit defaltam.* The Court on Debate ſet aſide the Nonſuit for Irregularity.

And

And feeing the *Tales* (*a*)\Men offer themfelves to us, we will tell them upon what Account they come, before they thruft themfelves into the Inqueft, commonly for the Love of eight Pence ; but it may be to do fome of their Neighbours a fhrewd Turn.

Venire facias de novo awarded, where intire Damages, and Part of the Words not actionable. *Pract. Reg. in C. P.*

Verdict fet afide, the *Venire* being returnable at a Day fubfequent to the Affizes, for till after the Return of the *Venire*, and Default by the Jurors, there could be no *Nifi prius*. Note, the Jury Procefs was returnable properly. 2 *Barnes's Notes* 377.

Return of *Venire facias*, if defective, within the Statutes of Amendment. 2 *Barnes's Notes* 3.

(*a*) *Tales*, is ufed in the Law for a Supply of Men impanelled on a Jury and not appearing, or on their Appearance challenged as not indifferent; when the Judge upon Motion orders a Supply to be made by the Sheriff, *&c.* of one or more *fuch* Perfons prefent in Court, equal in Reputation to thofe that were impanelled, to make up a full Jury. See *Poftea*.

CHAP.

CHAP. V.

Why the Venire Facias *runs to have the Jury appear at* Westminster, *though the Trial be in the Country. Of the Writ of* Nisi Prius, *when first given, when grantable, when not, and in what Writs. Of Justices of* Nisi Prius. *Of the* Tales *at Common Law and by Statute. When the Transcript of the Record of the* Nisi Prius *differs from the Roll, whereby the Plaintiff is nonsuited, he may have a* Distringas de novo.

BUT to observe the Method of the Writ, the next Words are *coram Justiciariis nostris de Banco apud Westminst. tali die.* And here first of all you may ask me, to what Purpose the Sheriff is commanded to cause the Jury to come to *Westminster,* when they are to try the Cause in the Country; and in Truth are not to come to *Westminster?* I must confess, The Resolution of this Question is not unnecessary. Wherefore we must know, That originally, before the Writ of *Nisi prius* was given, the Purpose for which the twelve Men were to be summoned upon the Writ of *Venire facias* to come to *Westminster,* was that contained in the Writ, *videl. ad faciend. quandam Juratam;* for then was the Trial intended to be there, if a full Jury appeared; if not, then a *Habeas Corpora,* (with a *Tales* sometimes annexed to it, the Form whereof you may see in the Register); and if they did not appear at

Why the *Venire facias* is to have the Jury appear at *Westminster.*
Hab. Corp.

Diſtringas. at the Return in the *Habeas Corpora*, then went out the *Diſtringas*. This I ſpeak of the *Common Pleas:* But the Courſe of the *King's Bench* and *Exchequer* is, after the *Venire facias*, to have a *Diſtringas*, leaving out the *Habeas Corpora*. Trials then were all at Bar. (I ſpeak not of Aſſizes.) But now, becauſe Jurors did not uſe to appear upon the *Venire facias*, it being with-

Trials at Bar. out Penalty, Trials at the Bar are appointed upon the *Habeas Corpora* and *Diſtringas*, be-cauſe the Jury will more certainly appear at the Day of the *Diſtringas*, through Fear of forfeit-ing Iſſues; which the Sheriff returns on the *Diſtringas*, not on the *Venire facias*. By the

Where a Jury is not compel-lable to ap-pear at Weſt-minſter. Statute of 18 *Eliz. cap. 5.* no Jury ſhall be compelled to appear at *Weſtminſter*, for the Trial of an Offence (upon any Penal Law) com-mitted above thirty Miles from *Weſtminſter*, except the Attorney General can ſhew reaſonable Cauſe for a Trial at Bar.

Thus it was at Common Law, before the giving of the Writ of *Niſi Prius*, when all Ju-rors, together with the Parties, came up to the King's higher Courts of Juſtice, where the Cauſe depended; which (when Suits multipli-ed) was to the intolerable Burden of the Country. 27 *E.* 1. *cap.* 4. Wherefore by the Statute of *Weſtminſter* 2. *cap.* 30. a Writ of

Niſi prius, when firſt gi-ven, and wherefore. Staundford's Pleas of the Crown 156. *Niſi Prius* was firſt given; and that in the *Ve-nire facias*, as we may ſee in the Form of the Writ there mentioned, *ſcil. Præcipimus tibi quod Venire facias coram Juſticiariis noſtris a-pud Weſtmon. in Octabis Sancti Michaelis, niſi tali die & loco ad Partes illas venerint 12 &c.* By which Writ it appears, that the *Venire fa-cias* was not returnable till after the Day of the

Niſi prius in the Venire fa-cias. *Niſi prius*. But the Miſchief thereof was ſo great

great, partly in respect that the Parties not knowing the Jurors Names, could not tell how to make their Challenges, and so were surprised; and partly in respect of the Jury, who were greatly delayed by the Essoigns of the Parties, that by the Statute of 42 *Ed.* 3. *cap.* 11. it is ordained, *That no Inquest, but Assizes and Deliverances of Goals, be taken by Writ of* Nisi Prius, *nor in other Manner at the Suit of great or small, before that the Names of all them that shall pass in the Inquest be returned in the Court.* And their Names must be returned upon a Panel annexed to the *Venire facias,* so that either Party may have a Copy of the Jury, that he may know whom to challenge; and the Jury not coming upon the *Venire facias,* make a feigned Default, which warrants the *Distringas, &c.* unless they appear at the Day of *Nisi prius.*

The Names of the Jurors must be returned into the Court before any Trial, and why.

So that by what hath been said, you may perceive to what Purpose the Sheriff is commanded to cause the twelve Men to come to *Westminster,* though the Trial be in the Country. And that, *ad faciend. quandam Juratam,* because it is in the Discretion of the Court, whether to grant a Writ of *Nisi prius,* or to have a Trial at the Bar. And for this, the Duke of *Exeter* being Plaintiff in Trespass, a *Nisi prius* was prayed for the Duke, and it was denied; for that the Duke was of great Power in that County. And if the Trial should be had in the Country, Inconvenience might thereupon follow, as you may read, 2 *Inst.* 424. and 4 *Inst.* 161. Nay, in some Cases (as if the Cause require long Examination, *&c.*) it is not in the Power of the Court to grant a *Nisi prius,* if the King please: For in such Cases, as appears by the Writ in the Register 186.

It is in the Court's Discretion, whether to grant a *Nisi prius* or not.

When the Court cannot grant a *Nisi prius.*

the

the King by his Writ may reftrain, and command the Juftices that they fhall not award any Writ of *Nifi prius*, and if they have, that they fuperfede it. *F. N. B.* 240, 241. No *Nifi prius* fhall be granted where the King is Party, without fpecial Warrant from the King, or the Attorney General's Confent. *Staundf.* 156. *F. N. B.* 241. 4 *Inft.* 161. 2 *Inft.* 424.

Where the King is concerned.

In a *Præcipe quod reddat*, if the Tenant after Aid of the King pleads to the Inqueft, the Plaintiff fhall not have a *Nifi prius*, becaufe the Tenant hath Aid of the King, and fo the King is in a manner Party. 25 *E*. 3. 39. Neither is a *Nifi prius* to be granted, if any of the Parties may have Prejudice by it. *Roll. Trial*, 629, *Q. pl.* 2.

Certification of Verdicts.

If the Juftices *de Nifi prius* die before the Day in Bank, yet the Record fhall be received from the Clerk of Affize, without a *Certiorari*, or other Form of Entry but the antient Form.

Alfo in that Cafe a *Certiorari* may be directed to the Executors or Adminiftrators of the Juftices, to certify the Record. *Dy.* 4. 5 *Ph. & Mar.* 163. 55. *Roll.* Tit. *Trial*, 629. *S. pl.* 1, 2.

What Things the Juftices of Nifi prius may do.

They have no Power to increafe Damages, nor allow or difallow Protections, nor to allow a Plea of Excommengement in the Plaintiff. But they may record the Protection and the Default; and this fhall be allowed or difallowed in *B. Roll, Trial,* 630.

Jurors fur peine fine.

They may demand the Jurors upon a *Peine*, they may amerce Jurors, and punifh a Trefpafs done in their Prefence, which is in Defpite of the King, and for this make Procefs, and may fine Offenders. *Ibid.*

In

In Ejectment the Defendant may plead at the Affizes, that the Plaintiff hath entered into Parcel of the Land mentioned in the Declaration *puis le darrein Continuance,* and the Juftices of *Nifi prius* may accept this Plea, for it is in their Election ; for if they perceive the Plea is dilatory, they may refufe it, for it is at their Difcretion. Sir *Hugh Brown's* Cafe, *in Scaccario, Mich. 8 Jac.* Roll. Tit. *Trial,* 630. *Plea puis darrein Continuance.*

If eleven Jurors be fworn, and the twelfth is challenged, and the Jurors cannot agree in the Challenge ; for ten affirm the Challenge, and the other denies it ; although the Party which did not take the Challenge, will not agree that the eleven fworn fhall have another to them in lieu of him that is challenged, yet the Court may do this. *Roll. Trial,* 675. *Y. pl.* 1.   *The Power of the Judge upon Difagreement or other Matter. Challenge.*

If a Challenge be taken to the Array before any Juror is fworn, and Triors be chofen, who cannot agree, yet they fhall not be commanded in Cuftody, becaufe they never were fworn upon the Principal. But the Court may difcharge them and chufe others. *Ibid. pl.* 2.   *Jurors difcharged.*

If there be three Triors who will not agree, the Court cannot take the Verdict of two, and command the other to Prifon. The fame Law in Cafe of a Verdict upon an Iffue. *Ibid. pl.* 2.

Where fourteen Jurors are impanell'd for the King, the Judge cannot difcharge any of them after they are fworn, if not, that they will not agree with their Companions. *Ibid.*

If the Jury fay, upon Demand of the Court, that they are agreed, and afterwards when they are oppofed, they fay the contrary in any Matter, they may be amerced for this. *Roll.* Tit. *Trial,* 675.   *Amercement.*

And

Nisi prius, why so called. And now since the *Nisi prius* (for so it is called, because the Word *Prius* is before *Venerint* in the *Distringas, &c.* which was not so in the *Venire facias* upon the Statute of *W.* 2. *cap.* 30. before rehearsed) must not be in the *Venire facias,* because the Names of the Jurors are to be returned to the Court, before the granting of the *Nisi prius* ; therefore the *Nisi*

No Nisi prius before the Venire facias returned. *prius* is now in the *Habeas Corpora* and *Distringas.* And if the Sheriff return not a Panel of the Jurors upon the *Venire facias,* there shall be no *Nisi prius* upon the *Tales,* until a Panel be returned, 27 *H.* 6. *f.* 10. 1 *H.* 5. *f.* 11. which brings me again to speak of the *Tales.*

After Verdicts, received of *Nisi prius,* and Writs of *habeas Corpora Jurat.* being lost by Mr. *Jacomb* the late Associate ; Rule for Defendant and *Jacomb* to shew Cause why new Records and Writs should not be made out agreeable to the old, and Verdicts returned according to the finding of the Jury, made absolute, no Cause being shewn to the contrary. *T.* 27 *&* 28 *Geo.* 2. *Lassiter* against *Harvey.* *Supplement to Barnes's Notes* 54.

If the Record of *Nisi prius* agrees with the Declaration, a Variation from the Issue is not material. 2 *Stra.* 1131.

The Tales at Common Law. A *Tales* is a Supply of such Men, as were impanelled upon the Return of the *Venire facias,* grantable when enough of the principal Panel to make a Jury do not appear ; or if a full Jury do appear, yet if so many are challenged, that the Residue will not make a Jury, then a *Tales* may be granted. And this at the Common Law was by Writs of *Decem tales, octo tales, &c.* (out of the King's Courts) one of them after another, as there was need, until there

there was a full Jury: But now by the Statutes
of 35 *H*. 8. 6.   4 *&* 5 *P. & M.* 7.   5 *Eliz.*
25. and 14 *Eliz.* 9.

The Juftices of Affize and *Nifi prius*, at the *Tales* by Sta-
Requeſt of Plaintiff or Demandant, Defendant tute.
or Tenant, or of the Profecutor *tam quam,* (if
two, more, or but one of the principal Panel
appear at the *Nifi prius)* may prefently caufe a
Supply to be made of fo many Men as are
wanting, of them that are there prefent ſtand-
ing about the Court ; and thereupon the very
Act is called a *Tales de circumſtantibus.* (*a*)

Note, the Difference between *Tales* at Common Law, and *Tales* by the Statute ; the firſt
called only [*Tales*] the fecond [*Tales de circumſtantibus*] the laſt of which cannot be granted
at a Trial at Bar, which is a Trial at Common
Law ; for there it muſt be only [*Tales*] by
Writ annexed to the *Venire facias.*   But *Tales
de circumſtantibus* is given by Statute to Trials
by Affize and *Nifi prius, per Stat.* 35 *H.* 8. 6.
Yet fuch a *Tales* to an Indictment in *Wales* was
out of that Statute, and helped by the 5 *Eliz.*
c. 25.

If the Iffue be to be tried by two counties, *Tales,* in what
and one full Inqueſt appear of one county, but Cafes it ſhall
the Inqueſt remain for Default of Jurors of the be granted.
other County, a *Tales* ſhall be awarded to the
County where the Default is, not to the other.
Roll. Trial, 671. *M. pl.* 1.

(*a*) A *Tales de circumſtantibus* is in fome Meafure taken
away, or rendered ufelefs, by the late Statute for regulating of Juries, 3 *Geo.* 2. *c.* 25. though it is faid to have
been held by *Raym.* Chief Juſtice, *Trin.* 5 *Geo.* 2. That
this Statute doth not exclude a *Tales,* but that it may ſtill
be granted upon fpecial Juries. *Vin. Trial,* 313.

If a Juror die after he is impanelled, a *Tales* fhall iffue, not a *Venire facias. Ibid. pl.* 2.

What Perfons may have a *Tales*. Upon a *Pluries Diftringas* three only appear, the Plaintiff prays another *Diftringas*, without praying a *Tales*, yet if the Defendant prays a *Tales*, the Court ought to grant it. *Dy.* 20 *El.* 359. 2. adjudged.

In what Cafes. A *Tales* fhall be granted in an *Attaint*, if all the Grand Jury make Default. *Roll. Trial,* 671. *O. pl.* 1. And it may be awarded in *Treafon*, where the King is Party, by Virtue of the Statute 4 & 5 *P.* & *M. c.* 7. though not without a Warrant from the Attorney General, or an exprefs Affignment from the Court before which the Inqueft is taken. *Vin. Trial,* 311, 316.

At what Time. It cannot be granted at the Day of the Return of the *Venire facias. Rolle fupra. pl.* 2.

If the *Venire facias* be good, and the *Habeas Corpora* ill, if the Panel be affirmed, yet the *Tales* is void, for in Effect there is only a *Venire facias* returned, and then no *Tales. Ibid. P. pl.* 1.

Tales with a Provifo. If the Defendant hath a *Habeas Corpora* with a Provifo, yet the *Tales* ought not to be granted with a Provifo, at the Defendant's Requeft, before a Default in the Requeft of a *Tales* in the Plaintiff. *Ibid.* 672.

At Common Law before the Statute, by Cuftom of a Court, a *Tales de circumftantibus* might be granted, for this is a good Cuftom. *Dubitatur, Roll.* Tit. *Trial,* 672.

Trefpafs *quare claufum fregit,* Verdict for Plaintiff; Error *in Cam. Scacc'.* The Error infifted on was, that but one of the principal Panel appeared at the Affizes; upon which, at the Plaintiff's Requeft, a Panel of *Tales de circumftantibus*

cumftantibus was returned by the Sheriff; the Title of it was, *Nomina decem talium, &c.* and eleven were returned: This was held well within the Statute 35 *H.* 8. *c.* 6. and that though there appeared but one of the principal Panel, a *Tales might* be prayed. 10 *Coke* 102.

If great Perfons are concerned, and by their *Tales denied;* labouring the Jury doth not appear, and *Tales* Men are prepared for their Turn, and there is a great Tumult *de circumftantibus*; the Juftices of their Difcretion may deny a *Tales,* and adjourn in Bank, notwithftanding the Statute. The principal Panel muft ftand, or elfe there can be no *Tales.*

If the Bailiff of the Franchife anfwer, that there be not fufficient of his Bailiwick, the Juftices may award a *Tales de circumftantibus* to be returned by the Sheriff.

If two Coroners or Eflifors return the Panel, one of them cannot return the *Tales, &c.*

If the Defendant fue the Writ of *Nifi prius* by Provifo, yet the Plaintiff may have a *Tales, &c.*

The Sheriff may return twenty-four, forty, *Attorney;* or any Number upon the *Tales de circumftantibus.* And it may be prayed by Attorney (although the Statute doth not mention an Attorney) as well as in proper Perfon. The Vouchee in *Præcipe quod reddat* may pray a *Tales,* though he be neither a Plaintiff nor Demandant in the firft Action.

If there be three Plaintiffs in *Replevin, &c.* and one of them makes Default at the *Nifi prius,* the other two cannot pray a *Tales;* otherwife of two copartners.

Mayor and Commonalty in their proper Perfons cannot pray a *Tales:* A Bifhop or Abbot may.

Two Plaintiffs in Trefpaſs; and at the *Niſi prius* the Defendant ſhews a Record to the Court, by which it appears that one of the Plaintiffs was outlawed after the laſt Continuance, the other cannot pray a *Tales*.

The Sheriffs upon the *Tales de circumſtantibus*, may impanel a Prieſt or Deacon, if he hath ſufficient Freehold of Lay-Fee ; but not an Infant, nor one of the Age of eighty Years.

What Perſons of the *Tales*. He may impanel Coroners, Capital Miniſters of any Corporation, Foreſters, Men blind, mute, (if they have their Underſtanding, but not deaf Men) excommunicated Perſons, but not outlawed or attaint, not Aliens, nor Clerks attainted, nor Perſons attainted of falſe Verdicts.

Challenge. The Coroners may put the Sheriff on the *Tales*.

It ſeems by the Statute, none of the Parties can challenge the Array of the *Tales*, but only to the Poll.

After a Challenge to the Poll tried, there ſhall be no other Challenge to the ſame Poll, for any Cauſe or Matter that is at the ſame Time.

In an Action of Trefpaſs for taking away the Plaintiff's Money, one of the *Tales* was challenged, becauſe he was a common Foſterer of Thieves, and dwelt in a ſuſpicious Place, and of ill Fame; and held a good Challenge.

For Challenges, ſee the Title *Challenge* at large.

What Iſſues ſhall be tried by *Tales de circumſtantibus*, ſee *William's* Reading, & *hic cap.* 7.

But ſince none can come after the Reporter, obſerve with me his *Nota Lecteur* in his 10th *Report* 104. That at Common Law, in the granting of a *Tales* five Things are to be confidered.

1. The Time of the granting, *&c.* thereof.
2. The Number of *Tales.*
3. The Order of them.
4. The Manner of Trial ; that is, where by them with others, and where by them only.
5. The Quality of them is to be confidered.

As to the firft, four Things are likewife to be confidered.

1. That the Time of granting them is upon Default of fo many of the principal Panel, that there cannot be a full Inqueft.

2. That at the Time of granting them, the principal Array ftand ; for *Tales* are Words fimilitudinary, and have Reference to the Refemblance, which then ought to be *in effe*; and therefore if the Array be quafhed, or all the Polls challenged and treited, no *Tales* fhall be awarded, for then there are not *Quales*; but in fuch a Cafe, a new *Venire facias* fhall be awarded. But if at the Time of granting the *Tales*, the principal Panel ftand, and afterwards is quafhed, as aforefaid, yet the *Tales* fhall ftand ; for it fufficeth if there were *Quales*, at the Time of granting the *Tales.*

3. It is to be obferved, that he which is meerly Defendant, cannot pray a *Tales* till the Plaintiff hath made Default.

4. In fome Cafes a *Tales* fhall be granted after a full Jury appear and is fworn ; as if a Jury be charged, and afterwards before a Verdict given in Court, one of them die, a *Tales* fhall be awarded, and no new *Venire facias* :

At *Wickham* Affizes in *Bucks,* 1684, Only one Juror appeared, who was challenged, but before he was fet afide, the Court granted a *Tales,* by *Mountague* Chief Baron.

G 3   And

And ſo if any of the Jurors impanelled die before they appear, and this appears by the Sheriff's Return, the Panel ſhall not abate; but if there be need, a *Tales* ſhall be awarded. And the Time for Challenge and Trial of the *Tales,* is after the principal Panel is tried; and if the principal Panel be affirmed, the ſame Triors ſhall try the *Tales*; but if it be quaſhed, then the two Triors of the Principal ſhall not try the *Tales.*

As to the ſecond, to wit the Number, two Things are to be obſerved.

1. That in all Caſes the *Tales* ought to be under the Number of the Principal in the *Venire facias* (unleſs in Appeals) as in Attaint, under twenty-four; and in other Actions where the *Venire facias* is of twelve, under twelve. And the Reaſon wherefore more than the Number may be granted in Appeals of the Plaintiff's Part, is becauſe the Defendant may challenge peremptorily; and if Default be in the Plaintiff, then the Defendant may pray a *Tales,* and the Reaſon is *in favorem vitæ,* and that he may expedite and free himſelf from Vexation, and the Queſtion of his Life, for fear that his Witneſſes ſhould die.

2. That the Number ought always to be certain, as ten, eight, ſix, or four, *&c.* But now by the Statute of 35 H. 8. a *Tales de circumſtantibus* may be granted, as well of an uncertain as a certain Number, and that by Force of theſe Words in the Statute 35 H. 8. *So many,* &c. *as ſhall make a full Jury.* In *capital Caſes* a *Tales* may be granted for a *larger Number* than were in the principal Panel, as for 60, 40, or any other even Number, in order to prevent Delay, which may be occaſioned by

peremptory

peremptory Challenges; and in this refpect the Law differs from other Cafes in which the *Tales* muft be for a *lefs Number* than the firft Procefs. *Vin. Trial*, 321.

As to the third, to wit, the Order, it is to be known, That always in every new *Tales*, the Number fhall be diminifhed, as if the firft be ten, the fecond fhall be eight, and fo always lefs. But if the *Tales* awarded be quafhed by Challenge, you may have another of the fame Number.

As to the fourth, to wit, the Manner of Trial, that is commonly by them with others; but by them only, when after the granting the *Tales*, the principal Panel is quafhed, then the Trial fhall be only by the *Tales*; or if the *Tales* do not amount to a full Inqueft, another *Tales* to fupply the former may be granted.

As to the fifth, to wit, the Quality of the *Tales*, they ought to be of the fame Quality as the *Quales* are; and therefore if the firft be *per medietatem Linguæ*, of Englifh and Aliens, fo ought the *Tales* to be; fo if the Principal be out of a Franchife; fo if the *Venire facias* be directed to the Coroners, fo ought the *Tales*; and all Things which are required by Law in the *Quales* are required in the *Tales*, as you may read in the aforefaid Statutes. *Vide Staundf. Pleas del Corone, f.* 155. 10 *Rep.* 105.

Therefore if the Venire facias be not de medietat. linguæ, the Tales cannot. 8 E. 4. 12.

Where a Juror is withdrawn, when the Plaintiff intends to bring the Caufe to Trial again, he may have a *Diftringas, &c.* with a *decem Tales.*

By the Statute of 23 *H.* 8. *cap.* 3. If there be not enough fufficient Freeholders as are required in an Attaint, in the County where fuch

Attaint.

Attaint is taken, a *Tales* may be awarded into the Shire next adjoining.

If the Tranfcript of the Record of the *Nifi prius* be miftaken, and not warranted by the Rolls, for which Caufe the Plaintiff becomes norfuit, he may have a *Diftringas de novo*, upon Motion to the Court, and the *Poftea* fhall not be recorded, *Cro.* 1 Part 204.   *Palmer's* Reports 378.   For there is but a Tranfcript of the Record fent to the Juftices of *Nifi prius*. Firft they were Juftices of *Affize*, and therefore they retain that Name ftill, though *Affizes* are very rarely brought; for this common Action of Ejectment hath ejected moft real Actions, and fo the *Affize* is almoft out of Ufe.

It fhall be lawful to return Perfons upon the *Tales* within any County of *England*, who fhall have 5 *l. per Annum* above Reprizes; and in *Wales* 3 *l. per Annum.* 4 & 5 *W.* & *M. c.* 24.

Where there fhall be Occafion for any *Tales*, the Sheriff or other Minifter, to whom it fhall appertain to return the *Tales* Men, fhall return Freeholders or Copyholders of the County where the Caufe is to be tried, who fhall be returned upon fome other Panel to ferve at the fame Affizes, and then attending to ferve upon fuch *Tales* ; and the Plaintiff or Defendant may have his Challenge to the Jurors fo named, in fuch Manner as if they had been impanelled upon the *Venire :* And the Judge of Affize fhall and may proceed to try the Iffue with thefe *Tales* Men fo newly added, as he might have done, if all the Jurors returned on the *Venire* had appeared: And in Cafe any Freeholder or Copyholder fo returned on the *Tales*, being prefent at fuch Return, fhall refufe to appear when called, or after Appearance fhall wilfully withdraw himfelf,

Margin notes

Nifi prius amendable.

Juftices of *Nifi prius*, and Juftices of Affize.

Tales Men, their Sufficiency.

Tales Men to be returned out of other Panels.

Challenge to the *Tales*.

Perfon on the *Tales* with drawing himfelf, to be fined.

himself, the Judge of Affize who awarded such *Tales* may fine him. 7 & 8 *W.* 3. *cap.* 32.

Bullock verfus *Parfons,* Paf. 4 *Ann.* B. R. In Debt, after Verdict for the Plaintiff, Mr. *Eyre* moved in Arreft of Judgment, that the *Diftringas* was with a Blank, and *Debiti* (the Caufe of Action) omitted ; fo it was a *Diftringas* in another Caufe: On the other Ssde, it was urged to be as no *Diftringas,* and aided by Verdict, and that it was amendable. *Hob.* 246. 2 *Cro.* 528. The Court made two Queftions, firft, Whether the Judge of *Nifi prius* had Authority to try this Iffue? *Et per Holt* Ch. J. The Authority of the Judge of *Nifi Prius* is not by the *Diftringas,* but by the Commiffion of Affize ; for it is 1 3 *E.* 1. *c.* 30. which gives the Trial by *Nifi prius,* and by that Statute the Trial by *Nifi prius* is given before the Juftices of Affize ; and at firft thefe Trials by *Nifi prius* were always had and made upon the *Venire facias* ; and indeed the Claufe of the *Nifi prius* is by 1 3 *E.* 1. *c.* 30. exprefly ordered to be inferted in the *Venire facias* ; and Trials by *Nifi prius* continued to be upon the *Venire facias* till 42 *Ed.* 3. *c.* 1 1. which requires that the Names of the Jurors be firft returned into Court.   By this Act two Inconveniencies were remedied ; 1*ft,* The Party might now be prepared to make his Challenges, the Panel being firft returned into Court, which was not before. 2*dly,* The Defendant was prevented by this Means to caft an Effoin at *Nifi prius,* which was frequently ufed before ; for by *Marlb. c.* 1 3. the Defendant was allowed one Effoin, and that after Iffue joined upon the Return of the *Venire :* By Confequence, when that was returned at *Nifi prius,* he could effoin at *Nifi prius* ; but

Diftringas with a Blank for the Caufe of Action, amendable.

Authority of a Judge of Nifi prius is by Commiffion of Affize.

now

now it is returned above, he muft effoin above, and cannot now effoin at the Trial, becaufe the Trial is upon the *Diftringas*, and not upon the *Venire*. 2*dly*, The Court held no *Diftringas*, or the Want of a *Diftringas*, to be aided by Verdict, but an ill *Diftringas* was not ; and remembered a Cafe, wherein *Saunders* of Counfel at the Bar, dropped the *Diftringas* out of his Hand, that he might want a *Diftringas*, which would be aided, and not keep and fhew an ill one, which would be naught. Alfo they held it amendable, and gave Judgment *pro Quer'*. Salk. 454.

Greeves verfus *Rolls, Paf. 4 Ann. B. R.* The Judge of *Nifi prius* may receive a *Non Prof.* at the Affizes; fo it was held by *two* Judges, and *that* Judgment was affirmed in the Houfe of Lords againft the Opinion of *Holt*, Ch. J. For before the Statute of *York*, the Juftices of *Nifi prius* had no Power to record a Nonfuit or Default in the Country, and confequently have no Power now to enter a *Non Prof.* which is not within that Statute. At Common Law they could not record a *Non Prof.* Default or Nonfuit. *Nota* ; The principal Cafe was Ejectment againft feveral, who all entered into the Rule of Leafe, Entry and Oufter ; at the Affizes fome would confefs, and others would not : The Plaintiff, as to thofe who would not confefs, entered a *Non Prof.* and went on againft the others, and recovered ; upon this a Rule was made, That in like Cafes the Plaintiff fhould go on againft thofe who would confefs, and as to thofe who would not, fhould be nonfuit ; but that the Caufe of the Nonfuit fhould be expreffed in the Record, *viz.* becaufe thofe Defendants would not confefs Leafe, Entry and Oufter ; and upon the Return of the

Sidenote (left margin): Where there is no *Diftringas*, it is aided by Verdict, but an ill *Diftringas* is not.

Sidenote (left margin): Judge of *Nifi prius* may receive a *Non-Prof.* at the Affizes.

Sidenote (left margin): In Ejectment againft feveral, if fome confefs Leafe, Entry, &c. and others do not, the Plaintiff may go on as to the former, and be nonfuit as to the latter.

Poſtea, the Court would be informed what Lands were in the Poſſeſſion of thoſe Defendants, that the Judgment might be entered againſt the caſual Ejector as to them. 2 *Salk.* 456, 457.

It was agreed in the arguing of this Cauſe, That where there are ſeveral Defendants, and they ſever in Plea, whereupon Iſſue is joined, that the Plaintiff may enter a *Non Proſ.* as to one Defendant at any Time before the Record is ſent down to be tried at *Niſi prius. Ibid.* 457.

Where Defendants ſever in Plea, Plaintiff may enter a *Non Proſ.* againſt one any Time before the Record ſent down.

Staple verſus *Hayden, Trin.* 2 *Ann.* Where the Defendant makes Default at *Niſi prius,* no Judgment can be given for him, nor Repleader awarded: If the Tenant make Default in a real Action, a *Grand Cape* is awarded; and upon the Return of it, if the Demandant inſiſts upon the Default, he muſt have Judgment final; but the Demandant may wave the Default, and take an Appearance upon the *Grand Cape,* and that is regular, becauſe the Tenant comes in by Proceſs: And ſo it is of a Default on a *Petit Cape,* but in a perſonal Action there is no Proceſs to bring the Party into Court again: Alſo the Day of *Niſi Prius* not being the ſame with the Day in Bank, a Default at *Niſi prius* cannot be waved at the Day in Bank; and the Bar was cautioned never to make Defaults at *Niſi prius,* becauſe no Judgment could be given for the Defendant afterwards. 1 *Salk.* 216, 217.

No Repleader awarded after Default at *Niſi prius.*

Default may be waved in real Actions, not in perſonal.

While the Jury were a ſwearing, Defendant's Counſel called for the Record, and finding a Miſtake in it, ſaid, they would make no Defence. Plaintiff's Counſel upon this, to avoid a Nonſuit, and to ſave the Coſts, refuſed to

pray

pray a *Tales*; and tho' Twelve had been fworn, yet there having been no actual Prayer of a *Tales*, the Caufe was fuffered to remain for want of Jurors. 1 *Str*. 707.

C H A P. VI.

Of the Number of the Jurors (a), and why the Sheriff returns Twenty-four, though the Venire Facias *mentions but Twelve: If he returns more or lefs, no Error, and of the Number Twelve.　And when the Trial fhall be* per primer *Jurors.　And of Inquefts of Office; and when to remain* pro defectu Juratorum. [*As to the Number of Jurors now to be returned, fee Stat.* 3 G. 2. c. 25. *at the End of this Chapter.*]

Of the Number Twelve.

NOW for the *Quales*; and thefe you fee for Number muft be Twelve, by the Common Law. *Doct. & Stud. fol.* 14.　For Quality, *liberos & legales Homines.*　And firft of their Number Twelve: And this Number is no lefs efteemed of by our Law than by Holy Writ.　If the twelve Apoftles on their twelve Thrones, muft try us in our eternal State, good Reafon hath the Law to appoint the Number of Twelve to try our Temporal.　The Tribes of *Ifrael* were Twelve, the Patriarchs were

Joth. 4.
Genef. 49.

(a) Juror (*Jurator*) is one of thofe Perfons that are fworn on a Jury; and the Law requires the Return of able and fufficient *Jurors.*　16 & 17 *Car.* 2.

Twelve,

Twelve, and *Solomon's* Officers were Twelve *(a)*. 1 *Kings* 4. 7. *Vide* Sir *Henry Spelman* verb. (*Jurata*). Therefore not only Matters of Fact were tried by Twelve, but of ancient Times, twelve Judges were to try Matters in Law, in the *Exchequer-Chamber,* and there were twelve Counsellors of State for Matters of State ; and he that wageth his Law must have eleven others with him who believe he says true. And the Law is so precise in this Number of Twelve, that if the Trial be by more or less, it is a Mistrial ; but in Inquests of Office *(b)*, as a Writ of Waste, there less than Twelve may serve. *F. N. B.* 107. *c.* And in Writs to inquire of Damages, the just Number of Twelve is not requisite, for they may be over or under ; and so it was resolved, *Trin.* 1651. *B. R. Abbot* versus *Holt,* that the Sheriff ought (in Writs of Inquiry) to summon Twelve by their Names, yet Damages assessed by a less Number is sufficient ; and in the Writ to the Sheriff, *quod ipse inquirat per Sacramentum proborum hominum,* omitting (*duodecim*) it is good and usual.

Finch 400, 484. Inquests of Office. *Vide hic, cap.* 13.

And in a Writ of Inquiry of Waste by thirteen it was holden good. 1 *Cro.* 414.

(a) The Privilege of Trial by *Jury,* is of great Antiquity in this Kingdom ; some Writers will have it that *Juries* were in Use among the *Britains* ; but it is more probable that this Trial was introduced by the *Saxons :* Yet some say, that we had our Trials by *Jury* from the *Greeks* ; (the first Trial of a *Jury* by Twelve being in *Greece.*) By the Laws of King *Ethelred,* it is apparent that *Juries* were in Use many Years before the Conquest ; and they are as it were incorporated with our Constitution, being the most valuable Part of it ; for without them no Man's Life can be impeached, (unless it be by Parliament) and no one's Liberty or Property ought to be taken from him.

(b) Plow. Com in Proœmio. Twelve Judges. Less than Twelve in Inquests of Office.

In

In Dower, if the Tenant come at the *Grand Cape*, and say he was always ready to render Dower, and Iffue is taken upon this, although Seifin of the Land be prefently awarded, yet no Inqueſt of Office, but the Jury upon the Trial of the Iffue ſhall affefs Damages. 22 *E*. 3. 15. *Roll. Trial*, 595.

In what Cafes there ſhall be an Inqueſt of Office, and in what not; fee *Roll*. Tit. *Trial*, 595.

Why the Sheriff returns twenty-four. And although there can be no Verdiƈt but by Twelve, yet by ancient Courſe and Uſage, (which, as the Lord *Coke* tells us, makes the Law in this Cafe. 1 *Inſt.* 155.) the Sheriff is to return Twenty-four. And this is for Expedition of Juſtice; for if Twelve ſhould only be returned, no Man ſhould have a full Jury appear or fworn, in refpeƈt of Challenges, without a *Tales*, which would be a great Delay of Trials; and for this Cauſe at Common Law, it was Error if the Sheriff returned lefs than Twenty-four.

If the Sheriff return lefs than twenty-four, it is no Error. But now it is remedied by the Statute of 18 *Eliz.* as a Mif-return. See *Cro.* 1 Part 223. *Lib.* 5. 36, 37. By which Books it appears, that if the Sheriff return but Twenty-three, &c. it ſhall not vitiate the Verdiƈt of Twelve, no, though a full Jury do not appear, fo that the Trial is by ten of the principal Pa-

Keble 1 Part 310. nel, and two of the *Tales*, notwithſtanding *Maynard*'s Opinion to the contrary, and *Cro.* 3 Part 587. After Verdiƈt it was alledged in Arreſt of Judgment, that neither upon the *Venire facias* or *Diſtringas* there was not made any Return; and it was held by the whole Court good Cauſe for the ſtaying the Judgment, and that it was not aided by the Statutes. The Sheriffs uſed to fummon above twenty-four, *ſcil. effrænatam*

natam multitudinem; but now they are prohibit- Muſt not reed by Statute to ſummon above twenty-four. turn above
Weſt. 2. *cap.* 38.   2 *Inſt.* 447. twenty-four.

If the Iſſue be to be tried by two Counties, In what Caſes
if but one of one County appear, although a the Inqueſt
full Inqueſt appear of the other, yet this ſhall ſhall remain
remain for Default, becauſe they cannot try that for Default of
which is in another County.   There ought to Jurors.
be ſix of each County.   And ſo of one Inqueſt Two Counties.
out of a Franchiſe, and another out of the
Guildable; and ſo of two Panels returned in an
Aſſize by ſeveral Bailiffs of Franchiſes to try
one Iſſue, and one Panel makes Default, the
Iſſue ſhall not be tried by the other Panel, for
the Jurors in one Franchiſe cannot make the
View in another Franchiſe.   *Roll.* Tit. *Trial,*
673.

If the Jury be of two Counties, or two Pa- The Manner
nels of the Guildable and Franchiſe, &c. they of Swearing
ſhall be ſworn interchangeably, firſt one of one, the Jurors.
then another of the other.

If a *Juryman* appear, and refuſe to be ſworn,
or refuſe to give any Verdict, if he endeavours
to impoſe upon the Court, or is guilty of any
Miſbehaviour after Departure from the Bar, he
may be fined, and Attachment iſſue againſt
him.   2 *Hawk.* P. C. 145, 146.

If the Jury go at large until another Day
after they are ſworn, and the Roll of the Entry
be not in Court, they may be ſworn anew.
Roll. Tit. *Trial,* 674.

To make a Jury in a Writ of Right, which Where there
is called the Grand Aſſize, there muſt be ſix- muſt be 16
teen, *ſcil.* four Knights, and twelve others; the and 24 in a
Jury in Attaint, called the Grand Jury, muſt Jury.
be twenty-four.   *Finch* 412, and 485.   But if
the Iſſue be upon a Matter out of the Point of
the

the Attaint, as upon a Plea of *Nontenure,* the Trial fhall be by twelve *Juratores.* 21 *E.* 3. 13.

There may be more than fixteen in a Writ of Right. *Roll.* Tit. *Trial,* 674.

Where Wit-nefles join with the Jury, the Number is uncertain. When Procefs ufed to be made out againft the Witneffes *in Carta nominat.* to join with the Jury in Trial of the Deed, as was ufed before the Statute of 12 *E.* 3. *c.* 2. (*his Teftibus*) being then Part of the Deed, then the Number was uncertain, according as the Number of Wit-neffes were in the Deed : Wherefore no At-tait lay, if the Deed were affirmed, becaufe more than twelve joined in the Verdict. But otherwife if the Deed was not found, becaufe **Cannot prove a Negative.** Witneffes cannot prove a Negative. *F. N. B.* 106. *b.* 1 *Inft.* 6. 2 *Inft.* 130, &c.

Juror departs and another fworn by Confent. If twelve are fworn, and one of them depart by Confent (*a*), another of the Panel may be fworn, and join with the other Eleven in the Verdict. 11 *H.* 6. 13.

A Jury of Six. It hath been frequently held, that a Cuftom in an inferior Court to try by fix Jurors is void ; and that though fuch Cuftom is ufed in *Wales,* yet that is by Force of the Stat. 34 *H.* 8. which appoints that fuch Trials may be by Six only, where the Cuftom hath been fo. *Cro. Car.* 259. 1 *Sid.* 233. 3 *Keb.* 326. See Stat. 3 *G.* 2. *c.* 25. *fect.* 9.

Per primer Jurors. Vide hic, cap. 4. If the Record be pleaded in Bar of the Af-fize, and the Party that pleads fays, the fame Tenements were put in View to the former Ju-rors : If the Plaintiff faith *nient comprife,* this

(*a*) After a Juror is fworn, he may not go from the Bar until the Evidence is given, for any Caufe whatfoever, without Leave of the Court ; and with Leave he muft have a Keeper with him. 2 *Lill.* 123, 127.

fhall

fhall be tried *per primer Jurors & auters.* 13 *H.*
4. 10. *Roll. Trial,* 592. *F. pl.* 1.

So if the Tenant faith, that thefe Lands are
not the fame Lands before recovered, this fhall
be tried *per primer Jurors & auters,* 22 *Affife*
16. and fo in a *Rediffeifin. Ibid.* 593. *pl.* 2.

So in an Affize, if the Defendant plead a
Recovery *per* View *de Jurors* in another Affize,
this fhall not be tried by the Affize, but *per
primer Jurors.* 13 *H.* 4. 10. *Ibid. pl.* 3.

And if at the Return of the former Jurors
and others, all the former Jurors appear, the
Trial fhall be by them only ; but if any do not
appear, they fhall be fupplied by the others.
40 *Affife* 4. *Ibid. pl.* 4.

In fuch Cafes where the Plaintiff is not to recover the Land, nor to defeat the former Judgment, if *nient comprife* be pleaded, upon a
Recovery pleaded, this may be tried by other
than the former Jurors. 1 *H.* 6. 5. *Ibid. pl.* 6.

As in Trefpafs for Trees cut, the Defendant
pleads, that he recovered before in an Affize,
the fame Land where, *&c.* and cut, *&c.* The
Plaintiff fays, this Land, where, *&c.* was not
put in View, and fo *nient comprife.* This fhall
not be tried by the firft Jurors, but by others,
becaufe this Action doth not defeat the former
Judgment, nor recover any Thing but Damages. *Note* the Difference, 1 *H.* 6. 5. Where
the Trial fhall be *per primer Jurors,* and where
by them and *Auters,* and where only *per auters.*
See *Roll.* Tit. *Trial,* 593. *pl.* 6.

Is a Writ granted for the re-examining of a
Matter paffed by *Affife* before Juftices : And
this is ufed where a Man appearing by his Bailiff to an *Affize* brought by another, hath loft
the Day ; and having fomething more to plead

*Certificate of
Affize of No-
vel Diffeifin.*

for himfelf, which the Bailiff did not, or might not plead for him, defires a further Examination of the Caufe, either before the fame Juftices, or others, and obtains Letters Patent to them to that Effect ; whereupon he brings a Writ to the Sheriff to call both the Party for whom the *Affife* paffed, and the Jury that was impanelled on the fame, before the faid Juftices at a certain Day and Place, when the fame is to be examined : And it is called a *Certificate,* becaufe therein mention is made to the Sheriff, that upon the Party's Complaint of the defective Examination, as to the *Affife* paffed, the King had directed his Letters Patent to the Juftices for the better *certifying* of themfelves, whether all the Points of the faid *Affife* were duly examined. *Reg. Orig.* 200. *F. N. B.* 181. *Bracton, lib.* 4. *c.* 13. *Horn's Mirror, lib.* 3.

Muft be twelve Jurors in a Writ of Inquiry. A Judgment out of an inferior Court was reverfed ; becaufe, being by Default, the Inquiry of Damages was only by two Jurors, and Cuftom alledged to warrant it ; and it was refolved by the Court, that there cannot be lefs than twelve, though the Writ of Inquiry faith only, *per Sacramentum proborum & legalium hominum,* and not *duodecim,* as in a *Venire.* 1 *Vent.* 113.

Rules in ftriking a fpecial Jury. *Trin.* 8 *W.* 3. A Rule was made in *B. R.* That when the Mafter is to ftrike a Jury, he fhould give Notice to the Attornies on both Sides to be prefent ; and if one comes, and the other does not, he that appears fhall ftrike out Twelve, and the Mafter fhall ftrike out other Twelve for him that is abfent. *Salkeld* 405.

If it be not expreffed in the Rule, that the Mafter fhall ftrike forty-eight, and each of the
Parties

Parties shall strike out Twelve, the Master is to strike twenty-four; and the Parties have no Liberty to strike out any. *Salk.* 405.

On a Motion granted for Leave to amend an Information in a Case of *Misdemeanor,* Leave was likewise granted for the Master to strike a Jury by Consent; *sed contra* in *capital Cases,* for then the Prisoner would lose his Challenges.

On Motion for a *special Jury* in a Case of Murder, it was denied *per Cur'*; for in Cases of Treason or Felony, there can be no special Jury, and the Party hath a right of challenging twenty without Cause; in Cases of special Juries there are forty-eight brought before the Master, who strikes off twenty-four, in which Case there cannot be a Rule for a good Jury.

If there be no legal Exceptions against the Sheriff, the Court cannot slip him, and order another to strike a special Jury *without Consent* of the Parties to be tried at the Assizes; but if there be any Objection against him, and that made out by Affidavit, a special Jury *may* then be struck by the Master without Consent; so to try a Cause at Bar, a special Jury may be struck without Consent. *Vin. Trial,* 301.

Formerly the Master and Under-Sheriff (who attends with the Book of Freeholders Names), had each a Guinea a side from the Plaintiff and Defendant; but see the Stat. 3 *G.* 2. *cap.* 25. by which the whole Charge lies on the Party applying for a special Jury.

By 3 *G.* 2. *c.* 25. *sect.* 15. reciting, ' That
' whereas some Doubt hath been conceived
' touching the Power of his Majesty's Courts of
' Law at *Westminster,* to appoint Juries to be
' struck before the Clerk of the Crown, Master
' of the Office, Prothonotaries, or other pro-

' per Officer of such respective Courts, for the
' Trial of Issues depending in the said Courts,
' without the Consent of the Prosecutor or Par-
' ties concerned in the Prosecution or Suit then
' depending, unless such Issues are to be tried
' at the Bar of the same Courts, Be it de-
' clared and enacted by the Authority aforesaid,
' That it shall and may be lawful to and for his
' Majesty's Courts of *King's Bench*, *Common*
' *Pleas*, and *Exchequer*, at *Westminster* respec-
' tively, upon Motion made on Behalf of his
' Majesty, his Heirs, or Successors, or on the
' Motion of any Prosecutor or Defendant in
' any Indictment or Information for any Mis-
' demeanor, or Information in the Nature of
' a *Quo Warranto* depending or to be brought
' or prosecuted in the said Court of *King's*
' *Bench*, or in any Information depending or to
' be brought or prosecuted in the said Court of
' *Exchequer*, or on the Motion of any Plaintiff
' or Plaintiffs, Defendant or Defendants in any
' Action, Cause, or Suit whatsoever, depend-
' ing or to be brought and carried on in the
' said Courts of *King's Bench*, *Common Pleas*,
' and *Exchequer*, or in any of them; and the
' said Courts are hereby respectively authorized
' and required, upon Motion as aforesaid, in
' any of the Cases beforementioned, to order and
' appoint a Jury to be struck, before the proper
' Officer of each respective Court, for the Trial
' of any Issue joined in any of the said Cases, and
' triable by a jury of twelve Men, in such Man-
' ner as special Juries have been, and are usually
· struck in such Courts respectively, upon Trials
' at Bar had in the said Courts; which said
' Jury so struck as aforesaid shall be the Jury
' returned for the Trial of the said Issue.

            ' And

And *Sect.* 16. It is further enacted, ' That
' the Perfon or Party, who fhall apply for fuch
' Jury to be ftruck as aforefaid, fhall bear and
' pay the Fees for the Striking fuch Jury, and
' fhall not have any Allowance for the fame,
' upon Taxation of Cofts.'

Sect. 17. Provided, ' That where any Special
' Jury fhall be ordered by Rule of any of the
' faid Courts to be ftruck by the proper Officer
' of fuch Court, in the Manner aforefaid, in
' any Caufe arifing in any City, or County of a
' City or Town, the Sheriff or Sheriffs, or Un-
' der Sheriff of fuch City, or County of a City
' or Town, fhall be ordered by fuch Rule to
' bring, or caufe to be brought before the faid
' Officer, the Books or Lifts of Perfons quali-
' fied to ferve on Juries within the fame, out
' of which Juries ought to be returned by fuch
' Sheriff or Sheriffs, in like Manner, as the
' Freeholders Book hath been ufually ordered to
' be brought, in order to the Striking of Juries
' for Trials at the Bar, in Caufes arifing in
' Counties at large; and in every fuch Cafe the
' Jury fhail be taken and ftruck out of fuch
' Books or Lifts refpectively.'

Since our Author wrote the following Stat.
of 3 G. 2. *c.* 25, hath been made, relating to
the Number of Jurors to be returned : And here
we fhall firft obferve that,

At Common Law in *Civil* Caufes, it feems
the Sheriff might have returned above 24 if he
pleafed; and therefore by the Stat. *Weft.* 2. *c.*
38. (*a*) It is recited, That whereas Sheriffs were
ufed to fummon an unreafonable Multitude of

(*a*) Note; this Stat. extends not to Jurors returned for
trial of *Criminal* Perfons. *Kel.* 16.

Jurors,

Jurors, to the Grievance of the People; it is ordained, that from thenceforth, in one *Affize*, no more fhall be returned than 24. See *Godb.* 370. 2 *Keb.* 310.

And now by the above mentioned Stat. of the 3 *G.* 2. *c.* 25. *fect.* 8. It is enacted, 'That ' every Sheriff or other Officer, to whom the ' Return of the *Venire facias juratores*, or other ' Procefs for the trial of Caufes before Juftices ' of Affize or *Nifi prius*, in any County in (*b*) *Eng-* ' *land*, doth or fhall belong, fhall, upon his Re- ' turn of every fuch Writ of *Venire facias* (un- ' lefs in Caufes intended to be tried at Bar, or in ' Cafes where a Special Jury fhall be ftruck by ' Order or Rule of Court) annex a Panel to the ' faid Writ, containing the Chriftian and Sir- ' names, Additions and Places of Abode of a ' competent Number of Jurors, named in fuch ' Lifts as qualified to ferve on Juries, the Names ' of the fame Perfons to be inferted in the Panel ' annexed to every *Venire facias*, for the Trial ' of all Iffues at the fame Affizes in each refpec- ' tive County; which Number of Jurors fhall ' be not lefs than Forty-eight in any County, ' nor more than Seventy-two, without direc- ' tion of the Judges appointed to go the Cir- ' cuit, and fit as Judges of Affize or *Nifi prius*, ' in fuch County, or one of them, who are re- ' fpectively hereby impowered and required, if ' he or they fee Caufe, by Order under his or ' their refpective Hand or Hands, to direct a

(*b*) By the ninth *Sect.* of this Stat. the Number in *Wales* for the Grand Seffions not to be lefs than *Ten*, nor more than *Fifteen* out of every Hundred, and to be fummoned eight Days before. By the 18th *Sect.* the Number in the Coun- ties Palatine, the fame as in other Parts of *England*, and to be fummoned 14 Days before.

' greater

' greater or leſſer Number, and then ſuch Num-
' ber as ſhall be ſo directed ſhall be the Num-
' ber to ſerve on ſuch Jury; and that the Writs
' of *Habeas corpora juratorum* or *Diſtringas*, ſub-
' ſequent to ſuch Writ of *Venire facias juratores*,
' need not have inſerted in the Bodies of ſuch
' reſpective Writs the Names of all the Perſons'
' contained in ſuch Panel; but it ſhall be ſuf-
' ficient to inſert in the Mandatory part of ſuch
' Writs reſpectively, *Corpora ſeparalium perſo-*
' *narum in panello huic brevi annexo nominata-*
' *rum*, or Words of the like Import, and to
' annex to ſuch Writs reſpectively Panels, con-
' taining the ſame Names, as were returned in
' the Panel to ſuch *Venire facias*, with their Ad-
' ditions and Places of Abode, that the Parties
' concerned in any ſuch Trials may have timely
' Notice of the Jurors, who are to ſerve at the
' next Aſſizes, in order to make their Challenges
' to them, if there be Cauſe; and that for the
' making the Returns and Panels aforeſaid, and
' annexing the ſame to the reſpective Writs, no
' other Fee or Fees ſhall be taken, than what
' are now allowed by Law to be taken, for the
' Return of the like Writs and Panels annexed
' to the ſame; and that the Perſons named in
' ſuch Panels ſhall be ſummoned to ſerve on Ju-
' ries at the then next Aſſizes or Seſſions of *Niſi*
' *prius*, for the reſpective Counties to be named
' in ſuch Writs and no other.'

CHAP. VII.

*Who may be Jurors, who not; who ex-
empted, and of their Quality and Sufficiency.*

Jurors muſt be
Liberi. Vide 2
Inſt. fol. 27.

SO much for their Number; next their Quality is to be conſidered; and for this the
Writ imforms you who they are to be, 1. *Liberos,* that is, Freemen, not Villeins or Aliens;
and that not only Freemen, and not Bond; but
alſo thoſe that have ſuch Freedom of Mind that

1 Inſt. 155.
Forteſcue,
cap. 25.

they ſtand indifferent, without any Obligation
of Affinity, Intereſt, or any other Relation what-
ſoever, to either Party: Sometimes the Word
Probos inſtead of *Liberos* is attributed to them;
they are both good Epithets for a Juror, but I
eſteem the firſt as moſt ſignificant.

Saunders a-
gainſt Leek.

Error of a Judgment in the *Marſhalſea,* the
Venire facias being *Probos & Legales,* not ſaying
as the Regiſter is, *Liberos homines, &c. ſed
non allocatur;* Judgment affirmed.   *Keble* 1
Part 563.

Legales.

2. They ought to be *Legales,* not outlawed,
nor ſuch as have loſt *Liberam Legem,* or become
infamous, as Recreants, Perſons attainted of Felony, falſe Verdict, Conſpiracy, Perjury, Pre-
munire or Forgery upon the Statute of 5 *Eliz.
cap.* 14. and not upon the Statute of 1 *H.* 5. 3.
Not ſuch as have had Judgment to loſe their
Ears, ſtand on the Pillory or Tumbrel, or have
been ſtigmatized or branded, nor Infidels'; neither can any ſuch be Witneſſes.   1 *Inſt.* 6.

3. *Homines;*

3. *Homines*; they ought to be Men, (yet there ſhall be a Jury of Women to try if a Woman be *Enſeint*, upon the Writ *de ventre inſpiciendo*): But what Kind of Men theſe ought to be, is worthy to be known. And for this ſome Men are exempted from ſerving on Juries, in Reſpect of their Dignity, as Barons, and all above them in Degree. Many are exempted by the Writ *de non ponendis in Aſſiſs*, *F. N. B.* 166. as aged Perſons Seventy Years old, and many others are exempted, as Clerks, Tenants in Ancient Demeſne, Miniſters of the Foreſt (out of the Foreſt) Coroners, Infants under the Age of fourteen Years, Officers of the Sheriff, ſick decrepit Men, and ſuch as are exempted by the King's Charter: Yet in a Grand Aſſize, Perambulation, Attaint, and ſome other Special Caſes, ſuch Men as are not exempted by Reaſon of their Dignity, ſhall be forced to ſerve, notwithſtanding their Exemption in other Caſes. See *Dalton*'s Office of Sheriffs, *fol.* 121. 52 *H.* 3. *cap.* 14. 2 *Inſt.* 127, 130, 378, 447, and 561. Counſellors, Attornies, Clerks, and other Miniſters of the King's Courts, are not to ſerve on Juries; but I find one Jury made of Attornies of the *Common Bench* and *Exchequer*, in a Caſe brought upon a Bill in the *Exchequer*, by Sir *Thomas Seton*, Juſtice, againſt *Luce C.* for calling of him Traitor in the Preſence of the Treaſurer and Barons of the *Exchequer*. And this Jury of Attornies gave the Juſtice one hundred Marks Damages. 30 *Aſſiſe* 19.

The Court frequently order a Jury of Merchants to try Merchants Affairs.

If the Charter of Exemption be, that he ſhall not be put *in Juratis, Aſſiſis ſeu recognitionibus aliquibus*, yet this ſhall not excuſe in a Writ of Right

Margin notes:

A Jury of Women.

Exemption of Juries.

Who are to be exempted from Juries.

A Jury of Attornies.

In what Caſes they ſhall be diſcharged by Charter.

Right upon Trial of the Grand Affize, for he comes not in, in this Cafe, by fuch Procefs as in otherCafes, but is chofen by the Oath of the four Chevaliers, and now he is in a Manner Judge in this Cafe. 39 *E.* 3. 15. *Roll. Trial,* 632. *B. pl.* 1.

Neither fhall it exempt him in an Attaint, nor in a Grand Inqueft, to inquire of Felonies, *&c.* becaufe the Charter hath not this Claufe. *Licet tangat nos & hæredes noftros.* 42 *Aff.* 5. *Ibid. pl.* 3.

At what Time, and how the Charter fhall be allowed.   At the *Nifi prius* the Bailiffs of a Vill may fhew a Charter, that to try Contracts, *&c.* within the Vill, the Inqueft fhall be all of Denizens, without Foreigners, and this fhall be allowed, and the Foreigners fhall be oufted. 29 *Aff.* 15. *Ibid.* 633.

So may the Burgeffes who are put upon a Jury out of the Borough, if they have fuch a Charter. 30 *Aff.* 1.

Allowed without Writ.   If a Man be impanelled of an Inqueft, and fhew fuch Charter of Exemption of the fame King in whofe Time he fhews it, this ought to be allowed without Writ. 39 *E.* 3. 15. *Roll. Ibid.* 633.

The Jurors ought to come in Perfon, and claim Privilege, the Sheriff cannot return it. 2 *Inft.* 130.

Vifne.   4. *De vicinet. de C.* It is not fufficient that they dwell in the County, but they are to be of the Neighbourhood, nay *le plus procheins* to the Place of the Fact, as by *Artic. fuper Chartas cap.* 9. it is appointed: They muft be moft near, moft fufficient, and leaft fufpicious. *Ibid.* as I fhall fhew hereafter.

Sufficiency of Jurors.   5. *Quorum quilibet habeat quatuor librat' terræ, tenement' vel reddit' per Annum ad mi-*

nus; this is their Sufficiency, where the Debt or Damages (or both together, 1 *Inst.* 272.) amount to 40 Marks or above. This Sufficiency of Jurors in o·her Cafes of leffer Moment, is ftill left to the Difcre·ion of the Juftices, *Fortefcue, cap.* 25. who (Experience tells us) never require Jurors under 4 *l. per Annum,* according to the Statute of 27 *Eliz. cap.* 6. before which, Men of 40 s. *per Annum* ferved; but neither this nor the Statute of 35 *H.* 8. extend to Juries in Cities, Towns corporate, or other privileged Places, or in the twelve Shires of *Wales*; fo that there they fhall be returned, as before they lawfully might have been. For the Jurors Sufficiency in Attaints, fee the Statutes 15 *H. 6.* 5. 18 *H. 6.* 2. and 18 *H. 8.* 3.

As to the Statute 35 *H.* 8. 6. the Trial ordained by that Statute, lies only in fuch Actions, which have their ordinary Trial by twelve Men, and not more; and by Writ of *Nifi prius*; and this only in thofe Actions in which the Procefs of *Vinire facias, Habeas corpora* and *Diftingas* lies againft the Jurors, and in no other Actions.

And although the Statute only mentions the Trial of Iffues joined in the King's Courts, commonly holden at *Weftminfter*; and if the Action be commenced in any other Court, yet if the Iffue be joined in any of the Courts at *Weftminfter*, it fhall be tried according to the faid Statute; and fo if thofe Courts are removed from *Weftminfter*, the Iffues joined in them fhall be tried as the faid Statute directs.

And the Words, *betwixt Party and Party*, fhall only be intended of common Perfons, and not betwixt the King and any other Perfon, nor when the King joins with any other Perfon, in any

any Action, which by the Releafe or Pardon, may be difcharged before the Action brought.

In an Information of Intrufion by the Queen, a Juror was challenged for Infufficiency of Freehold; he had but to the Value of 15 s. a Year. It was adjudged that the Statutes *H* 5. and 27 *Eliz.* extend only betwixt Party and Party, and not to the Queen; and if he had any Freehold, it was fufficient, but fome Freehold he muft have. *Cro. Eliz.* 38, 413. Sir *Chriftopher Blunt's* Cafe.

An Action on the Cafe was commenced in *Chancery,* and on Iffue joined there, a *Venire* iffued, *quorum quilibet habet quatuor Libras ad minus,* to try it in *B. R.* and on Trial it was found for Plaintiff; and now it was moved in Arreft of Judgment, that this *Venire* was wrong, and that the Statute 27 *Eliz. c.* 6. only extends to Iffues joined in *B. R. B. C.* or *Exchequer:* But it was held well, and that the Statute extended to all Iffues tried in *B. R.* wherever they were joined.

What is neceffary to be known, in Refpect of *Tales de circumftantibus, &c.* See *Williams* his Readings upon this Statute lately come out in Print; in which there are many ingenious Speculations; but becaufe they do not come often in Practice, and the Project of this Treatife is only to contain Matters ufeful for Practifers; that the Book may not fwell too big, I omit them, referring you to the Reading itfelf. See afterwards in the Chapter of Challenges.

It is the general Courfe of the World to efteem Men according to their Eftates; for *Quantum quifque fua nummorum fervat in arca, Tantum habet & fidei:* And fure I am, the

Makers of this Law had Caufe enough to do fo in this Cafe; for if Men of lefs Eftates fhould ferve on Juries, fuch Fellows would only be fhifted into Inquefts, as had more need to be relieved by the 8 *d.* than Difcretion to fift out the Truth of the Fact: 'Tis hard to get an un-biaffed Jury now; but furely lefs Rewards would fooner bribe and byafs meaner Men than thefe. Therefore, left Poverty or Neceffity fhould tempt, every Juror muft have 4 *l. per Annum* as aforefaid, of Freehold, out of Ancient De-mefne. And the Court may, in Matters of great Confequence, direct a *Venire facias* for a Jury above 4 *l. per Annum* a-piece, but not un-der. *Cro.* 2 Part 672. But in fuch Cafes (every one knows) the Court commonly orders the Pro-thonotary to chufe forty-eight, out of the She-riff's Book of Freeholders, of the moft fubftan-tial Men in the County, and the Parties ftrike out twelve a-piece, then the Sheriff returns the reft.

Note; In former Times, when Eftates of In-heritance were in few Men's Hands, fuch as had 40 *s. per Annum* were found fufficient Men to ferve on Juries. After, Eftates of Inheritance coming in greater Meafure to the Vulgar, it was by the faid Statute 27 *Eliz. cap.* 6. made 4 *l. per Annum*; and the fame Reafon improving in late Times, it was thought confifting with the Wifdom of a Parliament to raife it to 20 *l. per Annum*, to the End Men's Eftates might be trufted in the Judgment of more knowing Judges of the Fact, when they become litigious; and this was by an Act of 16 & 17 *Car.* 2. *cap.* 3. which being but a Probationer, and to continue but for three Years, and from thence to the End of the next Seffion of Parliament, it is ex-pired.   Such

Marginal notes:
Jurors of above 4 *l. per Annum.*

Jurors of 20 *l. per Annum.*

Such a Man who hath Land, Rent, Office, or other Profit *apprender*, out of Ancient Demefne, to the clear yearly Value of 4 *l.* of which he may have an Affife, he hath fufficient Freehold to be a Juror. *Vide* the faid Reading where you may know what Eftate is fufficient to make a Man a Juror. See the Chapter of *Challenges* in this work.

But now by the Statute 4 & 5 *Will. & Mariæ, c.* 24. *fect.* 15. all Jurors (other than Strangers *per medietat. linguæ*) returned upon Trial of Iffues joined in the *King's Bench, Common Pleas* or *Exchequer*, or before Juftices of Affize or *Nifi prius*, *Oyer* and *Terminer*, Gaol-Delivery, or General Quarter-Seffions of the Peace, fhall have in their own Name or in Truft, within the fame County, 10 *l.* a Year, above Reprifes, of Freehold or Copyhold Land, or in Ancient Demefne, or in Rents in Fee-fimple, Fee-tail, or for their own or fome other Perfon's Life; and in *Wales* 6 *l.* a Year. If any be returned of leffer Eftate, he may be difcharged by Challenge, or upon his Oath; nor fhall a Juror's Iffues be faved, but by Order of Court, for reafonable Caufe proved upon Oath.

The Sheriff, Coroner or other Minifter returning any Perfon of leffer Eftate, fhall forfeit 5 *l.* to their Majefties, for every Perfon fo returned.

They muft be fummoned fix Days before the Day of their Appearance, and none to take a Reward to excufe a Juror's Appearance, on Pain to forfeit 10 *l.* to their Majefties.

This Act extends not to Cities, Boroughs, and Towns corporate.

Tales Men in *England* fhall have 5 *l.* a Year, in *Wales* 3 *l.* a Year.

No

No Fee or Reward fhall be taken by any Perfons whatfoever, upon the Account of any *Tales* returned, upon Pain of 10 *l.* The one Moiety to the Profecutor, the other to his Majefty.

No Writ *de non ponendis in Affifis & Juratis* fhall be granted, unlefs upon Oath that the Suggeftions are true.

This Act to be in Force three Years, from the firft of *May* 1693, and is fince continued on.

Et qui nec D. E. *nec* F. G. *aliqua affinitate attingunt* ; the Law is very cautelous, in not leading Men into Temptation : Therefore, left Kindred and Affinity fhould wrong the Confcience to help a Friend, our *Jurors* muft not be related to any of the Parties ; and for this Reafon likewife the Statutes provide, that no Man of Law fhall ride Judge of Affize or Gaol-Delivery in his own Country. 8 *R.* 2. 2. 33 *H.* 8. *cap.* 24. [but this is fince altered by Stat.] And the contrary hereof was often done by a *Non obftante* ; but how confiftent with Integrity or Prudence, they know beft who procure it to be done. But becaufe moft Things concerning the Quality and Sufficiency of Jurors, will come more properly under the Title *Challenge,* I will refer you thither. *(Jurors muft not be of Affinity to the Party.)*

Rex verfus *Higgins, B. R.* The Caufe came to be tried at Bar, and a Challenge was made to the Jury in Behalf of the Defendants, for that the Jurymen were not Freeholders : And the Court faid it had been held, That for Juries within Corporate Towns, the Statutes that have been made, requiring that Jurymen fhould have fo much Freehold, do not extend to them ; and though to maintain the Challenge, it was faid, by the Common Law that Jurymen were to be Freeholders ; *(Jurors in Corporate Towns need not have Freehold.)*

Freeholders; the Court over-rul'd the Challenge.
1 *Vent.* 366.

In Waſte the Jury ſhall have the View.
If in a Writ of Waſte, the Defendant plead no Waſte done, and it appears upon Examination upon a *Voire dire,* That ſix of the Jury have view'd the Place waſted, it is ſufficient; if it appears upon Examination that none of the Jurors have had the View, the Trial ſhall be ſtay'd: If Waſte be aſſign'd in ſeveral Places, and of any of them the Jury have not had the View, they may find *Nul Waſte fait. Lutwich* 1558, 1559.

King may exempt Perſons from ſerving on Juries.
A Grant from the King to diſcharge one from ſerving on Juries is good, but a Grant to diſcharge a whole County is void. 1 *Siderfin* 127.

Grand Jury muſt find purſuant to the Indictment.
Rex verſus *Paine.* The Court held it was not in the Power of the Grand Jury to find one guilty of Manſlaughter on an Indictment of Murder. *Sid.* 230.

A whole City may be exempted from ſerving on Juries.
Rex verſus *Percival & al.* It was there held, That the King might grant the Privilege to a City, that they ſhould be exempt from ſerving on Juries *out of their own City.* But it was agreed by all, That by ſuch Grant they would not be exempt from ſerving in this Court *B R.* unleſs there were an expreſs Clauſe in the Charter, that they ſhould not ſerve *coram ipſo Rege. Sid.* 343.

Apothecaries exempted.
Every Perſon uſing and exerciſing the Art of an Apothecary in the City of *London,* or within ſeven Miles thereof, being free of the Society of Apothecaries in the ſaid City, and who ſhall have been duly examined and approved, *&c.* for ſo long Time as he ſhall exerciſe the ſaid Myſtery, and no longer, ſhall be exempted from

from ferving on any Jury or Inqueft. 6 *W.*
3. *cap.* 4.

Other Perfons exercifing the faid Art of an
Apothecary in any other Parts of this Kingdom,
who have ferved as Apprentices feven Years, according to the Statute of 5 *Eliz.* fhall likewife
be exempted from ferving on Juries, for fo long
Time as they fhall ufe and exercife the faid Art,
unlefs fuch Perfon voluntarily confent to ferve.
Ibid.

All Seamen alfo duly regiftred are exempted
from ferving on Juries by 7 & 8 *W.* 3. *cap.* 21.

Seamen ex-
empted.

All Conftables and Headboroughs fhall yearly at the General Quarter-Seffions of the Peace,
in the Week after *Michaelmas,* return and give
a true Lift in Writing of the Names and Abodes
of all Perfons within the refpective Places for
which they ferve, qualified to ferve on Juries,
between the Age of twenty-one and feventy
Years, which Lift they fhall deliver to the Juftices: And they fhall caufe the Clerk of the
Peace to deliver a Duplicate thereof to the Sheriff of the County or his Deputy, before the firft
of *January* next following, and caufe the faid
Lift to be fairly entred in a Book, and kept
among the Records of the Seffions: And no
Sheriff fhall impanel or return any Perfon to
ferve on any Jury at the Affizes, Gaol-Delivery
or Seffions of the Peace, who fhall not be named
in the faid Lift. Any Conftable or Headbo-
rough failing to make fuch Return as aforefaid,
to forfeit 5*l.* to the King. 7 & 8 *W.* 3. *cap.* 32.

Lifts of Jurors
to be exhibi-
ted by the
Conftables, to
the Juftices at
their Quarter-
Seffions
See Chap. 8. p.

No other to
be returned by
the Sheriff.

Every Summons of Perfons qualified to ferve
on Juries, fhall be made by the Sheriff or his
Officer, at leaft fix Days before the Day of Appearance, fhewing to the Perfon the Warrant
under the Seal of the Office, wherein he is no-

How to be
fummoned.

minated to ferve; and in cafe fuch Juror to be fummoned, be abfent from his ufual Habitation, a Note in Writing under the Hand of fuch Officer to that Effect, fhall be left at his Dwellinghoufe with fome Perfon there inhabiting. *Ibid.*

The Sheriff is excufable if he return any in the Conftables Lifts, though not qualified. The Return to the Seffions fhall be a good Excufe to the Sheriff, if he fummon one who is not qualified, and if an Action be brought thereupon, the Sheriff may plead the General Iffue, and give this Act in Evidence; and if the Plaintiff be nonfuit, &c. he fhall pay treble Cofts. And if the Sheriff, his Bailiff, or Deputy, fhall fummon any Freeholder or Copyholder, otherwife than as aforefaid, or neglect his or their Duty, or excufe any Perfon for Favour or Reward, or allow of any Exemption to any Perfon under the Age of feventy Years; *Penalty of Sheriff on his Mifbehaviour.* fuch Sheriff, his Deputy or Bailiff, fhall forfeit the Sum of 20 *l.* to the Party grieved, or to whomfoever fhall fue for the fame, in any Court of Record at *Weftminfter.* *Ibid.*

Quakers are incapable of ferving on Juries. 7 & 8 *W.* 3. *cap.* 34.

Special Writs where the Jury fhall have the View. The Courts of *Weftminfter* are impowered to order fpecial Writs of *Diftringas* or *Habeas Corpora,* to caufe fix or more of the firft twelve Jurors, to have the Matters in Queftion fhewn them, by two Perfons in the Writs named and appointed by the Court; and the Sheriff fhall return the View. 4 & 5 *Ann. cap.* 16.

For the Qualifications of Jurors as regulated by 3 *G.* 2. *c.* 25. and 4 *G.* 2. *c.* 7. fee the next Chapter towards the End.

C H A P.

C H A P. VIII.

Concerning the Vifne, *or Place from whence the Jury fhall come*, &c.

*V*Icinetum is derived of this Word *Vicinus*, Vifne.
and fignifieth Neighbourhood, or a Place
near at Hand, or a Neighbour Place, where the
Queftion abour the Fact is moved. And the
moft general Rule (faith *Coke* 1 *Inft.* 125,) is,
That every Trial fhall be out of that Town, Parifh or Hamlet, or Place known out of the Town,
&c. within the Record, within which the Matter of Fact iffuable is alledged, which is moft
certain and neareft thereunto, the Inhabitants
whereof may have the better and more certain
Knowledge of the Fact.

Some Place muft be alledged fo as an Iffue
may be taken; the Omiffion of it is incurable.

As in Debt for Rent, and *Nil debet* pleaded,
and Iffue join'd, at the Day of *Nifi prius*, the
Defendant pleaded a Releafe after the laft Continuance, but named no Place *where* the Plaintiff releafed, fo as no Iffue could be taken ; and
upon a Demurrer the Plaintiff had Judgment,
for the Fault was incurable.

So in Error on a Judgment in Debt, pleading
a Releafe of Errors without laying a *Venue* is ill;
and the Plea then amounts to a Confeffion of the
Errors.

So an Award pleaded in Bar, without faying
where the Award was made, was ruled ill upon
Demurrer.

Confideration *executory* is traverfable, and therefore a *Venue* muft be laid : But in Covenant

I 2 againft

against one as Assignee a *Venue* is not necessary
to be laid, for an Assignment is always intended
to be made on the Lands assign'd.

If a Place be alledged and no County where
it lies, no Issue can be upon it; as in a *Scire
facias* upon a Recognizance on a Breach of the
Peace. The Breach was assigned in a *Ville,* but
no County mentioned, and the Jury at the Bar
were discharged: But in some Cases the *Ville* alledged shall be intended in the County where
the Action is brought, as a Fact laid in *Middlesex* as done at *Islington*; in this Case *Islington*
shall be intended to be in *Middlesex,* for it is the
Gift of the Action: Indeed, if the Place mentioned be *collateral* to the Issue, it is then necessary to shew in *what* County it lies; it shall otherwise be intended to lie in any County.

So Act of Composition, and a Composition
in pursuance, being pleaded in Bar to Debt upon
a Bond, without reciting the Act, or laying a *Venue* for the Composition, was adjudged ill; and
Judgment for the Plaintiff.

But if Coverture be pleaded *to a Writ* it needs
no *Venue,* but may be tried where the Writ is
brought, and the Defendant must shew and prove
the Coverture. 'Tis the same in pleading *Infancy.*

So *Alien Enemy* pleaded in *Abatement* needs
no *Venue,* and so adjudged on Demurrer; for the
Plaintiff might have replied generally *born in
England,* but if pleaded *in Bar* a *Venue* is necessary; and this is the true difference, and according to *Coke,* though the Precedents be both
Ways.

The Want of a *Venue* may be aided *by pleading over*; as in Trespass, where the Defendant
pleads Performance of an Award, but lays no
Venue, and the Plaintiff replies a subsequent A-
ward

ward, on which the Defendant tenders an Issue, this is aided by the pleading over.

So in Debt upon a Bond, and the Defendant pleads a Release, this admits the Bond and aids the want of a *Venue.* *Vin. Trial,* 91, 92, 93.

And if a Thing be alledged in *D.* the *Venue* must not be of *D.* but *de vicineto de D.* for otherwise the Neighbourhood would be excluded. *Roll.* Tit. *Trial,* 622. *pl.* 33.

And if the Fact be alledged *in quadam platea vocat.* Kingstreet, *in parochia sanctæ Margaretæ in Civitate Westm. in Com. Midd.* in this Case the *Visne* cannot come out of *Platea,* because it is neither Town, Parish, Hamlet, nor Place out of the Neighbourhood, whereof a Jury may come by Law; but in this Case it shall not come out of *Westminster,* but out of the Parish of St. *Margaret,* because this is the most certain. But therein also it is to be noted, that if it had been alledged in *Kingstreet,* in the Parish of St. *Margaret* in the County of *Middlesex,* then should it have come out of *Kingstreet;* for then should *Kingstreet* have been esteem'd in Law a Town: For whensoever a Place is alledged generally in Pleading, (without some Addition to declare the contrary, as in this Case it is) it shall be taken for a Town.

1 Inst. 125.

Parish.

Town.

And albeit *Parochia* generally alledged, is a Place incertain, and may (as we see by Experience) include several Towns; yet if a Matter be alledged *in Parochia,* it shall be intended in Law, that it containeth no more Towns than one, unless the Party do shew the contrary. But when a Parish is alledged within a City, there without Question the *Visne* shall come out of the Parish, for that is more certain than the City.

Parochia.
1 Inst. 125. b.

Moor 559.

If a Matter be pleaded done *apud Bradford in Forfield in Parochia de Belbroughton,* the *Venue*

shall

shall be of *Belbroughton*, and not of *Brad-ford*; for *Belbroughton* shall be intended to be a Town, and one Town shall not be intended to be in another Town, and therefore *Bradford* shall not be intended to be a Town. *Roll.* Tit. *Trial*, 619. *pl.* 1.

The *Venue* shall ever be of the most certain Place; but a Writ of *Inquiry of Damages* is not of any *Visne* certain, it only says *per sacramentum proborum & legalium Hominum*, &c. *Vin. Trial* 90. and where there is a Judgment upon a *Nil dicit* the want of a *Venue* will not set it aside, for the Inquiry is not to be of any Thing besides Damages, which by any Jurors in the County may be inquired of. *Ibm.* 93.

So Matters touching the *Person*, as Privilege of Attorney, may be pleaded without a *Venue*. *Ibm.*

It is sufficient if the *Venue* be laid at a Place which has Reference to the County in the Margin; for since by Act of Parliament the *Venire* is *de corpore Com.* it is not necessary to lay any particular Place in the County.

Where no *Venue* is laid in the Body of the Declaration, the Reference then must be had to the Margin; but where a *Venue* is laid in the Body of the Declaration, the County in the Margin shall not vitiate, it shall help, but not hurt. *Vin. Trial*, 94.

In a *Quo warranto* for using a Warren in *D.* if the Defendant say the Vill *D.* is Parcel of the Manor of *S.* and prescribes to have a Warren within the said Manor and Demesnes thereof, Ibid. 619. pl. the *Venire facias* shall be of the Manor; for 6. the Manor by Intendment is more large than the Vill. If the *Visne* be *de D.* and *S.* and the *Ve-* Ibid. 620. pl. *nire facias* be *de D. S.* and *V.* this is not good, 8. because it is too large. If *apud Burgum de Pli-mouth,*

mouth, the *Venue* may be *de Plimouth* generally. If *apud Villam de Cambridge in Warda Fori*, and the *Venire facias* is *de Villa & Warda prædict.* this is helped by the Statute of *Jeofails.* *Ibid.* 621. *pl.* 21, 22.

If the Place be out of a Town, the *Venue* shall not be of the next Town, but from the Place itself, but the Sheriff ought to return the Jury *de plus prochein Ville.* *Ibid. pl.* 24.

In Ejectment of Land *in Foresta de Kevennon in Com. S.* the *Venue* may be *de vicineto Forestæ*, for this is a Place known ; and by Intendment, because the Defendant hath not pleaded in Abatement, that this is out of any Parish or Vill. *Ibid. pl.* 26.

In inferior Courts within Boroughs, the *Venire facias* is *quod Venire facias* 12 *liberos Burgenses Burgi & Parochiæ de* B. although there may be twelve Burgesses which are not Inhabitants. *Roll.* Tit. *Trial,* 622. *pl.* 34.

The *Venue* shall follow the Issue. *Vide Postea.*

In Trespass and Battery in *London*, if the Defendant justifie in *Midd.* by Process out of the *Marshal's* Court, that he arrested him, and because the Plaintiff would not go with him, he beat him, *&c. Absque hoc*, that he is guilty in *London vel alibi* out of the Jurisdiction of the Court. To which the Plaintiff replies, and acknowledges the Arrest, but says, that he beat him at *London, de injuria sua propria absque tali causa*, and Issue upon this ; this shall be tried in *London*, and the Words, *absque tali causa*, are void, the Issue being joined upon a Place certain, *scil. London :* Affirmed in a Writ of Error. *Roll. ib.* 624. But the Court said, that he might have demurred upon this Plea.

I 4   ✦ **If**

De Corpore Comitatus.
1 Inft. 125.b.
Manor.

If a Trefpafs be alledged in *D.* and *Nul tiel Ville* is pleaded, the Jury fhall come *de Corpore Comitatus.* But if it be al.edged in *S.* and *D.* and *Nul tiel Ville de D.* is pleaded, the Jury fhall come out *de vicineto de S.* for that is the more certain. So if a Matter be alledged within a Manor, the Jury fhall come *de vicineto Manerii.* But if the Manor be alledged within a Town, it fhall come out of the Town, becaufe that is moft certain, for the Manor may extend into divers Towns. And all thefe Points were refolved by all the Judges of *England,* upon Conference between them, in the Cafe of *John Arundel,* Efq; indicted for the Death of *William Parker.* 6 *Co.* 14.

De Corpore Com'.

Where there may be a fpecial *Vifne,* the Trial fhall never be *de Corpore Comitatus.* *Leon.* 1 Part 109.

If a *Venire facias* ought to be of one or more Vills in certain, in a County, and this is awarded *de Corpore Comitatus*; this feems to be aided by the Statute of 21 *Jac.* of *Jeofails*; for this comes from the Vills from whence it ought to come, and from others, inafmuch as it comes *de Corpore Comitatus, Roll.* Tit. *Trial,* 618. and many other Cafes concerning this Matter.

But in Ejectment of Land, called *S.* and no Place is named where the Land lies, and a *Venire* is awarded *de Corpore Com.* this is erroneous, and too large, becaufe there is a Place certain where the Land lies, and yet is not named in the *Nar.* as it ought to be. *Hob.* 121. *Roll.* *Trial,* 617. *pl.* 15.

But if the Iffue be taken upon a Title of Dignity, and whether *Chivaler* or not, this may come *de Corpore Comitatus,* becaufe that the *Place where, &c.* is not material. *Ibid. pl.* 16.

If

If *A.* by the Name of *A.* of the County of *Hampshire*, bring a *Scire facias* upon a Recognizance in *Chancery* in the County of *Middlesex* against *B.* and the Defendant plead that the Plaintiff is outlawed by the Name of *A.* in the County of *Chester*; to which the Plaintiff replies, that he is not *una & eadem Persona*, this may be tried by the Jury of the County of *Middlesex*, where the Writ is brought. *Roll. Trial,* 617. *pl.* 14.

In a *Quare Impedit* for the Church *de Uselbee*, and the Defendant pleads that there is no such Church, the *Venue* shall not come *de Corpore Comitatus*, but *de vicineto de Uselbee*; for this is a Place known, and it is intended the Church of *Uselbee* is within the *Ville* of *Uselbee*. *Hob.* 325. *Roll. Trial,* 616. *pl.* 7.

In a Prohibition, if the Parties be at Issue upon a Custom *de non decimando* of Wood in the Wild of *Sussex*, the *Venire facias* shall be *de Corpore Comitatus*; for the Wild is not such a Place, whereof the Court may have Conusance to be sufficient to have a Jury to come from this, for the Wild is a Wood by Intendment. *Hob.* 348. *Roll. Trial,* 617. *E. pl.* 2. *Wild.*

In a real Action where the Demandant demands Lands in one County, as Heir to his Father, and alledges his Birth in another County, if it be denied that he is Heir, it shall not be tried where the Birth is alledged, but where the Land lieth; for there the Law presumes it shall be best known who is Heir. But if the Defendant make himself Heir to a Woman (for that is the surer and more certain Side, and the Mother is certain, when perhaps the Father is incertain) it shall be tried where the Birth is alledged, *Heir tried where the Land lies, where not. 1 Inst. 125. b.*

Cro. 3 Part 818. *Cro. 2 Part* 303.

bailged, because they have more certain Cognisance, than where the Land lieth.

Bastardy.
1 Inst. 115 b.
And so it is where Bastardy is alledged, the Trial shall be in like Case, *Mutatis mutandis*.

No Countie,
where the
Letters bear Date
If a Man plead the King's Letters Patent, and the other Party plead *Non concessit*, it shall not be tried where the Letters bear Date; for they cannot be denied, but where the Land lieth.

Plea of a less
Place.
Every Trial must come out of the Neighbourhood of a Castle, Manor, Town or Hamlet, or Place known out of a Castle, Manor, Town, or Hamlet, as some Forest, and the like, as before.

Venire facias may be of a Forest, Burgh, Castle, Wards, Paris, &c. but not of a Leet, Rectory, Market, Wash, &c. nor *de bene esse*, without alledging this to be out of a Vill or Parish. *Jones fo. 326.* But after Verdict helped by the new Statute 16, 17 *Car. 2. c. 8.*

Where the
Writ is
brought at
Common
Law.
Every Plea concerning one Person, Plaintiff, &c. shall be tried where the Writ is brought. *1 Inst. 125 b.*

When the Matter alledged extendeth into a Place at the Common Law, and a Place within a Franchise, it shall be tried at the Common Law. *1 Inst. 125.*

Matters done
beyond Sea,
how triable in
England. Vide
cap. 10.
Matters done beyond Sea may be tried in England, and therefore a Bond made beyond Sea may be alledged to be made in any Place in England, if it bear Date in no Place; but if there be a Place, as at *Bourdeaux* in *France*, then it shall be alledged so be made in *quodam loco vocat.* *Bourdeaux* in *France*, in *Islington*, in the County of *Middlesex*, and from thence shall come the Jury, *1 Inst. 261. Latch 4. & 5.* So if the

Rob 1 Part
31 g.
Tenant plead that the Demandant is an Alien, born under the Obedience of the *French King*, and

and out of the Allegiance of the King of *England*; the Demandant may reply, that he was born at such a Place in *England*, within the King's Legiance, and hereupon a Jury of twelve Men shall be charged, and if they have sufficient Evidence that he was born in *France*, or in any other Place out of the Realm, then shall they find that he was born out of the King's Legiance. And if they have sufficient Evidence that he was born in *England*, or *Ireland*, or *Guernsey*, or *Jersey*, or elsewhere within the King's Obedience, they shall find that he was born within the King's Legiance. And this hath ever been the Pleading and Manner of Trial in that Case. So of other Things done beyond Sea, the adverse Party may alledge them to be done at such a Place in *England*, from whence the Jury shall come, and in a special Verdict, they may find the Things done beyond Sea. *Ibid. & Lib.* 7. 26.

Things done beyond Sea.

Lib. 7. 26.

So when Part of the Act is done in *England*, and Part out of the Realm, that Part that is to be performed out of the Realm, if Issue be taken thereupon, shall be tried here by twelve Men, and they shall come out of the Place where the Writ or Action is brought. *Ibid. Lib.* 6. 48.

Part without the Realm, and Part within.

Error, for that Judgment was given by Default against the Defendant, being an Infant; Issue was taken that he was of full Age. And *Godfrey* moved, whether the Trial should be in *Norfolk* where the Land was, or in *Middlesex*, where the Action was brought? And the Court held, That it should be tried in the County where the Land lay; and *Tanfield* said, it was so adjudged in the *King's Bench*, between *Thregmorton* and *Barford. Cro.* 3 Part 818.

Full Age tried where the Land lies.

Error

Error on a Judgment in Dower at the Grand Seffions in *Brecon* was affigned, for that the Tenant being under Age appeared by Attorney; and it was alledged that he was within Age at *Abergavenny* in the County of *Monmouth*; and Iffue being thereon joined, it was tried by a Jury *de Vicineto de Abergavenny*, and found for Plaintiff in Error. It was moved in Arreft of Judgment, that this was a Mif-trial; for being in a real Action, this Iffue ought to have been tried where the Land lay; but held well by all the Court; for the Alledging him to be within Age at *Abergavenny*, is the fame as alledging a Commorancy there; and a Difference was taken between where the Title depended on the Nonage, in which Cafe it fhould be tried where the Land lay, and where the Infancy is pleaded as a Matter *de hors*, as in the prefent Cafe. *Jones, T.* 170, 171.

Local Actions.   Queftions of Title of Land (except by fpecial Order of the Judges in fome Cafes) are to be tried in the County where the Land lies; for the Law is, that all real and mixt Actions, as Wafte, Ejectment, Trefpafs for breaking the Clofe, cutting down Trees, fpoiling the Corn, Grafs, &c. and Debt upon an Efcape, &c. muft be laid in the County where the Caufe of Action arofe, or where the Land lies.   If an Action be brought againft an Officer for a Matter relating to the Execution of his Office, the Action muft be laid in the proper County.   But if the Officer, after his Authority is expired, abufes the Party, or if he meets a Man and knocks him down, the Action of Trefpafs and Affault is not confined to the *proper* County.   1 *Str.* 446.

Tranfitory Actions.   Debt, Detinue, Annuity, Account, Actions of the Cafe, Battery, &c. are in their own Nature tranfitory, transitory, and yet they ought to be laid and tried in their proper County where the Fact was done, unless the Court order the contrary, for some special Reasons; and if they are laid out of the proper County, daily Practice tells us the Court may alter the *Venue*, upon *Affidavit* of the true Place of the Fact.

All *criminal* Matters are to be tried where the Offence is committed.

Criminal
Matters.

If the *Venue* arise in two Counties, the Jury upon two *Venire facias's* shall come from both, six out of one County, and six from the other. *Cro.* 3 Part 646. But by the Consent of Parties, entered upon Record, it may be by five out of one, and seven from the other, as appears, *Cro.* 3 Part 171. where in *Replevin* the the Defendant avows for *Damage feasant*; the Plaintiff by his Replication claims Common by Prescription *in loco quo, &c.* being *Broadway* in the County of *Worcester*, appurtenant to his Manor of *D.* in the County of *Gloucester*, and Issue thereupon, and two *Venire facias's* awarded to the Sheriffs of the several Counties; and now seven of the County of *Worcester* appeared, and five of *Gloucester*. And although there ought to have been six sworn of each County, to try that Issue, as appears 49 *Ed.* 3. 1. 31 *H.* 8. 46. yet by the Assent of Parties, those twelve who appeared, by the Advice of all the Justices were sworn, and tried the Issue. And it was commanded that this Assent should be entred upon Record; for otherwise it would be a strange Precedent.

This is called
a Joinder of
Counties.
Finch 410.
Jury out of
two Counties.

But out of
more than
two Counties
it cannot be
made.

In Assise of Common *in Confinio Comitatus,* and the Issue be, whether he had Common by Prescription in one County, appendant to a Ma- nor

nor in another County, this shall be tried by both Counties. *Roll. Trial,* 599. *N. pl.* 5.

The same Law is in Trespass brought in one County (which cannot be *in confinio*), upon such an Issue the Trial shall be *per ambideux* Counties, 49 *E.* 3. 20. See *Roll.* Tit. *Trial,* 599, *&c.* many Cases where the Jury shall come from two Counties.

In an Action upon the Statute of *Marlebridge,* for taking a Distress in one County and chasing in another County ; upon Not guilty the Trial shall be only by the County where the Chasing is, for this is all the Cause of the Action. 4 *H.* 6. 4. *Roll. Trial,* 601. *pl.* 1.

In an Action on Stat. 2 *W. & M. c.* 5. for rescuing a Distress for Rent ; the Lands demised lay in three Vills ; the Rescue was laid to be in one of them. The *Venire* shall be from that Vill only where the Rescue is laid ; for the Action is founded on the Tort, and the Demise is only Inducement. 1 *Lutw.* 215.

Escape.   In Escape upon Arrest in one County, and an Escape in another County, upon Not guilty, this shall be tried, where the Escape is laid, for the Action is upon the Escape. *Roll. ibid.* 602. *pl.* 8.

Covenant in P. to sell at R. tried at P.   In an Action of *Trover, apud Paxton in Com. Hunt.* the Defendant pleads a Bargain and Sale *apud Royston in Com. Hertford,* in the Market there, whereby he after converted them *apud P. in Com. Hunt.* The Plaintiff saith, that he was possessed of those Goods *apud P. in Com. Hunt.* and that *J. S.* there stole them from him, and by Covenant betwixt him and the Defendant, at *P. in Com. H.* he sold them to the Defendant as he hath pleaded : The Issue was upon the Sale made by Covenant, *&c.* And it was

tried

tried in the County of *Hunt.* and found for the
Plaintiff. And it was moved to be a Mis-trial;
for it ought to have been by a Jury of the
County of *Hertford*, or at leastwise by a Jury
of both Counties : But it was adjudged to be
well tried, because the Sale is confessed, and the
Issue is upon the Covenant alledged in *Hertford.*
Cro. 3 Part 511.

In Debt upon a Bond in *London*, the Defendant pleaded an usurious Contract in the County of *Warwick*; the Plaintiff replied, that the
Bond was made upon good Consideration ; *absque hoc*, that it was made for such usurious Contract : The Trial shall be in the County of
Warwick ; for the Bond is confessed, and the
Usury in *Warwick* is only in Question ; and so
if the Issue be, whether the Deed were made
by *Dures*, the Trial shall be where the *Dures*,
and not where the Deed is supposed to be made.
Cro. 3 Part 195.

Where Issue is taken upon a Surrender, it
shall be tried where it was alledged to be done,
and not where the Manor is, of which the
Copyhold is holden. *Ibid. f.* 260. *Br.* Tit.
Visne, 114.

In an *Assumpsit* laid at *London*, *in Warda de
Cheap*, the *Venire* was *de Parochia de Arcubus
in Warda de Cheap*, whereas no Parish was mentioned before in the Count ; and adjudged, that
the *Venire* was ill laid in the Count ; for a *Venire facias* may be of a Town, Parish, Manor,
or other Place unknown, but not of a Hundred
or Ward, *Cro.* 1 Part 165. for the Ward in a
City, is but as the Hundred in a County. The
Parish in *London* is in Lieu of a Vill, and the
Ward of a Hundred. *Roll.* Tit. *Trial*, 620,
pl. 15. *vide hic apres.*

Where

*Usurious
Contract in
another
County.*

*A Dures shall
be tried there,
not where the
Action is
brought.*

Surrender,

*Ward or
Hundred, to
good Visne.*

City.

Where the *Viſne* is laid to be at a City, in an Action brought in a ſuperior Court, or within the City, though it be both a City and County, the *Venire facias* may be *de vicinet. Civitatis. Latch* 258. Though it hath been held not good, but that the *Venire facias* may be *de Civitate*, leaving out *Vicinet.* as you may read in *Staundf.* 155. But now the Caſe in *Cro.* 2 Part 308. and *Bulſtr.* 1 Part 129. ſay, that all the *Venire facias's* are awarded *de vicinet. Civitatis*, which is intended as well *de Civitate* itſelf, as *de vicineto infra Juriſdictionem* of the City. And ſo it is *de vicinet. Civitatis*, or *de vicinet.* or *de Civitate Coventry, Eborum, Norwich, Sarum, Briſtol, Exon*, and all other Cities which are Counties in themſelves. In all Places beſides *London*, no Mention is made of the Pariſh or Ward. *Ibid.* 493. But in *London* the Pariſh and Ward is mentioned, and therefore it was adjudged *Cro.* 2 Part 150. that it was not good to alledge any Thing done in *London* generally ; but it muſt be in what Pariſh from which a *Venire* may be ; but where a Thing is laid in a City, *in alta Warda* there, and the *Venire facias* is from the City only, it is well, becauſe it ſhall be intended there be no more Wards in the ſame City. *Cro.* 3 Part 282.

Roll. 622, 623.

So in all inferior Courts, Style 2. March 125.

London.

City.

Hundred.

In an Action againſt the Hundred upon the Statute of *Winton, &c.* upon the Roll the *Venire facias* is awarded of *Bradley, quod eſt proximum Hundredum*, and the *Venire facias* is generally of *Bradley.* This is well, becauſe by the Roll it appears that *Bradley* and the Hundred are all one. *Roll.* Tit. *Trial*, 598.

If a Thing be laid done *apud Briſtol*, viz. *in Warda Sanctæ Mariæ in Warda de Ratliff*, and the

the *Venire facias* is *de Warda de Ratliff*, this is not good. *Ibid.* 619. *pl.* 5.

But if it be alledged in a Ward in the City of *Briftol, &c.* the *Venue* fhall be of the *Ward*, not *de Civitate*. *Ibid.* 621. *pl.* 28. Ward.

A *Venire facias* was awarded from *T.* and not *de vicinet. de T.* and for this Caufe refolved to be ill, and not amendable. *Cro.* 2 Part 399. *Bro.* Tit. *Ven. fac.* 8. De vicinet. left out, ill.

If the Iffue be *fi Rex conceffit per literas patentes*, the Trial fhall be, as hath been faid, where the Land lies, and not where the Patent was made, becaufe the Patent is of Record; and if it be traverfed, it fhall be tried by the Record, and therefore the Iffue being upon *Non conceffit*, the Iffue is not upon the Patent; but where the Iffue is upon *Non conceffit*, or *Non dimifit*, of a Thing which paffeth by Deed, the Trial fhall be where the Grant or Demife is alledged: But of a Feoffment, or Leafe for Life pleaded, the Iffue being *Non feoffavit*, or *Non dimifit*, Livery ought to be made, and therefore the Trial fhall be where the Land lies. *Cro.* 2 Part 376. 3 Part 269. Where the Land lies. 1 Inft. 125. *b.*

Where the Offence was laid in the Count to be in one County, and the Juftification in another County, and the Plaintiff replies *De injuria fua propria, &c.* The *Vifne* fhall be where the Juftification is alledged; as, one Example for all, to illuftrate. In an Action upon the Cafe, for Words fuppofed to be fpoken at *Bridge-North* in the County of *Salop*, the Defendant pleads, that he fpake them as a Witnefs upon his Oath upon an Iffue tried at *Chard* in the County of *Somerfet*. The Plaintiff replies *De fon tort demefne, &c.* And therefore it was tried by a *Venire facias* of *Bridge-North*, and Where the Action is laid in one County, and the Juftification in another, the Trial fhall be where the Juftification is.

Error thereof affigned, becaufe it ought to have been by a *Vifne* of *Chard*, where the Juftification arofe; and it was held clearly to be a Miftrial, and not aided by the Statute of *Jeofails*; wherefore the Judgment was reverfed. *Cro.* 3 Part, 468, 261, 870. *Moor* 410.

Vide poft.

Replevin, taking two Horfes at fuch a Place in *Denford in Com. Northampton*; the Defendant makes Conufance as Bailiff to the Lord *Mountague*, of his Manor of *S.* which Manor is holden of the Honour of *Gloucefter*, and that the Place in which, *&c.* is within the faid Honour, and alledges a Cuftom within the faid Honour, on which Cuftom the Parties were at Iffue, and the *Venire facias* was from *Denford* the Place of taking, which was moved after Verdict, for that the *Venue* was not fo large as the Iffue, which was the Honour; and of this Opinion was the whole Court of *C. B. Pafch.* 13 *Car.* 2. *Hill* verfus *Bunning,* 1 *Siderf.* 19.

But the great Queftion was, whence the *Venue* fhould arife in this Cafe; and by *Bridgman* Chief Juftice, and Juftice *Hide*, in no Cafe can a *Venue* arife from an Honour; and the Chief Juftice faid, he had caufed the Prothonotaries to fearch for Precedents, and they could not find that ever a *Venue* did arife from an Honour, which is a Bundle of Services, and an incorporeal Thing, from which no *Venue* can come; and yet an Honour may have Demefnes, as the Honours of *Grafton* and *Hampton* have, but *Gloucefter* not.

Honours.

Siderfin 19, 88.

Chief Juftice and Juftice *Hide* feemed to incline that the *Venue* fhould be *de corpore Comitat. Hob.* 266, 249. But when the Court was after moved for their Opinion, they bad them

3   tal e

take a *Venire facias* at their Peril, and would give no Opinion.

An Action of Debt was brought on a Bond to perform Covenants in an Indenture, whereby the Defendant had granted to the Plaintiff a Walk called *Shrob-Walk,* in the Forest of ———— *in Com. Northampton,* and covenanted for peaceable Enjoyment, *&c.* and he was ousted *per* Earl of *Northampton,* who had Right, on which Right Issue was joined, and the *Venire facias* was from *Shrob-Walk.*

Per Cur. It is not good, for it appears by the Record, that *Shrob-Walk* is not a Vill : but if the Obligation had been laid to be made at *Shrob-Walk,* the *Venue* should arise from thence, as a Vill. *Inter Stirt* and *Bales, Pasch.* 19 *Car.* 2. B. R.

The *Venue* shall follow, and be according to the Issue.

Out of what County, *vide hic antè & postea.*

As for Words in *Warwickshire, Thou art à Thief, and stoledst my Iron :* The Defendant justifies and says, the Plaintiff stole the Iron in *Liecesershire,* and brought it into *Warwickshire,* and therefore he spake the Words in *Warwickshire.* If the Plaintiff replies *De injuria sua propria absque tali causa,* the Jury shall come from *Leicesershire,* to which the *absque tali causa* refers, for the Words are acknowledged. See *Roll.* Tit. *Trial,* 598. *M. pl.* 3.

When Part of the Matter to be inquired of, is in one County or Place, and Part in another, the Trial shall be there where the best Conuzance of the Matter may be.

A Sheriff may assign a Bail Bond out of the County, and the Action may be brought where the Assignment was made. *Str.* 727.

K 2   As

From the
Place belt
known.

As in an Action upon the Cafe ; the Plain-tiff declares that the Defendant took the Horfe of *A.* at *S.* and fold him at *D.* to the Plaintiff as his proper Horfe, and afterwards *A.* retook the Horfe. If the Defendant plead, that the Property was in him, at the Sale, upon which Iffue is joined, the *Venue* fhall be *de S.* where the taking is fuppofed, for there the Property may be beft known, which is only in Queftion. 42 *Aff.* 8. *Roll. Trial*, 603.

If a tranfitory Action arife, Part in one County and Part in another, the Plaintiff has Election to lay it in which he pleafes. *Harri-fon's Pract. in K. B.* 85.

Where the
Counties can-
not join.

If the Iffue be whether *L.* did ride from *Lon-don* to *York*, and from *York* to *London*, five Times in fix Days, this may be tried in *London* only, although Part of the Matter to be inqui-red of, was done in each County. *Ibid.* 603.

In an Action of Battery in *London*, if the Defendant juftifies in Defence of his Poffeffion in *D.* in *Effex*, and the Plaintiff fays *de fon tort demefn fans tiel caufe*, this ought to be tried by both Counties, if they might join, be-caufe he may be found guilty at another Day, and therefore becaufe they may not join, this may be tried in *Effex. Ibid.* 603. *pl.* 8.

Of *Affifes in Confinio Com.* See 1 *Inft.* 154.

In Cafe for Words in one County, if the De-fendant juftify in another County, and the Plain-tiff reply *De fon tort demefn, &c.* although the Counties ought to join, if they could, and the Juftification is principally put in Iffue, yet the

Roll *Tit.*
Trial, 620.

Trial may be in either County, at the Election of the Plaintiff. *Ibid. pl.* 9.

London cannot
join with ano-
ther County.
49 *E.* 3. 20.

In Ejectment in *London*, upon a Leafe made there of Land in *Midd.* if the Defendant plead

2   Not

Not guilty, this may be tried in *London*; because the Counties cannot join, although the *Jury* ought to inquire of the Ejectment in *Midd.* and *Judgment* affirmed in a Writ of Error. See *Roll.* Tit. *Trial,* 603. *pl.* 10.

Two Counties may join although they be not nearest, nay, though twenty Counties be between them. *Finch, French* 59 a. 1 *Inst.* 154.

But if it be of a Lease at *Ickford* of Land in *Bury* in *Suffolk,* the *Venue* must be of *Bury,* not of *Ickford.* 619.

If the Issue be taken upon the Name or Condition of the Person, this shall be tried in the County where the Writ is brought. 21 *E.* 4. 8. for this may be well known there. *Roll. ibid.* 615.

Where the Writ is brought.

Where the Issue is to be tried upon a Point which shall be tried by two Counties, and one cannot join with the other, this shall be tried where the Writ is brought. 21 *E.* 4. 8. But for this, see before, where the Counties cannot join.

In Debt in *London* against *J. S.* of *D.* in *Essex,* if the Defendant saith that he was at *S.* in *Essex,* at the Time of purchasing the Writ, and not at *D.* this shall be tried in *Essex,* and not where the Writ is brought, for none can know where he dwelt so well as the County of *Essex.* 12 *H.* 6. 5.

Where in other County than where the Writ is brought.

Vide many Cases in *Roll. ibid.* 605, &c. about this Matter.

In an Action of the Case against a Sheriff, upon an Escape in *London,* and the Arrest laid to be in *Southampton*; adjudged, that the *Visne* shall be where the Escape was, because that is the Ground of the Action, and not where the Arrest was. *Cro.* 3 Part 271.

Where the Escape was, and not where the Arrest was.

Nota;

Deceit.
Efcape,

Nota ; In an Action of the Cafe for Deceit, or upon an Efcape, the Court will not change the *Vifne* out of the County where the Plaintiff fuppofes the Thing to be done. *Siderfin* 95.

Scandalum
Magnatum.

Nor in a *Scandalum Magnatum*, upon the common Affidavit. *Ibid.* 185. See *Str.* 807.

Informations.

Nor in Actions upon penal Statutes,. for they muft be brought in their proper County. *Ibid.* 287.

Two Counties.

Nor where the Caufe of Action is in two Counties, and the Plaintiff laid his Action in one of them. *Ibid.* 405.

If the Plaintiff will be bound to give no Evidence but what arifes in the County, where he lays his Action, the Court will not change the *Venue,* upon the common Affidavit. *Ibid.* 442.

A Counfellor at Law Plaintiff, his *Venue* fhall not be altered, becaufe of his Attendance at the Court. *Modern Rep.* 84. 2 *Show.* 176, 242.

A Barrifter has Privilege (in a tranfitory Action) to lay the *Venue* in *Middlefex* ; but a Mafter in *Chancery (as fuch)* has not. *Str.* 822. 2 *Ld. Raym.* 1556.

An *Attorney* has Privilege to change the *Venue* into *Middlefex,* as well as lay it here when Plaintiff. *(a) Str.* 1049. But a *Barrifter, Attorney* or Officer of the Court cannot change the *Venue* into *Middlefex,* when joined in an Action with unprivileged Perfons, or fue or are fued in *Auter droit,* as Executors, *&c. Ibid.* 610. *Ld. Raym.* 1556.

(a) Same Privilege has an Officer of the Court. But *Venue* may be changed from *Middlefex,* though the Plaintiff be an *Attorney,* if he fues by *Capias,* and not by *Attachment. Harrifon's Pract. C. P.* 137. So if he does not declare in Perfon. *Ibid.*

In

In Debt upon an Obligation, Payment was
pleaded *apud domum mansionalem Rectoriæ de
Much-Hadam,* and the *Venire facias* was *de vi-
cincto de Much Hadam,* where it ought to have
been *de vicinet. Rectoriæ de Much-Hadam*; but
it was adjudged good, because *Much-Hadam* is
here intended a Vill. *3 Cro.* 804. So you see
that where a Thing is alledged to be done at the
Capital House * of *D.* there the *Venire* shall be
of *D.* for that is intended to be all one with the
Vill. But where it is at the Castle of *Hertford,*
&c. there the *Venire facias* shall not be *de vicineto de Hertford,* but *de Castro de Hertford,* for
Castrum Hertford is intended a distinct Place by
itself; and so of all Castles. *Cro.* 2 Part 239.
Moor 216.

A *Venire facias* may be awarded of a Castle.
Roll. 618.

Where the Issue is not Parcel of the Manor
of *D.* or the Custom of a Manor is in Question,
the *Venire* ought to be of the Manor. *Hob.*
284. *Cro.* 2 Part 327. If the Manor be laid
to be in a Vill, the *Venire facias* may be of the
Manor in the Vill, as *de vicineto manerii de Stan-
sted-Hall* in *Windham. Cro.* 2 Part 405. *Moor*
518. *Arundel's* Case, *li.* 6. 14.

The *Venue* cannot be of a Scite of a Manor.
Roll. Tit. *Trial,* 618.

In the *Common Bench,* in Trespass, for taking
away a Bag of Pepper. The Defendant justi-
fied as a Servant of the Mayor and Commonalty
of *London,* for Wharfage due to them by the
Custom of *London,* which the Plaintiff refused
to pay. The Plaintiff replied that the Custom
did not extend to him, because he was a Freeman of the City, and ought not to pay Wharfage; to which the Defendant rejoined, that the

Marginal notes:
2 Salk. 665, 670.
2 Vent. 47.
* *Rectoriæ.*
Castle.
Roll. Tit. Trial, 621.
Manor.
Roll. Tit. Trial, 621.

K 4   Custom

Cuſtom extended to him as well as to Strangers; upon which Iſſue was joined.

Recorder. Reſolved, 1. That the Iſſue ſhould be tried *per Pais*, not by the Mouth of the Recorder, becauſe he certifies nothing but what the Mayor and Aldermen direct, who are concerned in the Cauſe.

Where the Trial ſhall be by the County nextadjoining. 2. That the *Venire facias* ſhall not be awarded to the Sheriffs of *London* or *Middleſex*, becauſe the Trials there are by Freemen. But it ſhall be to the County next adjoining, *viz.* the Sheriff of *Surrey*. So where any City is concerned, the *Venire facias* ſhall not be directed to the Officers of the City, but to the County next adjoining. *Hob.* 85. *Style* 137. *Moor* 171. *vide hic, cap.* 2. See *Hardres* Reports, f. 309. Good Learning concerning this Matter.

If the Iſſue concern the Mayor and Commonalty of a Town, the *Array* ſhall be made all of Foreigners. 31 *Aſſiſe* 19. *Vide Roll.* Tit. *Trial,* 596.

So if the Iſſue concern the Mayor and Commonalty, &c. although they are not Parties, yet the *Venire facias* ſhall be directed to the Sheriff of the next County. 15 *E.* 4. 18.

Information for Seizure. See *Hardres* Reports, f. 16, &c. Good Matter in an Information upon a Seizure, in what Place the *Viſne* ſhall be, and the Entry and Manner of quaſhing one *Venire facias*, and awarding a *Venire facias de novo*, &c.

Where a Man lends hisHorſe in one Place, and he is ſpoiled in another, Viſne where he is ſpoiled. Where a Man lends a Horſe to another to till his Land, and the Horſe dies with exceſſive Labour, the *Viſne* ſhall be from the Place where the exceſſive Labour was, and not where the Delivery was. *Moor* 887. *Vide Hob.* 188. *Roll.* Tit. *Trial,* 615. *Paſch.* 22 *Car.* 2. *B. R. Horſley* verſus *Potter.*

Where

Where a Promise is laid in one Place, and the Breach in another, the *Visne* must be according to the Event of the Issue, whether it be taken upon the Promise or Breach. But if no Place be alledged for the Breach, and Issue be taken upon it, the *Visne* must be from the Place of the Promise, which shall be intended right, where the contrary appears not. See *Godb.* 274. 36, 37. Promise in one Place, and Breach in another; *Visne* guided by the Issue.

Easter 39 *Eliz.* In the *King's Bench*; *Trespass, Assault* and *Battery* in *Wilts.* continuing the Assault in *Middlesex*; and adjudged that the *Jurors* shall come out of both Counties. *Moor* 538.

The Name of a Manor or *Land*, or other local Thing shall be tried where it lies, because it is local; but the Name or Addition of a Person shall be tried where the Action is brought, because this is transitory. *Bro.* Tit. *Visne*, 7. *lib.* 6. 65. Misnomer.

In Covenant upon an Indenture of *Demise* of the *Rectory* of *Stoken-Church* in the County of *Oxford, That the Defendant had good Power and Authority to demise*. The Indenture was alledged to be made at *London*, and the *Venire facias* was awarded to the Sheriff of *Oxon*; and this being assigned for Error, Judgment was affirmed, and this adjudged to be good. *Moor* 7·0. Because the Rectory was *in comitat. Oxon. vide Page* . Where the Land lies.

In Debt upon an Obligation in one County to perform Covenants in a Lease, and the Land and Payments were in another County; the Trial shall be where the Land and Payments are. 44 *E.* 3. 42. *Roll. Trial*, 607. *pl.* 1. Where the Land lies, and not where the Writ, &c.

In Debt upon a Lease in one County, and the Payment of the Rent upon the Lease limited there also, but the Land was in another County and the Payment upon the Land ; this fhall be tried where the Land and Payment was, for he was bound to pay this there upon the Diftrefs. *Ibid. pl.* 2.

But the Trial fhould have been where the Writ was brought, if the Payment had not been alledged to be where the Land was. *Ibid. pl.* 3.

Where the Land and Writ, &c.

If Debt be brought for Rent upon a Leafe for Years, and the Action is brought where the Land is, but the Deed of the Leafe bears Date in another County, the Trial fhall be where the Land and Writ is brought. 44 *E.* 3. 3. The Iffue being whether the Leffor had a conditional Eftate or not, and fo a lawful Eviction. *Ibid. pl.* 7.

Where the Land lies, and where not.

If the Iffue be in an Affize, whether the Tenant be the eldeft Son of *J. S.* and his Birth is alledged in another County, yet this fhall be tried where the Land is. 46 *Aff.* 5.

If an Infant bring an Affize, and a Releafe of his Anceftor is pleaded againft him, dated in another County, this muft be tried where the Releafe is dated, and not by the Affize, although the Plaintiff be an Infant, and the Circumftances are to be inquired. 21 *E.* 3. 23. See *Roll. ibid.* 611. *pl.* 37.

Where from two Places in one Country, and where not, *vide cap.* 10.

In Cafe, if the Plaintiff declare upon a Truft at *D.* and of a Wrong at *S.* Upon not guilty, if it appear the Truft is not material, the *Venue* fhall only come from *S.* and not from both Places, one not being material.

In Cafe, for ftopping a Way from fuch a Place to fuch a Place, and that the Obftruction was at *D.* Upon Not guilty, the *Venue* fhall not come from *D.* only, for all the Way is put in Iffue.

If

If the *Nar.* be *apud A. in Com. B.* and the The *Venire* as
Venire is *de Vill. & paroch. de A.* 'tis ill. *Yelv.* large as the
104. 2 *Cro.* 586. *Nar.* and no
Venire from

When the *Venue* shall be from two Vills. 2 two Vills.
Cro. 599. *Yelv.* 26, 182, 187.

In Trespass in one Vill, and a Release pleaded
in another Vill, within the same County, upon
Non est factum, this shall be tried *per ambideux.*
Roll. ibid. 624. *Vide hic ante.* See *Roll. ibid.*
615. many Cases about this.

Where the *Venue* cannot be from a Vill, Ham- *De Corpore*
let or *Lieu Conus,* (a) there it may be *de Cor-* *Com.*'
pore Comitatus, for if it might not be so, the
Cause could not be tried.

Debt for Rent, and the Demise was laid *in &*
super Acclivitatem de Hampstead-Hill; and held
not a good *Venue.* 2 *Vent.* 249, 270.

A Custom of a County is to be tried *de Cor-*
pore Comitatus, for the Custom runs through
the whole County.

Where the Parish is named by way of Deno- Parish.
tation, or Explanation of the Place where the
Fact is alledged to be done, as at the Parish-
Church of *Hauk-bucknol,* there the *Venire fa-*
cias shall be of the Town, not of the Parish.
Bulstr. 1 Part 60, 61.

If the Fact be alledged in *Kingstreet* in the Town.
Parish of St. *Margaret in Com. Midd.* you have
already heard that the *Visne* shall be from *King-*
street, because it is intended to be a Town;
but where it is alledged to be done at *Gray's*

(a) A *Lieu Conus* is a Castle, Manor, or other notorious
Place well known, and generally taken Notice of by those
who dwell about it, and not a Close or Pasture of Ground,
or such like Place of no Repute.

I:2n

Inns of Court. **Inn Hall**, or *Lincoln's Inn Hall, &c.* in *Holborn,* the *Viſne* ſhall be from *Holborn,* which is the Town ; for as *Yelverton* ſaid, it was never heard of any *Venire facias* to be had of any of the Inns of Court. *Bulſtr.* 2 Part 120. eſpecially

Not from Houſe or Hall.

of the *Hall,* becauſe it cannot be of a *Houſe,* much leſs of a *Hall.*

In Ejectment upon a Demiſe made at *Denham;* of Lands *in Parochia de Denham prædict* ; the *Viſne* may be of *Denham,* or of the Pariſh of *Denham;* becauſe *Denham* and *Parochia de Denham Prædict.* are all one by Intendment of Law. *Bulſtr.* 2 Part 209. *Moor* 709. *Hob.* 6. But when it appears by the Record, or is intend-

Pariſh.

ed that the Pariſh is more ſpacious than the Town, as the Caſe in *Moor* 837. where in Ejectment the Leaſe was alledged to be made at *Bredon* of Tithes in *W.* and *W.* Hamlets within the Pariſh of *Bredon,* there the *Venire facias* muſt not be of *Bredon,* but of the Pariſh, becauſe it appears, that the Pariſh extends fur-ther than the Town. *Hob.* 326.

For Rent where the Land lies, and where not.

Where an Action of Debt for Rent is brought upon the *Privity of the Contract,* by the Leſſor, or againſt the Leſſee, or his Executors, for Ar-rearages due in the Life-time of the Teſtator, the *Viſne* may be laid in any Place ; but where the Action is brought upon the *Privity in Eſtate,* as againſt the Aſſignee of the Leſſee, or his Exe-cutors, for Rent due after the Teſtator's Death, the *Viſne* muſt be where the Lands lie. *Latch* miſprinted 197, 262, 271. *Vide li.* 3. 24. (*a*).

(*a*) Debt lies for Rent either in the County where the Deed was made, or the Lands lie, if the Action be againſt the Leſſee ; but if brought (by or) againſt an *Aſſignee,* it muſt be brought in the County where the Land lies ; for the Aſſignee is only on the *Privity* of Eſtate, and not upon the Contract. *Str.* 776.

And

And so it was adjudged in the Case of *Hall and Arnold,* 1656. *B. R.* And it was further adjudged there, the Case being of a Lease made at *London,* of Lands in *Monmouthshire,* rendring Rent payable at the *Old Exchange,* for which an Action is brought by the Heir. If there had been no Place of Payment, the Heir must have brought his Action where his Lands lie, but the Place of Payment being in another County, he has his Election, as on a Lease for Years of Lands in two Counties.

Venue not to be changed in an Action of Debt for Rent. *Per tot. Cur. M. 4 Geo.* 2. *MS. Rep. Str.* 878. In all Actions of Debt *Venue* unchangeable, *per Ch. Justice. MS. Rep.*

Walker's Case, in Debt upon a Lease of Land in another County, *Nihil debet* shall be tried where the Action is brought. *Bro.* Tit. *Visne,* 119. **Debt for Rent of Land in another County.**

In *Replevin* brought by *Strede* against *Hartly,* for taking a Distress at *Baildon,* the Defendant made Conusance as Bailiff, because the *locus in quo, &c.* was holden of *W. H.* as of his Manor of *Baildon*; and upon Issue *hors de son fee,* the *Venire facias* was *de vicineto de Baildon*; and upon Motion that the *Venire facias* ought to have been as well from the Manor as the Town, the Court adjudged it to be well enough, for that the Court shall not intend the Manor was larger than the Town, because it doth not appear so to be, though possibly it might, as like the Case of a Town and Parish. *Hob.* 305, 306. **Manor.**

If the Sheriff return, that there are no Freeholders of that *Visne,* or if the *Visne* be where the King's Writ runs not, as in the *Cinque Ports, &c.* or in a Place where the Men are privileged from serving on Juries out of that Place, as the Isle of *Ely, &c.* the Plaintiff may **Visne next adjoining, in what Cases. Cinque Ports.**

pray

pray a *Venire facias* of the *Vifne* next adjoining

Wales.
And if the *Vifne* be in *Wales*, (*ou Brief le Roy ne court*) the *Venire facias* fhall be directed to the Sheriff of the next *Englifh* County, to caufe the Jury to come *de propinquiori Vifne* of his County to the *Vifne* in *Wales* adjoining ; for the Court fhall not be oufted of the Plea. *Fitz. Abr* Tit. *Vifne*, 8. *Jurifdict.* 24.

In an Action againft a Hundred, the *Venire facias* may come from the next Hundred generally. *Vide Comb. Rep.* 332.

In Trefpafs, if the Defendant plead Not guilty to Part, and to the Refidue a Plea, which caufes the Trial of that to be by a Jury *de prochein* Hundred ; the *Venire* fhall be awarded at *prochein* Hundred for both Iffues, becaufe there ought not to be two *Venire facias's* in one Action. *Vide Roll.* Tit. *Trial*, 596. *pl.* 4.

In an Appeal of Murder committed in the *Cinque Ports*, although the King be concerned, yet becaufe this is betwixt common Perfons, the *Venire facias* fhall be to the next adjoining Vill. *Ibid. pl.* 6.

Ireland.
If the Iffue be joined of Matter in *Ireland*, this fhall be tried by a Jury of the next County in *England*. *Ibid.* 587. *pl.* 8.

If the Iffue be to be tried by the *Venue* of a Manor, and the Plaintiff fuggefts that he is Prochein Hundred. Lord of the Hundred in which the Manor is, and that all within the Hundred are within his Diftrefs, if the Defendant acknowledge this, the *Venue* fhall not be *de Corpore Comitatus*, but of the next Hundred, for if it fhould be *de Corpore Comitatus*, this fhould be tried by the Tenants of the Manor.

Vifne mifawarded in Part.
If the *Vifne* is in fome Part mifawarded, or fued out of more Places or fewer than it ought

to

to be, so as some Place be right named, this is aided by the Statute of *Jeofails*, which hath ended the Differences in many Cases reported in our Books concerning this Point; wherefore I purposely omit them.

Error, for that the Judgment was given by Default against the Defendant, being an Infant, upon Issue, that he was of full Age: Adjudged, That the Trial should be in *Norfolk* where the Land was, and not in *Middlesex*, where the Action was brought. *Cro.* 3 Part 818. **Infancy, where the Land lies.**

If the *Visne* cometh from a wrong Place, yet if it be *ex assensum partium*, and so entred of Record, it shall stand; for *Omnis Consensus tollit errorem.* 1 Inst. 125. **May be out of a wrong Place by Consent.**

Where the Issue is local, the *Visne* cannot be changed by Consent. *Siderfin* 339.

Holmes versus *Saunders, Hill.* 22, 23 *Car.* 2, *B. R.* Error to reverse a Judgment given in the *King's Bench* in *Ireland,* in Debt for Rent brought by the Assignees of a Reversion; the Plaintiff declared of a Lease of Land in such a Parish in the Suburbs of *Dublin;* on *Nil debet* pleaded, the *Venire facias* was from the said Parish *in Civitate Dublin,* and Judgment there *pur* Plaintiff; it was assigned for Error, because the Land lies in the Suburbs of the City, and the *Venire facias* was from a Parish in the City.

Per Cur. It is all one, for the Suburbs are always within the Franchise of the City, as *Fleet-street* is within the Suburbs of *London,* but the *Strand* not, though so reputed.

Note; It was adjudged Error in an inferior Court, that the *Venire facias* was awarded *secundum consuetudinem Curiæ,* which ought to be *per Curiam. Reader* versus *Moore, Mich.* 1650, *B. R.*

By

By the Statute of 16 & 17 *Car.* 2. After Verdict, Judgment shall not be stayed or reversed, for that there is no right *Venue*, so as the Cause were tried by a Jury of the proper County or Place where the Action is laid. This Act doth not extend to Appeals, Indictments of Felony, &c. nor to Actions upon Penal Statutes, other than concerning Customs and Subfidies, &c.

Cafe, for that whereas the Plaintiff had let the Defendant a Horfe to ride from *Swaffham* in *Norfolk* to *Ipfwich* in *Suffolk*, the Defendant *in itinere illo tam immoderate equitavit Equum præd.* that he died. It was tried at *Norfolk*; after Verdict it was moved in Arreft of Judgment, that no Place was laid where the immoderate Riding was, and the Journey is in two Counties; but held aided by Stat. 17 *Car.* 2.

Cafe for Scandalous Words, which were laid to be fpoken at *London*, charging the Plaintiff with ftealing Plate out of *Wadham* College at *Oxford*. The Defendant juftifies, for that the Plaintiff *apud Oxon in Com. Oxon* ftole Plate out of *Wadham* College: The Plaintiff replied *De injuria fuâ propriâ*; and upon that Iffue was joined and tried in *London*, and a Verdict for the Plaintiff. Upon which it was moved in Arreft of Judgment, that this was a Mif-trial; but it was held by *Keeling* C. J. and *Rainsford* and *Moreton*, that this was a good Trial within Stat. 16, 17 *Car.* 2. being tried by a Jury of the proper County where the Action was laid. 1 *Saund.* 246. 1 *Vent.* 22.

Cafe for fcandalous Words, faying he was perjured; and it was laid in *Devonfhire*. The Defendant juftified, that the Plaintiff made a falfe Oath at *Launcefton* in *Cornwall*; and Iffue

was

was taken on that, and tried in *Devonshire*, and held aided by Stat. 16, 17 *Car.* 2. 1 *Vent.* 263. 2 *Lev.* 121.

Covenant for Non-payment of Rent of Allom Mines was brought in *London*, where the Deed was supposed to be made: The Defendant pleads, that the Plaintiff had inclosed the Mine, so that he could not enter to work it; and Issue being taken on that, it was tried in *London*; and being found against the Defendant, it was moved in Arrest of Judgment that this was a Mis-trial; but it was answered, that it was aided by Stat. 16, 17 *Car.* 2. *Jones T.* 82.

Earl of *Shaftsbury* versus *Graham & al*, B. R. *Venue altered where a Peer was Party.* Resolved in *Easter* Term 34 *Car.* 2. That the Court had Power to alter the *Venue*, in Case of a Peer; especially if there be no Likelihood of an indifferent Trial in the Place where the Action is laid. 1 *Vent.* 363, 364, 365.

Every *Venire* out of the Courts of Record at *Westminster*, shall be awarded of the Body of the County, where the Issue is triable: Provided that this Clause shall not extend to Appeals of Felony or Murder, or to any Indictment or Presentment of Treason, Felony, or Murder; or to any Process on any of them; or to any Writ, Bill or Information on any Penal Statute. 4 & 5 *Ann. cap.* 16. *(a). Venire to be awarded de Corpore Com.*

Debt *qui tam*, on the Stat. 9 *Ann.* against *Gaming*, and a Verdict for Plaintiff: It was moved in Arrest of Judgment, that the *Venire* was *de Corpore Com.* and that Penal Actions are

---

(a) The Court said, that since this Statute it seems unnecessary in the Declaration to set forth a particular *Parish* or *Vill* for a *Venue*. *E.* 13 *Geo.* 1. in the Case of *Crabtree* and *Moorcroft*, MS. *Rep.*

excepted in the Statute for the Amendment of the Law, but held well and aided by the Jury Act, and S:ar. 5 *Geo.* 1. *French* qui tam, v. *Wiltſhire,* H. 11 *Geo.* 2. *B. R.*

Since our Author wrote, there has been a great Alteration in the Law, as to Jurors, for by the Statute 3 *Geo.* 2. *cap.* 25. for the better Regulation of Jurors, it is enacted, ' That the ' Perſon or Perſons, required by a Statute made ' the Seventh and Eighth Years of the Reign ' of his late Majeſty King *William* the Third, ' [intitled, *An Act for the Eaſe of Jurors,* ' *and better regulating of Juries,*] and by a ' Clauſe in another Act, made in the third and ' fourth Years of the Reign of the late Queen ' *Anne* [intitled, *An Act for making perpetual* ' *an Act for the more eaſy Recovery of ſmall* ' *Tithes*; and alſo *an Act for the more eaſy* ' *obtaining Partition of Lands in Coparcenary,* ' *Joint-Tenancy, and Tenancy in Common*; and ' alſo *for making more effectual and amending* ' *ſeveral Acts relating to the Return of Jurors,*] ' to give in, or who are by Virtue of this ' Act to make up true Liſts in Writing of ' the Names of Perſons qualified to ſerve on ' Juries, in order to aſſiſt them to complete ' ſuch Liſts, purſuant to the Intent of the ſaid ' Act, ſhall (upon Requeſt by him or them ' made to any Pariſh Officer or Officers, who ' ſhall have in his or their Cuſtody any of the ' Rates for the Poor or Land-Tax, in ſuch Pa-' riſh or Place) have free Liberty to inſpect ' ſuch Rates, and take from thence the Name ' or Names of ſuch Freeholders, Copyholders, ' or other Perſons qualified to ſerve on Juries, ' dwelling within their reſpective Pariſhes or ' Precincts, for which ſuch Liſt is to be given

Liſts of Ju-rors qualified according to the Act 7 & 8 *W.* 3.

and 3 & 4 *Ann.*

to be made from the Rates in each Pariſh,

3 ' in

' in and returned, pursuant to the said Acts;
' and shall yearly and every Year, twenty
' Days at least before the Feast of Saint Mi-
' chael the Archangel, upon two or more Sun-
' days, fix upon the Door of the Church, Cha-
' pel, and every other publick Place of reli-
' gious Worship, within their respective Pre-
' cincts, a true and exact List of all such Per-
' sons intended to be returned to the Quarter-
' Sessions of the Peace, as qualified to serve on
' Juries, pursuant to the Directions of the said
' Act, and leave at the same Time a Duplicate
' of such List with a Church-warden, Chapel-
' warden, or Overseer of the Poor of the said
' Parish or Place, to be perused by the Pa-
' rishioners without Fee or Reward, to the
' End that Notice may be given of Persons so
' qualified, who are omitted, or of Persons in-
' serted by Mistake, who ought to be omitted
' out of such Lists; and if any Person or Per-
' sons, not being qualified to serve on Juries,
' shall find his or their Name or Names men-
' tioned in such List, and the Person or Per-
' sons required to make such List shall refuse to
' omit him or them, or think it doubtful
' whether he or they ought to be omitted, it
' shall and may be lawful to and for the Justices
' of the Peace for the County, Riding, or Divi-
' sion, at their respective General Quarter-Sessi-
' ons, to which the said Lists shall be so returned,
' upon Satisfaction from the Oath of the Party,
' complaining, or other Proof, that he is not
' qualified to serve on Juries, to order his or their
' Name or Names to be struck out, or omitted
' in such List, when the same shall be entred in
' the Book to be kept by the Clerk of the Peace
' for that Purpose, pursuant to the said Act.

(marginal notes:) and yearly fixed upon Church Doors.

Persons not qualified may be relieved at the Quarter-Sessions.

L 2   ' It

Wilfully o-
mitting, or
inserting
wrong Per-
fons, forfeits
20s. for every
Perfon fo o-
mitted or in-
ferted

§. 2. ' It is further enacted, That if any Perfon
' or Perfons, required by the faid Acts to return
' or give in, or by Virtue of this Act to make
' up any fuch Lift, or concerned therein, fhall
' wilfully omit, out of any fuch Lift, any Per-
' fon or Perfons, whofe Name or Names ought
' to be inferted, or fhall wilfully infert any Per-
' fon or Perfons, who ought to be omitted, or
' fhall take any Money or other Reward for omit-
' ting or inferting any Perfon whatfoever; he or
' they fo offending fhall, for every Perfon fo
' omitted or inferted in fuch Lift, contrary to the
' Meaning of this Act, forfeit the Sum of
' twenty Shillings for every fuch Offence, upon
' Conviction before one or more Juftice or
' Juftices of the Peace of the County, Riding
' or Divifion, where fuch Offender fhall dwell,
' upon the Confeffion of the Offender, or Proof
' by one or more credible Witnefs or Wit-
' neffes on Oath; one Half thereof to be paid
' to the Informer, and the other Half to the
' Poor of fuch Parifh or Place, for which the
' faid Lift is returned; and in cafe fuch Pe-
' nalty fhall not be paid within five Days after
' fuch Conviction, the fame fhall be levied by
' Diftrefs and Sale of the Offender's Goods,
' by Warrant or Warrants from one or more
' Juftice or Juftices of the Peace, returning the
' Overplus, if any there be; and the faid Ju-
' ftice or Juftices, before whom fuch Perfon
' fhall be convicted of fuch Offence, fhall, in
' Writing under their Hands, certify the fame
' to the Juftices at their next General Quarter-
' Seffions, which fhall be held for the County,
' in which the Perfon or Perfons fo omitted or
' inferted fhall dwell, which Juftices fhall di-
' rect

' rect the Clerk of the Peace for the Time be-
' ing to insert or strike out the Name or Names
' of such Person or Persons, as shall by such
' Certificate appear to have been omitted or in-
' serted in such Lists, contrary to the Meaning Duplicates of
' of this Act ; and Duplicates of the said Lists, the Lists to be
' when delivered in at the Quarter-Sessions of transmitted to
' the Peace, and entred in such Book, to be the Sheriff,
' kept by the Clerk of the Peace for that Pur-
' pose, shall, during the Continuance of such
' Quarter-Sessions, or within ten Days after, be
' delivered or transmitted by the Clerk of the
' Peace to the Sheriff of each respective County,
' or his Under-Sheriff, in order for his returning
' of Juries out of the said Lists ; and such She-
' riff or Under-Sheriff shall immediately take
' care, that the Names of the Persons contained
' in such Duplicates, shall be faithfully entred
' alphabetically, with their Additions and Places by the Clerk
' of Abode, in some Book or Books to be kept of the Peace,
' by him or them for that Purpose ; and that on Pain of
' every Clerk of the Peace neglecting his Duty 20 *l.*
' therein, shall forfeit the Sum of twenty
' Pounds to such Person or Persons as shall in-
' form or prosecute for the same, until the
' Party be thereof convicted upon an Indict-
' ment before the Justices of the Peace, at any
' General Quarter-Sessions of the Peace to be
' holden for the same County, Riding, Divi-
' sion, or Precinct.

' And it is further enacted, That in case Sheriff, &c.
' any Sheriff, or Under-Sheriff, Bailiff, or o- returning any
' ther Officer, to whom the Return of Juries Person whose
' shall belong, shall summon and return any in the Dupli-
' Person or Persons to serve on any Jury, in cate,
' any Cause to be tried before the Justices of
' Assize, or *Nisi prius,* or Judges of the said

' Great Seffions, or the Judge or Judges of the
' Seffions for the faid Counties Palatine, whofe
' Name is not inferted in the Duplicates fo
' delivered or tranfmitted to him or them by
' fuch Clerk of the Peace, if any fuch Duplicate

' fhall be delivered or tranfmitted; or if any
' Clerk of Affize, Judge's Affociate, or other
' Officer, fhall record the Appearance of any
' Perfon fo fummoned and returned as afore-
' faid, who did not really and truly appear,
' then and in fuch Cafe any Judge or Juftice of
' Affize or *Nifi prius,* or Judge or Judges of the
' faid Great Seffions, or the Judge or Judges of
' the Seffions for the faid Counties Palatine,
' fhall and may, upon Examination, in a fum-
' mary Way, fet fuch Fine or Fines upon fuch
' Sheriff, or Under-Sheriff, Clerk of the Affize,
' Judge's Affociate, or other Officer, for every
' fuch Perfon fo fummoned and returned as afore-
' faid; and for every Perfon, whofe Appearance
' fhall be fo falfly recorded, as the faid Judge
' or Juftice of Affize, *Nifi prius,* or of the faid
' Great Seffions, or the Judge or Judges of the
' Seffions for the faid Counties Palatine, fhall
' think meet, not exceeding ten Pounds, and
' not lefs than forty Shillings.'

' And for preventing Abufes by *Sheriffs, Un-*
' *der-Sheriffs, Bailiffs, or other Officers concerned*
' *in the fummoning or returning of Jurors,* it is en-

' acted, That no Perfons fhall be returned as Ju-
' rors to ferve on Trials at any Affizes, or *Nifi*
' *prius,* or at the faid Great Seffions, or at the
' Seffions for the faid Counties Palatine, who
' have ferved within the Space of one Year be-
' fore in the County of *Rutland,* of four Years
' in the County of *York,* or of two Years before
' in any other County, not being a County of
' a City

' a City or Town ; and if any such Sheriff shall
' wilfully transgress therein, any Judge or Ju-
' stice of Assize or *Nisi prius,* or of the said
' Great Sessions, or the Judge or Judges of the
' Sessions for the said Counties Palatine, may,
' and is hereby required on Examination and
' Proof of such Offence, in a summary way, to
' set a Fine or Fines upon every such Offender,
' as he shall think meet, not exceeding five
' Pounds for any one Offence. (*a*)

' It is further enacted, That the Sheriff, Un- Sheriff, &c. to
' der-Sheriff, or other Officer, to whom the enter the
Names of
' Return of Juries shall belong, shall from Time those who
' to Time enter or register in a Book to be kept have served :
' for that Purpose, the Names of such Persons
' as shall be summoned, and shall serve as Ju-
' rors on Trials at any Assizes, or *Nisi prius,* or
' in the said Courts of Great Sessions, or Sessi-
' ons for the said Counties Palatine, together
' with their Additions and Places of Abode al-
' phabetically, and also the Times of their Ser-
' vices ; and every Person so summoned and at- and give Certificates.
' tending, or serving as aforesaid, shall (upon
' Application by him made to such Sheriff, Un-
' der-Sheriff, or other Officer) have a Certifi-
' cate testifying such his Attendance or Service
' done, which Certificate the said Sheriff, Un-
' der-Sheriff, or other Officer, is hereby di-
' rected and required to give without Fee or
' Reward ; and the said Book shall be transmit-
' ted by such Sheriff, Under-Sheriff, or other
' Officer, to his or their Successor or Successors,
' from Time to Time.'

(*a*) Note ; by the 4 *Geo.* 2. *c.* 7. this Clause is repealed
as to the County of *Middlesex,* and no Person to serve who
has served within *the two* Terms before. See this Act *Postea.*

' It

No Money or Reward to excuse any Person from serving.

"It is further enacted, That no Sheriff, Under-Sheriff, Bailiff or other Officer, or Person whatsoever, shall directly or indirectly take or receive any Money or other Reward, to excuse any Person from serving, or being summoned to serve on Juries, or under that Colour or Pretence, and that no Bailiff or other Officer appointed by any Sheriff or Under-Sheriff to summon Juries, shall summon any Person to serve thereon, other than such, whose Name is specified in a Mandate signed by such Sheriff or Under-Sheriff, and directed to such Bailiff or other Officer; and if any Sheriff, Under-Sheriff, Bailiff or other Officer, shall wilfully transgress in any the Cases aforesaid, any Judge or Justices of Assize, Nisi prius or Great Sessions aforesaid, or the Judge or Judges of the Sessions for the said Counties Palatine, may and is hereby impowered on Examination and Proof of such Offence, in a summary Way, to set a Fine or Fines upon any Person or Persons so offending, as he shall think meet, not exceeding ten Pounds, according to the Nature of the Offence."

Penalty.

And whereas by the said Act 7 & 8 W. 3. and by the 3 & 4 Ann. all Constables, Tythingmen and Headboroughs, are obliged to return true Lists at the respective Quarter Sessions of the Peace holden for each County, Riding or Division, of the Names and Places of abode of all Persons within their respective Precincts or Places, qualified to serve on Juries, to the Justices of Peace in open Court, which hath by Experience been found inconvenient and expensive to several Constables, Tythingmen and Headboroughs, such Quarter Sessions being often held at a great Distance from their Abodes; For Remedy whereof

whereof it is enacted. ' That from and after the
' said first Day of September one thousand seven
' hundred and thirty, it shall be lawful and suf-
' ficient for all or any Constables, Tithingmen,
' or Headboroughs, after they shall have made
' and compleared such Lists of Persons qualified
' to serve on Juries for their respective Parishes
' or Precincts, according to the Manner direct-
' ed by the before mentioned Acts, and this
' present Act, to subscribe the same in the Pre-
' sence of one or more Justice or Justices of the
' Peace for each respective County or Place,
' and also at the same Time to attest the Truth
' of such Lists upon Oath to the best of their
' Knowledge or Belief, which Oath such Justice
' or Justices respectively are hereby impowered
' and required to administer; and the said Lists
' shall (being first signed by the said Justices re-
' spectively, before whom the same shall be at-
' tested on Oath, and subscribed as aforesaid)
' be delivered by the said Constables, Tithing-
' men or Headboroughs, to the Chief or High
' Constables of the Hundreds or Divisions where-
' unto the same shall respectively belong, who
' are hereby directed and required to deliver in
' such Lists to the Justices of the Peace for the
' County, Riding or Division, at their respec-
' tive General Quarter-Sessions in open Court,
' attesting at the same Time upon Oath their
' Receipt of such Lists from the Constables,
' Tithingmen or Headboroughs respectively,
' and that no Alteration hath been therein made
' since their Receipt thereof; and the said Lists
' so delivered in and attested, shall be deemed
' as effectual as if they had been delivered in
' by the Constables, Tithingmen, or Headbo-
' roughs, for their respective Parishes or Pre-
' cincts.'   And

Constables,
&c. to de-
liver their
Lists before
Justices, on
Oath, &c.

Sheriff, &c. on Return of Writs of *Venire facias* to annex a Panel of Jurors, &c.

' And it is alfo further enacted, That from ' and after the twenty-fifth Day of *December* ' one thoufand feven hundred and thirty, every ' Sheriff, or other Officer, to whom the Re- ' turn of the *Venire facias juratores*, or other ' Procefs for the Trial of Caufes before Juftices ' of Affize, or *Nifi prius*, in any County in *Eng-* ' *land*, doth or fhall belong, fhall, upon his Re- ' turn of every fuch Writ of *Venire facias* (unlefs ' in Caufes intended to be tried at Bar, or in ' Cafes where a fpecial Jury fhall be ftruck by ' Order or Rule of Court) annex a Panel to the ' faid Writ, containing the Chriftian and Sur- ' names, Additions, and Places of Abode, of ' a competent Number of Jurors, named in fuch ' Lifts as qualified to ferve on Juries, the Names ' of the fame Perfons to be inferted in the Pa- ' nel annexed to every *Venire facias*, for the ' Trial of all Iffues at the fame Affizes in each ' refpective County ; which Number of Jurors ' fhall not be lefs than forty-eight in any County, ' nor more than feventy-two, without Direc- ' tion of the Judges appointed to go the Circuit, ' and fit as Judges of Affize, or *Nifi prius*, in ' fuch County, or one of them, who are refpec- ' tively hereby impowered and required, if he ' or they fee Caufe, by Order under his or their ' refpective Hand or Hands, to direct a greater ' or leffer Number, and then fuch Number as ' fhall be fo directed fhall be the Number to ' ferve on fuch Jury ; and that the Writs of *Ha-* ' *beas Corpora juratorum*, or *Diftringas*, fubfe- ' quent to fuch Writ of *Venire facias juratores*, ' need not have inferted in the Bodies of fuch ' refpective Writs the Names of all the Perfons ' contained in fuch Panel ; but it fhall be fuffi- ' cient to infert in this Mandatory Part of fuch

                ' Writs

' Writs respectively, *Corpora separalium perso-*
' *narum in panello huic brevi annexo nominatarum,*
' or Words of the like Import, and to annex
' to such Writs respectively, Panels containing
' the same Names as were returned in the Panel
' to such *Venire facias,* with their Additions and
' Places of Abode, that the Parties concerned
' in any such Trials may have timely Notice of
' the Jurors, who are to serve at the next As-
' sizes, in order to make their Challenges to
' them, if there be Cause; and that for the ma-
' king the Returns and Panels aforesaid, and an-
' nexing the same to the respective Writs, no
' other Fee or Fees shall be taken, than what
' are now allowed by Law to be taken, for the
' Return of the like Writs and Panels annexed
' to the same; and that the Persons named in
' such Panels shall be summoned to serve on Ju-
' ries at the then next Assizes or Sessions of *Nisi*
' *prius,* for the respective Counties to be named
' in such Writs, and no other.'

' And it is enacted, That every Sheriff, or Return of Ju-
' other Officer, to whom the Return of Juries rors in *Wales;*
' for the Trial of Causes in the Court of Grand
' Sessions in any County of *Wales* do or shall
' belong, shall, at least eight Days before every
' Grand Sessions, summon a competent Num-
' ber of Persons qualified to serve on Juries, out
' of every Hundred and Commote within every
' such County, so as such Number be not less
' than ten, or more than fifteen, without the
' Directions of the Judge or Judges of the Grand
' Sessions held for such County, who is and are
' hereby impowered, if he or they shall see
' Cause, by Rule or Order of Court, to direct
' a greater or lesser Number to be summoned
' out of every such Hundred and Commote re-
' spectively;

' fpectively; and that the faid Officer and Offi-
' cers, who fhall fummon fuch Perfons, fhall
' return a Lift containing the Chriftian and Sur-
' names, Additions and Places of Abode, of
' the Perfons fo fummoned to ferve on Juries,
' the firft Court of the fecond Day of every
' Grand Seffions ; and that the Perfons fo fum-
' moned, or a competent Number of them, as
' the Judge or Judges of fuch Grand Seffions
' fhall direct, and no other, fhall be named in
' every Panel to be annexed to every Writ of
' *Venire facias juratores, Habeas Corpora jura-*
' *torum,* and *Diftringas,* that fhall be iffued out
' and returnable for the Trial of Caufes in fuch
' Grand Seffions.'

and Counties   ' And it is further enacted, That every She-
Palatine of   ' riff or other Officer, to whom the Return of
Chefter, Lan-   ' the *Venire facias juratores,* or other Procefs
cafter and   ' for the Trial of Caufes before the Juftices of
Durham.   ' the Courts or Seffions to be held for the
' Counties Palatine of *Chefter, Lancafter* or
' *Durham,* doth belong, fhall, fourteen Days
' at the leaft before the faid Courts or Seffions
' fhall refpectively be held, fummon a compe-
' tent Number of Perfons qualified to ferve on
' Juries, fo as fuch Number be not lefs than
' forty-eight, nor more than feventy-two, with-
' out the Direction of the Judge or Judges of
' the Courts or Seffions to be held for fuch
' Counties Palatine refpectively, and fhall, eight
' Days at leaft before fuch Courts or Seffions
' fhall refpectively be held, make or caufe a
' Lift to be made of the Perfons fo fummoned
' to ferve on Juries, containing their Chriftian
' and Surnames, Additions and Places of Abode;
' and the Lift fo made fhall forthwith be pub-
' lickly hung up in the Sheriff's Office, to be
                                        ' infpected

‘ inspected and read by any Person or Persons
‘ whatsoever; and that the Persons named in
‘ such List, and no other, shall be summoned
‘ to serve on Juries at the next Courts or Ses-
‘ sions to be held for the said respective Coun-
‘ ties Palatine; and the said Sheriff, or other
‘ Officer, is hereby required to return such List
‘ on the first Day of the Court or Sessions to be
‘ held for the said Counties Palatine respectively;
‘ and the Persons so summoned, or a compe-
‘ tent Number of them, as the Judge or Judges
‘ of such Courts or Sessions respectively shall
‘ direct, and no other, shall be named in every
‘ Panel, to be annexed to every Writ of *Venire*
‘ *facias juratores*, *Habeas corpora juratorum* and
‘ *Distringas*, that shall be issued out and return-
‘ able for the Trial of Causes in such Courts or
‘ Sessions respectively.’

‘ And it is further enacted, That the Name
‘ of each and every Person, who shall be sum-
‘ moned and impanelled as aforesaid, with his
‘ Addition and the Place of his Abode, shall be
‘ written in several and distinct Pieces of Parch-
‘ ment or Paper, being all, as near as may be,
‘ of equal Size and Bigness, and shall be deli-
‘ vered unto the Marshal of such Judge of As-
‘ size, or *Nisi prius*, or of the said Great Sessi-
‘ ons, or of the Sessions for the said Counties
‘ Palatine, who is to try the Causes in the said
‘ County, by the Under-Sheriff of the said
‘ County, or some Agent of his; and shall, by
‘ Direction and Care of such Marshal be rolled
‘ up all, as near as may be, in the same Man-
‘ ner, and put together in a Box or Glass, to
‘ be provided for that Purpose; and when any
‘ Cause shall be brought on to be tried, some
‘ indifferent Person, by Direction of the Court,

Names of Persons impanelled to be written, and delivered to the Marshal of the Assize, and put in a Box to be drawn, *&c.*

‘ may

' may and fhall in open Court draw out twelve
' of the faid Parchments or Papers one after an-
' other; and if any of the Perfons, whofe Names
' fhall be fo drawn, fhall not appear, or be chal-
' lenged and fet afide, then fuch further Num-
' ber, until twelve Perfons be drawn who fhall
' appear, and after all Caufes of Challenge fhall
' be allowed as fair and indifferent; and the
' faid twelve Perfons fo firft drawn, and appear-
' ing and approved as indifferent, their Names
' being marked in the Panel, and they being
' fworn fhall be the Jury to try the faid Caufe;
' and the Names of the Perfons fo drawn and
' fworn fhall be kept apart by themfelves in fome
' other Box or Glafs to be kept for that Purpofe,
' till fuch Jury fhall have given in their Verdict,
' and the fame is recorded, or until fuch Jury
' fhall, by Confent of the Parties, or Leave of
' the Court, be difcharged; and then the fame
' Names fhall be rolled up again, and returned
' to the former Box or Glafs, there to be kept
' with the other Names remaining at that Time
' undrawn, and fo *toties quoties*, as long as any
' Caufe remains then to be tried.'

Where the Jury have not brought in their Verdict, twelve others to be drawn.
' Provided always, That if any Caufe fhall
' be brought on to be tried in any of the faid
' Courts refpectively, before the Jury in any
' other Caufe fhall have brought in their Ver-
' dict, or be difcharged, it fhall and may be
' lawful for the Court to order twelve of the
' Refidue of the faid Parchments or Papers, not
' containing the Names of any of the Jurors, who
' fhall not have fo brought in their Verdict, or
' be difcharged, to be drawn in fuch Manner as
' is aforefaid, for the Trial of the Caufe, which
' fhall be fo brought on to be tried.

' And

' And it is further enacted, That every Per- Penalty on
' son or Persons, whose Name or Names shall Defaulters.
' be so drawn as aforesaid, and who shall not ap-
' pear after being openly called three Times,
' upon Oath made by some credible Person that
' such Person so making Default had been law-
' fully summoned, shall forfeit and pay for every
' Default in not appearing upon Call, as afore-
' said (unless some reasonable Cause of his Ab-
' sence be proved by Oath or Affidavit, to the
' Satisfaction of the Judge, who sits to try the
' said Cause) such Fine or Fines not exceeding
' the Sum of five Pounds, and not less than forty
' Shillings, as the said Judge shall think rea-
' sonable to inflict or assess, for such Default.

' Provided always, That where a View (*a*) Method in
' shall be allowed in any Cause, that in such Case case of View.
' six of the Jurors named in such Panel, or more,
' who shall be mutually consented to by the Par-
' ties or their Agents on both Sides, or if they
' cannot agree, shall be named by the proper
' Officer of the respective Courts of *King's Bench*,
' *Common Pleas, Exchequer*, at *Westminster*, or
' the Grand Session in *Wales*, and the said Coun-
' ties Palatine, for the Causes in their respective
' Courts, or if need be, by a Judge of the re-
' spective Courts where the Cause is depending,
' or by the Judge or Judges before whom the
' Cause shall be brought on to Trial respectively,
' shall have the View, and shall be first sworn,
' or such of them, as appear upon the Jury to
' try the said Cause, before any Drawing, as
' aforesaid, and so many only shall be drawn to
' be added to the Viewers who appear, as shall,

(*a*) Note; that a Juror withdrawn in order to a View
may be sworn on the Jury afterwards. 1 *Str.* 70.

' after

' after all Defaulters and Challengers allowed,
' make up the Number of twelve to be fworn
' for the Trial of fuch Caufe.'

 ' And whereas fome Doubt hath been conceiv-
' ed touching the Power of his Majefty's Courts
' of Law at *Weftminfter*, to appoint Juries to be
' ftruck before the Clerk of the Crown, Mafter
' of the Office, Prothonotaries, or other proper
' Officer of fuch refpective Courts, for the Trial
' of Iffues depending in the faid Courts, without
' the Confent of the Profecutor or Parties concern-
' ed in the Profecution or Suit then depending,
' unlefs fuch Iffues are to be tried at the Bar of the
' fame Courts; It is declared and enacted by the

In Trials of ' Authority aforefaid, That it fhall and may be
Iffues at *Weft-* ' lawful to and for his Majefty's Courts of *King's*
minfter, on ' *Bench*, *Common Pleas* and *Exchequer*, at *Weft-*
Motion of ' *minfter*, refpectively, upon Motion made on
Parties, ' Behalf of his Majefty his Heirs or Succeffors,
Judges may ' or on the Motion of any Profecutor or Defen-
order a fpe- ' dant in any Indictment or Information for any
cial Jury. ' Mifdemeanor or Information in the Nature of
' a *Quo Warranto*, depending or to be brought
' or profecuted in the faid Court of *King's Bench*,
' or in any Information depending or to be
' brought or profecuted in the faid Court of *Ex-*
' *chequer*, or on the Motion of any Plaintiff or
' Plaintiffs, Defendant or Defendants in any
' Action, Caufe or Suit whatfoever, depending
' or to be brought and carried on in the fame
' Courts of *King's Bench*, *Common Pleas* and *Ex-*
' *chequer*, or in any of them ; and the faid Courts
' are hereby refpectively authorized and requi-
' red upon Motion as aforefaid, in any of the
' Cafes before mentioned, to order and appoint
' a Jury to be ftruck, before the proper Officer
' of each refpective Court, for the Trial of any
         ' Iffue

' Iſſue joined in any of the ſaid Caſes, and tria-
' ble by a Jury of twelve Men, in ſuch Man-
' ner as ſpecial Juries have been and are uſually
' ſtruck in ſuch Courts reſpectively, upon Trials
' at Bar had in the ſaid Courts; which ſaid Jury
' ſo ſtruck as aforeſaid, ſhall be the Jury re-
' turned for the Trial of the ſaid Iſſue.

' And it is enacted, That the Perſon or Party, Perſon apply-
' who ſhall apply for ſuch Jury to be ſtruck as ing for ſuch
' aforeſaid, ſhall bear and pay the Fees for the Jury, to pay
' ſtriking ſuch Jury, and ſhall not have any the Fees.
' Allowance for the ſame, upon Taxation of
' Coſts.'

' Provided always, and it is thereby further Where ſpecial
' enacted, That where any ſpecial Jury ſhall be Juries in Cities
' ordered by Rule of any of the ſaid Courts to are appointed,
' be ſtruck by the proper Officer of ſuch Court, taken out of
' in the Manner aforeſaid, in any Cauſe ariſing Liſts of Per-
' in any City, or County of a City or Town, ſons qualified.
' the Sheriff or Sheriffs, or Under-Sheriff of ſuch
' City, or County of a City or Town, ſhall be
' ordered by ſuch Rule to bring, or cauſe to be
' brought before the ſaid Officer, the Books or
' Liſts of Perſons qualified to ſerve on Juries
' within the ſame, out of which Juries ought to
' be returned by ſuch Sheriff or Sheriffs, in like
' Manner, as the Freeholders Book hath been
' uſually ordered to be brought, in order to the
' ſtriking of Juries for Trials at the Bar, in
' Cauſes ariſing in Counties at large; and in
' every ſuch Caſe the Jury ſhall be taken and
' ſtruck out of ſuch Books or Liſts reſpec-
' tively.'

' And it is enacted, That any Perſon or Per- Who are qua-
' ſons, having any Eſtate in Poſſeſſion in Land, lified to be in-
' in their own Right, of the yearly Value of ſerted in the
' twenty Pounds or upwards, over and above Liſts,

' the referved Rent payable thereout, fuch Lands
' being held by Leafe or Leafes for the abfolute
' Term of five hundred Years or more, or for
' ninety-nine Years, or any other Term, de-
' terminable on one or more Life or Lives, the
' Names of every fuch Perfon or Perfons fhall
' and may, and are hereby directed and requi-
' red to be inferted in the refpective Lifts as afore-
' faid, in order to their being inferted in the
' Freeholders Book; and the Perfons appointed
' to make fuch Lifts are hereby directed to in-
' fert them accordingly; and fuch Leafeholder
' or Leafeholders fhall and may be fummoned
' or impanelled to ferve on Juries, in like Man-
' ner as Freeholders may be fummoned and im-
' panelled by Virtue of this, or any other Act
' or Acts of Parliament for that Purpofe, and
' be fubject to the like Penalties for Non-ap-
' pearance; any Law, Statute, Ufe, or Cuftom
' to the contrary notwithftanding.'

or to ferve in London.

' And it is further enacted, That the Sheriffs
' of the City of *London,* for the Time being,
' fhall not impanel or return any Perfon or Per-
' fons, to try any Iffue joined in any of his Ma-
' jefty's Courts of *King's Bench, Common Pleas*
' and *Exchequer,* or to be or ferve on any Jury
' at the Seffions of *Oyer* and *Terminer,* Gaol-
' Delivery, or Seffions of the Peace, to be had
' or held for the faid City of *London,* who fhall
' not be an Houfholder within the faid City,
' and have Lands Tenements, or perfonal Eftate
' to the Value of one hundred Pounds; and the
' fame Matter and Caufe alledged by Way of
' Challenge, and fo found, fhall be taken and
' admitted as a principal Challenge, and the Per-
' 'fon or Perfons fo challenged, fhall and may be
' examined on Oath of the Truth of the faid
' Matter.'   ' And

' And it is further enacted, That the Sheriffs,
' or other Officers, to whom the returning of
' Juries doth or shall belong, for any County,
' City, or Place respectively, shall not impanel
' or return any Person or Persons to serve on Return of Ju-
' any Jury for the Trial of any Capital Offence, ries in Capital
' who, at the Time of such Return, would not Cases.
' be qualified in such respective County, City,
' or Place, to serve as Jurors in Civil Causes for
' that Purpose ; and the same Matter and Cause
' alledged by Way of Challenge, and so found,
' shall be admitted and taken as a principal
' Challenge, and the Person or Persons so chal-
' lenged shall and may be examined on Oath of
' the Truth of the said Matter.'

This Act was made perpetual by Stat. *6 Geo.*
2. *c.* 37.

' And by Stat. 4 *Geo.* 2. *c.* 7. It is enacted, After 1 *May*
' That from and after the first Day of *May* in 1731. Clause
' the Year of our Lord one thousand seven hun- in the Jury
' dred and thirty-one, the fourth Section of the Act not to ex-
' said Act, or any Part thereof, shall not extend tend to *Mid-*
' or be construed to extend to the County of *dlesex.*
' *Middlesex.*'

' Provided always, and it is enacted by the Au-
' thority aforesaid, That no Person shall be re- None to be
' turned to serve as a Juror at any Session of returned, who
' *Nisi prius* in the County of *Middlesex*, who has been re-
' has been returned to serve as a Juror at any turned in the
' such Session of *Nisi prius* in the said County, two Terms
' in the two Terms or Vacations next immedi- preceding.
' ately preceding, under such Penalty upon the
' Sheriff, Under-Sheriff, Bailiff or other Offi-
' cer employed or concerned in the summoning
' or returning of Jurors in the said County of
' *Middlesex*, as might have been inflicted upon
' them, or any of them, for any Offence against
' the said recited Clause.'

' And

Leaseholders, where the improved Rents amount to 50 *l. per Ann.* liable to serve on Juries.

'And whereas by the very frequent Occa-
'sions there are for Juries in the County of
'*Middlesex,* and by the small Number of Free-
'holders, that are in the said County, the She-
'riffs of the said County may be under Difficul-
'ties in procuring Juries to answer the Purposes
'of this Act; for Remedy whereof it is en-
'acted by the Authority aforesaid, That all
'Leaseholders upon Leases, where the impro-
'ved Rents or Value shall amount to fifty
'Pounds, or upwards, *per Annum,* over and
'above all Ground-Rents, or other Reserva-
'tions, payable by Virtue of the said Leases,
'shall be liable and obliged to serve upon Ju-
'ries, when they shall be legally summoned for
'that Purpose; any Thing in this or any for-
'mer Act to the contrary notwithstanding.'

CHAP. IX.

Of Challenges (a) to the Array, &c.

1 Inst. 155. *b.* 156. Challenges.

YOU have already seen of what *Visne* the
Jury ought to be: The next Thing to be
considered is concerning *Challenges.*

Challenge is a Word common, as well to the
English as to the *French,* and sometimes signifieth to claim, and the *Latin* Word is *Vindicare;* sometimes in Respect of Revenge, to
challenge into the Field, and then it is called
in *Latin, Vindicare* or *provocare;* sometimes in
Respect of *Partiality or Insufficiency,* to chal-

(a) One challenged sworn as a Tales-Man, ill. *Str.*
640.

lenge

lenge in Court Perfons returned on a Jury. And feeing there is no proper *Latin* Word to fignify this particular Kind of Challenge, they have framed a Word anciently written *Chalumniare,* and *Columpniare,* and *Calumpniare,* and now written *Calumniare,* and hath no Affinity with the Verb *Calumnior,* or *Calumnia,* which is derived of that, for that is of a quite other Senfe, fignifying a *falfe Accufer*; and in that Senfe *Bratton* ufeth *Calumniator,* to be a falfe *Calumniator.* Accufer: But it is derived of the old Word *Caloir* or *Chaloir,* which in one Signification is to care for, or forefee. And for that to challenge Jurors, is the Mean to care for, or forefee, that an indifferent Trial be had, it is called *Calumniare,* to challenge, that is, to except againft them that are returned to be Jurors, and this is its proper Signification. But fometimes a Summons, *Summonitio,* is faid to be *Calumniata,* and a Count to be challenged, but this is improperly. And forafmuch as Mens Lives, Fames, Lands and Goods, are to be tried by Jurors, it is moft neceffary that they be *Omni exceptione majores*; and therefore I will handle this Matter more largely.

A Challenge to the Jurors is twofold, either *Ibid.* to the Array, or to the Polls: To the Array *Challenge is* of the *principal Panel,* and to the Array of *two fold.* the *Tales.* And herein you fhall underftand *To the Array.* that the Jurors Names are ranked in the Panel one under another, which Order or Ranking the Jury, is called the Array, and the Verb, *to array* the Jury, and fo we fay in common Speech *Battail Array,* for the Order of the *Array.* Battail. And this Array we call *Arraiamentum,* to make the Array, *Arraiare,* derived of the *French* Word *Arroier*; fo as to challenge

M 3   the

the Array of the Panel, is at once to challenge or except against all the Persons so arrayed or impanelled, in Respect of the Partiality or Default of the Sheriff, Coroner, or other Officer that made the Return.

Ibid.
Principal
-Challenges.

And it is to be known, that there is a *principal Cause* of Challenge to the Array, and a Challenge to the *Favour*; principal in Respect of Partiality; as first, If the Sheriff or other Officers be of Kindred or Affinity to the Plaintiff or Defendant, if the Affinity continue. Secondly, If any one or more of the Jury be returned at the Denomination of the Party, Plaintiff or Defendant, the whole Array shall be quashed. So it is, if the Sheriff return any one, that he be more favourable to the one than to the other, all the Array shall be quashed. Thirdly, If the Plaintiff or Defendant have an Action of Battery against the Sheriff, or the Sheriff against either Party, this is a good Cause of Challenge. So if the Plaintiff or Defendant have an Action of Debt against the Sheriff; (but otherwise it is, if the Sheriff have an Action of Debt against either Party); or if the Sheriff have Parcel of the Land depending upon the same Title, or if the Sheriff, or his Bailiff which returned the Jury, be under the Distress of either Party; or if the Sheriff or his Bailiff be either of Counsel, Attorney, Officer in Fee, or of Robes, or Servant of either Party, Gossip, or Arbitrator in the same Matter, and treated thereof. And where a Subject may challenge the Array for Unindifferency, there the King being a Party, may also challenge for the same Cause, as for Kindred, or that he hath Part of the Land, or the like; and

where

where the Array ſhall be challenged againſt the King, you may read in our Books.

The Challenge to the Array is, in Reſpect to the Cauſe of *Indifferency or Default* of the *Sheriff* or other *Officer that made the Return*, and not in Reſpect of *the Perſons returned*. For if the Challenge to the *Array* be found againſt the Party that takes it, he ſhall yet have his particular Challenge to the *Polls*; and the Reaſon why the Array or Panel may be challenged, is, becauſe the Cauſe doth not appear *upon Record*, and there is no other Way to take Advantage of it, which is likewiſe the Reaſon of challenge to the Polls. *Vin. Trial*, 224.

A Challenge was offered to the Array, for that it was made by *J. S.* as Sheriff of *Bucks*, who was made Sheriff in *Mich.* Term 1687. and had not taken the Oaths required by Stat. 25 *Car.* 2. and ſo his Office was made void; but it was diſallowed by the Court, for he is *de facto* Sheriff. 2 *Vent.* 58.

The Defendant challenged the Array becauſe it was returned by *J. S.* as Sheriff, two Days after he had received his Writ of Diſcharge; and the Court diſallowed the Challenge, becauſe contrary to the Record. *Cro. Eliz.* 369.

In Ejectment, the Plaintiff ſuggeſteth that his Leſſor, the Sheriffs and Coroners were Tenants to a Dean and Chapter, whoſe Intereſt was concerned, and prayed the *Venire facias* to *Eliſors*, and had it, being confeſſed by the Defendant, and the Court took it as a principal Challenge. *Vide Hut.* 24. *Moor* 470. *Roll. Rep.* 328. *Duncomb* and *Ingleby, Trin.* 15 *Car.* 2. *B.R.*

Challenging the Array of a ſpecial Jury for the Sheriff's being intereſted, not a Contempt. 2 *Str.* 1000.

A Prayer

A Prayer to *Elisors* in Trials at Bar may be at the Suit of the Defendant or Plaintiff, but in *Nisi prius* at the Prayer of the Plaintiff only ; and *per Cur',* It is a principal Challenge that the Plaintiff's Lessor is Sheriff or Kindred, and if the Plaintiff doth not pray, &c. the Defendant may challenge the Array at the Assizes. Lord *Brook*'s Case, *Trin.* 1657. *B. R.*

It is a good Challenge to the Array, that the Array is made and returned by two Coroners only, when there are four in the County, and that the Writ is returned by one of the Sheriffs of *London* only.   So if a Bailiff return them that are out of his Franchise, or if an Array be to be, of Persons out of a Franchise and Guildable, and the Bailiff return them, for the Sheriff ought to make it ; and that some of the Panel were returned by the Bailiff of a Franchise, where the whole Panel is returned as Array by the Sheriff, this is a good Challenge to the Array, for otherwise the Parties would lose their Challenge to the Array made by the Bailiff.   *Roll.* Tit. *Trial,* 636.

By what Person.

If the Defendant sue the Writ of *Habeas Corporas* by *Proviso,* at the Return, the Plaintiff may challenge the Array for Kindred between the Defendant and the Sheriff. *D.* 15 *Eliz.* 319. 13. *Rol. Trial,* 637.

What Consanguinity is sufficient.

D. 15 *Eliz.* 319. The Array was quashed although the Sheriff was the *Ninth* in Descent, and the Tenant in the *seventh* Descent from the Ancestor of whom both descended, Cousin to the Party's Wife, although herself no Party. So if the Wife be dead, if Issue be alive, these are good Challenges to the Array. *Dyer* 37. *Roll. Trial,* 637, 638.

Alliance

Alliance to one Party is a good Challenge. For Affinity.

It the Sheriff be allied at the making of the At what
Panel, and be dead at the Challenge, yet this Time.
is a good Challenge. It is no Challenge that
the Sheriff became of Kin after making the
Panel: Nor can the Array be challenged after
a Juror is sworn, or appear full, for it then
comes too late. *Vin. Trial,* 241.

It is no Challenge to the Array, if all the
Jurors be of Affinity.

It may be after a *Tales* prayed, for no Chal- Roll. Trial,
lenge can be until the Jury is full. If the Sug- 644. *pl.* 6.
gestion of Coufinage to have the *Venire facias*
to the Coroners, be denied, and the *Venire facias* is awarded to the Sheriff, the fame Challenge shall not be allowed to the Array, but any
other Cause may be alledged, than what was
before denied.

Favourably made by the Sheriff or his Bai- For Favour.
liff, or the Bailiff of a Franchise, is a good 1 Inft. 156.
Challenge. That the Sheriff is within the Di- Roll. Trial,
ftrefs of a Party, or Servant to the Plain iff, of 638.
the Robes of the Plaintiff, was Arbitrator for a
Party, is Procurator, and Maintainer of a Party:
That the Sheriff purchafed Part of the Land in
Queftion: That the Panel was made by the
Bailiff of the Franchife of the other Party:
Thefe are good Challenges to the Array.

It is no principal Challenge that one Party is *Ibid.*
Tenant or Servant to the Sheriff, but it is a
good Challenge for Favour.

It is a good Challenge to the Array. That
the Sheriff made the Array, or put a Juror into the Panel at the Denomination of any of the Denomina-
Parties, in Favour to them, or of their Ser- tion.
vants, or of one interefted, or of a Maintainer, or
of the Counfel, or of a Procurator. *Ibid.* 640.

Not

Not if Strangers by the Sheriff's Leave make the Panel, or it be made at the Requeſt of both Parties. *Ibid. pl. 13.* 1 *Inſt.* 156.

For Malice. It is a good Challenge to the Array, that one of the Parties has brought an Action of Debt againſt the Officer that returns that Panel, or that there is a Difference betwixt the Officer *Ibid.* 642. and the Party; that the Officer killed his Servant. *Ibid.*

Ibid. But not that the Officer has Debt againſt the Party, for he may demand his Debt without Malice.

An Action brought for *every Debate* will not be the Cauſe of a principal Challenge, unleſs it be in ſuch Actions, in which there is either *Malice, Grief,* or *Revenge*; in ſuch Caſes theſe are principal Challenges, but not otherwiſe.

So if an Action be brought in which the *good Name* and Fame of the Party be touched, or in Actions which concern *Life, Honeſty, Maihem,* it is a principal Challenge to ſuch that he hath ſuch Action depending againſt the Sheriff. *Vin. Trial,* 235.

Where a Man challenges the Array, and does not verify his Plea with *Et hoc paratus eſt verificare,* yet the Challenge is good; for the Entries do not direct it, and the Court will not vary from the Entries. *Ibid.* 237.

How, and in what Manner the Challenge is to be made, Roll. Trial, 642. The Challenge ought to be, *quod tempore Panelli prædict' Arraiati* the Sheriff was Couſin to the Wife of the Defendant, &c. not afterwards nor before, unleſs you aver that ſhe was alive, or had Iſſue at the making the Panel.

Ibid. If the Challenge be taken for Couſinage, it ought to be ſhewn *coment* Couſin, but in ſuch a Challenge to be a Juror, it is not neceſſary to
ſhew

shew *coment* Cousin: But *per Br. Challenges*, pl. 56. he ought to shew *coment*.

The Matter and Conveyance of the Cousi- *What Coun-*
nage alledged in a Challenge, is not traversable. *terplea of a*
You may traverse the Cousinage *prout* without *Challenge is*
modo & forma. If the Challenge be, that the *good, and*
Sheriff was Cousin to the Plaintiff, or within *pleaded.*
his Distress; it is no Counterplea to say he is
likewise of Kin to the Defendant, or within his
Distress also.

In Trespass against *B* Feoffee to the Use of
C. The Sheriff is Cousin to *B.* but not to *C.*
the Plaintiff may challenge the Array. So
where the Panel was returned by *H.* the Sheriff
and *M. the Under Sheriff*, and *M.* was Cousin to
the Plaintiff, and shews *coment*, this was allowed a principal Challenge to the Array. But in
Case upon a Surmise *by the Plaintiff*, that the
Under Sheriff was his Cousin, and shewed *coment*,
and because the Defendant did not deny it, the
Venire was awarded to the Coroners; and after
Verdict and Judgment, the Judgment was held
erroneous, and not aided by the Statute. *Vin.*
Trial, 227.

So in Ejectment after Not guilty pleaded, it
was surmised that the Sheriff was of *Consangui-*
nity to the Lessor of the Plaintiff, which being
confessed, the *Venire* was awarded to the Coroners. This Challenge was afterwards adjudged
insufficient, and a new *Venire* awarded, for it
was no principal Challenge, and did not conclude to the Favour; and it is no *principal*
Challenge, that the Sheriff is *Cousin* to the Lessor
of the Plaintiff, as the Lessor cannot hinder the
Action of the Lessee. *Ibid.*

If a Panel be returned by the Sheriff who is a
Party concerned, or Member of a *Body politick*
concerned,

concerned, it is a good Caufe of Challenge, of which the Court is to be apprifed by Suggeftion of the Party, and the *Venire* then goes to the Coroners at firft ; but the Want of a proper *Venue* was never yet a Challenge to the Array, as it is in the *Cafe* of *Affinity* to either Party, or *interefted*, or *not qualified* to make a Return, or had made it at the *Requeft* of either Party, or where the Caufe concerns a Corporation of which the Sheriff is a Member. *Ibid.* 232.

If it be prefented that *J. S.* hath made a Nufance to *London* and *le gents,* it is no Challenge to the Array, to fay the Sheriff of *Middlefex* is deputed and removable by the Commonalty of *London*, becaufe this is the Suit of the King.

The King may make his Challenge, that the Sheriff is within the Party's Diftrefs, although every Subject owes greater Favour and Obedience to the King, by Reafon of his Allegiance, than to any Lord by Reafon of Tenure.

In a Writ of Right, or any other Writ, a Baron of the Realm may excufe himfelf.

What Perfons may be impanelled.   In a Writ of Right, the Inqueft ought to be all Knights. A Banneret may be impanelled in this Writ ; fo may a Serjeant, if there be not Chivalers covenable.

In an Attaint upon a Recovery by falfe Verdict in an Affife, fome Knights ought to be returned ; and if there be not any in the Hundred where the Land lies, they fhall be returned out of the County.

By Default of the Sheriff ; as when the Array of a Panel is returned by a Bailiff of a

1 Init. 156.   Franchife, and the Sheriff return it as of himfelf, this fhall be quafhed, becaufe the Party fhall lofe his Challenges. But if a Sheriff return

turn a Jury within a Liberty, this is good, and the Lord of the Franchise is driven to his Remedy against him.

If a Peer of the Realm, or Lord of Parliament be Demandant or Plaintiff, Tenant or Defendant, there must be two or more Knights returned of his Jury, be he Lord Spiritual or Temporal, or else the Array may be quashed: But if they be returned, although they appear not, yet the Jury may be taken of the Residue. And if others be joined with the Lord of Parliament, yet if there be no Knight returned, the Array shall be quashed against all. So in an Attaint, there ought to be a Knight returned to the Jury.
only the Privilege of a Peer.

Where there must be a Knight returned of the Jury. 1 Inst. 156. Note; This Challenge may be taken by the Peer, but not by the other Party, who is not a Peer, for it is *Modern Reports 2, 26.*

In an Assise between *Newdigate*, Plaintiff, and the Earl of *Darby* and others Defendants; the Array was challenged by the Earl because he was a Peer of the Realm, and had a Seat in Parliament; and that the Array was made by *A.* and *B.* Sheriff of *Middlesex, Nullo Milite in eodem panello nominato nec retornato.* To this the Plaintiff demurred; and the Court held the Challenge good, and ordered a new Panel to be made. *Q.* If he was Plaintiff, and would not challenge for that Cause, if the Defendant shall have such Challenge; it seemeth that he shall not. *Dyer* 107. *b. Vin. Trial,* 225.

In Ejectment in *Ireland* of Lands on the Demise of Lady *Conway*; at the Trial the Defendant challenged the Array, for that the Lessor of the Plaintiff was a Countess; that the Ejectment was to try her Title, and that she bore the Costs of the Suit, and prosecuted the same; and that the Sheriff had made that Array *Nullo Milite*

Milite in eodem exiften' retornat'. To this the
Plaintiff demurred ; and upon a Writ of Error
in *B. R.* here the Court held, that the Defendant might take Advantage of the two Knights
not being returned, as well as the Plaintiff, notwithftanding the Opinion in *Dyer* 107. *b*. And
that in Ejectment, as well as in any other Action ; the Leffor being the real, and the other
only the nominal Plaintiff. 2 *Show*. 423.

In an Information for a Riot againft feveral ;
at the Trial a Challenge was offered, becaufe the
Lord *Grey* was one of the Defendants, who was
a Peer, and that no Knights were returned on
the Panel ; and held a good Challenge. 2 *Show*.
262.

If two *Peers* fue as *Gentlemen*, and admit
themfelves fo in Pleading ; 'tis no Challenge to
fay, no Knight is returned ; for the Sheriff is in
no Fault.

Where the   And when the King is Party, as in Traverfe
King is Party. of an Office, he that traverfeth may challenge
1 Inft. 156. the Array, as hereafter in this Section fhall appear, and fo it is in Cafe of Life : And likewife
the King may challenge the Array, and this fhall
be tried by Triors, according to the ufual Courfe.
The Array challenged on both Sides fhall be
quafhed.

Ibid.   And if two Eftrangers make a Panel, and not
in a favourable Manner for the one Party or the
other, and the Sheriff returns the fame, the Array was challenged for this Caufe, and adjudged
good. It is therefore common for the Officers
of the Court, by the Direction of the Judges to
give a Panel to the Sheriff which he returns ;
whence it feems the Court hath the Power to
compel the Sheriff to make his Return, and

                              3   they

they may fine him if a sufficient Jury doth not appear according to the Precept of the Writ.

It is no good Cause of Challenge to the Array to say, that the Jury should come out of different Counties. *Vin. Trial*, 224, 5.

If the Bailiff of a Liberty return any out of his Franchise, the Array shall be quashed, as an Array returned by one that hath no Franchise shall be quashed. *Ibid.*

Challenge to the Array for Favour: He that taketh this must shew in certain the Name of him that made it, and in whose Time, and all in Certainty; this Kind of Challenge being no principal Challenge, must be left to the Discretion and Conscience of the Triors; as if the Plaintiff or Defendant be Tenant to the Sheriff, this is no principal Challenge, for the Lord is in no Danger of his Tenant; but *e converso* it is a principal Challenge; but in the other he may challenge for Favour; and leave it to Trial. So Affinity between the Son of the Sheriff, and the Daughter of the Party, or *e converso*, or the like, is no principal Challenge, but to the Favour; but if the Sheriff marry the Daughter of either Party, or *e converso*, this (as hath been said) is a principal Challenge, or the like. But where the King is Party, one shall not challenge the Array for Favour, &c. because in respect of his Allegiance, he ought to favour the King more. But if the Sheriff be a Vadelect of the Crown, or other menial Servant of the King, there the Challenge is good, and likewise the King may challenge the Array for Favour. *Challenge to the Favour. 1 Inst. 156.* *For the King.*

Note; Upon that which hath been said it appeareth, that the Challenge to the Array is in Respect of the Cause of Unindifferency, or Default of the Sheriff, or other Officer that made the *To the Array. 1 Inst. 156.*

the Return, and not in the Refpect of the Perfons returned, where there is no Unindifference
or Default in the Sheriff, &c. for if the Challenge to the Array be found againft the Party
that takes it, yet he fhall have his particular
Challenge to the Polls.

To the Polls.
1 Inft. 156. b.

In fome Cafes a Challenge may be had to the
Polls, and in fome Cafes not at all. Challenge
to the Polls is a Challenge to the particular Perfons, and thefe be of four Kinds, that is to fay,
Peremptory, Principal, which induce Favour,
and for Default of Hundredors.

Peremptory
Challenge.
Ibid.

Peremptory ; this is fo called, becaufe he may
challenge peremptorily upon his own Diflike,
without fhewing of any Caufe ; and this only is
in Cafe of Treafon or Felony, *in favorem vitæ*;
and by the Common Law, the Prifoner upon
an Indictment or Appeal might challenge thirty-
five, which was under the Number of three Juries ; but now by the Statute of 22 *H.* 8. the
Number is reduced to twenty in Petit Treafon,
Murder and Felony ; and in Cafe of High Treafon, and Mifprifion of High Treafon, it was
taken away by the Statute of 32 *H.* 8. But now
by the Statute of 1 & 2 *Phil.* & *Mar.* the Common Law is revived, for in Treafon, the Prifoner fhall have his Challenge to the Number of
thirty-five ; and fo it hath been refolved by the
Juftices, upon Conference between them in the
Cafe of Sir *Walter Raleigh* and *George Brooks:*
But all this is to be underftood when any Subject, that is not a Peer of the Realm, is arraigned for Treafon or Felony. But if he be a Lord
of Parliament, and a Peer of the Realm, and is

No Challenge
of Peers.

to be tried by his Peers, he fhall not challenge
any of his Peers at all ; for they are not fworn
as other Jurors be, but find the Party Guilty

or

or Not guilty, upon their Faith or Allegiance to the King, and they are Judges of the Fact, and every of them doth feparately give his Judgment, beginning at the loweft. But a Subject under the Degree of Nobility may, in Cafe of Treafon or Felony, challenge for juft Caufe, as many as he can, as fhall be faid hereafter.   In an Appeal of Death againft divers, they plead Not guilty, and one joint *Venire facias* is awarded; if one challenge peremptorily, he fhall be drawn againft all; otherwife it is of feveral *Venire facias's.*

The King, or any on his Behalf, may on fuf- ficient Caufe, challenge either the Array or the Polls, in the fame Manner as a private Perfon may; alfo by the Common Law, the King, without affigning any Reafon, but barely alledging *quod non funt boni pro Rege*, might have challenged peremptorily as many as he thought proper. Of Challenges by the King.

But this is remedied by 33 *E.* 1. which enacteth as follows; ' Of Inquefts to be taken be-
' fore any of the Juftices, and wherein our Lord
' the King is Party, howfoever it be, it is agreed
' and ordained by the King and all his Counfel,
' that from henceforth, notwithftanding it be
' alledged by them that fue for the King, that
' the Jurors of thofe Inquefts, or fome of them,
' be not indifferent for the King, yet fuch In-
' quefts fhall not remain untaken for that Caufe;
' but if they that fue for the King will challenge
' any of thofe Jurors, they fhall affign of their
' Challenge a Caufe certain, and the Truth of the
' fame Challenge fhall be inquired of according
' to the Cuftom of the Court.'

It hath been clearly fettled, that the Words of this Stat. being general, it extends to all

Caufes, as well *Criminal* as Civil, whereto the King is Party. *Moor* 595. *Co. Lit.* 159.

The King may challenge the Array for Favour, fo he may the Polls; but a Man fhall not have fuch Challenge *againft* the King. *Vin. Trial*, 243.

In an Information for Forgery the King's Counfel challenged a Juror, and being preffed to fhew the Caufe, the Court held, that if the Panel fhould be gone through firft, and if there were Jurors enough without thofe challenged, the King is not to fhew any Caufe. 1 *Vent.* 309. And the like was done in Lord *Grey's Cafe, Raymond* 473. See alfo *Co. Lit.* 156. *Skin.* 82. 2 *H. H. P. C.* 271.

Principal Challenge to the Polls. 1 Inft. 156. b.

Principal; fo called, becaufe, if it be found true, it ftandeth fufficient of itfelf without leaving any Thing to the Confcience or Difcretion of the Triors. Of a principal Caufe of Challenge to the *Array*, we have fpoke fomewhat already; now it followeth with like Brevity, to fpeak of principal Challenges to the *Polls*, (that is) feverally to the Perfons returned.

A principal Challenge is nothing elfe but fuch Matter which proves evident Favour or Enmity in the Juror; and therefore it belongeth to the Juftices to draw the Juror, and not to leave the Dicifion to Triors. 21 *Ed.* 4. 11. *Roll. Trial,* 649. *pl.* 1.

To the Polls. 1 Inft. 156. b.

Principal Challenges to the Polls may be reduced to four Heads; Firft, *Propter Honoris refpectum*, for refpect of Honour. Secondly, *Propter Defectum*, for Want or Default. Thirdly, *Propter Affectum*, for Affection or Partiality. Fourthly, *Propter Delictum*, for Crime or Delict.

Firft,

Firſt, *Propter Honoris reſpectum:* As any Peer of the Realm, or Lord of Parliament, as a Baron, Viſcount, Earl, Marqueſs and Duke; for theſe in reſpect of Honour and Nobility, are not to be ſworn on Juries; and if neither Party will challenge him, he may challenge himſelf; for by *Magna Charta* it is provided, *Quod nec ſuper eum ibimus, nec ſuper eum mittemus, niſi per legale judicium parium ſuorum, aut per legem terræ.* Now the Common Law hath divided all the Subjects into Lords of Parliament, and into the Commons of the Realm. The Peers of the Realm are divided into Barons, Viſcounts, Earls, Marqueſſes and Dukes; the Commons are divided into Knights, Eſquires, Gentlemen, Citizens, Yeomen and Burgeſſes: And in Judgment of Law any of the ſaid Degrees of Nobility are Peers to another: As if an Earl, Marqueſs or Duke be to be tried for Treaſon or Felony, a Baron, or any other Degree of Nobility, is his Peer. In like Manner a Knight, Eſquire, &c. ſhall be tried *per Pares,* and that is by any of the Commons, as Gentlemen, Citizens, Yeomen or Burgeſſes; ſo as when any of the Commons is to have a Trial, either at the King's Suit, or between Party and Party, a Peer of the Realm ſhall not be impanelled in any Caſe.

Marginal notes: Principal Challenges to the Polls. *Ibid.* Propter honoris reſpectum. — A Peer may challenge himſelf. — Peers and Commons.

Secondly, *Propter Defectum.*
1. *Patriæ,* As Aliens born.
2. *Libertatis,* As Villeins or Bondmen, and ſo a Champion muſt be a Freeman.
3. *Annui cenſus, i. e. liberi tenementi.*

Marginal notes: Ibid. Challenge, Propter defect'.

Firſt, What yearly Freehold a Juror ought to have, that paſſeth upon Trial of the Life of a Man, or in a Plea real, or in a Plea perſonal,

Marginal notes: Ibid. See before cap. 7.

where

where the Debt or Damage in the Declaration amounteth to forty Marks. *Vide Littleton, sect.* 464. Secondly, This Freehold must be in his own Right, in Fee-simple, Fee-tail, for Term of his own Life, or for another Man's Life, although it be upon Condition, or in Right of his Wife, out of Ancient Demesne; for Freehold within Ancient Demesne will not serve: But if the Debt or Damage amounteth not to forty Marks, any Freehold sufficeth. Thirdly, He must have Freehold in that County where the Cause of the Action ariseth, and though he hath in another, it sufficeth not. Fourthly, If after his Return he selleth away his Land, or if *Cestuique vie*, or his Wife dieth, or an Entry be made, for the Condition broken, so as his Freehold be determined, he may be challenged for Insufficiency of Freehold.

In Cases of Treason and Felony, at Common Law, Want of Freehold was no Cause of Challenge; *probos & legales homines* was sufficient. The Statute of 2 *H.* 5. is gone as to that by the Statute of 1 *&* 2 of Queen *Mary*. See the Lord *Russel*'s Trial, *July* 13, 1683. *State Trials,* Vol. 3. p. 135.

It seems before the Statute 2 *H.* 5. in Actions where the Freehold was concerned, the Jurors ought to have some Freehold. 3 *H.* 4. 4. By that Statute in all Pleas real and personal, where the Debt or Damage, or both together amount to forty Marks, the Juror must have forty Shillings Freehold. In an Attaint they must be able to expend twenty Pounds *per Annum. Roll.* Tit. *Trials, f.* 648.

In an Account, upon the Receipt of one hundred Shillings, if he count to his Damage two hundred Shillings, if the Juror hath but twenty Shillings, or under forty Shillings, 'tis

sufficient,

fufficient, becaufe he fhall not recover Damages; and fo this is not within the Statute 10 *H.* 6. 18. For the Sufficiency of Jurors, fee *Roll.* Tit. *Trials*, 648. *pl.* 14.

A Man feifed of a Manor of *Dale*, enfeoffs a Stranger upon Condition to pay yearly to *J. S.* and his Heirs, forty Shillings Rent. *J. S.* dies feifed of this Rent, and then his Heir takes it, yet the Heir hath not fufficient Freehold.

Land to the Value of forty Shillings is given to the Hufband and Wife, and the Heirs of their two Bodies begotten, who had Iffue a Son; the Hufband gives the Land by Fine to an E-ftranger and his Heirs, and dies, the Wife enters and dies feifed; the Son hath not fufficient Freehold to be a Juror.

A Man feifed of Land to the Value of forty Shillings within the County of *Middlefex*, and of Land to the Value of twelve within the County of *Suffex*, and grants a Rent-Charge of forty Shillings, iffuing out of all the faid Land to a Stranger in Fee; the Grantee hath fufficient Freehold to be a Juror in both Counties. See many fpeculative Cafes upon this Subject, in *Williams* his Reading upon the Statute 35 *H.* 8. *cap.* 6.

It was held that the Statute, as to Jurors being Freeholders, don't extend to Juries in Corporate Towns. 1 *Ventris* 366. *Raymond* 485.

4. *Hundredorum:* Firft, By the Common Law in a Plea real, mix'd and perfonal, there ought to be four of the Hundred (where the Caufe of Action arifeth) returned for their better Notice of the Caufe; for *Vicini vicinorum facta præfumuntur fcire.* And now, fince *Littleton* wrote, in a Plea perfonal, if two Hundre-

1 Inft. 157. Challenges *propter defectum hundredorum.*

N 3   dors

dors appear, it fufficeth; and in an Attaint, though the Jury is double, yet the Hundredors are not double. Secondly, If he hath either Freehold in the Hundred, though it be to the Value of but Half an Acre, or if he dwell there, though he hath no Freehold in it, it fufficeth.

Hundredors.   Thirdly, If the Caufe of the Action rifeth in divers Hundreds, yet the Number fhall fuffice as if it had come out of one, and not feveral Hundredors out of each Hundred. Fourthly, If there be divers Hundreds within one Leet or Rape, if he hath any Freehold, or dwell in any of thofe Hundreds, though not in the proper Hundred, it fufficeth. Fifthly, If the Jury

No Hundre-dors.   come *de Corpere Comitatus*, or *de proximo Hundredo*, where one Party is Lord of the Hundred, or the like, there need no Hundredors be returned at all. Sixthly, If a Hundredor, after he be returned, fell away his Land within that Hundred, yet fhall he not be challenged for the Hundred, for that his Notice remains; otherwife, as hath been faid, for his Infufficiency of Freehold, for his Fear to offend, and to have Lands wafted, &c. which is one of the Reafons of Law, is taken away. Seventhly, He that challengeth for the Hundred, muft fhew in what Hundred it is, and not drive the other Party to fhew it. Eighthly, His Challenge for the Hundred is not *fimpliciter*, but *fecundum quid*; for though it be found that he hath nothing in the Hundred, yet fhall he not be drawn, but remain *præter H.* that is befides for the Hundred; and albeit he dwelleth, or hath Land in the Hundred, yet muft he have fufficient Freehold.

Note; This Challenge for Want of Hundredors muft be given in Writing prefently,

.and

and the other Party is to demur thereto, if oppofed.

If a Challenge be, that there is not any Hundredor returned, it may be averred to the Court,
that there is not any fufficient within the Hundred,
which is not within the Fee of the Plaintiff; although this be not returned by the Sheriff, and
if this be found true by Triors, the Array fhall
be affirmed. 45 *Aff.* 1. *Roll. Trial,* 634.
pl. 6.

If the King be made Party by Aid Prayer,
and fufficient Hundredors do not appear, nor
are returned, yet the Panel fhall not be quafhed,
but a *Tales* of the Hundred fhall be returned.
But betwixt common Perfons in fuch Cafes, the
Panel fhall be quafhed, and this fhall not only
be a Challenge to the Heads. 25 *E.* 3. 43.
Ibid. pl. 7, 8.

If the Sheriff return *quod non funt pluries del
Hundred,* he fhall take of the Hundred adjoin-
ing, which fhall be fufficient. 19 *H.* 6. 43.
Ibid. pl. 5.

If the Juror hath fufficient Land within the
Hundred, although he doth not dwell within
the Hundred, yet he is a fufficient Hundredor.
9 *H.* 6. 66. *Ibid.* 635. Nay, though he dwell
in another County.

If he be not Hundredor at the Return of the
Venire, but at the Return of the *Diftringas,* yet
this doth not take away the Challenge.

After four are fworn, or after a Challenge to At what Time
the Polls, there can be no Challenge for the the Challenge
Hundred. *Roll.* Tit. *Trial,* 636. *pl.* 15.   muft be.

Who fhall be fufficient *Hundredor,* fee *Williams* his Reading aforefaid.

If he dwell or have Aſſets within the Leet, Rape, Franchiſe or Vill, where the *Venue* is, he is a ſufficient Hundredor.

If he hath Aſſets in Rent, Common of any Sort, Market, Fair, Piſcary, Toll, Paſſage, Leet, Office of Bailiwick, &c. he is a ſufficient Hundredor; otherwiſe of an Advowſon, &c.

A Jury being ready at the Bar in *B. R.* Serjeant *Earl* challenged the Array for want of Hundredors. *Econtra:* It was inſiſted that the Jury by Rule of Court was returned by the Secondary, and that the Hundredors were ſtruck out by Conſent; but the Court held it a good Challenge notwithſtanding the Conſent. *Style* 233.

In an Information in the Nature of a *Quo warranto* againſt the Defendant for acting as Mayor of *Tiverton*, the Defendant entered into the common Rule, by Conſent, for the Maſter to ſtrike the Jury, who accordingly ſtruck forty-eight: The Defendant ſtruck out twelve of theſe, and the Proſecutor ſtruck off twelve more; and the Sheriff returned the remaining twenty-four as the Jury to try the Cauſe; but the Defendant having artfully ſtruck out all the Hundredors named by the Maſter at the Aſſizes, challenged the Array for want of Hundredors. The Court held that the Challenge was good, but that the Rule being made by the Defendant's Conſent, this Challenge was a Contempt of the Court; and granted an Attachment againſt the Defendant for the ſame. *Rex* v. *Burridge, T.* 10 *Geo.* 1. *B. R.*

1 Inſt. 157.
Challenge
*propter affec-
tum.*

3. *Propter affectum*; and this is of two Sorts, either working a principal Challenge, or to the Favour. And again a principal Challenge is of two Sorts, either by Judgment of Law, with-

2   out

out any Act of his, or by Judgment of Law upon his own Act.

And it is said, that a principal Challenge is, *Ibid.* when there is express Favour, or express Malice. **Principal** First, without any Act of his; as if the Juror **Challenge.** be of Blood or Kindred to either Party, *Con-sanguineus,* which is compounded *ex con & san-guine, quasi eodem sanguine natus,* as it were is-sued from the same Blood; and this is a princi-pal Challenge; for that the Law presumeth that **Kindred, Sid.** one Kinsman doth favour another before a Stran- **2 Part 155.** ger; and how far remote soever he is of Kin-dred, yet the Challenge is good. And if the Plaintiff challenge a Juror for Kindred to the Defendant, it is no Counter-plea, to say that he is of Kindred also to the Plaintiff, though he be in a nearer Degree. For the Words of the *Ve-nire facias* forbid the Juror to be of Kindred to either Party.

If a Body Politick or Incorporate, sole or ag- **Bodies Poli-** gregate of many, bring any Action that con- **tick.** cerns their Body Politick or Incorporate, if the **1 Inst. 157.** Juror be of Kindred to any that is of that Body, although the Body Politick or Incorporate can have no Kindred, yet, for that those Bodies con-sist of natural Persons, it is a principal Chal-lenge. A Bastard cannot be of Kindred to any, and therefore it can be no principal Challenge. And here it is to be known, that *Affinitas,* Af- **Affinity.** finity, hath in Law two Senses. In its proper Sense it is taken for that Nearness that is gotten by Marriage, *Cum duæ cognationes inter se divisæ per nuptias copulantur, & altera ad alterius fines accedit, & inde dicitur Affinis.* In a larger Sense *Affinitas* is taken also for Consanguinity and Kin-dred, as in the Writ of *Venire facias,* and other-where. Affinity or Alliance by Marriage is a
principal

principal Challenge, and equivalent to Confanguinity, when it is between either of the Parties; as if the Plaintiff or Defendant marry the
Daughter or Coufin of the Juror, or the Juror
marry the Daughter or Coufin of the Plaintiff
or Defendant, and the fame continues, or Iffue
be had. But if the Son of the Juror hath married the Daughter of the Plaintiff, this is no
principal Challenge, but to the Favour, becaufe
it is not between the Parties. Much more may
be faid hereof; *fed fumma fequor faftigia rerum.*

Peremptory Challenge upon Record.　　As if he hath formerly tried the Caufe, although reverfed by Error, or upon the fame
Title ; if the Record be not fhewed, this Challenge is not peremptory. *For he that grounds
a Challenge upon a Record,* &c. *ought to have the
Record ready.* 33 *H.* 6. 55. The Record ought
to be exemplified. 21 *E.* 4. 74. *Roll. Trial,*
649. *pl.* 1.

'Tis a good Challenge to fay the Juror was
attainted in an Attainder, or Writ of Confpiracy; but Attainder in a Writ of Forgery of
falfe Deeds upon the Statute 1 *H.* 5. 2. (but 'tis
upon 5 *Eliz.* 14.) is not, becaufe this Attainder
is given of late Time by the Statute 33 *H.* 6.
55. *Ibid. pl.* 2, 4, 5.

In a Writ of Confpiracy, 'tis a principal
Challenge, That the Juror was one of the In-
dictors, although the Trial is now of the Confpiracy, and not upon the firft Point, *viz.* the
Felony. *Ibid. pl.* 9.

In Trefpafs, if one juftify as Mafter, and the
other as Servant; 'tis not a principal Challenge
to fay the Juror paffed in the firft Iffue for the
Mafter, but he ought to conclude, *& iffint* favourable. 18 *E.* 4. 12. *Ibid. pl.* 7.

If

If two plead Not guilty, and firſt one Iſſue is tried, and then the other is tried, 'tis no Challenge to ſay the Juror tried the other Iſſue, and gave Damages, of which Damages he ſhall be charged if he be attainted in an Attaint; for perhaps the Defendant will be found Not guilty. *Ibid. pl.* 8.

That the Juror is within the *Diſtreſs* of any *Diens* Diſtreſ. of the Parties, is a good Cauſe of Challenge. And ſo it is, if he be within the *Diſtreſs* of any Perſon concern'd, although no Party to the Action. As within the *Diſtreſs* of *A.* the Maſter of the Defendant, who juſtifies as Servant to *A.* by Reaſon of his Freehold; and the Iſſue is *ſur le franktenement.* So for him in Reverſion received, within the Diſtreſs of the Tenant for Life. And ſo in an Action by the Tenant for Life, within the Diſtreſs of him in Reverſion: Theſe are good Challenges. *Ibid.* 650. *pl.* 1, 2, 3.

So in an Action by Dean and Chapter, within the Diſtreſs of the Chapter, or one of the Chapter, are good Challenges. *Ibid. pl.* 8.

Conſanguinity of the Half Blood is a princi- Principal for pal Challenge: If the Juror be at the ninth De- Conſanguinity gree, if it can be ſhewed, it is good. *Ibid.* 652. *pl.*
1, 3,
In an Action by the Dean and Chapter, or *Ibid.pl.*10,11. Mayor and Commonalty, Brother to one of the Commonalty, or to one of the Canons, is a good Challenge: So to any Perſon concerned in Intereſt, although no Party to the Action. As Couſin to the Patron, or the Parſon, &c. ſo in Attaint to one of the *Petit* Jury. *Ibid.* 653. *pl.* 36.

But in an *Ejectione firmæ,* and Not guilty pleaded, 'tis no Challenge to the Array, that the Sheriff is Couſin to the Leſſor of the Plaintiff;

tiff; for it doth not appear that the Title of him in Reverſion ſhall be in Queſtion, and he in Reverſion is no Party to the Action: See it ſo adjudged upon Demurrer, *Roll.* Tit. *Trial,* 653. But now in our feigned Ejectments it is otherwiſe, becauſe the Title of the Leſſor is only in Queſtion.

Principal for
Affinity.
1 Inſt. 157. b. 'Tis a good Challenge that the Juror is Goſ‑ ſip to the Plaintiff, *& ſic e converſo*; and ſo although the Son be dead; for the Spiritual Af‑ finity remains, and ſo is *Curat* of the Juror. That the Juror hath married the Siſter of the Party; that the Daughter of the Uncle of the Juror hath married the Uncle of the Party; Couſin to the Wife of the Party; theſe are good Challenges, although the Wife, *&c.* is dead, if her iſſue be alive; otherwiſe if ſhe be dead with‑ out Iſſue, for then the Cauſe of the Favour is determined.

But it is no Challenge to ſay, the Juror is Brother to one who married the Siſter of the Party, nor that the Son of the Party married the Siſter of the Juror, becauſe theſe are not Parties to the Action. *Roll. Trial,* 654. *pl.* 10. 11.

In an Attaint it is a good Challenge to the Juror, that he hath married the Siſter of the Wife of one of the *Petit* Jury, for the Alliance. *Ibid. pl.* 17.

Principal for
Favour. If a Juror declare the Right of one Party, or give his Verdict before-hand, or take Money, this is a principal Challenge; but if he promiſe a Party, this is not a principal Challenge, but for Favour. *Ibid.* 655. *pl.* 6, 7, 8.

Principal for
Malice. If the Action depending betwixt the Party and Juror, be ſuch as implieth Malice, this is
a good

a good Challenge; but not if it imply no Malice. *Ibid.* 656. *pl.* 1.

That the Party hath an Appeal depending againſt the Juror, or the Juror againſt him, or Action of Battery. That they are in Debate and Wrangling, &c. are good Challenges. Not Actions of Debt or Treſpaſs *Quare Clauſum fregit,* &c. Nor that the Brother, &c. of the Party, hath Actions againſt the Juror. *Ibid.*

That the Juror was born out of the King's Ligeance; for although he came into *England* an Infant, and is ſworn to the King, yet he continues an Alien; and that he is outlawed, for then he is not *legalis homo,* are good Challenges. *Ibid.* 657. *pl.* 2.

Peremptory.

Alien.

If the Juror ſays, That he will paſs for one Party becauſe he knows the Verity of the Matter, this is no Challenge; but if he ſays it is for Favour, it is a good Challenge, if the Triors find he ſpoke for Favour, and not for Truth. *Ibid. pl.* 2, 3.

For Favour.

In an Action betwixt the King and a Party, the Subject cannot take any Challenge for Favour, as in an Indictment of Barretry, &c. the Defendant cannot challenge a Juror for Favour to the King. *Ibid. pl.* 1, 2.

King.

After the Array is affirmed, there ſhall not be ſuch Challenge to a Juror, which would have been a ſufficient Challenge to the Array. As it is not a good Challenge that the Juror was impanelled at the Denomination of a Party, for this had been a good Challenge to the Array. *Ibid.* 658. *pl.* 1, 2.

At what Time Challenges may be taken.

If a Man challenge a Juror for Non-ſufficiency of Freehold, and this is adjudged againſt him, yet he may challenge for Favour; and this ſhall be tried. 10 *H.* 6. 18. *Ibid. pl.* 3.

If

If the Jury upon finding of the principal do not tax the Damages, for which the *Venire fa-cias* iſſues to the ſame Jurors, to tax the Damages, the Parties cannot take any Challenge for a Cauſe before the firſt Trial. But for a Cauſe ariſing after they may. And ſo againſt *les primer Jurors. Ibid. pl.* 5, 6.

King. The King cannot challenge a Juror after he is ſworn, unleſs it be for a Cauſe ariſing after he is ſworn. *Ibid. pl.* 9.

In what Caſes he which challenges ought to ſhew the Cauſe preſently. If the Defendant challenge the Array which is found againſt him, or he releaſe the Challenge, and the Array is affirmed, and afterwards he challenge a Juror; he ought to ſhew the Cauſe preſently. *Ibid.* 659. *pl.* 1, 2.

But if there be two Defendants, and one challenge the Array, and afterwards both challenge a Juror; the other ſhall not ſhew Cauſe preſently. *Ibid. pl.* 3.

If a Juror be challenged, and there be enough of the Panel beſides, the Cauſe of Challenge need not be ſhewed unleſs the other Side challenges *touts peravail.*

If any of the Jurors be ſworn, and there be not ſufficient, for which a *Tales* is granted, and at the Return one of the *primer* Jurors is challenged, the Cauſe ought to be ſhewed preſently, he being ſworn before. *Roll. Trial,* 659. *pl.* 4.

King. In an Action between the King and a common Perſon, as in an Indictment of Barretry, Preſentment of Nuſance, &c. the Defendant, if he challenges any Juror, muſt ſhew the Cauſe preſently. *Ibid. pl.* 5.

But in an Inqueſt betwixt the King and a Stranger, the Stranger need not ſhew the Cauſe preſently ;

presently; for in this Case the King is as a common Person of the Realm. *Ibid. pl.* 9.

Cause ought to be shewed before the *Tales* be perused in Case of a common Person. *Ibid.* 660. *pl.* 1.

If both Parties challenge, although for several Causes, as if one be for Favour, and the other Peremptory; yet the Juror shall be drawn without shewing Cause. *Ibid. pl.* 2. *Treat.*

It may be in an Inquest before the Sheriff to inquire of Waste, both to the Array and Polls. *Ibid. P. pl.* 1. *In what Inquest a Challenge may be.*

But not in an Inquest of Office, as in a Writ of Inquiry of Damages. *Ibid. pl.* 2.

In a Writ of Right, a Challenge may be to the Polls *del* 4 *Chivalers* returned. *Ibid.* 661. *pl.* 4.

Not of Cosinage to the Witnesses coming to try the Deed in an Affize. *Ibid. pl.* 5.

If one Party challenge the Array, which is affirmed, and afterwards challenge a Juror, he ought to shew Cause presently; and this shall be tried presently; but otherwise of the other, who did not take the Challenge to the Array. *Ibid.* 661. *S. pl.* 1, 2. *Trial and Triors, and Challengers.*

The Challenge of him who first challenged, shall be first tried; although the first be for Favour, and that of the others be *Riens diens H.* *Ibid. T. pl.* 1.

If the *Venue* be of two Counties, and both Panels challenged, the *Eslisors* shall be one of one Panel, and the other of the other. *Ibid.* 663. *pl.* 1.

If the Array be challenged, the Court to try the Array may choose two Triors, according to their Discretion.   29 *Aff.* 15.   19 *H.* 6. 9.

If an Action be depending between the Juror and one of the Parties, and for this he is challenged, and the other says, that this is brought *What Challenge they may try.*

by

by Covin; the Triors may try this; for although the Action is of Record, yet the Covin is not. *Roll. Trial,* 664. *pl.* 10.

Evidence.

The Juror may be examined upon a *Voier dire,* to any Challenge that is not to his Dishonour; but the Triors are not bound by his Oath. *Ibid.* 665. *A.*

The Triors after they are sworn may go at large by Assent of the Parties until another Day. *Ibid.* 666. *pl.* 9.

In what Cases a Challenge or Affirmance by one shall serve for others.

In Trespass against two who plead to Issue, and a *Venire facias* is returned, although one accept the Array, yet the other may challenge it; and if it be found, the Array shall be quashed against all. So in an Appeal against Principal and Accessary, for one shall not disinherit the other. *Ibid.* 662. *pl.* 8.

But in an Appeal by two, if the Defendant challenge a Juror, and one of the Plaintiffs agree to this, the other shall not be received to say, that this is by Covin, but the Juror shall be drawn, in Favour to the Life of Man.

And yet in a *Præcipe quod reddat* by two, and the Tenant challenge the Array, because the Sheriff is Gossip to one of the Demandants, and one Demandant acknowledge the Challenge, the other may say that this is not so, and have it tried. *Roll.* Tit. *Trial,* 662, &c. *pl.* 7.

Ley Gager.

In *Gager de Ley* none shall be challenged for Favour or Insufficiency, &c.

Cousinage.

If there be a Challenge for Cousinage, he that takes the Challenge must shew how the Juror is Cousin. But yet if the Cousinage, that is, the Effect and Substance be found, it sufficeth; for the Law preferreth that which is material before that which is formal. 1 *Inst.* 157.

If

If the Juror have Part of the Land that de- pendeth upon the same Title. *Ibid.* Depending on the same Title.

If a Juror be within the Hundred, Leet, or any Way within the Seigniory, immediately or mediately, or any other Distress of either Party, this is a principal Challenge. But if either Party be within the Distress of the Juror, this is no principal Challenge, but to the Favour. *Ibid.* Distress.

If a Witness named in the Deed be returned of the Jury, it is a good Cause of Challenge of him. So if one within Age of one and twenty be returned, it is a good Cause of Challenge. *Ibid.* Witness. Infant.

Upon his own Act, as if the Juror hath given a Verdict before for the same Cause, albeit it be reversed by Writ of Error, or if after Verdict Judgment were arrested. So if he hath given a former Verdict upon the same Title or Matter, though between other Persons. But it is to be observed, that I may speak once for all, that in this or other like Cases, he that taketh the Challenge must shew the Record, if he will have it take Place as a principal Challenge, otherwise he must conclude to the Favour, unless it be a Record of the same Court, and then he must shew the Day and Term. *Ibid.* Challenges arising from the Juror's own Act. Former Verdict.

So likewise one may be challenged, that he whas Indictor of the Plaintiff or Defendant, either of Treason, Felony, Misprision, Trespass, or the like in the same Cause. Indictment. 1 Inst. 157.b.

If the Juror be Godfather to the Child of the Plaintiff or Defendant, or *e converso,* this is allowed to be a good Challenge in our Books. Godfather. *Ibid.*

If a Juror hath been an Arbitrator chosen by the Plaintiff or Defendant, in the same Cause, and hath been informed of, or treated of the Matter, this is a principal Challenge. Otherwise Arbitrator. 1 Inst. 157.b.

wife if he were never informed, nor treated thereof; and otherwife if he were indifferently chofen by either of the Parties, though he trea-
Commiffioner. ted thereof. But a Commiffioner chofen by one of the Parties, for Examination of Witneffes in the fame Caufe, is no principal Caufe of Challenge; for he is made by the King under the Great Seal, and not by the Party as the Arbitrator is, but he may upon Caufe be challenged for Favour.

Arbitrator in another Matter, is no Caufe of Challenge.

Counfel.   If he be of Counfel, Servant, or of Robes
1 Inft. 157.b. or Fee of either Party, it is a principal Challenge.

Eat or drink   If any, after he be returned, do eat and drink,
at the Parties   at the Charge of either Party, it is a principal
Charge.   Caufe of Challenge; otherwife it is of a Trior
1 Inft. 157. b. after he be fworn.

In an Information of Forgery, the Defendant challenged one of the Jury, for that the Profecutor had been lately entertained at his Houfe; and held a good Challenge to the Favour. 1 *Vent.* 309.

Actions of   Action brought either by the Juror againft
Malice.   either of the Parties, or by either of the Par-
1 Inft. 157.b. ties againft him, which may imply Malice or Difpleafure, are Caufes of principal Challenge, unlefs they be brought by Covin, either before or after the Return; for if Covin be found, then it is no Caufe of Challenge; other Actions which do not imply Malice or Difpleafure, are to the Favour; as an Action of Debt, &c.   *Moor* 3.

Parfon and   In a Caufe where the Parfon of a Parifh is
Parifhes.   Party, and the Right of the Church cometh in
Ibid.   Debate, a Parifhioner is a principal Challenge. Otherwife it is in Debt, or any other Action, where

where the Right of the Church cometh not in
Queſtion.

If either Party labour the Juror, and give him To labour the
any Thing to give his Verdict, this is a prin- Jury.
cipal Challenge. But if either Party labour the *Ibid.*
Juror to appear, and to do his Conſcience, this
is no Challenge at all, but lawful for him to do
it.

That the Juror is a Fellow-Servant with ei- Fellow-Ser-
ther Party, is no principal Challenge, but to vant.
the Favour. *Ibid.*

Neither of the Parties can take that Challenge To the Polls.
to the Polls, which he might have had to the *Ibid.*
Array.

Note; If the Defendant may have a principal *Ibid.*
Cauſe of Challenge to the Array, if the Sheriff
return the Jury, the Plaintiff in that Caſe may
for his own Expedition alledge the ſame, and
pray Proceſs to the Coroners, which he cannot *Venire facias*
have, unleſs the Defendant will confeſs it; but to the Coro-
if the Defendant will not confeſs it, then the ners.
Plaintiff ſhall have a *Venire facias* to the Sheriff,
and the Defendant ſhall never take any Challenge for that Cauſe, and ſo in like Caſes. But
on the Part of the Defendant, any ſuch Matter
ſhall not be alledged, and Proceſs prayed to the
Coroners, becauſe he may challenge the Jury
for that Cauſe, and can be at no Prejudice.

Challenge concluding to the Favour, when Challenge to
either Party cannot take any principal Challenge, the Favour.
but ſheweth Cauſes of Favour, muſt be left to *Ibid.*
the Conſcience and Diſcretion of the Triors,
upon hearing their Evidence, to find him favourable, or not favourable. But yet ſome of
them come nearer to principal Challenges than
other; as if the Juror be of Kindred, or under
the Diſtreſs of him in the Reverſion or Remain-

der, or in whofe Right the Avowry or Juftification is made, or the like: Thefe be principal
Challenges, becaufe he in Reverfion, Remainder, or in whofe Right the Avowry or Juftification is, is not Party to the Record; otherwife it is, if they were made Parties by Aid,
Receipt or Voucher, and yet the Caufe of Favour is apparent; fo it is of all principal Caufes,

Favour.   if they were Party to the Record.   Now the
Caufes of Favour are infinite, and thereof fomewhat may be gathered of that which hath been
faid, and the reft I purpofely leave the Reader
to the Reading of in our Books concerning that
Matter.   For all which the Rule of Law is,
That he muft ftand indifferent, as he ftands un-
fworn.

King.   The Subject may challenge the Polls, where
Ibid.   the King is Party.   And if a Man be outlawed
of Treafon or Felony at the Suit of the King,
and the Party for avoiding thereof alledgeth Imprifonment, or the like, at the Time of the
Outlawry, though the Iffue be joined upon a
collateral Point, yet fhall the Party have fuch
Challenges, as if he had been arraigned upon
the Crime itfelf, for this by a Mean concerneth
his Life alfo.

Challenges   *Propter delictum :* As if the Juror be attain-
propter delict.
1 Inft. 158. ted or convicted of Treafon or Felony, or for
any Offence to Life or Member, or in Attaint
for a falfe Verdict, or for Perjury as a Witnefs,
or in a Confpiracy at the Suit of the King, or
in any Suit (either for the King or for any Subject) be adjudged to the Pillory, Tumbrel, or
the like, or to be branded, or to be ftigmati-
zed, to have any other corporal Punifhment,
Infamous. whereby he becometh infamous, (for it is a
Maxim in Law, *Repellitur a facramento infamus*);

thefe

thefe and the like are principal Caufes of Challenge. So it is if a Man be outlawed in Tref- *Outlawed.*
pafs, Debr, or any other Action, for he is
Exlex, and therefore is not *legalis homo*. And
old Books have faid, That if he be excommunicate, he could not be of a Jury.

A Baftard may be of a Jury, yet may be *Baftard.*
challenged if he be of Kindred. *Jenk. Cent.* 1.
cap. 90.

See the Statutes of *W.* 2. and *Artic. fupra Who ought to*
Chartas, what Perfons the Sheriff ought to re- *be on Juries.*
turn on Juries. And fee *F. N. B. breve de non* *1 Inft.* 158.
ponendis in Affifis & juratis; and the Regifter
in the fame Writ. And fee there what Remedy the Party hath that is returned againft Law.

It is neceffary to be known, the Time when *Ibid.*
the Challenge is to be taken. Firft, he that hath *At what Time*
divers Challenges muft take them all at once, *Challenges*
and the Law fo requireth indifferent Trials, that *muft be taken.*
divers Challenges are not accounted double. Secondly, If one be challenged by one Party, if
after he be tried indifferent, it is Time enough
for the other Party to challenge him. Thirdly,
After Challenge to the Array, and Trial duly
returned, if the fame Party take a Challenge to
the Polls, he muft fhew Caufe prefently. Fourthly,
So if a Juror be formerly fworn, if he be challenged, he muft fhew Caufe prefently, and that
Caufe muft rife fince he was fworn. Fifthly,
When the King is Party, or in an Appeal of
Felony, the Defendant that challengeth for
Caufe, muft fhew his Caufe prefently Sixthly,
if a Man, in Cafe of Treafon or Felony, challenge for Caufe, and he be tried indifferent, yet
he may challenge him peremptorily. Seventhly, A Challenge for the Hundred muft be taken *Hundredors.*

O 3 before

before so many be sworn as will serve for Hundredors, or else he loseth the Advantage thereof.

Writ of Right.
Ibid.

In a Writ of Right, the Grand Jury must be challenged before the four Knights, before they be returned in Court; for after they be returned into Court, there cannot any challenge be taken upon them.

The Array of the *Tales*.
Ibid.

Nota; The Array of the *Tales* shall not be challenged by any one Party, until the Array of the principal be tried; but if the Plaintiff challenge the Array of the Principal, the Defendant may challenge the Array of the *Tales*. After one hath taken Challenge to the Polls, he cannot challenge the Array.

Ibid.

Now it is to be seen how Challenge to the Array of the principal Panel, or of the *Tales*, or of the Polls shall be tried, and who shall be Triors of the same, and to whom Process shall be awarded.

Ibid.

Coroners.

Elisors.

If the Plaintiff alledge a Cause of Challenge against the Sheriff, the Process shall be directed to the Coroners; if any Cause against any of the Coroners, Process shall be awarded to the rest; if against all of them, then the Court shall appoint certian *Elisors* or *Eslisors*, (so named *ab eligendo*) because they are named by the Court, against whose Return no Challenge shall be taken to the Array, because they were appointed by the Court, but he may have his Challenge to the Polls. *Note*; If Process be once awarded for the Partiality of the Sheriff, though there be a new Sheriff, yet Process shall never be awarded to him; for the Entry is, *Ita quod Vicecomes se non intromittat.* But otherwise it is, for that he was Tenant to either Party, or the like.

Ibid.
Array.

If the Array be challenged in Court, it shall be tried by two of them that be impanelled, to

2   be

be appointed by the Court; for the Triors in that Case, shall not exceed the Number of two, unless it be by Consent. But when the Court names two, for some special Cause alledged by either Party, the Court may Name others; if the Array be quashed, then Process shall be awarded *ut supra*. If there be a Demurrer to a Challenge, the Judge before whom the Cause is to be tried, may determine it, or adjourn it to be heard another Time. *Style* 464. *Vide Bulstr.* 1 Part 114.

Two Triors.

Demurrer to a Challenge, how determinable.

If a Panel upon a *Venire facias* be returned, and a *Tales*, and the Array of the Principal is challenged, the Triors which try and quash the Array, shall not try the Array of the *Tales*; for now it is, as if there had been no Appearance of the principal Panel; but if the Triors affirm the Array of the Principal, then they shall try the Array of the *Tales*. If the Plaintiff challenge the Array of the Principal, and the Defendant the Array of the *Tales*, there the one of the Principal, and the other of the *Tales*, shall try both Arrays. For other Matter concerning the *Tales*, see in *Coke's* Reports, Matters worthy of Observation. When any Challenge is made to the Polls, two Triors shall be appointed by the Court; and if they try one indifferent, and he be sworn, then he and the two Triors shall try another; and if another be tried indifferent, and he be sworn, then the two Triors cease, and the two that be sworn on the Jury shall try the rest.

Array of the Principal and *Tales*.
1 Inst. 158.

1 Inst. 158.
Two Triors.

If any of the Jury, after some of them be sworn, be challenged, those that are sworn are to say, whether he that is challenged be indifferent or not. But if the first or second Man be challenged, then the Court doth use to appoint

Trials of Challenges.

O 4   some

fome of them, (whom it pleafeth) that fhall be afterwards fworn to try the Indifferency of the Perfon challenged.

Rules concerning Challenges.

1. All Challenges muft be taken before the Jurors are fworn.

2. If one challenge a Juror, and it be found againft the Challenger, he may not challenge the Juror for a fecond Caufe.

3. If one challenge the Array, and it be found againft him, he may not afterward challenge any of the Polls, without fhewing Caufe prefently; and this fhall be tried prefently.

4. No Challenge fhall be admitted againft the Triors appointed by the Court.

Trial of Challenges.
1 Inft. 158.

If the Plaintiff challenge ten, and the Defendant one, and the twelfth is fworn, becaufe one cannot try alone, there fhall be added to him one challenged by the Plaintiff, and the other by the Defendant. When the Trial is to be had by two Counties, the Manner of the Trial is worthy of Obfervation, and apparent in our Books. If the four Knights in the Writ of Right be challenged, they fhall try themfelves, and they fhall chufe the Grand Affize, and try the Challenges of the Parties. If the Caufe of Challenges touch the Difhonour or Difcredit of

Juror examined.

the Juror, he fhall not be examined upon his Oath, to inform the Triors. If an Inqueft be awarded by Default, the Defendant hath loft his Challenge; but the Plaintiff may challenge for juft Caufe, and that fhall be examined and tried.

View.
1 Inft. 158. b.

Wherefoever the Plaintiff is to recover *per vifum juratorum,* there ought to be fix of the Jury that have had the View, or known the Land in Queftion, fo as he be able to put the Plaintiff in Poffeffion, if he recover.

Trail

Trait doth fignify the fame as taken out or *Trait, what.* withdrawn, and is applied to a Juror, that is withdrawn by Confent, or removed and difcharged by Challenge.

A Juror fick was withdrawn, and another fworn. *Palmer's Rep.* 411.

After Evidence given, the King cannot draw *King.* a Juror, but before he may; but after Evidence on his Prayer, the Court may difcharge the Jury. *Keb.* 2 Part 506.

If the Defendant do not appear at the Trial *Challenge loft.* when he is called, he lofeth his challenge to the Jurors, although he doth afterwards appear.

'Tis a good Challenge to a Juror to fay, he *A wrong* is returned by another Name in the Panel.   *Name.*

A Juror appeared, and faid he had no Free- *No Freehold.* hold, and prayed that he might not ferve, yet the Judge would not fpare him, for he may have an Action againft the Sheriff for returning him. *Roll.* 2 Part, *Reports* 483.

The Challenge *pro defectu Hundred.* muft be written in Parchment, and the Counfel muft arraign it in *French,* upon which the Defendant may take Iffue or Demur. The Clerk or Affociate in Court muft call the Jury over, and afk if they have any Lands within the Hundred, or had at the Time of the Array of the Panel, and whether they dwell, or did dwell in the fame. And upon Examination, if 'it appear clearly, that they have no Lands or Tenements, nor dwell in the Hundred; then the Clerk is to mark them by the Side of every of their Names thus, [*præter Hundred.*] but if he find there be too few Hundredors, he is to refort back to the *præter Hundred.* and fwear them in order. So that you fee the Trial whether Hundredors or not, is determined by the Court's Examination

by

by the Poll feverally. But if the Counfel demur, and the other Side join in Demurrer, the Judge of Affizes may affirm the Challenge, and over-rule the Demurrer, or allow the Demurrer good, and proceed to the Trial of the Caufe; or if the Judge doubt, it may be determined in Bank; but this is great Delay. If the Challenge be adjudged Good, the Court awards, *Que le panel il foit caffe*, i. e. that the Panel be quaſhed.

In Cities, Cor-porations, Bo-roughs and Towns, and Counties, this Challenge cannot be.　At Common Law there ought to have been four Hundredors returned and appear in all Ac-tions, *pro meliori notitia caufæ in controverfia*, for *vicini vicinorum faſta melius fcire præfumuntur*. But by the Statute 35 *H.* 8. *cap.* 6. fix are to be re-turned and appear. But fince, by the Statute 27 *Eliz. cap.* 6. if two Hundredors be returned and appear, it is fufficient in all perfonal Actions: But in real Actions there muft be fix, or elfe *Remanet pro defeſtu Jur'*.

Hundredors.　*Note*; In an Information of Forgery to be tried at Bar, upon the Attorney General's Mo-tion, that the Defandant might not challenge for want of Hundredors; (*a*) it was denied him. *Keb.* 3 Part 740.

The Court fhall appoint two Triors in a Challenge to the Poll, and if they find two in-different, the firft Triors fhall be difcharged; and the two that are found indifferent, being fworn to try the Iffue, fhall alfo be fworn to try the reft of their Fellows. 1 *Inft.* 158.

At Common Law there ufed to be returned twenty-four upon the *Venire*, and afterwards a *Habeas Corpora* with a *Decem Tales*; and if a full Jury did not appear or were challenged, then

(*a*) Challenging for want of Hundredors, or contrary to the Special Jury Rule, a Contempt. *Str.* 593.

a *Di-*

a *Distringas* with an *Octo Tales*, and so to the
Duo Tales, if there were not a full Jury.   And
this was the Course until the Statute 35 *H.* 8.
which gives the *Tales de Circumstantibus* at the
Assizes, &c. and by the Statute 5 *Phil.* & *Mar.*
cap. 7. where the King, Queen or Informer, &c.
are Parties.

Tales de Circumstantibus may be in the Case of Aliens.

A Challenge may be taken to those of the
Tales de Circumstantibus.

The King, or any one authorized for him,
may release his Challenge.   Where the Party
may challenge, the King may challenge.

'Tis no Challenge to say, the Juror is the
King's Tenant, or that he is favourable to the
King; but it is good to say, the Sheriff or Juror bears Grudge or Malice to the Defendant
where the King is Party.   If the Juror hath
any Freehold 'tis sufficient, although not to 40 *s.*
a Year: For the Statute which injoins that,
speaks only betwixt Party and Party.

The first who challenges, be he Plaintiff or
Defendant, shall have the Preference and Advantage of his Challenge.   If a Juror be once
challenged and withdrawn upon the Principal,
he cannot serve upon the *Tales*; if he doth, 'tis
Error, and Judgment may be stayed; and so if
he be challenged, and a Jury remain *pro defectu
Juratorum*, if he be sworn upon a new *Distringas*, 'tis Error, not helped by any Statute of
Jeofails, and a Mis-trial, and a *Venire facias de
novo* may be awarded. *Cro. Eliz.* f. 429. *Whit-
by*'s Case.

Eslisors may be sworn in some Cases to return
and impanel all Juries, as should upon any *Venire facias, Habeas Corpora*, or *Distringas Jur.*
come to their Hands, impartially, indifferently,
                                    and

and without Favour or Affection, nor at the Denomination of any Person.

In High Treason the Prisoner may peremptorily challenge to the Number of thirty-five, which is under the Number of three Juries; but in Petit Treason, Murder or Felony, the Number is reduced to twenty. The Prisoner may challenge any that are Witnesses against him.

Where the King is Party, the Defendant must shew the Cause of his Challenge instantly.

After a Challenge for Cause, the Prisoner may challenge the same Person peremptorily.

Grand Jury. One of the Petty Jury was challenged, because he had been of the Grand Jury, and found the Bill. *Siderfin* 244. 'Tis a good Challenge.

Prosecutor entertained by a Juror, Cause of Challenge. In an Information of Forgery, the Defendant challenged one of the Jury, for that the Prosecutor had been lately entertained at his House: This was admitted to the Favour, though against

Challenge by the King without shewing Cause. the King. And then the Counsel for the King challenged another, and were pressed to alledge the Cause, for 33 *Ed.* 1. takes away the general Challenge; but the Court (save *Wylde,* who seemed to be of another Opinion) ordered the Panel to be first gone through, and if there were enough, the King is not to shew any Cause. 1 *Vent.* 309. *T. Raym.* 473, 4.

Jurors found others guilty in the same Indictment: No Cause of Challenge. The Jurors were challenged by the Prisoners, because they had already given a Verdict, and found others guilty, who were indicted in the same Indictment: But held to be no Cause of Challenge. *Kelynge* 9.

One challenged thirty-six and adjudged to be hanged. One was arraigned of Felony, who challenged thirty-six peremptorily; and adjudged to be hanged, and not pressed to Death. *Kelynge* 36.

Upon

Upon a Trial at Bar, *Trin.* 1 *W. & M.* the Queftion was, Whether the Fair called *Waybill* Fair, fhould be kept at *Waybill*, or at *Anderry?* And one of the Jury was challenged, becaufe he lived at *Waybill:* This being a Challenge to the Favour, two of the Jurors were fworn to be Triors, and their Oath was, *You fhall well and truly try whether* A. *(the Juryman challenged) ftand indifferent between the Parties to this Iffue.* Salkeld 144.

Cook being indicted for High Treafon, and the Jury called, he offered to ask the Jurors, in order to challenge them, if they had not faid he was guilty, or would be hanged? *Et per Cur*, this is a good Caufe of Challenge, but then the Prifoner muft prove it by Witneffes, and not out of the Mouth of the Juryman: A Juryman may be asked upon a *Voir (a) dire, (b)* whether he hath any Intereft in the Caufe, or whether he hath a Freehold, *&c.* For thefe do not make him criminal; but you fhall not afk a Witnefs, or a Juryman, Whether he hath been whipped for Larceny, or convict of Felony? Or whether he was ever committed to *Bridewell, &c.* becaufe that would make a Man difcover that of himfelf which tends to make him

---

(a) Voire, a *French* Word fignifying truly.

(b) Voire dire, (Fr. *Veritatem dicere*) is when it is prayed upon a Trial at Law, that a Witnefs may be fworn upon a *Voire dire*; which is, that he fhall on his Oath fpeak the *Truth*, whether he fhall gain or lofe by the Matter in Controverfy; and if it appears that he is unconcerned, his Teftimony is allowed, otherwife not. On a *Voire dire*, a Witnefs may be examined by the Court, if he be not a Party interefted in the Caufe, as well as the Perfon for whom he is Witnefs; and this has been often done, where a bufy Evidence, not otherwife to be excepted againft, is fufpected of Partiality.

infamous;

infamous; and in this Cafe the Anfwer might charge him with a Mifdemeanor. *Et per Powel* Juftice: In a Civil Caufe, you may perhaps ask a Man if he has not given his Opinion before-hand upon the Right? For he might have done that as Arbitrator between the Parties. *Salkeld* 153.

It was held, that a Challenge to the Array is no Part of the Record, and ought to be determined whether good or bad by the Judge who fhould have tried the Caufe, if the Challenge had not been taken; and has been fo held in *B. C.* It was alfo faid, That if a Demurrer be to a Challenge at the Affifes, the Judge of Affife may determine it there, or adjourn it to be heard another Time. *Style* 464.

Precedents, containing the Forms of Challenges to the Array, *&c.* And the Proceedings thereupon. Pleas *Puis le Darrein Continuance*; Bills of Exception, *&c.*

A Challenge to the Array, becaufe the Sheriff is Coufin to one of the Defendants.

AND now here at this Day came, as well the faid *Henry Vernon,* the now Demandant, as the faid *John Manners, &c.* by their Attornies aforefaid; and the Jury thereupon impanelled being called likewife came: And thereupon the faid *Henry Vernon* challenges the
Array

Array of the Panel aforesaid; because he saith, that that Panel was arrayed by one Sir *John Zouch*, Knight, now, and at the Time of making the said Array, Sheriff of the said County of *Derby*, which said Sheriff is the Cousin of the said *John Manners*; to wit, the Son of *George Zouch*, Esq; the Son of Sir *John Zouch*, Knight, the Son of *John Zouch*, Esq; the Son of *John Zouch*, Esq; the Son of *William* Lord *Zouch*, the Son of *Allen* Lord *Zouch*, the Son of *William* Lord *Zouch*, the Son of *Elizabeth* the Daughter of *William* Lord *Roos*, the Father of *Thomas* Lord *Roos*, the Father of *Thomas* Lord *Roos*, the Father of *Eleanor* the Mother of Sir *George Manners*, Knight, the Father of *Thomas* Earl of *Rutland*, the Father of the said *John Manners*. And this the said *Henry* is ready to verify. Wherefore he prays Judgment, and that the said Panel may be quashed. *Coke*'s Entries 340. *c.*

A Suggestion on the Roll by the Plaintiff, that the Sheriff is Tenant to the Plaintiff.

And thereupon the said *John* Lord *St. John* says, That *John Dyve*, Esq; is now Sheriff of the said County; and that the said *John Dyve* holds twelve Acres of Meadow, with the Appurtenances in *Budenham* in the County aforesaid, of the said *John* Lord *St. John*, at will, by the Rent of forty Shillings, to be paid to the said *John* Lord *St. John* yearly; and for that Cause, he prays a Writ of our Sovereign Lord the King, to cause to come twelve, &c. to try the said Issue above joined, to be directed to the *Coroners* of our said Lord the King, of
the

the faid County.   Whereupon the faid *Thomas*
(the Defendant) fays, That the faid *John Dyve*
doth not hold the faid twelve Acres of Meadow,
with the Appurtenances, or any Part thereof,
of the faid *John* Lord *St. John*, at will, as the
faid *John* Lord *St. John* hath above alledged.
Therefore, notwithftanding the aforefaid Challenge of the faid *John* Lord *St. John* to the faid
Sheriff, it is commanded the faid Sheriff, that,
&c.   Coke's Entries 397. *a.*

A Precedent of a Challenge for Default of Hun-dredors.

And thereupon the faid *A. B.* by *C. D.* his
Attorney, comes and challenges the Array of
the Panel aforefaid; becaufe he faith, That the
Vill of *Dale* in the County aforefaid, in which
the faid Caufe of Action arifes, and is laid in
the faid Declaration to arife, at the Time of
making the faid Array, was, and now is within
the Hundred of *Downs*, in the County aforefaid;
and that the prefent Sheriff of the County aforefaid, hath not returned or impanelled any Hundredors of the Hundred of *Downs* aforefaid, to
try the Iffue now joined between the faid Parties; neither have the Jury now impanelled and
returned, or any of them, nor had they, or any
of them at the Time of making the faid Array,
or at any Time fince, any Lands or Tenements
within the faid Hundred of *Downs*; neither do
the faid Jury, or any of them now, nor did they,
or any of them at the Time of making the faid
Array, dwell or inhabit within the faid Hundred.   And this the faid *A. B.* is ready to verify.

rify. Wherefore he prays Judgment, and that the said Panel may be quashed.

This must be under Council's Hand, and the Proceedings herein you may read before; if they demur, thus,

Moratur in Lege
W. T.
Joinder in Demurrer
G. D.

A Challenge by the Defendant, because the Sheriff is Cousin to the Lessor of the Plaintiff.

And thereupon the said Defendant, by *A. B.* his Attorney, comes and *challenges* the Array of the Panel aforesaid; because he saith, That that Panel was made and arrayed by *C. D.* Esq; now, and at the Time of making the Array of the said Panel, Sheriff of the County aforesaid; which said Sheriff is the *Cousin* of *E. F.* Gentleman, the Lessor of the Plaintiff named in the said Declaration, To wit, The Son of *G. H.* the Son of *K. L.* the Daughter of *M. N.* the Son of *O. P.* the Father of *Q. R.* the Mother of the said *E. F.* the Lessor of the said Plaintiff named in the said Declaration. And this the said Defendant is ready to verify. Wherefore he prays Judgment, and that the said Panel may be quashed, *&c.*

If the Plaintiff deny the Kindred and Affinity, then thus,

Nient Cousin par le manner
W. T.
est Cousin
G. D.

Then are two or more Triors sworn, but seldom more than two, and (after they have heard the Proofs and Evidence given to make good the Defendant's Plea) they give their Verdict accordingly.

Note; *The Plaintiff may, if he please, demur upon the Challenge.*

A Challenge to the Array by a Peer, because no Knight was returned upon the Jury; and a Demurrer to the same, and Joinder in Demurrer.

And thereupon the said Earl *challenges* the Array of the Panel of the said Affize; becaufe he faith, That he now is, and at the Time of fuing out the faid Writ of Affife, and long before, was one of the Nobles and Peers of this Realm, having a Seat and a Vote in every Parliament of the faid Realm; and that the Array of the Panel of the faid Affife was arrayed by *T. O.* and *W. H.* late Sheriff of the faid County of *Middlefex*, no *Knight* being named or returned in the faid Panel of that Array, as there ought to have been according to the Law of this Realm. And this he is ready to verify. Wherefore he prays Judgment, and that the Panel may be quafhed.

And the faid *J. N.* fays, That the faid Challenge of the faid Earl above made by the faid Earl to the Array of the Panel of the faid Affife, is not fufficient in Law to quafh the Array of the faid Panel; and that by the Law of the Land he is not bound to anfwer to the faid Challenge in Manner and Form aforefaid alledged. And this he is ready to verify. Wherefore he prays
Judgment,

Judgment, and that the Array of that Panel may be affirmed.

And the said Earl, for as much as he hath alledged a sufficient Challenge to quash the Array of the said Panel, which he is ready to verify; which said Challenge the said *J. N.* hath not denied, neither doth he any ways answer thereto, prays Judgment, and that the Array of the Panel of that Assise may be quashed. *Plowd.* 117. and Judgment was given to quash the Panel.

A Challenge to the Array, because returned at the Denomination of the Plaintiff.

And thereupon the said *A. B.* by *C. D.* his Attorney, comes and *challenges* the Array of the said Panel; because he saith, That that Panel was made and arrayed by *E. F.* the present Sheriff of the said County and his Officers, at the *Denomination* and Instance of the said Plaintiff, in Favour of the said Plaintiff. And this he is ready to verify. Wherefore he prays Judgment, and that that Panel may be quashed, &c.

To which the Plaintiff may plead, that the Array of the Panel was well and equally made and arrayed by the said Sheriff and his Officers, according to the Duty of his Office.

Or the Plaintiff, if he will, may confess it; but if he plead, then the Judges immediately assign Triors to try the Array, which seldom exceed two, who being chose and sworn, the Associate or Clerk in Court doth declare and rehearse unto them

the

the Matter and Caufe of the Challenge, and after he hath fo done, concludes to them thus. And fo your Charge is to inquire whether it be an even and impartial Array, or a favourable one: *And if they affirm it, then the Clerk enters underneath the Challenge,*

Affirmatur.

But if the Triors find it favourable, then thus;

Calumpnia vera.

A Challenge becaufe the Caufe of Action arofe within an Hundred, of which the Plaintiff is Lord, and praying a Writ to the next Hundred.

And thereupon the faid *A.* faith, That the faid Vill of *Dale*, in which the faid Trefpafs was done, is within the Hundred of *B.* and that he is Lord of the faid Hundred ; and that all the Freeholders within the faid Hundred are within the *Diftrefs* of the faid *A.* and for that Reafon he prays a Writ of our faid Lord the King to caufe to come, *&c.* to try the faid Iffue from the next *Neighbourhood* in the faid County, out of the *Hundred* next adjoining to the faid Vill of *Dale*, to be directed to the Sheriff of the faid County; and becaufe the Defendant doth not deny this, it is granted to him; therefore it is commanded, *&c.*

A Chal-

A Challenge becauſe the Sheriff and two of the Co-
roners are Tenants of the Plaintiff, and a Ve-
nire prayed to the other Coroners.

And thereupon the ſaid *A. B.* ſaith, That as
well *C. D.* Knight, Sheriff of the ſaid County,
as *E. F.* and *G. H.* two of the Coroners of the
ſaid County, are Tenants of the ſaid Plaintiff,
and within his *Diſtreſs*; and for that Reaſon
he prays a Writ of our ſaid Lord the King to
cauſe to come, *&c.* to be directed to *E. A.*
and *R. P.* the reſt of the Coroners of our ſaid
Lord the King in the ſaid County; and becauſe
the ſaid Defendant doth not deny the ſame, it is
granted to him, *&c.*

A Challenge, becauſe after the laſt Continuance the
Couſin of the Plaintiff is made Sheriff.

At which Day here came the ſaid Parties, *&c.*
the Sheriff did not return the Writ. And there-
upon the ſaid Plaintiff faith, that *after the laſt*
Continuance of the ſaid Plea, to wit, after the
Octaves of St. *Martin* laſt paſt, from which
Day the ſaid Plaint was continued here until this
Day, to wit, *ſuch a Day* laſt paſt, the preſent
King by his Letters Patent did grant the Cu-
ſtody of the ſaid County to Sir *A. B.* Knight; by
Virtue of which Letters Patent the ſaid *A. B.*
is now Sheriff of the ſaid County; which ſaid
A. B. is the Couſin of the ſaid Plaintiff, to wit,
the Son, *&c.* And for that Reaſon he prays a
Writ, *&c.* to be directed to the Coroners of
our ſaid Lord the King, of the ſaid County,
&c.

P 3   *A Chal-*

A Challenge becaufe the Sheriff is of Council with the Plaintiff, and hath a Salary.

And thereupon the faid Plaintiff faith, That *A. B.* is now Sheriff of the faid County ; which faid *A. B.* is one of the Council of the faid Plaintiff, and hath of him the yearly Rent or Fee of 20*l.* and for that Caufe he prays a Writ, *&c.* to be directed to the Coroners, *&c.* And becaufe the faid Defendant denies this, therefore, notwithftanding the faid Allegation of the faid Plaintiff, the Sheriff is commanded, *&c.*

A Challenge, where the Plaintiff is Sheriff, and one of the Coroners his Tenant.

And thereupon the faid Plaintiff faith, That he is now Sheriff of the faid County ; and that there are in the faid County two Coroners, to wit, *R. H.* and *R. D.* and that *R. H.* one of the faid Coroners, holds of him one Meffuage, *&c.* at the yearly Rent of, *&c.* And for thefe Reafons he prays a Writ, *&c.* to be directed to the faid *R. D.* the other Coroner of the faid County, *&c.*

A Challenge, becaufe the Plaintiff is one of the Sheriffs of London, *and a* Ven. fac. *awarded to the other Sheriff alone.*

And thereupon the faid Plaintiff faith, That he and one Sir *John Blunt,* Knight, are Sheriffs of *London;* and becaufe he is one of the Sheriffs of *London,* he prays that a Writ, *&c.* may be directed to the faid Sir *John Blunt,* the other Sheriff,

Sheriff, only, &c. And the said Defendant was asked if he could say any Thing why the said Process should not be directed to the said Sir *J. B.* the other Sheriff alone; who said that he could not. Therefore it was commanded the said Sir *J. B.* that he should cause to come, &c. so that the said Plaintiff should in no wise intermeddle therewith.

A Challenge because the Panel was made by the Under-Sheriff, at the Denomination of the Plaintiff.

And thereupon the said Defendant challenges the Array of the Panel of the said Jury, because he saith, That that Panel was made and arrayed by *T. W.* Under-Sheriff of the said County, at the Denomination of the said Plaintiff, in Favour of the said Plaintiff. And this he is ready to verify, &c.

Mich. 23 & 24 *Eliz. Rot.* 109. Therefore came thereupon the Jury before our Lady the Queen at *Westminster*, the Day, &c. who neither, &c. to recognize, &c. because as well, &c. The same Day is given to the said Parties there, &c. At which Day, before the said Queen at *Westminster*, came the said Parties by their said Attornies, and the Sheriff sent not the Writ; and upon this, the same Plaintiff saith, That *after the last Continuance* of the said Plea, that is to say, after the *Saturday* next after, &c. now last past; from which Day the said Plaintiff was continued here until this Day, that is to say, the Day, &c. *R. P.* Esq; late Sheriff of the said County of *E.* from the same Office

Entry of a Challenge after Issue joined, where the Sheriff is a-moved, &c.

Between Barkley and Jefferson,

of

of Sheriff of that County was duly *amoved*; and the said Queen now by her Letters Patent, hath committed unto one *T. P.* Knight, the Custody of the said County of *E.* by Pretence of which said Letters Patent the said *T. P.* now remaineth Sheriff of that County, which said *T. P.* of *A.* at *A.* aforesaid took his Wife *Anne*, of the Blood of *M.* now the Wife of him the Plaintiff; that is to say, the Daughter of *R. D.* the Son of *W. D.* Knight, Father of *Anne*, Mother of the said *M.* now Wife of him the Plaintiff; which said *T. P.* Knight, and *A.* had Issue between them *A. P.* yet alive, and in full Life remaining, at *A.* aforesaid; and this he is ready to prove, *&c.* And for that Cause he prayeth a Writ of our Lady the now Queen, of *Venire facias*, to try the said Issue in Form aforesaid joined, to be directed to the Coroners of the said County; and

Challenge gainsaid. because the said Defendant doth gainsay, and doth not grant that to be true; therefore, notwithstanding the same Challenge, a Command is to the Sheriff, that he make to come twelve, *&c.* of the *Visne* of *B.* by whom, *&c.*

Challenge to the Array, because the Coroners made the Panel at the Denomination of the Plaintiff. *Easter* Term 38 *H.* 8. *Rot.* 558. And hereupon the Defendant doth challenge the Array of the Panel of the said Jury, because he saith, That that Panel was made and arrayed by *A.* and *C. Coroners* of the said County, at the *Denomination*, and in Favour of the said Plaintiff; and this he is ready to verify, and requesteth that the same Panel may be quashed. And the said Plaintiff saith, That the said Panel by the said Coroners was well and equally made; and not at the Denomination, or in Favour, nor in Promotion of the said Plaintiff; whereupon the said Justices, by the Consent of the said Parties, did chuse and assign *D.* and *E.* two of the said Jury now

now appearing, to try the said Challenge; which said Triors being elected and tried, say upon their Oaths, that the said Panel was well and faithfully made and arrayed by the said Coroners, and not at the Denomination, neither in Favour, nor in Promotion of the said Plaintiff; whereupon the Jurors of the said Jury being called, tried and sworn, say, &c.

A Precedent of a Plea after the last Continuance.

And now at this Day, &c. comes such a one Defendant, by *J. C.* his Counsel, and saith, This Action the Plaintiff against the Defendant ought not to maintain; for that after the *Quinden'* of the Holy *Trinity* last past, from which Day, until such a Day in *Michaelmas* Term next, unless the Justices of Assizes come before such a Day, &c. the Action aforesaid is continued, &c. the Plaintiff by his Deed dated, &c. did release, &c. and shew, &c. the Matter what it is, whether in Abatement, in Bar dilatory, or peremptory, as the Case is, &c. and this he is ready to aver. *To this Plea must be annexed an Affidavit of the due Execution of the Deed, Release,* &c.

Note; *Brook* in his *Abridgment*, Tit. *Continuance*, 61 and 83, says, That after the Inquest is awarded to inquire of Damages, the Defendant cannot plead a Plea *Puis le darrein Continuance*, because he hath no Day in Court to plead.

The Day of *Nisi prius* and Day in Bank are all one; so that a Release made betwixt these Days cannot be pleaded in Bank; but it seems that a Release made between the Day of the *Venire facias* returned, and the Writ of *Nisi prius* awarded,

Of a Release.

awarded, and the Day of the *Nifi prius*, may be pleaded at the Day of the *Nifi prius*, but not after the Verdict. 21 *H.* 6. f. 10. *Bro.* Tit. *Juror*, &c. 31. Tit. *Continuance*, 76, 42, 27, 13.

A Man fhall have but *one Plea* after the laft Continuance; for the Plaintiff fhall not be delayed *ad infinitum.* 16 *H.* 7. 11. *Bro.* Tit. *Continuance*, 59, 41, 45, 46, 5, 21.

After the Inqueft taken by Default, and before Judgment, the Defendant came and pleaded an Arbitrament made after the laft Continuance; and by the Opinion of the Court, he had no Day in Court to plead this Plea; and it was faid, that he could plead no Plea in fuch Cafe, but as *Amicus Curiæ*, and of Matter apparent, he fhall be received; otherwife he muft refort to his *Audita Querela.* 21 *H.* 7. 33. *Brook, ibid.* 38.

But if the Jury remain for Default of Jurors, the Defendant may plead a Releafe, &c. at the Day in Bank *Puis le darrein Continuance*, although he did not offer it at the *Nifi prius*; otherwife if the Jury had been taken at the *Nifi prius.* 22 *H.* 6. 1. *Brook, ibid.* 30.

If it be pleaded at the *Nifi prius*, the Court may record the Plea, and difcharge the Inqueft, and give Day to the Parties in Bank. *Ibid.* 34. 8.

In Debt after Iffue joined, the Defendant at the *Nifi prius* pleaded Payment of Part after the latter Continuance in Abatement.   And the Jury being difcharged, and the Plea adjourned in Bank, for that no Place of Payment was pleaded, the Plaintiff had Judgment to recover his Debt, becaufe after Iffue joined, no *Refpondeas oufter* can be awarded. *L.* 5 *E.* 4. 139. *Aleyn's Rep.* 69. in the Cafe of *Beaton* and *Foreft.*

If

If after a Plea in Bar the Defendant pleads a Plea *Puis darrein Continuance*, that is a Waver of his Bar; and no Advantage shall be taken of any Thing in the Bar.   1 *Salk.* 178.

One may plead *Puis darrein Continuance*, that the Plaintiff brought a second Action for the same Cause, and recovered; though he might have pleaded the former in Abatement of the second Action.   *Per Holt* C. J. *Comberb.* 357.

To an Action brought by an Administrator *de bonis non cum testamento annexo*, during the Minority of *R. W.* it is a good Plea for the Defendant, *Puis darrein Continuance*, that *R. W. puis darrein Continuance*, had attained the Age of twenty-one Years; for by that the Administrator's Power is determined, and of Consequence the Action also.   1 *Lutw.* 342.

A ⌈Release pleaded *puis darrein Continuance* must be pleaded in Bar, and pray Judgment if the Plaintiff ought further to have or maintain his said Action; being this is a Collateral Matter that happened since the Action was brought, and thereby the Defendant admits that the Action was well brought at first; but that by reason of this new Matter the Plaintiff ought not to proceed any further.   2 *Lutw.* 1143.

Now, although, when Difficulty arises in the Evidence, the Matter is most commonly (of late) found specially, and Demurrers on the Evidence are seldom used; yet inasmuch as it is sometimes done, and that our Practiser may be prepared with an Authentick Precedent for that Purpose, I shall transcribe one out of *Coke's Entries, f.* 134. *viz.*

Afterwards, at the Day and Place within named, before Sir *James Dyer*, Knight, Chief Justice, Demurrer on the Evidence.

Juſtce, &c. and *N. B.* Juſtices of our ſaid Lady
the Queen, aſſigned accordng to the Form of
the Statute, &c. to hold the Aſſizes in the
County of *Northampton*, &c. came, as well the
within named *J. A.* as he within written *H. C.*
by their ſaid Attornies. And the Jurors of the
Jury within mentioned being called likewiſe
came; who were elected, tried and ſworn to
ſpeak the Truth concerning the Premiſſes.
Whereupon the ſaid *H.* by *J. B.* his Council,
in order to maintain the Iſſue within joined, gave
in Evidence to the ſaid Jury before the ſaid
Juſtices, That (*here inſert the Evidence* verba-
tim.)And ſo the ſaid *H.* ſaith that, &c. as he
hath within in his Plea alledged: Wherefore he
prays Judgment; and that the ſaid Jurors may
give their Verdict of and concerning the Matters within contained for the ſaid *H.*

And the ſaid *J. A.* by *C. Y.* his Council ſaith,
That the Matter aforeſaid by the ſaid *H.* above
given in Evidence to the ſaid Jury, is not ſufficient to prove the Iſſue above joined on the
Part of the ſaid *H.* And that he to the ſaid
Matter ſo given in Evidence in the Form aforeſaid, is not bound by the Law of the Land to
anſwer: And this he is ready to verify. Wherefore for want of ſufficient Matter ſhewn to the
ſaid Jury in that Behalf, the ſaid *J. A.* prays
Judgment, and that the Jurors aforeſaid may be
diſcharged from giving their Verdict on the ſaid
Iſſue, and that his Debt within mentioned, together with his Damages by reaſon of the de-
taining that Debt, may be adjudged to him.

And the ſaid *H.* ſince he hath above given in
Evidence to the ſaid Jury, ſufficient Matter in
Law to maintain the Iſſue within mentioned on
the

the Part of the faid *H.* which he is ready to verify, which faid Matter the faid *J.* hath not denied, nor any wife anfwered thereto, prays Judgment; and that the faid *J. A.* may be barred
from having his faid Action againft him, and
that the faid Jurors may be difcharged from giving their Verdict upon the faid Iffue: *And at
the Day in Bank Judgment was given for the
Plaintiff, that the Evidence was fufficient.*

A Precedent of a Demurrer upon the Evidence.

And now at this Day the faid Plaintiff and
Defendant by their Attornies did appear, and
the Jury likewife did appear and were fworn,
&c. upon which Sir *T. W.* Serjeant at Law, of
Council with the Plaintiff, gave in Evidence fo
and fo, [*here repeat it truly*] and did require the
Jurors to find for the Plaintiff; upon which *J.
C.* of Counfel with the Defendant faith, That
the Evidence and Allegations aforefaid alledged,
were not fufficient in Law to maintain the Iffue
jointed for the Plaintiff, to which the Defendant
need not, nor by the Laws of the Land is not
holden to give any Anfwer; wherefore, for Default of fufficient Evidence in this Behalf, the
Defendant demands Judgment, that the Jurors
aforefaid of giving their Verdict be difcharged,
&c. and that the Plaintiff be barred from having a Verdict, &c. Then the Plaintiff joins
and fays, That he had given fufficient Matter
in Evidence, to which the Defendant hath given
no Anfwer, &c. and demands Judgment, and
that the Jury be difcharged, and that the Defendant be convicted; then the Jury may give
Damages, if Judgment fhall happen to be for Clayton's
the Plaintiff, &c.   Rep. 154.

A Bill

A Bill of Exception.

—— To wit. Be it remembered, That the Day of in the Year of our Lord before *T. B.* and *W.* Juſtices of our ſaid Lord the King, for taking Aſſizes in the ſaid County aſſigned, in a Plea of Treſpaſs and Ejecment, which *J. S.* in the Court of our ſaid Lord the King before himſelf, by Bill, doth proſecute againſt *E. B.* ſuppoſing by the ſaid Bill, that the aforeſaid *T. B.* &c. [*And recite the Subſtance of the Declaration, or what it is,* &c. *and the Iſſue, and then what the Evidence to prove the Defendant guilty was, which here was a Surrender of a Copyhold out of Court,* &c.] and that he deſired the Jury aforeſaid to give their Verdict for the ſaid *T. B.* of and upon the Premiſſes, and that he likewiſe deſired the Judges aforeſaid, that they would inform the Jury aforeſaid, that the Surrender aforeſaid out of Court made, was good and effectual in Law ; and the aforeſaid Juſtices the aforeſaid Surrender of the Land aforeſaid, with the Appurtenances, made out of Court of the Manor aforeſaid, in Form aforeſaid, did affirm to the ſaid Jurors was not good in Law, by which the ſaid *Thomas*, for that the aforeſaid Matters to the ſaid Jurors in Evidence ſhewed, do not appear, &c. did requeſt of the ſaid Juſtices, according to the Form of the Statute in ſuch Caſe provided, this preſent Bill, which doth contain in it the Matter aforeſaid, above by him to the Jurors aforeſaid ſhewed ; by which the ſaid Juſtices, at the Requeſt of him the ſaid *Thomas*, this Bill have ſealed at *D.* aforeſaid.

Vide a Bill of Exceptions in the *King's Bench*, upon a Trial at the Aſſizes in *Sam. Vernon's* Caſe,

in

in *Brownlow's Entries Latine Rediviv. f.* 129. where the Declaration, Plea, and Continuances are set forth, and then the Exception. A very useful Precedent.

Hillary Term in the 33d and 34th Year of the Reign of our Lord Charles *the Second, the present King of* England, *&c.*

Kent, to wit, Samuel Vernon, &c. [*here recite all the Pleadings and Continuances of the Record.*] Which said several Issues in Manner aforesaid respectively joined between the said Parties, afterwards, to wit, at the Assizes held at the Castle of *Canterbury* in the County aforesaid, before *W. Montague,* Chief Baron of the *Exchequer* of our said Lord the King, and Sir *H. Windham,* Knight, one of the Justices of our said Lord the King, of the Court of *Common Pleas,* the Justices of our said Lord the King assigned to hold the Assizes for the said County, according to the Form of the Statute, *&c.* on *Tuesday* the 14th Day of *March* in the 34th Year of the Reign of our said Lord the present King, came to be tried. At which Day before the said Justices, come as well the said *S. V.* in his proper Person, as the said *J. T.* by his said Attorney; and the Jurors of the Jury impanelled being called likewise came, and were sworn to try the said several Issues in Manner aforesaid respectively joined. And upon that Trial in Manner aforesaid had, to maintain the said Issues, the said *S. U.* gave in Evidence to the Jury so impanelled and sworn, That, *&c.* [*here recite the Evidence*]. And thereupon the Counsel on the Part of the said *J. F.* interposed and insisted, That the said Matter,

so

fo as aforefaid given in Evidence to the Jurors
aforefaid, was not fufficient in Law to maintain
the faid Iffues on the Part of the faid *S. U.* and
thereupon prayed of the faid Judges, That the
faid Matter might be found fpecially. Notwithftanding which the faid Judges declared
their Opinion, That the faid Matter, fo as aforefaid given in Evidence to the Jurors aforefaid,
was fufficient in Law to maintain the faid Iffues
on the Part of the faid *S. U.* if the Jurors fhould
believe it; and find that, *&c.* And thereupon
the faid Juftices, by their Direction to the Jury,
according to their Opinion aforefaid, left the
Confideration thereof to the faid Jurors: Whereupon the Counfel of the faid *J. F.* conceived,
that by the Law of the Land the Matters aforefaid, fo as aforefaid, on the Part of the faid *S.
U.* given in Evidence to the faid Jurors, (although
the Jurors fhould believe and find, That, *&c.*)
were not fufficient in Law to maintain thofe Iffues on the Part of the faid *S. U.* Therefore
they made their Exception to the faid Opinion
of the faid Juftices, and prayed that the faid Juftices would fet their Hands and Seals to this Bill,
according to the Form of the Statute in the like
Cafe lately made and provided: And thereupon
the faid *H. Windham* fet his Hand and Seal
thereto, according to the Form of the faid Statute. At the Caftle of *Canterbury*, 14th *March*
in the 35th Year of the faid King.

1. *Weft.* 2. 31. or 13 *E.* 1. 31. When the Juftices will not allow a Bill of Exception upon
Prayer, if the Party impleaded tender the fame
unto them in Writing, and requires there Seals
thereunto, they or one of them fhall do it.

2. If

2. If the Exception fealed be not put into the Roll, upon Complaint thereof to the King, the Juftice fhall be fent for, and if he cannot deny the Seal, the Court fhall proceed to Judgment according to the Exception.

This Bill of Exception is given by the Statute of *Weftm.* 2. *cap.* 31. before which Statute a Man might have had a Writ of Error; for Error in Law, either *in redditione Judicii, in redditione Executionis,* or *in Proceffu, &c.* which Error in Law muft be apparent in the Record; or for Error in *Fait,* by alledging Matter out of the Record, as the Death of either Party, *&c.* before Judgment. But the Mifchief was, if either Party did offer any Exception, praying the Juftices to allow it, and the Juftices over-ruled it, fo as it was never entred of Record, this the Party could not affign for Error, becaufe it neither appeared within the Record, nor was any Error in *Fait,* but in Law; and fo the Party grieved was without Remedy until this Statute was made.

2 Inft. 426.

This Act extendeth to all Courts, to all Actions, and to both Parties, and to thofe who come in their Places, as to the Vouchee, *&c.* who comes *in loco tenentis.*

It extendeth not only to all Pleas dilatory and peremptory, *&c.* to Prayers to be received, *Oyer* of any Record or Deed, and the like; but alfo to all Challenges of Jurors, and any Material Evidence given to any Jury, which by the Court is over-ruled. 2 *Inft. f.* 427.

All the Juftices ought to feal the Bill of Exceptions, yet if one doth it, it is fufficient; if all refufe, it is a Contempt in them all. And the Party grieved may have a Writ grounded upon this Statute, commanding them to put their Seals *juxta formam Statuti, & hoc sub periculo quod incumbit nullatenus omittatis.*   *Ibid.*

The Party muft pray the Juftices to put their Seals before Judgment; but if they deny it they may be commanded, and may do it after Judgment. *Ibid.*

If the Party be dead, his Heirs or Executors, *&c.* according to the Cafe, may have a Writ of Error upon this Bill of Exceptions. And no Diminution can be alledged, for the Parties are confined to the Matter in the Bill. *Ibid.*

If the Juftice die before he acknowledgeth the Seal according to the Aft, a *Scire facias* fhall go to his Executor or Adminiftrator, for the Death of the Judge is the Aft of God, which fhall not prejudice the Party: As in the Cafe of a Certificate of the Marfhal of the King's Hoft, that the Perfon outlawed was in the King's Service beyond Sea, in a Writ of Error a *Scire facias* fhall go to the Marfhal's Executor or Adminiftrator upon fhewing the Certificate. 2 *Inft.* 428.

If the Judge denieth his Seal, the Party may prove it by Witneffes. *Ibid.*

Error of a Judgment at the Grand Seffions in the County of *Pembroke,* in an Affize of *darrein Prefentment,* by *Henry Cort,* againft the Bifhop of St. *David's, Dorothy Owen* and others, for the Church of *Stackpool.*

The fourth Error affigned was, becaufe the Iffue being, whether *H. Cort* did laft prefent one *R. D.* the laft Incumbent, who was inftituted and inducted upon this Prefentation: The Plaintiff offered in Evidence Letters of Inftitution, which appeared to be, and fo mentions that they were fealed with the Seal of the Bifhop of *London,* becaufe the Bifhop of St. *David's* had not his

Seal

Seal of Office there, and thofe Letters were made out of the Diocefe; and the Defendant had demurred thereupon, that thofe Letters were infufficient, and the Demurrer was denied; which *Jones* faid was an Error, becaufe they ought to have permitted the Demurrer, and fhould have adjudged upon it. But it was held, That the not admitting of the Demurrer ought not to be affigned for Error; for when upon the Evidence, the Matter was over-ruled by the Juftices of Af-fize, that was a proper Caufe of a Bill of Excep-tions, and the Remedy which the Statute ap-points in that Cafe: And for the Matter of the Letters of Inftitution, fealed with another Seal, and made out of the Diocefe, it was held they were good enough; for the Seal is not material, it being an Act made of the Inftitution, and the Writing and Sealing is but a Teftimonial there-of, which may be under any Seal, or in any Place. But of that Point they would advife. *Cro.* 1 Part 340.

The Party grieved may have a Writ of Er-ror, and may affign Error upon that Bill fealed, and alfo in the Record, or in one of them at his Pleafure, *F. N. B.* f. 21. N. *Ex rigore juris*, it need not be allowed in Arreft of Judgment. 27 *H.* 8. in *Tatum*'s Action upon the Cafe.

Sir *Henry Vane* being indicted of High Trea-fon tendered a Bill of Exceptions, which the Court refufed to accept: And held that a Bill of Exceptions did not lie in Criminal Cafes, but only in Actions between Party and Party. 1 *Lev.* 68. *Keyling* 15. 1 *Sid.* 84.

The Bifhop of *Coventry* and *Litchfield* was in-dicted for a Trefpafs, and the Court allowed him a Bill of Exceptions. 1 *Leon.* 5.

Error

Error of Judgment in *C. B.* in *Ireland,* in Ejectment. The Question was upon the Bill of Exceptions, for that the Justices there would not direct the Jury, that a Probate of a Will before the Archbishop of *Canterbury,* and also before the Bishop of *Fernes,* were sufficient *concluding* Evidence, but only affirmed that they were *good* Evidence, leaving it to the Jury, to which the other Party shewed in Evidence Letters of Administration under the Seal of the Primate of *Ireland*; whereupon the Jury found no fuch Will, and Judgment there given for the Plaintiff, and Error brought here by Defendant; and Judgment affirmed. *T. Raym.* 404, 405.

A Bill of Exceptions does not extend where Prisoners are indicted at the Suit of the King. *T. Raym.* 486.

The Justices of the Peace having removed a *Pauper* and his Family from the Parish of *Nanesbrough* to the Parish of *Preston on the Hill* in *Cheshire, Preston* appeals to the Sessions, who confirmed the Orders; but the Counsel for the Appellants, at the hearing of the Appeal, tendred a Bill of Exceptions, stating a special Fact; which was returned up under the Seals of two of the Justices, together with the Order into *B. R.* by Virtue of a *Certiorari.* And the Court of *King's Bench,* upon great Debate, held, that a Bill of Exceptions did not lie in this Cafe, by reafon no Writ of Error lay; and for that Reafon confirmed the Order of Sessions. The King *verfus* Inhabitants of *Preston on the Hill* in *Cheshire,* M. 9 G. 2. and P. 9 G. 2. in *B. R.*

In an Information in the Nature of a *Quo warranto,* againft *Higgins* and Others, Citizens of the City of *Worcefter,* for ufing feveral Liberties and Franchifes within the faid City; the

Court

Court of *King's Bench* upon a Trial at Bar allowed a Bill of Exceptions. *T. Raym.* 484, 486. 1 *Vent.* 366.

Note; This Bill is to prevent the Precipitancy of the Judges, and ought to be allowed in all Courts, and in all Places of Pleadings, and may be put in at any Time before the Jury have given their Verdict.

But this Bill is rarely ufed, there being *impar congreffus* betwixt the Judge and the Council; and the Prudence of the Judges induces them to find fpecial Verdicts in Cafes of Doubt and Difficulty.

After a Bill of Exceptions is figned, the Party who preferred the Bill may bring Error in Parliament.

CHAP. X.

Of what Things a Jury may inquire; when of Spiritual, when of Things done in another County, or in another Kingdom; when of Eftoppels, and when not; when of a Man's Intent, &c.

THE next Words in the Writ, which have not yet been taken Notice of, are thefe, *per quos rei veritas melius fciri poterit*; and this is the chief End of their meeting together: No Court can give a Right Judgment, unlefs the Truth of the Fact be certainly known; and to find out this Truth, no Way is like to this of Juries; for they do not only go upon their own

See more of this Matter, *cap.* 13.

Ex facto Jus oritur.

Q 3   Know-

Knowledge, though they are Neighbours to the Place where the Queſtion is moved, and ſo are preſumed to have a better Knowledge of the Fact, than any others; for *vicinus, facta vicini, praſumitur ſcire.* But leſt this Preſumption ſhould fail, the Law allows other Evidence to be given to them, by which they may more certainly and confidently give their Verdict of the Iſſue, which is meant by this Word *Rei.*

And here it will not be amiſs to give you a brief Deſcription, *de quibus rebus,* what the Inqueſt may inquire of and find.

Of the Law.   Wherefore, though it be true, that a Jury ſhall not be charged, or meddle with a Matter of Law ; and if they do, and find it, their Verdict as to this ſhall be void ; yet daily Experi-
1 Inſt. 228.   ence (as well as *Littleton, Sect.* 368.) tells us, that they may take upon them the Knowledge of the Law, and give a general Verdict ; though to find the ſpecial Matter is the ſafeſt Way for them ; becauſe, if they miſtake the Law, they run into the Danger of an Attaint.

In the Caſe of *Manby* and *Scot,* adjudged *Trin.* 13 *Car.* 2. *B. R.* one Queſtion was, If the Verdict was well found, in an Action of the Caſe againſt the Huſband for Wares bought by the Wife ; the Verdict finding, that the Wares were Neceſſaries, and according to her Degree, whereas (as was objected) they ought to have found the Degree of the Party, and the Value of the Wares, and left it to the Court to judge.

But it was anſwered and reſolved, that the Court, *i. e.* the Judge before whom it is tried, informs the Jury of the Matter of Law, and accordingly they find, and ſo it belongs not to this Court.

Broughton

Broughton, a Reader of the *Temple*, brought a Bill by *Quo minus* in the *Exchequer*, against *Prince*, for maintaining a Suit against the Statute, *&c. Prince* pleads, that he was admitted in the *Inner Temple*, and Student for many Years there, that he was *Confiliarius in lege eruditus*, and took his Fee in that Caufe. *B.* replied, *de injuria fua propria, abfque hoc quod in lege eruditus, &c. & hoc petit, &c. & defendens fimiliter.*

It was moved, that the Defendant fhould demur to the Replication. *Atkinfon* excepted to the Traverfe and conclufion ; for it cannot be tried by a Jury ; for (fays he) if Matters in law be to be tried by the Judges, *à fortiori* the Learning of the Law ought to be tried by them.

Per Manwood Chief Baron, it fhall be tried by the Country, 3 *Leo.* 237. *Broughton* verfus *Prince* ; which Cafe is cited, 3 *Cro.* 728. to be otherwife ruled ; yet it was allowed there a good Iffue, whether a Parfon of a Parifh could fpeak *Welfh*.

Hut. 20, 21. Whether a Plaint was levied according to the Cuftom, was tried by a Jury who are directed by the Court, as to the Plaint, and whether it were purfuant to the Cuftom, and are to find according to fuch Directions.

In many Cafes the Jury are to inquire of Of a Man's the Knowledge and *Intent* of a Man, as where Intent. the *Nar.* is that the Defendant kept a Dog which killed the Plaintiff's Sheep, *fciens canem fuum ad mordendos oves confuetum* ; though *fciens* be not traverfable, yet the Jury upon Evidence muft inquire of it. *Lib.* 4. 18.

Of spiritual Things.

In some Cases a Jury may try and find a *spiritual* Thing, as a Divorce, Matrimony, &c. and must take Notice thereof, upon Pain of Attaint. *Lib. 4. 29. Lib. 7. 43. Lib. 9. Vide hic, cap. 2.*

Bastard.

The Jury may find Bastardy, but it was pleaded it must be tried by Certificate.

Divorce.

So they may find a Divorce, for it is not Matter of Record, but a Matter in *Fait.*

In Trespass *Quare clausum fregit* in the County of D. where the Trespass was committed in the County of S. upon Not guilty, if the Jury find the Defendant guilty in the County of S. their Verdict is void. But if they find him guilty generally, an Attaint lieth, *Finch* 400. because this Trespass is *local*; and what is local cannot be inquired of by Men of another County, for they can have no Cognisance of it. *cap.* 8.

The Jurors of one County may find any transitory Thing done in another County : Nay sometimes they *must* find local Things in another County ; as if the Heir pleads *riens per descent*, and the Plaintiff replies, Assets in a Parish and Ward within *London*, the Jury may find Assets in any County ; the same Case against an Executor, who pleads *Plene Administravit* ; the Jury may likewise find Assets in any Part of the World. And the Reason is, because the Place is only named for necessity of Trial. But where the Place is *Part of the Issue*, it is otherwise. And therefore, if I promise in one Place to do a Thing in another, and Issue is upon the Breach, the Jury ought to come from the Place of the Breach. But if I promise in *London* to do a Thing at *Bourdeaux* in *France*, and issue upon the Breach, yet this shall be tried in *London for necessity* ; because otherwise it would want Trial ; the Jury must inquire of the Breach at *Bourdeaux*. But if I promise in *France* to do a Thing in *France*, so that both Contract and Performance is beyond Sea, this wants Trial in our Law. *Lib. 6. 47. Lib. 7. 23, 26, 27.* Of Things done in another County or Country, *vide* Roll. *Tit.* Trial, *f.* 571, 624.

If

If an Act be to be done all beyond Sea, it cannot be tried in *England*; but where Part is to be done in *England*, and Part beyond Sea, the whole shall be tried in *England*. *Vin. Abr.* Tit. *Trial*, 3. *pl.* 4.

When Part of the Act, especially the original, is to be done in *England*, and Part out of it, that Part that is to be performed out of it shall be tried here by twelve Men, if issue be taken thereupon; and those twelve Men shall come out of the Place where the Writ is brought. As where it was covenanted by Indenture by *Charter-party*, that a Ship should sail from *Blackney Haven* in *Norfolk* to *Muttrel* in *Spain*, and there remain by certain Days; in an Action of Covenant brought upon this *Charter-party*, the Indenture was alledged to be made at *Thetford* in the County of *Norfolk*, and upon pleading the Issue was joined; whether the Ship remained at *Muttrel* in *Spain* by the said certain Days. And it was adjudged that the Issue should be tried at *Thetford* where the Action was brought, because there the Contract took its *original* by making of the *Charter-party*, and so it has been often adjudged in the like Case *Co. Lit.* 261. *b.* 4 *Inst.* 141, 142. *Pasch.* 28 *Eliz. S. C.* by the Name of *Gyne* v. *Constantine.* 6 *Rep.* 48. *a. S. C.* cited as adjudged. *S. C.* cited *Godb.* 204. *pl.* 292. *per Coke,* Ch. J. as adjudged, that where the *original Act* was in *England*, and the subsequent Matter upon the Sea, the Trial shall be where the original Act is done. And so it was agreed that the Trial should be in the principal Case there. *Mich.* 11 *Jac. C. B. Leighton* v. *Green* and *Garret. Vin. Abr.* Tit. *Trial,* 3.

If a Man in Consideration of 100 *l.* promises in *London* to transport certain Commodities to *Turkey*, in an Action for not transporting, this may be tried in *London*. *Per Curiam. Vin. Abr.* Tit. *Trial,* 3. *pl.* 1.

S. P. per Fineux and *Townsend. Br.* Trials *pl.* 154. cites 11 *H.* 7. 16. but *Brian* contra.

If a Man be bound to do a Thing beyond Sea, the Bond is good, and the Condition void; for it is not triable in *England*, and so in effect impossible. *Vin. Abr.* Tit. *Trial,* 3. *pl.* 2. cites *Br.* Obligation *pl.* 70. cites 21 *E.* 4.

But *per Brian,* if a Man be bound in 20 *l.* to pay 10 *l.* at *Bourdeaux,* the Plaintiff may declare upon all the Deed. But if Defendant pleads Payment at *Bourdeaux, extra Regnum,* the Plaintiff shall be barr'd, because it is Parcel of the Count of the Plaintiff. *Ibid.*

A Con-

A Contract, made Part beyond Sea and Part here, fhall be tried here *in toto. Vin. Abr.* Tit. *Trial,* 4. *pl.* 6.

Where an Agreement is at Land, and a Performance is at Sea, it fhall be tried where the Agreement is made ; and faying in *Partibus tranfmarinis infra Paroch'* is idle.   12 *Mod.* 34. *Hill.* 4 *W. & M.* 1692. *Can.* v. *Cary.*

In Debt upon Bond, Condition to pay 20 l. within 40 Days next after his perfonal Being at *Rome,* and his Return into *England,* the Defendant pleaded that the Plaintiff never was at *Rome.* It was objected that the Iffue fhould be upon his Return into *England,* for the other was not triable: But to this it was replied, that if one was not triable, the other could not, becaufe the Condition was in the *Copulative* ; but that had it been in the *Disjunctive* it had been otherwife ; and thereupon the Juftices *doubted* how the Law fhould be in this Cafe.   *Mich.* 24 *Eliz. Mullineaux's* Cafe, *Vin. Abr. Trial,* 4. *pl.* 6.

4 Inft. 142.   Cafe upon an Affumpfit grounded upon a
cap. 22. S. C.   Policy made between Merchants for affurance
in *B. R.*   of their Goods, whereby the Undertaker did affume, that fuch a Ship fhould fail from *Melcome Regis* in the County of *Dorfet* unto *Abvile* in *France* fafely without violence, *&c.* and declared that the faid Ship in failing towards *Abvile,* viz. towards the River of *Some,* in the Realm of *France,* was arrefted by the *French* King, *&c.* whereupon iffue was taken, and tried where the Action upon the Affumpfit was brought.   It was infifted that this Iffue arifing merely from a Place out of the Realm, cannot be tried: But it was refolved that this Iffue fhall be tried where the Action was brought.   And it was well agreed, that where the contract,
and

and alfo the Performance thereof, is wholly done or to be done beyond Sea, and it fo appears to be, there wants Trial in our Law. But here the Affumpfit, which is the Ground of the Action, was at *London,* and therefore muft neceffarily be tried (where the Action is brought) or fhall not be tried at all. And the Arreft which is in Iffue is not the Ground of the Action but the Affumpfit, and the Arreft is the Breach of the Affumpfit, and fo muft neceffarily be tried where the Affumpfit, which is the Ground of the Action, was made. *Vin. Abr.* Tit. *Trial,* 4. *pl.* 8. cites 6 *Rep.* 47. *b.* in *Dowdale's* Cafe cites *Mich.* 30 & 31 *Eliz.*

An Obligation with Condition that if the Obligor brings the Merchandizes of the Obligee from *Norway* beyond Sea to *Lynn* in *England,* that then, &c. this may be tried in *England;* per *Vavifor* and *Fineaux* accordingly. *Br. Trials,* *pl.* 154. cites 11 H. 7. 16.

Retainer in *England* to ferve beyond Sea fhall be tried in *England. Br. Trials, pl.* 93. cites 7 *H.* 7. 8. *per Huffey* Ch. J.

In the Cafe of *Drake* and *Beere, Trin.* 15 *Car.* 2. *B. R.* 1 *Siderf.* 151. 1 *Keb.* 528. this Difference was agreed by the Court, *viz.* That a Jury in an inferior Court may inquire of Things out of the Jurifdiction, if they be *but* for Increafe of Damages, as is 1 *Cro.* 571. *Ireland* verfus *Blackwell;* but if they inquire of any Thing iffuable out of that Jurifdiction, it is naught. 1 *Cro.* 101. 2 *Cro.* 503.

Error was brought to reverfe a Judgment Jurifdiction given in the Palace-Court, in *Indebitat.* for that of Courts. the Defendant was indebted to the Plaintiff *infra Jurifdictionem,* for nurfing of a Child,

not

not saying, the Nursing was *infra Jurisdictionem.*

Wadh. Windham, Justice, held it good, for that it is a Debt every where, and not like a Debt that ariseth by Matter collateral: But *Twisden* Justice doubted. *Whitehead* versus *Brown, Pasch.* 15 *Car.* 2. *B. R.* 1 *Keb.* 512.

Vide Saunders's Reports, 1 Part, 73. *Peacock* against *Bell* and *Kendall.* The Plaintiff declared the Defendant *infra Jurisdictionem indebitatus fuisset* to the Plaintiff in 39 *l. pro diversis Merchandizis per quer. eidem Defendenti ante tempus illud vendit. & deliberat.* Held **Inferior Courts.** nought in an inferior Court, for not saying *ibidem vendit. &c.* but good in a superior Court, and in the County Palatine of *Durham,* for that is an original and superior Court.

Estoppels. The Jury may find *Estoppels,* as the taking of a Lease of a Man's own Land, by Deed **When the Estoppel is found, the Court may judge according to the especial Matter.** indented, or the Delivery of a Deed before the Date; as in Debt by an Administrator, upon a Bond dated 4 *Aprilis* 24 *Eliz.* the Defendant pleaded that the Intestate died before the Date of the Obligation, and *issint nient son fait*; upon which they were at iss̄ue; and adjudged that the Jury might find that the Bond was delivered the third of *April,* because they are sworn *ad veritatem dicendam*; though the Parties are estopped to plead a Deed was delivered before the Date; but they may plead a Delivery after the Date, because it shall never be intended that a Deed was delivered before the Date, but after it may.

Estoppel. But if the Estoppel or Admittance be within the same Record, in which Issue is joined, then the Jurors cannot find any Thing contrary to this, which the Parties have affirmed and admitted

mitted of Record, though it be not true, for the Court may give Judgment upon Matters *confessed* by the Parties; and the Jurors are not to be charged with any such Thing, but only with such in which the Parties *vary*. *Lib.* 2. 4. *Lib.* 4. 53. *Co. Lit.* 227.

A Decree in *Chancery* shall be tried by a Jury, and not by itself; for it is not a Record, but a Decree recorded. The *Chancery*, as it is a Court of Equity, is not a Court of Record, but touching Things agitated in the *Petty-Bag* Office, it is a Court of Record. *Decree.*

Exemplification of a Decree in *Chancery*, which has Bill and Answer, allowed good Evidence. *Keb.* 1 Part 21. Deeds, *&c.* *Exemplification.*

The Jury may find Deeds or Matter of Record, if they will, though not shewed in Evidence. *Finch* 400. They may inquire of Things done before the Memory of Man. *Lib.* 9. 34. *Records not shewed.*

The Jury in many Cases may find Matters in a foreign County, Conditions, Records, Releases, *&c.* As in Battery of the Plaintiff's Servant in one County, and Loss of Service in another County, this Damage in the other County may be inquired of by the Jury of the County where the Battery is laid. The like of Assets, because transitory; otherwise of a local Trespass, *&c.* *Foreign County.*

Nul tiel Record is not to be tried by a Jury, but upon the General Issue, *&c.* they may find a Record.

The Jury may find a Warranty, being given in Evidence, though it be not pleaded: Nay, the Jury may find that which cannot be pleaded; as in Trespass, upon Not guilty, the Jury may find that the Defendant leased Lands *Warranty.*

for

Condition.

for Life, upon Condition, and entred for the Condition broken; though this cannot be pleaded without Deed, yet the Jury may find it. *Lit. Sect.* 366.

Where a collateral Warranty binds, this may well be given in Evidence; for although it doth not give a Right, yet in Law this shall bar and bind a Right. *Lib.* 10. 97.

Jury is bound by Estoppel unless the Party leaves the Fact at large by Pleading.

Where the Plaintiff's Title is by Estoppel, and the Defendant pleads the General Issue, the Jury are bound by the Estoppel; for here is a Title in the Plaintiff, that is a good Title in Law, and a good Title, if the Matter had been disclosed and relied on in Pleading; but if the Defendant pleads the special Matter, and the plaintiff will not rely on the Estoppel when he may, but take issue on the Fact, the Jury shall not be bound by the Estoppel; for then they are to find the Truth of the Fact which is against him. Thus in Debt for Rent on an Indenture of Lease, if the Defendant plead *Nil debet*, he cannot give in Evidence, That the Plaintiff had nothing in the Tenements; because, if he had pleaded that specially, the Plaintiff might have replied the Indenture and estopped him; but if the Defendant plead *Nihil habuit, &c.* and the Plaintiff will not rely on the Estoppel, but reply *habuit, &c.* he waves the Estoppel, and leaves it at large; and the Jury shall find the Truth notwithstanding his Indenture. *Salkeld* 276, 277.

CHAP.

CHAP. XI.

The Juries Oath; why called Recogni-
tors in an Assize, and Jurors in a
Jury. Of the Trial per medietatem
linguæ; when to be prayed, and when
grantable. Of a Trial betwixt two
Aliens, by all English. Of the Venire
facias, per medietatem linguæ, and of a
Challenge to such Juries.

THE Jury having heard their Evidence, let them now consider of their Verdict: But first they must remember their Oath, which in Effect is, *To find according to their Evidence,* and therefore they should have had it before the Evidence, but that the Form and Order of the *Venire facias* (which I have tied myself to follow) leads me to it after their Evidence, in these Words, *Ad faciend. quandam Juratam.* I have already shewed the Derivation of this Word *Jurata,* and what is the legal Acceptation of it; only observe with our Great Master *Littleton,* That the Word *Assise* is sometimes taken for a Jury; so, as the learned Commentator doth well paraphrase, that the Word *Assise* is *Nomen Æquivocum Æquivocans,* because sometimes it signifieth a Jury, sometimes the Writ of Assise, and sometime an Ordinance or Statute; but *Jurata* is *Nomen Æquivocum Æquivocatum,* because we always understand that Word (according to the aforesaid Definition) to be a Jury of twelve Men, so called, by reason of the Oath they take, *Truly to try the Suit of* Nisi prius, be- *tween*

Assize, Enquest and Proof, are taken for the Word Jury. Vide 28 E. 3. 13.

See Chap. 1.

1 Inst. 154.

Assisa for Jurata.

The Juries Oath.

tween Party and Party, according to their Evidence.

Why called Recognitors in an Affize, and Jurors in a Jury.

And as in an Affife, the Jurors are called Recognitors, from thefe Words in the Writ of Affife. *facere Recognitionem*; fo upon a *Nifi prius*, they are called *Juratores*, from thefe Words in the *Venire facias*, *Ad faciend' quandam Juratam*.

12 Knights.

In ancient Time, the Jury, as well in Common Pleas, as in Pleas of the Crown, were twelve Knights, as appears by *Glanvil, Lib.* 2. *cap.* 14. and *Bracton, fol.* 116.

The next Words of the *Venire facias* are, *Inter partes prædictas.* In the fourth Chapter, I have inftanced, That in fome Cafes, a Jury fhall be awarded betwixt the Party and a Stranger to the Writ and iffue; I will now fhew what the Jury fhall be, when one of the Parties is an Alien, the other a Denizen; and when both Parties to the Iffues are Aliens.

Jury *per medietatem linguæ.*

This Trial is called in *Latin, Triatio bilinguis*, or *per medietatem linguæ* (a).. And this Trial by the Common Law was wont to be obtained of the King, by his Grant made to any

2 Keb. 315.

Company of Strangers, as to the Company of *Lumbards* or *Almaigns*, or to any other Company, that when any of them was impleaded, the Moiety of the Inqueft fhould be of their own Tongue. *Staund. Pleas of the Crown, Lib.* 3. *cap.* 7.

(a) People are diftinguifhed by their Language, and *Medietas Linguæ* is as much as to fay, half *Englifh*, and half of any other Tongue or Country whatfoever.

And

And this Trial in fome Cafes, *per medietatem* Its Antiquity.
linguæ, was before the Conqueſt, as appears by
Lamb. fol. 91. 3. *Viri duodeni Jure conſulti,*
Angliæ ſex, Walliæ totidem, Anglis & Wallis
jus dicanto. And of ancient Time it was called
Duodecim-virale judicium. 1 *Inſt.* 155. *b.*

But afterwards this Law became univerſal:
Firſt, by the Statute of 27 *Ed.* 3. *c.* 8. it was
enacted, That in Pleas before the Mayor of Stamf. P. C.
the Staple, if both Parties were Strangers, the 158. b.
Trial ſhould be by Strangers. But if one
Party was a Stranger, and the other a Denizen, then the Trial ſhould be *per medietatem*
linguæ. But this Statute extended but to a
narrow Compaſs, to wit, only where both
Parties were Merchants or Miniſters of the
Staple, and in Pleas before the Mayor of the
Staple: But afterwards, in the 28th Year
of the fame King's Reign, *cap.* 13. it was
enacted,

' That in all Manner of Enqueſts and Proofs,
' which be to be taken or made among A-
' liens and Denizens, be they Merchants or
' other, as well before the Mayor of the Staple,
' as before any other Juſtices or Miniſters, al-
' though the King be Party ; the one Half of
' the Enqueſt or Proof ſhall be Denizens, and
' the other Half Aliens, if fo many Aliens and
' Foreigners be in the Town or Place where
' fuch Enqueſt or Proof is to be taken, that
' be not Parties, nor with the Parties in Con-
' tracts, Pleas, or other Quarrels, whereof ſuch
' Enqueſt or Proof ought to be taken ; and
' if there be not fo many Aliens, then ſhall
' there be put in fuch Enqueſts or Proofs,
' as many Aliens, as ſhall be found in the fame

VOL. I.   R   ' Towns

' Towns or Places, which be not thereto Par-
' ties, nor with the Parties, as aforesaid is said,
' and the Remnant of Denizens which be good.
' Men, and not suspicious to the one Party nor
' to the other.

Ibid.

So that this is the Statute which makes the Law universal, concerning the *medietatem lin- guæ*; for though the King be Party, yet the Alien may have his Trial. And it matters not, whether the Moiety of Aliens be of the same Country as the Alien, Party to the Action, is: For he may be a *Portugal* and they *Spaniards*, &c. because the Statute speaks generally of Aliens. See *Dyer* 144.

The Return of a *Venire de medietate linguæ* ought to (a) shew which of the Jurors are Denizens, and which Aliens, and a full Number of each must appear to be sworn; if there be not sufficient to make up a full Number of six Denizens and six Aliens, the Justices of *Nisi prius* (b) may, by Construction of the Statutes, which give a *Tales de Circumstantibus*, award such a *Tales* for so many Denizens and Aliens as shall be wanting. *Cro. Eliz.* 818.

St. P. C.
159. b.

Resolved, That if both Parties be Aliens, the Inquest shall be all *English*; for though the *English* may be supposed to favour themselves more than Strangers, yet when both Parties are Aliens, it will be presumed they favour both alike, and so indifferent. 21 *H.* 6. 4. But if the Plea be before the Mayor of the Staple, and both Parties Alien Mer-

(a) But this being only a Misreturn, is helped by Verdict in Cases within the Statutes of *Jeofail*. *Cro. Eliz.* 84.

(b) 10 Co. 104. *Cro. Eliz.* 305.

chants

chants of the Staple, it shall be tried by all
Aliens. *Staundford's Pleas del Corone* 159. A
Scotchman is a Subject, and shall not have
this Trial. *Egyptians* are also excluded, when
tried for Felony made by the Statute against
them. 1 *Phil. & Mar. cap.* 4. 5 *Eliz. cap.* 20.

Where an Alien is Party, yet if the trial be by all *English*, it is not erroneous, because it is at his Peril, if he will slip his Time, and not make use of the Advantage which the Law giveth him when he should. *Dyer* 144. All English.

When an Alien is Plaintiff, and Defendant a
Denizen; the Plaintiff, before the Awarding of
the *Venire*, ought to suggest on the Roll, that
he is an Alien born, and pray procefs according
to the Statute; he ought also to suggest in what
Parts beyond Sea he was born, that Men of the
same Country might be upon the Jury, if they
could be found; but if he do not suggest this
before the *Venire* is awarded, he shall not suggest it afterwards; neither shall he challenge the
Array or Polls for that Caufe. *St. P. C.* 159.
Dyer 144. *b.*

If an Alien neglect to pray the Benefit of the
Statute (*a*) before the Return of a common
Venire, he can neither except to such a *Venire*,
nor pray a subfequent Procefs *de medietate lin-
guæ*. 3 *Bac. Abr.* 263. When the Alien should pray a *Venire facias per me-dietatem.*

(*a*) If upon an Indictment of Felony against an Alien
he plead guilty, and a common Jury be returned, if he
doth not furmife his being an Alien, before any of the
Jury fworn, he hath lost that Advantage; but if he alledge
that he is an Alien, he may challenge the Array for that
Caufe, and thereupon a new Precept or *Venire* shall issue,
or an award be made of a Jury *de medietate linguæ*; But
it is more proper for him to furmife it upon his Plea pleaded, and thereupon to pray it. 2 *Hal. Hist. P. C.* 272.

Tales. If he hath a general *Venire facias*, he cannot pray a *Decem Tales*, &c. *per medietatem linguæ*, upon this; becaufe the *Tales* ought to purfue the *Venire facias*, 3 *E.* 4. 11, 12. And fo if the *Venire facias* be *per medietatem linguæ*, the *Tales* ought to be *per medietatem linguæ*; as if fix Denizens and five Aliens appear of the principal Jury, the Plaintiff may have a *Tales per medietatem linguæ. Lib.* 10. 104. But if in this Cafe the *Tales* be general, *de circumftantibus*, it hath been held good enough; for there being no Exception taken by the Defendant, upon the awarding thereof, it fhall be intended well awarded. *Cro.* 3 Part 818, 841.

Where the Trial of an Alien's Caufe fhall be by Englifh.

If the Plaintiff or Defendant be Executor or Adminiftrator, &c. though he be an Alien, yet the Trial fhall be by *Englifh*, becaufe he fueth *in auter droit*; but if it be averred that the Teftator or Inteftate was an Alien, then it fhall be *per medietatem linguæ. Cro.* 3 Part 275.

Part Englifh, and Part Aliens.

Mich. 40 & 41 *Eliz.* The Queen's Attorney exhibited an Information againft *Barre* and divers other Merchants, fome whereof were *Englifh* and fome Aliens: After Iffue, the Aliens prayed a Trial *per medietatem linguæ*. But all the Juftices of *England* refolved, That the Trial fhould be by all *Englifh*, and likened it to the Cafe of Privilege, where one of the Defendants demands Privilege, and the Court, as to his Companion, cannot hold Plea, there he fhall be oufted of his Privilege. *Sic hic. Moor* 557.

By the Statute of 8 *H.* 6. *cap.* 29. Infufficiency or Want of Freehold is no Caufe of Challenge to Aliens, who are impanelled with the
Englifh,

English, (notwithſtanding *Staundford*'s Opinion, *Pl. Coron.* 160.) for this Statute ſaith, That the Statute 2 *H.* 5. 3. ſhall extend only to Enqueſts betwixt Denizen and Denizen.

If the Defendant do not inform the Court that he is an Alien, upon awarding the *Venire facias*, and ſo pray a *Venire facias per medietatem linguæ*, he cannot challenge the Array for this Cauſe at the Trial, if the Jury be all Denizens ; (notwithſtanding *Staundford*'s Opinion to the contrary, and the Books cited by him, *fol.* 159. *Pl. Cor.*) For the Alien at his Peril ſhould pray a *Venire facias per medietatem linguæ. Dyer* 357. *Vide Roll.* Tit. *Trial,* 643.

If the *Plaintiff* be an Alien, he muſt ſuggeſt it before the Awarding of the *Venire facias* ; but if the *Defendant* be an Alien, the Plaintiff is allowed to ſurmiſe that, before or after the *Venire facias*, becauſe the Defendant's Quality may not be known to him before. 21 *H.* 7. 32.

If the Defendant be an Alien, on Notice given by his Attorney to the Plaintiff or his Attorney, the Plaintiff ought to enter it on the Roll, to have a Trial *de medietate* at his Peril ; but the Court refuſed to award it for the Defendant, on his *Affidavit* that he is an Alien. *Keb.* 1 Part 547.

No *medietas linguæ* was at Common Law, but introduced by 28 *Ed.* 3. *c.* 13. for Contracts and Felonies.   In what Caſes.

Denizens are as well thoſe who are *Engliſh* born, as thoſe who are Aliens and made Denizens by Patent.

On a Writ of Inquiry of *Damages*, the Inqueſt ſhall be all of *Engliſh*, and no Part of Aliens, for it is out of the Statute.

It feems agreed that the fubfequent Statutes, which require Jurors to have Tenements to a greater Value, no way repeal the former Statute, though the *Englifh half* of the Jury ought to have Value as in other Cafes.

Where Iffue is joined between an Alien and an *Englifhman*, upon the Prayer of the Party, but not otherwife, a *medietas linguæ* fhall be granted; but in the Cafe of an Alien arraigned *of Treafon done here* he fhall be tried by *all Englifh*; for by 1 *Ma.* 10. the Trial in all Treafons is according to the Common Law: But it is otherwife in a Cafe of Felony, Petit Treafon or Murder. *Vin. Trial,* 187.

There is no need in Cafe of an *Indictment* for any of the Grand Jury to be Aliens.

In Trials where *Medietas linguæ* is required, the Alien may be aided *de circumftantibus.* The Return upon the *Venire* ought to be *diftinct,* 12 of each, and to be fworn *alternately.*

Wherever a *Medietas linguæ* is, a fpecial Jury is to be returned: And where a Jury is *de medietate linguæ,* the Plaintiff is not bound unlefs the Jury be by fix of the one and fix of the other.

It muft be prayed on the Award of the *Venire facias,* or it will not be allowed; for the Sheriff hath otherwife by the *Venire* no Power to return Aliens, or Conufance that an Alien is in the Cafe.

In this Trial the Court ought to be informed that one of the Parties is an Alien *before* the Award of the *Venire.*

If the *Defendant* be an Alien, the Plaintiff's Attorney on Notice ought to enter it on the Roll for a Party Jury at his Peril; but the Court will not award it for the Defendant on the Defendant's Affidavit that he is an Alien. *Vin. Trial,* 288, 289, 290.   CHAP.

CHAP. XII.

*How the Jury ought to demean themselves,
whilst they consider of their Verdict;
when they may eat and drink, when
not; what Misdemeanor of theirs will
make the Verdict void: Evidence given
them, when they are gone from the Bar,
spoils their Verdict: For what the Court
may fine them, and where the Justices
may carry them in Carts, till they agree
of their Verdict. An Amercement affeered by the Jury.*

THERE is a Maxim, and an old Custom
in the Law, That the Jury shall not eat
nor drink after they be sworn, till they have
given their Verdict, without the Assent and Li-
cence of the Justices; and that is ordained by
the Law for eschewing of divers Inconveniences
that might follow thereupon; and that especially if they should eat or drink at the Costs of
the Parties; and therefore if they do so, it may
be laid in Arrest of Judgment.

  But with the Assent of the *Justices* they may
both eat and drink; as if any of the Jurors
fall sick before they be agreed of their Verdict,
so sore that he may not commune of the Verdict,
then by the Assent of the Justices he may have
Meat or Drink, and also such other Things as
be necessary for him; and his Fellows also at
their own Costs, or at the indifferent Costs of
the Parties, if they so agree, or by the Assent

*Jurors ought
not to eat or
drink.
Dr. and Stu-
dent 158.*

*For by Assent
of the Justices
they may eat
and drink.*

of the Juſtices, may both eat and drink: And if the Caſe ſo happen, that the Jury can in no wiſe agree in their Verdict; as if one of the Jurors knoweth in his own Conſcience the Thing to be falſe, which the other Jurors affirm to be true, and ſo he will not agree with them in giving a falſe Verdict; and this appeareth to the Juſtices by Examination; the Juſtices may in ſuch Caſe ſuffer the Jury to have both Meat and Drink for a Time, to ſee whether they will agree. And if they will in no wiſe agree, the Juſtices may take ſuch Order in the Matter as ſhall ſeem to them by their Diſcretion to ſtand with Reaſon and Conſcience, by awarding of a new Inqueſt,

New Inqueſt when the Jury cannot agree. and by ſetting Fine upon them, that they ſhall find in Default, or otherwiſe, as they ſhall think beſt by their Diſcretion; like as they may do, if one of the Jury die before the Verdict, &c. *Doct. and Student* 158.

If the Jury, after their Evidence given unto

Where, if the Jury eat or drink, it ſhall avoid the Verdict, and where only fineable. them at the Bar, do at their own Charges eat or drink, either before or after they be agreed on their Verdict, it is fineable, but it ſhall not avoid the Verdict; but if before they be agreed on their Verdict, they eat or drink at the Charge of the Plaintiff, if the Verdict be given for him, it ſhall avoid the Verdict; but if it be given for the Defendant, it ſhall not avoid it; & *ſic e converſo*. But if after they be agreed on their Verdict, they eat or drink at the Charge of him for whom they do paſs, it ſhall not avoid the Verdict. 1 *Inſt.* 227. *b*.

To give the Jury Money, makes their Verdict void; by two Juſtices. *Leon.* 1 Part 18.

If

If the Plaintiff, after Evidence given, and the Jury departed from the Bar, or any for him, do deliver any Letter from the Plaintiff to any of the Jury, concerning the Matter in Iffue, or any Evidence, or any Efcrow, touching the Matter in Iffue, which was not given in Evidence, it fhall avoid the Verdict, if it be found for the Plaintiff; but not if it be found for the Defendant; & *fic e converfo.* But if the Jury carry away any Writing unfealed, which was given in Evidence in open Court, this fhall not avoid their Verdict, albeit they fhould not have carried it with them. 1 *Inft.* 227. *b.*

Marginal note: What delivered to the Jury after Evidence, fhall avoid their Verdict. *Litleton's Rep.* 69. *Keb.* 1 Part 824.

By the Law of *England,* a Jury after their Evidence given upon the Iffue, ought to be kept together in fome convenient Place, (a) without Meat or Drink, or Fire (c) (which fome Books call an Imprifonment) and without Speech with any, unlefs it be the Bailiff, and with him only, if they be agreed. After they be agreed, they may in Caufes between Party and Party, give a Verdict; and if the Court be rifen, give a privy Verdict before any of the Judges of the Court, and then they may eat and drink, and the next Morning in open Court they may either affirm, or alter their privy Verdict; and that which is given in Court fhall ftand. But in criminal Cafes of Life or Member, the Jury can give no privy Verdict, but they muft give it openly in Court. *Ibid.*

Marginal notes: How the Jury ought to be kept by the Bailiff.

When they may eat and drink, fee *Smith's Com-wealth* 74.

Where there can be no privy Verdict.

(a) When the Jury depart from the Bar, (b) a Bailiff ought to be fworn to keep them together, and not to fuffer any to fpeak to them. 2 *H. H. P. C.* 296.

(b) That a Bailiff is to be fworn in a *Civil* as well as in a *Criminal* Cafe. *Palm.* 380.

(c) 2 *H. H. P. C.* 297.

A privy

A privy Verdict may be taken in a *Quo warranto*, Perjury *c* wherever the King is Party, unless in Case of Life and Death. *Keb.* 3 Part 459.

Where the Jury cannot be discharged before Verdict.
The King cannot be nonsuit.
1 Inst. 227. b.

Neither can a Jury, sworn and charged in Case of Life or Member, be discharged by the Court, or any other, but they ought to give a Verdict. And the King cannot be nonsuit, for he is, in Judgment of Law, ever present in Court; but a common Person may be nonsuit. And in Civil Actions, the Justices, upon Cause, may discharge the Jury. *Br. Inquest,* 68, 47, 39, &c.

But this is against common Practice; and I have known, that after a Jury of Life and Death have been sworn, and charged with Prisoners arraigned, the Judge having been credibly informed, that it was a Jury pack'd to favour some Prisoner, has discharged that Jury, and made the Sheriff return another presently.

Information.

In an Information by an Informer, *qui tam,* &c. the Informer may be nonsuited. *1 Inst.* 139. *Coke's Entries,* Tit. *Information,* 394.

In *Hillary* Term *Sexto H.* 8. *Rotul.* 358. It was alledged in Arrest of the Verdict at the *Nisi Prius,* That the Jurors had eat and drank. And upon Examination it was found, that they had first agreed, and that returning to give their Verdict, they saw *Rede* Chief Justice in the Way, going to see a Fray, and they followed him, *Et in veniendo viderunt scyphum & inde biberunt.* And

Jurors fined.

for this every one of them was fined 40 *d.* And the Plaintiff had Judgment upon the Verdict. *Dyer* 37.

Jurors at the Nisi Prius fined in Bank, for eating Pears, and drinking Ale.

And *Dyer* 218. At the *Nisi Prius,* the Jury after their Charge given, returned and said, That they were all agreed except one, who had eat a

Pear,

Pear, and drank a Draught of Ale, for which he would not agree; and at the Requeft of the Plaintiff, the Jury was fent back again, and found the Iffue for the Plaintiff. And the Matter aforefaid being examined by the Oath of the Jurors *feparatim*, and the Bailiff who kept them, and found true, the Offender was committed, and afterward found Surety for his Fine. *Si, &c.* And *Fitzherbert*, the then Juftice of Affife, gave him Day *in Banco, &c.* At which Day a Fine of twenty Shillings was then affeffed. *Et quoad Ball. Curia advifare vult.* But the Plaintiff had his Judgment.

In Trefpafs by *Mounfon* againft *Weft*, the Jury was charged, and Evidence given, and the Jurors being retired into a Houfe for to confider of their Evidence, they remained there a long Time without concluding any Thing; and the Officers of the Court who attended them, feeing their Delay, fearched the Jurors, if they had any Thing about them to eat; upon which Search it was found, that fome of them had Figs, and others Pippins, for which, the next Day the Matter was moved to the Court, and the Jurors were examined upon Oath, and two of them did confefs, that they had eaten Figs before they had agreed of their Verdict; and three other of them confeffed, that they had Pippins, but did not eat of them, and that they did it without the Knowledge or Will of any of the Parties. And afterwards the Court fet a Fine of 5 *l.* upon each of them which had eaten; and upon the others which had not eaten, 40 *s.* But upon great Advice and Confideration had, and Conference with the reft of the Judges, the Verdict was held to be good, notwithftanding the faid Mifdemeanor. *Leon.* 1 Part 1 33.

Fined for having Figs and Pippins about them.

And

Fined for eating Raisins and Dates.

And fee the Book of *Entries* 251. The Jurors, after they went from the Bar *ad feipfos* of their Verdict to advife *comederunt quafdam fpecias, fcil.* Raifins, Dates, *&c.* at their own Cofts, as well before as after they were agreed of their Verdict. And the Jurors were committed to Prifon, but their Verdict was good, although the Verdict was given againft the King.

Fineable for having Sweetmeats, &c. about them, tho' they do not eat them. See *Plo. Com.* 519. One fined and imprifoned for having Sugarcandy and Liquorifh about him.

'In *Ejectione firmæ* it was found for the Defendant ; three of the Jurors had Sweet-meats in their Pockets, and thofe three were for the Plaintiff, until they were fearched and the Sweet-meats found, and then did agree with the other nine, and gave Verdict for the Defendant. It was the Opinion of the Juftices, That whether they eat or not, they were fineable for having of the Sweet-meats with them, for that is a very great Mifdemeanor. *Godbolt* 353.

Jurors carted.

40 *Affife Placito* 11. The Juftices faid, That if the Jurors will not agree in their Verdict, the Juftices may carry them in a Cart along with them, till they are agreed.

The fame Evidence given to the Jury, after they were gone from the Bar, fpoils the Verdict.

The Jury were gone from the Bar to confer of their Verdict, and one of the Witneffes before fworn on the Defendant's Part, was called by the Jurors, and he recited again his Evidence to them, and after they gave their Verdict for the Defendant. And Complaint being made to the Judge of the Affifes of this Mifdemeanor, he examined the Inqueft, who confeffed all the Matter, and that the Evidence was the fame in Effect that was given before, *& non alia nec diverfa*. And this Matter being returned by the *Poftea*, the Opinion of the Court was, That the Ver-

Verdict was not good, and a *Venire facias de novo* was awarded. *Cro.* laſt Part 189.

Trinity-Term 1653. between *Web* and *Taylor*, Copies of a Bill, Anſwer and Depoſitions were proved, but not all read, and delivered to the Jury, who carried them with them from the Bar in a Bundle, which they laid by them and did not look on; yet their Verdict at the Bar was ſet aſide for this Cauſe, and the Court would not regard their ſaying, that they did not read them, for they might ſay that to ſave themſelves; it being a Fault to take any Thing without the Court's Knowledge. *Roll. Trial,* 714. *pl.* 6.

If the Names of the Jurors be tranſpoſed in the Panel of the *Habeas Corpora,* as thoſe which were firſt in the Panel of the *Venire facias,* be ſet laſt in the *Habeas Corpora,* 'tis good Cauſe for a new Trial. So held in the *Exchequer,* 1694.

If the *Venire* be returned, but not filed, the Panel may be changed; but by *Wyndham,* Not reaſonable the Jury returned ſhould be changed without Motion. *Keb.* 1 Vol. 562.

If one of the Parties ſay to the Jury after they are gone from the Bar, *Your are weak Men, it is as clear of my Side as the Noſe in a Man's Face*; this is new Evidence, for his Affirmation may much perſwade the Jury, and therefore ſhall quaſh the Verdict. *Roll. Trial,* 716. *pl.* 20.

If a Party ſpeak to them.

So if any of the Party's Servants ſpeak to the Jury, and the Verdict goes for his Maſter, it may be quaſhed; but if for the other Side, 'tis only fineable. *Keb.* 300, 1 Part.

So if any Thing be read to them, which they ought not to have with them, as a Book of Depoſitions, ſome whereof were read in Evidence. *Prat*'s Caſe 21 *Jac. Roll. Trial* 716. *pl.* 19.

The

Efcrow deli-
vered to a Ju-
ror before he
was fworn,
vitiates the
Verdict.

The Plaintiff delivered an Efcrow to a Juror impanelled, before he was fworn, who afterwards being fworn, and gone with the Jury from the Bar, to confider of the Verdict, fhewed the fame Efcrow to his Companions, who found for the Plaintiff. The Minifter who kept the Inqueft, informed the Court hereof, and the Jury being examined confeffed the Matter aforefaid, upon which Judgment was ftayed; for after the Jury are fworn, they ought not to fee nor carry with them any other Evidence but what was delivered to them by the Court: Afterwards the Plaintiff faid, That the Efcrow proved the fame Evidence which was given to them at Bar by him; wherefore it was not fo bad as if it had been new Evidence not given before: *Sed non allocatur.* 11 *H.* 4. 17. *Roll. Trial,* 714. *pl.* 8.

Church Book
delivered to
the Jury, Act
of Court.

Pafch. 38 *Eliz. Inter Vicary* and *Farthing,* at the *Nifi Prius.* The Iffue was about Nonage, and two Church Books were given in Evidence, one whereof was delivered to the Jury in Court, by the Affent of Parties, and afterwards the other was delivered to the Jury out of the Court, by the Solicitor of the Plaintiff, without the Affent of the Court; and a Verdict for the Plaintiff; and this was indorfed on the *Poftea*; the Queftion was, Whether this fhould make the Verdict void, or no? For the Juftices differed in Opinion, *Popham* and *Gawdy* that it fhould not, *Fenner* and *Clench* that it fhould; the Negative Juftices gave thefe Reafons; That the Book was delivered in Evidence in the Court, and fo the other Party might anfwer to it, and that the Court had informed the Jury of the Validity thereof, how far they were to believe, with many other Reafons: But the Affirmative was urged, becaufe

becaufe there might be fome Matter in this Book
to induce them otherwife than was intended before, and becaufe it was delivered on his Part;
for whom the Verdict paffed, without the Court's
Affent; yet Judgment was afterwards given for
the Plaintiff. *Cro. Eliz.* 411. *Roll. Trial,*
715. *pl.* 11. See *Moor's Reports* 452. The
Books differ, for *Cro.* makes *Clench* give his Opinion for the Verdict. But *Moor* brings him on
the other Side, which I conceive is trueft; and
for my Part, I know no Reafon why foifting of
Evidence to the Jury, without the Court, fhould
have any Favour at all.

In the Cafe of *Taylor* and *Webb, Trin.* 1653. Confider the Reafons in the former Cafes.
B. R. Twifden moved to fet afide a Verdict given
at Bar, becaufe that after Evidence, when the
Writings were delivered to the Jury, fome Writings which were not fealed (and therefore ought
not to be delivered to the Jury) were delivered
by a Stranger to the Jury.

Hale, Counfel of the other Side, produces an
Affidavit of the Foreman of the Jury, that they
made no ufe of them in giving their Verdict,
and that moft of thofe Writings were read in
Court, in Evidence upon the Trial; and *Hale*
faid, That if this fhould avoid the Verdict, then
it would be in the Power of any Stranger unknown, and againft the Mind of the Parties,
to avoid any Verdict.

Rolle Chief Juftice: The *Affidavit* of the Jury
ought not to be allowed to make good their own
Verdict, for now they are (as it were) Parties,
and have offended, and fhall not be allowed by
their own Oath to take off their Offence; and
it is the Duty of the Jury to look what Writings they receive before they go from the Bar;
and if any fuch Paper be wrap'd up among other

3   Papers

Papers delivered to them by the Court, so soon
as they have discovered it, they should call in the
Tipstaff who keeps them, and deliver it to him,
and to testify they made no use of it; and he
said it would be dangerous to give the least Way
to the delivering of any Writings to a Jury.

And at another Day, *Rolle* cited 11 *H.* 4. 18.
The Plaintiff (before the Trial) delivered a Bre-
viate of his Evidence to the Jury, which contained no more than was proved in Court, yet
by this the Verdict was avoided: So *Mich.* 31
Eliz. C. B. Metcalf and *Dean.* After the Jury
were gone from the Bar, they sent for one of
the Witnesses and re-examined him, who gave
the very same Evidence that he had before given
in Court, yet the Verdict was avoided; and the
Reason of both is, a Fear and Jealousy that other
Matters might be given, &c. *Roll. Trial*, 715.
pl. 13.

37 *Eliz. Farthing*'s Case: A Paper not under
Seal, which was given in Evidence, was delivered to the Jury; this did not avoid the Verdict, because here can be no such Fear; and by
Rolle, if any Writing (though not given in Evidence) be delivered to the Jury by the Court, it
shall not avoid the Verdict. And in the principal Case the Verdict was avoided.

Escrow from one who was no Party.   *Hill.* 40 *Eliz. Rot.* 147. In Arrest of Judgment after Verdict, it was alledged, that a Ju-
ror delivered to his Companions an Escrow for
Evidence to them, which was not given in Evidence at the Trial; and adjudged no Cause to
arrest Judgment, unless it had been received from
one of the Parties, which did not appear, *Moor*
546. but otherwise if it had been given by a
Party, and the Jury had found for him. *Roll.
Trial*, 715. *pl.* 15, 16.

In

The Jury ought not to *fee or carry with them any other Evidence*, than that which is delivered them by the Court, and by the Party himfelf brought into Court and given in Evidence, for it is Caufe to arreft the Judgment; as upon Evidence to a Jury to prove *J. S.* to be Heir to *W. S.* a *Pedigree* drawn by a Herald at Arms is not Evidence, nor will the Court fuffer the Jury to have it with them; for it is only private Information without any Proof by Office or other fubftantial Matter.

A Jury may have with them an Exemplification of Witneffes examined in Chancery upon Oath *who are dead*; but if the Exemplification comprehends fome Witneffes who are dead and *fome who are living*, they fhall not have it with them.

No Deed or Writing fhall be *privately* delivered to a Jury that was not *openly* fhewed; nor Copies of Books, &c. but with the *Affent of Parties.*

Writings or Books *not under Seal,* or a Fine indented not exemplified, cannot be delivered to the Jury *without Affent of Parties*; though if delivered by the Court without fuch Affent, this will not avoid the Verdict, where they are before given in Evidence.

Nothing can be delivered to a Jury *without Affent* but that which is of *Record or under Seal,* as the *Chirograph of a Fine,* though it may be given in Evidence, is not to be delivered to a Jury, and indeed if Evidence *under Seal* be read in Court, the Jury regularly ought to have it with them, but not if it be not under Seal.

Where there are feveral Depofitions under *the Great Seal* given in Evidence, fome of them are read, fome not, thefe the Jury may have with them as being under the Great Seal, and might be all relative to the same Purpose. *Vin. Trial,* 372.

In the Case of *Duke* and *Ventris, Mich.* 1656. B. R. tried at Bar, one Mr. *Beverley* of *Suffolk,* a Barrister, was returned of the Jury, who (having been at a Trial of the same Cause above twenty Years before, in the *Exchequer,* and heard there great Evidence to make a Deed fraudulent, which was now the Contest) demanded of the Court, whether he ought to inform the rest of the Jury privately of this, or conceal it, or declare it in open Court? The Court ordered him to come into Court, and deliver all his Knowledge which he heard then proved (which Evidence was not now given, because the Parties were dead); and so he did, being not sworn again, but only upon the Oath taken as a Juryman.

Nota.

And certainly it is of dangerous Consequence to receive a Verdict against Evidence, given on Supposal that some of the Jury knew otherwise, or on private Information given by one Juryman to the Rest, where he cannot be cross-examined; and let such Jurors beware of Attaint, but the best Way is (as before) in open Court.

Jury adjourned.

In a Writ of Error, the first Error assigned was, That *Termino Trin.* ten Jurors, and no more, did appear. This *ex assensu partium* was adjourned until *Crastino Animar.* on which Day two others came in and were sworn, being of the first Panel.

The Court were all clear of Opinion, That this is no Error, this being good enough, they being all to be called again. *Leon.* 3 Part 38.

If

If a Juror depart after he is fworn, he fhall be fined and imprifoned, and by Affent of Parties, another Juror may be fworn. *Bro. Jurors* 46. *Lib.* 5. 40.

If a Man be nonfuited after the Jury is ready ro give their Verdict, the Court may caufe the Amercement of the Plaintiff to be prefently affeered by the Jurors. *Lib.* 8. 39.

If a Jury give their Verdict by Lot, it is a Mifdemeanor and Caufe of a new Trial, although in *Prior* and *Powel's* Cafe, *Keble* 1 Vol. 811. a new Trial was denied, becaufe the Lot feemed there very innocent.

But fee *Keble's* 3 Part 805. A Jury, on *Affidavit*, that they gave their Verdict on throwing Crofs and Pile, were bound to appear to an Information; which 'tis faid broke one of the Jurors Hearts. *Keb.* 1 Part 811.

Upon a Motion for a new Trial, on the Judge's Certificate that the Verdict was againft Evidence in Perjury; the Court faid, there could be no new Trial for or againft the King, and denied it, but faid, the Certificate might mitigate the Fine.

Nota; The Court will not award new Trials on the Jurors gainfaying their Verdicts, unlefs the Judge, before whom it is tried, conceived the Verdict to be given againft Evidence, *Per Cur.* 13 *Car.* 2. *B.* 5.

The Jury appearing and fworn in an Information of Extortion, the Court would not difcharge the Jury upon a *Ceffat Proceffus*, fo the Attorney General caufed the Clerk of the Crown to enter a *Noli profequi*.

The Duke of *Richmond* verfus *Wife*, *Pafch*, 23 *Car.* 2. *B. R.* In an Ejectment the Parties had a Trial at Bar, and a Verdict for the Plaintiff.

tiff. The Court was moved to fet afide this Verdict, upon an *Affidavit* made of thefe Mifdemeanors in the Jury, *viz.* That they had Bottles of Wine brought them before they had given their Verdict, which were put into a Bill together with Wine and other Things, which were eat and drunk by the Servants of the Jury, and the Tipftaffs that attended them at the Tavern where they were confulting of their Verdict. That this Bill (after the Verdict given) was paid by the Plaintiff's Solicitor; and that after they had given up their privy Verdict, they were treated at the Tavern by the Plaintiff's Solicitor before the Affirmance of it in Court.

Council being heard on both Sides as to thofe Matters, the Court delivered their Opinion *feriatim*, that the Verdict fhould ftand. They faid, they were not upon a difcretionary fetting afide of the Verdict, as when the Jury goes againft Evidence: But whether thefe Mifcarriages fhall avoid it in Point of Law?

They all agreed, That if the Jury eat or drink at the Charge of the Party for whom they find the Verdict, it difannuls the Verdict; but here it doth not appear, That the Wine they drank was had by the Order of the Plaintiff, or any Agent for him: 'Tis true, in regard his Solicitor paid for it afterwards, it doth induce a Prefumption that he befpoke it; but that again is extenuated by its being put into a Bill with other Things that were allowable; and if the Verdict fhould be quafhed for this Caufe, it muft be entred upon the Roll, that it was for drinking at the Plaintiff's Charge; and it is not proved that this Wine was provided by him: And as to the other Part, That they received a Treat from the Plaintiff, after their privy Verdict given, and before

[Marginal notes:]
Mifdemeanor of a Jury.

Eating at the Party's Charge fpoils the Verdict.

Being treated by the Plaintiff after a privy Verdict, does not fpoil the Verdict.

before it was given up in Court, that fhall not avoid the Verdict.

But if the Defendant had treated them, and they had changed their Verdict, as they might have done in Court, it fhould then have been void. *Co. Lit.* 227. *b.* If after the Jury be agreed on their Verdict (which the Chief Juftice faid muft be intended fuch an Agreement as hath the Signature of the Court put upon it, *viz.* a privy Verdict) they eat and drink at the Charge of him for whom they do pafs it, it fhall not avoid the Verdict; and if it fhould, the Court faid, moft Verdicts given at the Affizes would be void, for there 'tis ufual for the Jury to receive a Collation after the privy Verdict given, from him for whom they find.

Unlefs it induces them to change their Verdict.

But fuch Practice ought not to be, and if any of the Parties, their Attornies or Solicitors fpeak any Thing to the Jury, before they are agreed relating to the Caufe, *(viz.) That it is a clear Caufe, or I hope you will find for fuch a one,* or the like, and they find accordingly, it fhall avoid the Verdict; but if Words of Salutation, or the like, pafs between them, (as was endeavoured to be proved) it fhall not.   Alfo if, after they depart from the Bar, any Matter of Evidence be given them, as Depofitions, or the like, though the Jury fwear they never looked on them, yet that fhall quafh their Verdict.   But they all held in this Cafe, that though there was great Matter of Sufpicion, yet there was not Matter of clear Proof (as there ought to be) fufficient to difannul this Verdict; but they faid, it was a great Mifdemeanor in the Jury, for which they ought to be fined, and that the Plaintiff's Solicitor had carried himfelf with much Blame and

Speaking to the Jury by a Party converned, where it avoids the Verdict.

Words of Salutation do not.

Papers given them after their Departure from the Bar, will avoid it.

Indif-

Tipftaffs fin'd Indifcretion; and the two Tipftaffs which at-
for not keep- tended the Jury, for that they were not more
ing the Jury
from Wine. careful, but connived at thefe Matters, were
fined the one forty Shillings (who appeared moft
in Fault) and the other twenty Shillings. 1
Vent. 124.

One commit- *Anonymus, Mich.* 21 *Car.* 2. *B. R.* One was
ted for fending committed for fending a Note to a Juryman, (af-
to know the
Privy Verdict. ter a privy Verdict given) to know what Verdict they gave. 1 *Vent.* 49.

The Jury being in great Doubt agreed to try
the Event by toffing up a Sixpence; and the
Chance being for the Plaintiff, they found a Verdict accordingly. The Court fet their Verdict
afide, and granted a new Trial; and ordered the
Jury, who were of the County of *Northumber-
land,* to attend the Court the next Term. *Jones
T.* 83. 2 *Lev.* 208.

C H A P.

CHAP. XIII.

What Punishment the Law hath pro-
vided for Jurors offending; as ta-
king Reward to give their Verdict.
Of Embraceors. Decies tantum. At-
taint. Several Fines on Jurors. What.
Issues they forfeit, and of Judgment
for striking a Juror in Westminster, &c.

YOU have already heard how the Court
may fine the Jurors for their Misdemeanors in giving up their Verdict; I will proceed
in shewing what Punishments they are liable
unto, if they neglect their Duty ; and doubtless
no Men have more need of knowing what Penalties the Law inflicts on their Offences, than
common Jurors, who too often being pre-en-
gaged with Favour to the Plaintiff, or Malice
against the Defendant, *& sic e converso*, or with
common Interest (as they call it) where Tithes
or Commons are in Question, will neither hear-
ken to their Evidence nor Direction of the Judge,
but subvert the whole Drift of the Common Law,
which will have them of the Neighbourhood
where the Fact was committed, to the End that
they knowing most of the Fact, may consequently give the best Verdict; yet contrariwise, Jurors who live nearest, do now-a-days, most commonly so fetter themselves with Favour or Ani-
mosities to the Parties; that those which live
farthest off (as Juries from other Counties) for
the most part give the clearest Verdicts. And
how

how fhould the Judges remedy this Mifchief but by feverely punifhing thofe Juries which offend? The Law in this will be their Guide, for without Doubt, (excepting Life and Member) the Law hath provided more fevere Punifhments againft Juries, than againft any other Offenders whatfoever, as well knowing that *corruptio optimi eft peffima :* And common Jurors generally have nothing to do with this Verfe, *Oderunt peccare boni, virtutis amore* ; therefore it is fit they fhould be concerned in the next, *Oderunt peccare mali, formidine Pœnæ* ; wherefore the Defcription of what this *Pœna* is, fhall be the Subject of this Chapter.

The Penalty of Jurors taking Rewards. If any Juror take a Reward to give his Verdict, and be thereof attainted, at the Suit of other than the Party, and maketh Fine, he which fueth fhall have Half the Fine ; and if any of the Parties to the Plea bring his Action againft fuch Juror, he fhall recover his Damages. And the Jurors fo attainted fhall have Imprifonment for one Year, which Imprifonment fhall not be pardoned for any Fine : This is by the Statute of 34 *E.* 3. *cap.* 8.

Shall not ferve of any other Inqueft. 5 *E.* 3. *cap.* 10. it is accorded, That if any Juror in Affizes, Juries or Inquefts, take of the one Party, or of the other, and be thereof duly attainted, that hereafter he fhall not be put into any Affizes, Juries or Inquefts ; and neverthelefs he fhall be commanded to Prifon, and fur-

Imprifoned and ranfomed, (that is) fined. ther ranfomed at the King's Will. And the Juftices, before whom fuch Affizes, Juries and Inquefts, fhall pafs, fhall have Power to inquire and determine according to this Statute.

A Man would think that thefe Statutes fhould have frighted any Juror from taking Rewards to give his Verdict. But,

—— *Quid*

—— *Quid non mortalia pectora cogis*
Auri sacra fames?

So sacred is this Love of Money, that Conscience herself must vail to it, and not stand in Competition with such Allurements: Wherefore the Law did redouble its Force; nay more, produced a *Decies tantum, scil.* That a Juror taking Reward to give his Verdict, shall pay ten Times as much as he hath taken; which Forfeiture, methinks, should make even those who love Money best, refuse to take Money upon such an Account, because it is like a Canker in their Estates, depriving them in the End, of ten Times more than it brought; for which hear the Statute 38 *E. 3. cap.* 12.

Item, As to the Article of Jurors, in the 34th *Decies tantum.* Year, it is assented and joined to the same, that if any Jurors in Assizes sworn, and other Inquest to be taken between the King and Party, or Party and Party, do any Thing take by them or other of the Party, Plaintiff or Defendant, to give their Verdict, and thereof be attainted by Process contained in the same Article, be it at the Suit of the Party that will sue for himself, or for the King, or any other Person, every of the said Jurors shall pay ten Times as much as he hath taken: And he that will sue shall have the one Half, and the King the other Half; and that all the Embraceors, that bring or procure *Embraceors.* such Inquests in the Country, to take Gain or Profit, shall be punished in the same Manner and Form as the Jurors. And if the Juror or Embraceor so attainted have not whereof to make grée, in the Manner aforesaid, he shall have the Imprisonment of one Year. And the Intent of
the

the King, of great Men, and of the Commons, is, that no Juſtice or other Miniſter ſhall inquire of Office, upon any of the Points of this Article, but only at the Suit of the Party, or of other, as afore is ſaid.

Upon which Statute there is a Writ called a *Decies tantum*; and who will may bring it, for it is a popular Action, and lies, (as you ſee) where any of the Jurors, after he is ſworn, taketh of one Party or of the other, or of both *Ambidexter.* (and then he is called *Ambidexter*) any Reward to give his Verdict, &c. And it may be brought againſt all the Jurors and Embraceors, although they take ſeveral Sums of Money, and although the Jury give no Verdict, or a true Verdict. So *F. N. B.* But it doth not lie againſt an Embraceor, if he faith; but for taketh no Money, and embaces, or taketh Moeth he is ney, and doth not embrace. See *Bro.* Tit. *De-* miſtaken, for *cies tantum* 13. and *F. N. B.* 171. the Statute mentioneth nothing of his taking Money; and in my Opinion, the Caſe of 37 *H.* 6. 13. is full againſt him.

A *Decies tantum* lies againſt the Jurors, though they do not give a Verdict, if they take Money. *F. N. B.* 171.

Embracery Embracery is defined in general to be an Atdefined. tempt by either Party, on a Stranger, to corrupt or influence a Jury, or to incline them to favour one Side, by Gifts or Promiſes, Threats or Perſwaſions, or by inſtructing them in the Cauſe, or any other Way, except by opening and enforcing the Evidence by Counſel at the Trial, whether the Jurors give any Verdict or not, and whether the Verdict be true or falſe. 3 *Bac. Abr.* 284.

Alſo

Also it is an Offence of this Kind barely to labour a Juror to appear and act according to his Conscience, or for any Person to labour a Juror not to appear; but it is no Offence for the Party himself, or for any Person, who can justify an Act of Maintenance, to labour a Juror to appear and give a Verdict according to his Conscience. *Ibid.*

Also it is an Offence to give Money to a Juror after the Verdict, unless it be openly and fairly given to all alike in Consideration of the Expences of their Journey and Trouble of their Attendance. *Ibid.*

So the bare giving of Money to another to be distributed amongst the Jurors favours of Embracery, whether any of it be distributed or not; and it is an Offence of the like Kind for a Person, by indirect Means, to procure himself, or another, to be sworn of a *Tales*, in order to serve one Side; also it is as Criminal in a Juror, as in any other Person, to endeavour to prevail on his Companions to give a Verdict on one Side, by any other Arguments besides the Evidence produced, and the general Obligations of Conscience. *Ibid.*

The Offence of Embracery is punishable at Common Law by Indictment or Action; and if it were not known before the Trial, will be a good Cause to set aside the Verdict. *Ibid.*

How Embracery is further restrained and punished by Statute, *vide* 5 *E.* 3. *cap.* 10. 34 *E.* 3. *c.* 8. 38 *E.* 3. *c.* 12. and 1 *Hawk. P. C.* 260, &c.

If a full Jury appear and some are challenged off, so that the Jury remains for Default of Jurors, the Defaulters shall lose their Issues.

Issues. Roll. Trial, 4 *H.* 631. pl. 1, 4. 6. 7. Other-

6. 7.   Otherwife if a Jury be fworn, and one is withdrawn by Confent.

Ibid. pl. 2.
But if there be a Joinder of Counties, and a Jury of one County appear, and not of the other; the Defaulters of that County from which enough came, fhall not lofe their Iffues, becaufe the Inqueft doth not remain for their Default, but for the Default of them of the other County. 48 *Aff.* 5. *Mes quære.*

Amercement.
If the Jurors at the Return of the *Venire facias* make Default, yet they fhall not be amerced, becaufe the Parties may be claimed at the firft Day, but at the Return of the *Habeas Corpora* they fhall. 10 *E.* 4. 19. 1 *E.* 3. 12.

Demand for Peine.
If any of the Jurors appear, the Court may charge them to inquire if any of the other Jurors were within the Town after the Return; and if they find they were, they fhall be demanded upon a *Peine*, and if they come not, they fhall be amerced. *Roll.* Tit. *Trial*, 632.

Juror fined for departing when he was challenged.
A Juror was challenged, and fix other Jurors were fworn to try the Challenge, who found him indifferent, and thereupon the Juror was demanded, but did not appear; for which Default he was fined the Value of his Lands for a Year; and the other Jurors inquired of the Value, &c. although the other Party then would have challenged him when he was demanded, fo that he might have been *treit*; but the Court would not admit this, becaufe then the King would have loft his Fine. 36 *H.* 6. 27.

Juror adjourned upon Pain.
If a Juror appear, and is adjourned upon Pain, and makes Default, in this Cafe, becaufe he fhall be fined to the Value of his Land *per Annum*, this fhall be inquired by his Companions of the Jury, becaufe the Court knows not the Value of his Land. *Lib.* 8. 41.

2   A Ver-

A Verdict was taken from the Foreman of the Jury, to which one of them did not assent, and Damages assessed to twenty Shillings, in Trespass and Assault; and afterwards, every one of the eleven were fined, for giving their Verdict before they were all agreed. 40 *Assize* 10.

Where a Jury are to be fined, a Fine jointly imposed on them, is not legal, but they must be severally fined, because the Offence of one, is not the Offence of another. *Et nemo debet puniri pro alieni delicto.* For then it might be said, *Rutilius fecit, Æmilius plectitur.* Lib. 11. 42.

A Man struck a Juror at *Westminster*, (sitting in the Court) who passed against him, and he was thereof indicted and arraigned at the King's Suit, and attainted; his Judgment was That he should go to the *Tower*, and stay there in Prison all Days of his Life, and that his right Hand should be cut off, and his Lands seised into the King's Hands. 41 *Assise, p.* 25. And now our Juror sees what Punishment it is to strike him in the Face of the Court, let him hold his Hands from others left the same Judgment light on him.

By the Statute of 27 *Eliz. c.* 6. It is enacted, That upon every first Writ of *Habeas Corpora* or *Distringas*, with a *Nisi Prius*, ten Shillings shall be returned as Issues, upon every Person impanelled, and upon the second Writ, twenty Shillings, and upon the third, thirty Shillings. And upon every Writ that shall be farther awarded to try any Issue, to double the Issues last afore specified, until a full Jury be sworn.

And these Issues being returned upon a Tenant in Fee-simple, in Tail, or for Life of another, or of himself, or in the Right of his Wife;

the

the Land he then hath will be chargeable for it, and any Man's Cattle upon this Land may be diftrained for it.

Not fummon-
ed.
But if the Under-Sheriff, &c. return a Juror fummoned, who in Truth was not legally fummoned, and therefore doth not appear, and fo lofeth Iffues, the Under-Sheriff fhall pay him double the Value of the Iffues loft. See the Statutes of 35 H. 8. 6. and the 2 E. 6. 32.

And *Note*; The Law hath been fo careful to punifh all Offenders, who would endeavour to biafs and corrupt the Jury; and to punifh the Juries themfelves, if they receive Money to give their Verdict, or any otherwife pre-ingage themfelves to any of the Parties, all which is to the End that a true an honeft Verdict may be given: What Punifhment fhall that Jury have which gives a falfe Verdict?

Such a Punifhment, that (as I faid before) in Civil Caufes, it is without Example: And furely, if the Jurors did bear it in their Minds, their Verdicts would be always grounded upon their Evidence; and not upon their own Intereft, or any Partiality to either of the Parties.

Attaint.
Wherefore, if the Jurors give a falfe Verdict (which is Perjury of the higheft Degree) upon an Iffue joined between the Parties in any Court of Record, and Judgment thereupon, the Party grieved may bring his Writ of Attaint, in the *King's Bench* or *Common Pleas*; upon which twenty-four of the beft Men in the County are to be Jurors, who are to hear the fame Evidence which was given to the *Petit* Jury, and as much as can be brought in Affirmance of the Verdict, but no other againft it. And if thefe twenty-four (who are called the Grand Jury) find it a falfe Verdict; then followeth this terrible and

heavy

heavy Judgment at Common Law upon the *Petit* Jury.

1. That they shall lose *Liberam legem* for ever, that is, they shall be so infamous, as they shall never be received to be a Witness, or of any Jury.

2. That they shall forfeit all their Goods and Chattels.

3. That their Lands and Tenements shall be taken into the King's Hands.

4. That their Wives and Children shall be thrown out of Doors.

5. That their Houses shall be rased and thrown down.

6. That their Trees shall be rooted up.

7. That their Meadow Grounds shall be ploughed up.

8. That their Bodies shall be cast into the Gaol, and the Party shall be restored to all that he lost, by reason of the unjust Verdict. So odious is Perjury in this Case, in the Eye of the Common Law; and the Severity of this Punishment is to this End, *Ut pœna ad paucos, metus ad omnes perveniat;* for there is *Misericordia puniens,* and there is *Crudelitas parcens.* And seeing all Trials of real, personal and mixt Actions depend upon the Oath of twelve Men, prudent Antiquity inflicted this severe Punishment upon them, if they were attainted of Perjury. 1 *Inst.* 294. *b.*

But now by the Statute of 23 *H.* 8. *cap.* 3. The Severity of this Punishment is moderated, if the Writ of Attaint be grounded upon that Statute.

Judgment in Attaint.

Put

But the Party grieved may, at his Election, either bring his Writ of Attaint, at the Common Law, or upon that Statute; wherefore let the Juror expect the greatest Punishment, when he offends.   3 *Inst.* 163, 222.

And so I conclude as to the Jurors, only with the Words of *Fortescue, Quis tunc (etsi immemor salutis animæ suæ fuerit) non formidine tantæ pœnæ, & verecundia tantæ infamiæ, veritatem non diceret sic Juratus?*

Who then, though he regard not his Soul's Health, yet for fear of so great Punishment, and for Shame of so great Infamy, would not upon his Oath, declare the Truth?

But as to our Practiser, I would give this one farther Advertisement, which relates also to Jurors.

When a Verdict has been given by a former Jury in the same Cause, and on the same Evidence, it is allowed to give the former Verdict in Evidence, and I have known this introduced by the Counsel, as obliging to the latter Jury to find accordingly; intimating, that otherwise they do (in Effect) perjure the former twelve Men; which may amuse tender Minds, and draw them from the strict Inquiry into the Merits of the Cause, in Favour of their Predecessors; which is a palpable Mistake and Misinformation for these Reasons.

1. The same Evidence in the former Cause and Trial (perhaps) was not so perspicuously delivered as in this.

2. This latter Jury may be of more sagacious and comprehensive Judgment than the former.

3. The

3. The Directions of the Court (which the Jury moft heed) may be more clearly delivered to this Jury.

4. The Matter in Conteft (perhaps) was not in the former Trial fo clearly managed by the Council, being not fo well inftructed as afterwards.

5. And laftly, fuppofing the Evidence equally delivered by the Witneffes, apprehended by the Jury, directed by the Court, managed by the Council, yet it is no Perjury or Fault to differ in Judgment; for if twenty-four Jurymen were to try a Matter of Fact, and twelve were of one Opinion, and twelve of another, who is in Fault, while they judge according to the beft of their Knowledge and Skill, to which (only) they are fworn? And it is a reafonable Kindnefs to Jurymen, to make good Conftructions of differing Judgments among them, while we fee how oft Judges themfelves differ in their Opinions, on a Matter ftated equally to them all, and that not only as to Matter of Law, but as to Matter of Fact; as attending Practifers may obferve in Trials at Bar, in the feveral Judges feveral Directions.   And this I thought good to advertife, for that I have known Verdicts gained on this unwarrantable Suggeftion, againft clear and exprefs Evidence, and could inftance fome Cafes: *Sed verbum fat, &c.*

As to the Difference betwixt the Judge and the Jury, and that Queftion which has made fuch a Noife, *viz. Whether a Jury is fineable for going againft their Evidence in Court, or the Direction of the Judge?* I look upon that Queftion as dead and buried, fince *Bufhel*'s Cafe, in my Lord *Vaughan's Reports* 135; yet fome of the Afhes thereof I may fprinkle here without Offence.

fence. It doth appear there to have been refolved by all the Judges, upon a full Conference
at *Serjeants Inn, That a Jury is not fineable for
going againſt their Evidence, where an Attaint lies.*
And that it is evident by feveral Refolutions of
all the Judges, *That where an Attaint lies, the
Judge cannot fine the Jury for going againſt their
Evidence or Direction of the Court, without other
Miſdemeanor.*

And where an Attaint doth not lie, as in Criminal Caufes upon Indictments, &c. my Lord
Vaughan fays thefe Words, *That the Court could
not fine a Jury at the Common Law, where Attaint
did not lie, I think to be the cleareſt Poſition that
ever I confidered, either for Authority or Reaſon of
Law.* And one Reafon for this (which can never be anfwered) is, the Judge cannot fully know
upon what Evidence the Jury give their Verdict;
for they may have other Evidence than what is
fhewed in Court. They are of the *Vicinage*, the
Judge is a Stranger: They may have Evidence
from their own perfonal Knowledge, that the
Witneffes fpeak falfe, which the Judge knows
not of; they may know the Witneffes to be ftig-
matized and infamous, which may be unknown
to the Parties or Court.

And if the Jury know no more than what
they heard in Court, and fo the Judge knew fo
much as they, yet they might make different
Conclufions, as oftentimes two Judges do; and
therefore, as it would be a ftrange and abfurd
Thing to punifh one Judge for differing with another in Opinion or Judgment; fo it would be
worfe for the Jury, who are Judges of the Fact,
to be punifhed for finding againft the Direction
of him who is not Judge of the Fact. But he
that would be better fatisfied in this Point, may
read

read that Case, and the Authorities and Reasons given by my Lord *Vaughan.*

It is shewed in that Case, That much of the Office of Jurors, in order to their Verdict, is Ministerial, as not withdrawing from their Fellows after they are sworn; not receiving from either Side Evidence after their Oath, not given in Court; not eating and drinking before their Verdict, refusing to give a Verdict, and the like; wherein if they trangress, they are fineable: But the Verdict itself when given, is not an Act Ministerial but Judicial, and according to the best of their Judgment; for which they are not fineable, nor to be punished but by Attaint.

Nor can any Man shew, that a Jury was ever punished upon an Information either in Law or the Star-Chamber, where the Charge was only, *For finding against their Evidence, or giving an untrue Verdict,* unless Imbracery, Subornation, or the like were joined.

But the *Fining and Imprisoning of Jurors for* Keb. 2 Part *giving their Verdicts,* hath several Times been 180. 1 Part declared in Parliament an illegal and arbitrary 162. Innovation, and of dangerous Consequence to the Government, the Lives and Liberties of the People; this celebrated Trial by Juries having been confirmed by many Parliaments.

Littleton, Sect. 368. tells us, That as the Jury Hardres may find the Matter at large, that is, a Special Rep. 409. Verdict, (which the Court cannot refuse, if it 1 Inst. 228. be pertinent to the Matter put in Issue) and leave the Law to the Court; so if the Jury will, they may take upon them the Knowledge of the Law upon the Matter, and may give their Verdict generally, as is put in their Charge. As for Example; upon all General Issues, as Not guilty pleaded in Trespass, *Nil debet* in Debt, *Nul tort, Nul diſſeiſin* in Aſſiſe, *Ne diſturba pas* in *Quare impedit, &c.* though it be Matter of Law, whether the Defendant be a Treſpaſſer, a Debtor, Diſſeiſor or Diſturber, in the particular Caſes in Iſſue; yet the Jury find not (as in a ſpecial Verdict) the Fact of every Caſe by it ſelf, leaving the Law to the Court, but find for Plaintiff or Defendant upon the Iſſue to be tried, wherein they reſolve both the Law and the Fact complicately, and not the Fact by itſelf. And ſo upon Not guilty to an Indictment of Felony, Breach of the Peace, Treſpaſs, &c. and other Caſes where the Law and the Fact are complicate and joined, they may determine upon both; yet I muſt give them my Lord *Coke's* Caution, which is, That although the Jury, if they will, may take upon them the Knowledge of the Law, and give a general Verdict, yet it is dangerous for them ſo to do; for if they do miſtake the Law, they run into the Danger of an Attaint. Therefore to find the Matter ſpecially, is the ſafeſt Way where the Caſe is doubtful.

And to end, as I began, That *Decantatum* in our Books (as my Lord *Vaughan* calls it) *Ad quæſtionem facti non reſpondent Judices, ad quæſtionem legis non reſpondent Juratores*, literally taken, is true; for if it be demanded what is the Fact? the Judge cannot anſwer it. If it be asked what the Law is in that Caſe? the Jury cannot anſwer it. But upon the General Iſſue, if the Jury be asked the Queſtion, Guilty or not? which includes the Law, they reſolve both Law and Fact, in anſwering Guilty or Not guilty. So as tho' they anſwer not ſingly to the Queſtion what is the Law? yet they determine the Law in all Matters where Iſſue is joined and tried, but where the Verdict is ſpecial. But in ſuch Caſes
the

the Judge cannot of himself anfwer or determine one Particle of the Fact, but muft leave it
to the Jury, with whom let it reft and continue for ever, as the beft Kind of Trial in the
World for finding out the Truth; and the
greateft Safety of the juft Prerogatives of the
Crown, and the juft Liberties of the Subject;
and he which defires more for either of them, is
an Enemy to both.

Abufes by others, in relation to Juries, are
punifhable by Fine and Imprifonment; as if a
Man affault or threaten a Juror for having given
a Verdict againft him, he may be indicted as a
Difturber of the Adminiftration of Juftice, and
one who is guilty of a Contempt to the King's
Courts.   2 *Hawk. P. C.* 58, 9.

Alfo the Court of *King's Bench* granted an
Information againft a Town Clerk, for publifh-
ing an Order of the Court againft Jurors who
had found a Perfon guilty of Manflaughter only
upon an Indictment of Murder, by which Order the faid Jurors were declared to be juftly fu-
pected of Bribery.   *H.* 10 *Ann.* The *Queen* v.
Wakefield.

CHAP.

C H A P. XIV.

The Learning of General Verdicts, Special Verdicts, Privy Verdicts, and Verdicts in open Court; and where the Inquest shall be taken by Default, Inquests of Office, &c. Arrest of Judgment, Variance betwixt the Nar. and the Verdict, &c.

Verdict.

VERDICT, (*veredictum, quasi dictum Veritatis*) is the Answer of a Jury given to the Court, concerning the Matter of Fact in any Cause committed to their Trial; wherein every one of the twelve Jurors must agree, or it cannot be a *Verdict*. And this is the Foundation upon which the Judgment of the Court is built, for *ex facto jus oritur*; the Law ariseth from the Fact; wherefore it is no Wonder, that the Law hath ever been so curious and cautelous, as not to believe the Matter of Fact, until it is

The Credit of Verdicts.

sworn by twelve sufficient Men of the Neighbourhood where the Fact was done, whom the Law supposeth to have most Cognizance of the Truth or Falshood thereof, which being sworn (for the Words are, *Juratores praedict. dicunt super sacramentum, &c.*) is the *Verdict* whereof we now treat: And such Credit doth the Law give to Verdicts, that no Proof will be admitted to impeach the Verity thereof, so long as the Verdict stands not reversed by Attaint. And therefore upon an Attaint, no *Supersedeas* is grantable by Law. *Pla. Com. 496.*

And

And it is worth our Observation, that the Law seems to take more Care of the Fact, than or hereof; for the major Part of the Judges give the Judgment of the Law, though the other Judges diffent. But every one of the twelve Jurors muft agree together of the Fact, before there can be a Verdict, which muft be delivered by the firft Man of the Jury. 29 Affiæ, pl. 27.

Verdicts are either *General* or *Special*.

General or Special.

A General *Verdict* is that which is brought into the Court in like general Terms to the General Iffue; as if a Defendant pleads Not guilty, or no Wrong, then the Iffue is general, whether he be Guilty, or the Fact be a Wrong or not; which being committed to the Jury, they, upon Confideration of the Evidence, fay for the Plaintiff that the Defendant is guilty of a Wrong, or for the Defendant that it is no Wrong, &c. 1 Inft. 228.

General Verdict.

A Special Verdict is where the Jury find the Matter at large, according to the Evidence given, that fuch a Thing is done by the Defendant; and declaring the Courfe of the Fact, as in their Opinions it is proved, pray the Judgment of the Court as to what the Law is in fuch a Cafe. And as a Special Verdict may be found in Common Pleas, fo may it alfo be found in Pleas of the Crown, or Criminal Caufes that concern Life or Member.

Special Verdict.

And it is to be obferved, that the Court cannot refufe a Special Verdict, if it be pertinent to the Matter in Iffue. 1 Inft. 228.

The Court cannot refufe it.

It hath been queftioned, whether the Jury could find a Special Verdict, upon a Special Point in Iffue, or no, as they might upon the General Iffue. But this Queftion hath been fully refolved

A Special Verdict may be found upon any Iffue, as upon an objection, &c. &c.

T 4

refolved in many of our Books; firft in *Plo. Com.* 92. It is refolved, That the Jury may give a Special Verdict, and find the Matter at large, *en chefcun iffue en le monde,* fo that the Matter found at large, tend only to the Iffue joined, and contain the Certainty and Verity thereof. *Lib.* 9. 12.

In all Special Verdicts the Judges will not adjudge upon any Matter of Fact, but what the Jury declare to be of their own finding, as upon an Inquifition or fuch like found at large in a Special Verdict; for their finding of it, is not an Affirmation that all which is in it, is true.

It is a *certain Rule* in all *Special Verdicts,* That if the Jury find the Point in Iffue, and only put a Special Doubt to the Court in a Matter of Law, it is a good Verdict; but if they don't find a fufficient Matter of Fact, to bring Light enough to the Court to refolve that Doubt; then it is an imperfect Verdict and an immaterial Iffue, and a *Venire facias de novo* fhall be awarded.

This Rule is founded on undeniable Authority, and on clear and evident Reafon, becaufe the Jury are Judges of the Fact, though the Judges are to judge of the Law arifing on that Fact; and the Jury, in finding the Gift of the Action, have taken upon them to find every Thing neceffary to make the Defendant guilty, if the Point of the Law be refolved for the Plaintiff. *Vin. Trial,* 398, 399, 403.

And in 2 *Inft.* 425. upon Collection of many Authors, it is faid, That it hath been refolved, that in all Actions real, perfonal and mixt, and upon all Iffues joined, General or Special, the Jury might find the fpecial Matter of Fact, pertinent and tending only to the Iffue joined, and thereupon pray the Direction of the Court for
the

the Law. And this the Jurors might do at Common Law, not only in Cases between Party and Party, but also in Pleas of the Crown at the King's Suit, which is a Proof of the Common Law And the Statute of *Westminster* the 2. *cap.* 30. is but an Affirmative of the Common Law.

And as this Special Verdict is the safest for the Jury, 1 *Inst.* 228. so in many Cases it is most advantageous to the Party, and helps him where his own Pleading cannot. As for Example, saith *Littleton*, Sect. 366, 367, 368. Albeit a Man cannot in any Action plead a Condition, which toucheth and concerns a Freehold, without shewing Writing of this; yet a Man may be aided upon such a Condition, by the Verdict of twelve Men, taken at large in an Assize of *Novel disseisin*, or in any other Action, where the Justices will take the Verdict of twelve Jurors at large: As put the Case, a Man seised of certain Land in Fee, letteth the same Land to another for Term Life, without Deed, upon Condition to render to the Lessor a certain Rent, and for Default of Payment, a Re-entry, *&c.* By Force whereof the Lessee is seised as of Freehold; and after, the Rent is behind, by which the Lessor entreth into the Land, and after the Lessee arraigns an Assize of *Novel disseisin* of the Land against the Lessor, who pleads that he did no Wrong nor *Disseisin*. And upon this an Assize is taken. In this Case, the Recognitors of the Assize may say, and render to the Justices their Verdict at large, upon the whole Matter; as to say, that the Defendant was seised of the Land in his Demesne as of Fee, and so seised let the same Land to the Plaintiff for Term of his Life, rendring to the Lessor such a yearly Rent,

A Freehold upon Condition, without Deed, may be found by Verdict, though it cannot be pleaded.

payable

payable at fuch a Feaft, *&c.* upon fuch Condition, that if the Rent were behind at any fuch
Feaft, at which it ought to be paid, then it
fhould be lawful for the Leffor to enter, *&c.*
By Force of which Leafe the Plaintiff was feized
in his Demefne as of Freehold ; and that afterwards, the Rent was behind at fuch a Feaft,
&c. By which the Leffor entred into the Land,
upon the Poffeffion of the Leffee. And pray
the Difcretion of the Juftices, if this be a Diffeifin done to the Plaintiff or not. Then, for
that it appeareth to the Juftices, that this was no
Diffeifin to the Plaintiff, infomuch as the Entry of the Leffor was congeable on him, the
Juftices ought to give Judgment, that the
Plaintiff fhall not take any Thing by his Writ
of Affize ; and fo in fuch Cafe the Leffor
fhall be aided, and yet no Writing was ever
made of the Condition ; for as well as the Jurors may have Conufance of the Leafe, they
alfo may as well have Conufance of the Condition, which was declared and rehearfed upon
the Leafe.

Littleton,   In the fame Manner it is of a Feoffment in
Sect. 367. Fee, or a Gift in Tail, upon Condition, although no Writing was ever made of it. And
as it is faid of a Verdict at large, in an Affize,
&c. in the fame Manner it is of a Writ of Entry, founded upon a Diffeifin, and in all other
Actions where the Juftices will take the Verdict
at large, there where fuch Verdict at large is
made, the Manner of the whole Entry is put
in Iffue.

But in Affize of Rent, it cannot be found
to be upon Condition, unlefs they alfo find
the Deed of the Condition. *Roll. Trial,* 690.
P. *pl.* 4.

So

So of a Confirmation in Fee to Leffee for Years. *Ibid. pl. 5.*

Per Hale Chief Juftice, *Guildhall, Hill.* 1671. A fpecial Verdict may be found as to Damages in an Action of the Cafe; as the Cafe was there, *viz. Pro Quer*, and if fo, *&c.* then fuch Damages; if fo, *&c.* then Damages fuch; and he faid, *He had known it fo done in Debt, and the Damages three Ways.*

Alfo in fuch Cafe where the Inqueft may give their Verdict at large, if they will take upon them the Knowledge of the Law upon the Matter, they may give their Verdict generally, as is put in their Charge; as in the Cafe aforefaid, they may well fay, that the Leffor did not diffeife the Leffee, if they will, *&c.*

General Verdict. Lit. Sect. 368. *Note;* The Court cannot refufe a general Verdict, if the Jury will find it; it was fo held before

Juftice *Wyndham*, Lent Affizes 1681. in *Verdon*'s Cafe, at *Cambridge.*

In *local Trefpaffes* the Jury cannot find the Defendant guilty in *another County*; becaufe it is local, but they may find Acts in any other Place in the *fame* County, for a Jury may thereof have Conufance: The Finding of *Affets* is *not* local, and may be found in a foreign County, even in *Ireland*; for Affets is the Subftance of the Iffue. Refignation, Divorce, *&c.* may be found in a foreign County, fo may a Deed, Leafe, and Releafe, or Grant of Rent, *&c.* in one County be found in another where Locality is not *fpecially* put in Iffue, or where the Place is not material, but is only put for the Venue. *Vin. Trial.* 379, 380.

The Jury may likewife find Eftoppel, which cannot be pleaded, as in the fecond Report, f. 4. it well appears, where one *Goddard*, Adminiftrator ſtrator of *James Newton*, brought an Action of Debt againſt *John Denton*, upon an Obligation made to the Inteſtate, bearing Date the 4th Day of *April, Anno* 24 *Eliz.* The Defendant pleaded, that the Inteſtate died before the Date of the Obligation, and ſo concluded, that the ſaid *Eſcript* was not his Deed ; upon which they were at Iſſue.

And the Jury found, that the Defendant delivered it as his Deed, *July* 30 *Anno* 23 *Eliz.* and found the Tenor of the Deed *in hæc verba, Noverint Univerſi, &c. Dat.* 4 *Aprilis Anno* 24 *Eliz.* And that the Defendant was alive 30 *July Anno* 23 *Eliz.* And that he died before the ſaid Date of the Obligation, and prayed Conſideration of the Court, if this was the Defendant's Deed : And it was adjudged by *Anderſon* Chief Juſtice, *Windham, Periam* and *Walmſley*, that this was his Deed ; and the Reaſon of the Judgment was, that although the Obligee in pleading cannot alledge the Delivery before the Date, as it is adjudged in 12 *H.* 6. 1. which Caſe was affirmed to be good Law, becauſe he is eſtopped to take an Averment againſt any Thing expreſſed in the Deed ; yet the Jurors, who are ſworn *ad veritatem dicend.* ſhall not be eſtopped. For an Eſtoppel is to be concluded to ſpeak the Truth, and therefore Jurors cannot be eſtopped, becauſe they are ſworn to ſpeak the Truth.

Note; That a Deed may be pleaded to be delivered after the Date, not before, becauſe it ſhall not be intended written before the Date, which may be after the Date, 12 *H.* 6. 1. As in Waſte ſuppoſed in *A.* to plead that *A.* is a Hamlet in *B.* and not a Town of itſelf, admitteth the Waſte, &c. 9 *H.* 6. 66. and the Jury cannot find No Waſte, for that would be againſt the Record.

Eſtoppel, 1 Cro. 110. lib. 4. 53. But if the Eſtoppel, or Admittance, be within the ſame Record in which the Iſſue is joined,

2

joined, upon which the Jurors give their Verdict, there they cannot find any Thing against this, which the Parties have affirmed and admitted of Record, although it be not true; for the Court may give Judgment upon a Thing confessed by the Parties, and the Jurors are not to be charged with any such Thing, but only with Things in which the Parties vary. 2 *Coke* 4.

So Estoppels which bind the Interest of the Land, as the taking of a Lease of a Man's own Land by Deed indented, and the like, being specially found by the Jury, the Court ought to judge, according to the special Matter; for albeit Estoppels regularly must be pleaded and relied upon, by apt Conclusion, and the Jury is sworn *ad veritatem dicend.* yet when they find *veritatem facti,* they pursue well their Oath, and the Court ought to judge according to Law. So may the Jury find a Warranty being given in Evidence, though it be not pleaded, because it bindeth the Right, unless it be in a Writ of Right, when the Mise is joined upon the meer Right.   1 *Inst.* 227.   *1 Inst. 227. a.*   *Warranty not pleaded.*

Verdicts ought to be such, that the Court may go clearly to Judgment thereon, and therefore Verdicts finding Matter incertainly, or ambiguously, are insufficient and void, and no Judgment shall be given thereupon.   As if an Executor plead *Plene Administravit,* and Issue is joined thereon, and the Jury find that the Defendant hath Goods within his Hands to be administred, but find not to what Value, this is an Uncertainty, and therefore an insufficient Verdict. *Lib.* 9. 74. 1 *Inst.* 227.   *Uncertain Verdicts.*

In all special Verdicts, the Judges will not adjudge of any Matter of Fact, but this which   *Special Verdict.*

the

the Jury declare to be true of their own finding. And therefore the Judges will not adjudge upon an Inquisition, or *aliquid Tale* found at large in a special Verdict, for their finding of this is not an Affirmation, that all which is in this is true.　*Siderf.* 2 Part 86.

The Office of the Jury.　It is the Office of the Jurors to shew the Verity of the Fact, and leave the Judgment of the Law to the Court. And therefore, upon an Indictment of Murder, *Quod felonice percussit,* &c. If the Jury find *percussit tantum,* yet the Verdict is good; for the Judges of the Court are to resolve upon the Special Matter, whether it was *felonice,* and so Murder, or not, *Lib.* 9. 69. And if the Court adjudge it Murder, then the Jurors, in the Conclusion of their Verdict, find the Felon guilty of the Murder contained in the Indictment.

A Jury may take Conusance of a Deed *without Date,* and made before Time of Memory, and find it if they will, though they are not bound to do it.

Intention.　The Jury cannot determine the *Intention* in Deeds or Wills; this belongs to the Court, who is to construe by the Rules of Law: But what is, or is not, *an Intent* to do a Thing within an Act of Parliament, this a Jury is to determine because the *Intent* is to be collected from Facts and Circumstances of which they are the proper Judges.

Matter of *Record* may be found by a Verdict at large, but the Jury are not compellable to find it; Recovery hath been found by Verdict without shewing of it under Seal; as also a Fine not pleaded or given in Evidence. So a *Note of a Fine,* or a Recovery without the Record itself, *sub pede sigilli,* or the Number Roll may be
given

given in Evidence, if the Jury will accept of it. Indeed these ought either *to be pleaded*, and made Part of the Record to be tried, or else given in Evidence *sub pede sigilli*, and then the Jury are bound to take Conusance of them. *Vin. Trial*, 384, 385.

A Verdict that finds Part of the Issue, and finding nothing for the rest, is insufficient for the whole, because they have not tried the whole Issue wherewith they are charged : As if an Information of Intrusion be brought against one, for intruding into a Messuage and an hundred Acres of Land : Upon the General Issue, the Jury find against the Defendant for the Land, but say nothing for the House; this is insufficient for the whole.

Verdict finding Part of the Issue. 1 Inst. 127. Moor 406.

But if the Jury give a Verdict of the whole Issue, and of more, &c. that which is more is Surplusage, and shall not stay Judgment : For *Utile per inutile non vitiatur. Leon.* 1 Part 66. *Cro.* 1 Part 130. But necessary Incidents required by Law, the Jury may find. *Siderfin* 232.

Finding more than the Issue. 1 Inst. 227. Where fatal, Sid. 96. Keb. 1 Part 289.

If the Issue be upon a Descent, and the Jury find the same, and a continual Claim, that as to the continual Claim is Surplusage. 7 *H.* 6. 8, 9, 10.

An Action of the Case on Deceit was brought, for that he sold unto the Plaintiff two Oxen, and warranted them to be sound ; on not guilty, the Jury found him Guilty as to one, and Not guilty as to the other; and good ; for that the Action was founded not on the Contract, but the Deceit. 3 *Cro.* 884. *Gravenor* and *Mete.*

In Debt the Plaintiff declares, that he had Judgment against Baron and Feme for a Debt

of

of the Wife's, *dum fola, &c.* that they were in Execution, and fuffered to efcape ; the Jury found the Hufband only in Execution, and efcaped, and Judgment for the Plaintiff. *Roberts* verfus *Herbert, Hill.* 12 *Car.* 2. *C. B.* 1 *Sid.* 5.

Plaintiff where barred though Verdict for him. In fome Cafes the Verdict may be found for the Plaintiff, and yet he may be barred.

As 40 *Aff.* 6. in a *Mortdanceftor*, all the Points of the Writ found for the Plaintiff, and yet he was barred for this Reafon; for although he was Heir to his Father, yet becaufe the elder Brother by the Half Blood did enter, he was barred.

Where the Verdict ought to be of more than is in the Iffue. Yet in many Cafes, nay almoft in all, the Jury ought to find more than is put in Iffue, otherwife their Verdict is not good ; and therefore they are to affefs Damages and Cofts, becaufe it is Parcel of their Charge, as a Confequent upon the Iffue, though it be not Part of the Iffue *in Terminis. Lib.* 10. 119.

A Verdict muft be fufficient in Matter and Form, be the fame Special or General, and therefore they muft find Damages and Cofts where the fame ought to be found.

Damages by the firft Inqueft. So in Trefpafs againft two, one comes and pleads Not guilty, and is found Guilty. In this Cafe, the firft Inqueft fhall affefs Damages for the whole Trefpafs, by both Defendants ; and afterwards the other comes and pleads Not guilty, and is found Guilty : The finding of Damages by the firft Inqueft, to which he was **Attaint.** not Party, fhall bind him ; and therefore if the Damages are outrageous and exceffive, the Defendant in the laft Inqueft fhall have an Attaint. *Lib.* 10. 119.

So

So in Trespass, *Quare clausum fregit,* if Issue be joined upon a Feoffment, and the Jury give outrageous Damages, an Attaint lies; for the Inquiry of Damages is consequent and dependent upon the Issue, and Parcel of their Charge. *Ibid.*

In the 11th Report, fol. 5. It was resolved, Damages by That in Trespass against two, where one comes the first In- and appears, &c. against whom the Plaintiff quest. declares with a *simul cum,* &c. who pleads, and is found Guilty, and Damages assessed by the Inquest, and afterwards the other comes and pleads, and is found Guilty; the Defendant which pleaded last shall be charged with the Damages taxed by the first Inquest ; for the Trespass which the Plaintiff had made joint by his Writ and Count, and done at one Time, cannot be severed by the Jurors, if they find the Trespass to be done by all, at one and the same Time as the Plaintiff declared.

So in Trespass against divers Defendants, if Several Da- they plead Not guilty, or several Pleas, and mages. the Jury find for the Plaintiff in all, the Jurors *Vide Devant,* cannot assess several Damages against the De- *cap.* 4. fendants, because all is but one Trespass, and 11 Coke 5. made joint by the Plaintiff, by his Writ and Count. And although that one of them was more malicious, and *de facto* did more and greater Wrong than the others, yet all came to do an unlawful Act, and were of one Party, so that the Act of one is the Act of all of the same Party being present. But in Trespass a- gainst two, if the Jurors find one Guilty at one Time, and the other at another Time, there se- veral Damages may be taxed. But if the Plain- tiff bring an Action of Trespass against two,

and declare upon a feveral Trefpafs, his Action
fhall abate.   And this is the Diverfity between
the finding of the Jury, and the Confeffion of
the Party.

Ibid. 7.

And in Trefpafs, where the Defendants plead
feveral Pleas, all triable by one Jury, and they
find generally for the Plaintiff, the Jurors cannot fever the Damages ; if they do, their Verdict is vicious.

Detinue.

If the Declaration be on feveral Damages,
touching every Part in feveral, the Verdict
ought to find the Damage feveral, as the Declaration is.

Wafte.

So in Wafte, for every feveral Parcel.

Præmunire.

So in a *Præmunire,* againft the Principal and
Acceffary.

Forcible
Entry.

So in a forcible Entry, where fome are
found to detain forcibly, and others to enter
forcibly.

Trefpafs,

If one be found Guilty of feveral Trefpaffes,
the Damages may be intire.

Jeofail.

If one of the Iffues be a Jeofail, and the Damages intirely affeffed, 'tis ill in both.

Coft.

But Coft in thefe Cafes muft be intire.

Judgment
*de melioribus
dampnis.*

But in Trefpafs againft two, where one appears and pleads Not guilty to a Declaration
againft him, with a *Simul cum, &c.* and afterwards the other appears, and pleads Not guilty
to a Declaration againft him alfo, with a *Simul
cum, &c.*   Whereupon two *Venire fac.* iffue
out, and one Iffue tried after the other, and feveral Damages affeffed ; In Judgment of the
Law, the feveral Juries give one Verdict, all at
one Time, and the Plaintiff hath his Election
to have Judgment *de melioribus dampnis,* by either of the Inquefts.   And this fhall bind all,
but *fiat nifi una Exccutio.*

It

. It is a Maxim, That in every Case where an Inquest is taken by the Mise of the Parties, by the same Inquest shall Damages be taxed by all. And in *Mich.* 39 H. 6. *fol.* 1. in an Action of Trespass against many, (who pleaded in Bar the Term before) and one of them made Default, which was recorded : There it is resolved by all the Court, That for saving of a Discontinuance, a Writ of Inquiry of Damages shall be award-ed, but none shall issue out, because he shall be contributory to the Damages taxed by the Inquest, at the Mise of the Parties, if it be found for the Plaintiff : And if it be found against the Plaintiff, then the Writ of Enquiry shall issue forth.

Damages.
11 Coke 6.

Writ of In-quiry.

And the Reason wherefore no Writ shall is-sue out at first, to inquire of Damages, until, &c. is, because that if a Writ should issue out, and be executed, this is nothing but an Inquest of Office, and not at the Mise of the Parties; and yet this Inquiry (if it might be allowed) ought to serve for all the Damages; for Inqui-ry of Damages shall not be twice, and the others which have pleaded to the Inquest, if the Issue be found against them, shall be chargeable to those Damages which are found by the Inquest of Office, and if they be excef-sive they shall have no Remedy, although there be no Default in them : For they cannot have an Attaint, because it is but an Inquest of Office.

Ibid.

So in Trespass of *Assumpsit* against two, if one confess the Action, or let it go by *Nil dic.* and the other plead, the Jury upon the Issue shall assess the Damages against both. *Keb.* 1 Part 623.

But

where any Point is omitted, whereof an Attaint
lieth, there this shall not be supplied by a
Writ of Inquiry, upon which no Attaint li- Keb. 1 Part
eth. And therefore in Detinue, if the Jury 882.
find Damages and Cost, and no Value, as they
ought, this shall not be supplied by Writ of Inquiry of Damages, for the Reason aforesaid.
Et sic in similibus. Ibid.   •

   The Plaintiff was nonsuit. And upon the In Replevin.
Statute 17 *Car.* 2. 7. the Jury inquired of the
Value of the Cattle, *scil.* 55. *l.* and *da.* 12 *d.*
But they did not inquire what Rent was ar-
rear : And it was moved to supply it by a new
Writ of Inquiry, as in a *Quare Impedit* ; but
it was answered, that the Statute says, in Case
of a Nonsuit, the same Jury shall inquire of the
Value of the Cattle, and the Rent arrear.
Sid. 480. *Keb.* 2 Part 409.

   A Verdict upon an Issue of Misnomer, plead- Abatement.
ed in Abatement, is peremptory ; and if the
Jury omit to find Costs, they cannot be sup- Costs.
plied by a Writ of Inquiry, *&c. Keb.* 2 Part
545.

   But how then ? What, shall the Plaintiff lose Verdict set
the Benefit of his Verdict, because the Jury aside, because
assessed no Damages, or did insufficiently assess the Damages
them ? Certainly in such Cases where Damages not well af-
are only to be recovered, he must lose the whole feffed.
Benefit of his Verdict; but where any Thing
else is to be recovered besides Damages, as in
Debt, Ejectment, *&c.* he may release his Da- Releafe Damages, and have Judgment upon his Verdict as mages.
to the rest. And so where Damages are to be
recovered, if Part of them are assessed insuffi- Carter's Rep.
ciently, and Part well, he may have Judgment 51.
for those Damages well assessed. And often-

Verdict set aside in Part, for Insufficiency in the Declaration.

times the Insufficiency of the Declaration shall set aside the Verdict ; as if an Action upon the Case be brought upon two Promises, and one of them be insufficiently laid, and the Verdict give intire Damages, this is naught for the whole ; but if the Damages had been severally assessed upon the several Promises, then the Verdict as to the Promise well laid should have stood. *Litt. Rep.* 6. 2 *Keb.* 488.

Release of Damages where none were assessed.

In the 11th *Report, f.* 56. *Marsh* brought a Writ of Annuity against *Bentham*, and the Parties descended to Issue, which was tried for the Plaintiff, and the Arrearages found, *&c.* But the Jurors did not assess any Damages or Costs ; which Verdict was insufficient, and could not be supplied by Writ of Inquiry of Damages : Wherefore the Plaintiff released his Damages and Costs, and upon this had Judgment ; upon which the Defendant brought a Writ of Error, and assigned the Error aforesaid, *scil.* the Insufficiency of the Verdict ; *sed Judicium affirmatur,* because the Plaintiff had released his Damages and Costs, which is for the Benefit of the Defendant.

In *Detinue* of Charters, on *Non detinet,* Verdict for the Plaintiff, and Damages, but the Jury did not find the Value of the Deeds, and a Writ of Inquiry was awarded to that Purpose, and returned, and ruled good ; and by *Twisden* Justice, Debt against Executor, who pleads *Plene, &c.* and it is found against him, and the Jury gave no Damages, that cannot be aided by Writ of Inquiry. *Burton* versus *Robinson, Pasch.* 17 *Car.* 2. *B. R.*

1 *Sid.* 246.

Release of Damages where they were not well assessed.

In *Dyer,* 22 *Eliz.* 369, 370. in a Writ of *Ejectione Custodiæ terræ & hæredis,* the Jurors assessed Damages intirely, which was insufficient,

cient, for it lay not for the Heir; yet the Plaintiff released his Damages, and had Judgment for the Land: And *Note,* That insufficient Assessment of Damages, and no Assessing is all one.

The Jury ought to assess no more Damages *pro injuria illata,* than the Plaintiff declares for; but they may assess so much, and more-over give Costs, which is called *Expensæ litis*; tho' in the proper and general Signification *Dampnum* also comprehends Costs of Suit, as the Entry, reciting both Damages and Costs, well affirms, *scil. Quæ dampna in toto se attingunt ad, &c.* Damages and Costs.

But if the Jury do assess more Damages than the Plaintiff declares for, the Plaintiff may remit the Overplus, and pray Judgment for the Residue, as in the 10th Report, *f.* 115. In Trespass, the Plaintiff declared *ad dampnum, &c.* 40 *l.* At the Trial the Jury assessed Damages *occasione transgressionis prædict'* ad 49 *l.* And for Costs of Suit 20 *s.* Upon which Verdict the Plaintiff, at the Day in Bank, remitted 9 *l.* Parcel of the said 49 *l.* assessed for Damages, and prayed Judgment for 40 *l.* (to which Damage he had counted) with Increase of Costs of Suit, and had 9 *l. de Incremento* added by the Court, which in all amounted to 50 *l.* and had his Judgment accordingly; upon which a Writ of Error was brought, and the Judgment affirmed. More Damages than the Plaintiff declares for.

Damages remitted.

For as in real Actions, the Demandant shall not count to Damages, *&c.* because it is incertain to what Sum the Damages will amount, by reason he is to recover Damages *pendant le Brief*; so in the Case of Costs, he shall recover *Ibid.* 117.

ver

ver for the Expences depending the Suit, which being uncertain cannot be comprehended in the Count, becaufe the Count extends to Damages paft, and not to Expences of Suit. For in per-

Damages in real and per- fonal Actions. fonal Actions he counts to Damages, becaufe he fhall recover Damages only for the Wrong done, before the Writ brought, and fhall not recover Damages for any Thing *pendant le Brief.* But in real Actions, the Demandant never counts to Damages, becaufe he is to recover Damages al- fo, *pendant le Brief,* which are incertain.

Damages and Cofts intirely affeffed. The Jury may, if they will, affefs the Da- mages and Cofts intirely together, without making any Diftinction, 18 E. 4. 23. But then they muft not affefs more Damages and Cofts than the Damages are which the Plaintiff counts to, for if they do, the Plaintiff fhall recover only fo much as he hath declared for, without any Increafe of Cofts, becaufe the Court cannot diftinguifh how much they intend- ed for Coft, and how much for Damage.

10 Coke 117. As in 13 *H.* 7. 16, 17. one *Darrel* brought a Writ of Trefpafs, and counted to his Damage twenty Marks; the Defendant pleaded Not guilty, and the Jury taxed the Damages and Cofts of Suit jointly to twenty-two Marks, and the Verdict was held to be good for twenty Marks, and void for the Refidue, becaufe it doth not appear how much was intended for Damages, and how much for Cofts; fo that there may be more Damages than the Plaintiff declared for, or lefs, and fo the Court knows not how to increafe the Coft; wherefore he fhall have Judgment but for twenty Marks, by reafon of the Incertainty.

Verdict a- mended by the Notes. Where a fpecial Verdict is not entered ac- cording to the Notes, the Record may be

2   amended

amended and made agree with the Notes at any Time, though it be three or four, *&c.* Terms after it is entered. *Lib.* 4. 52. *lib.* 8. 162. *Cro.* 1 Part 145.

In the Case of *Turnor* and *Thalgate, Mich.* 1658. *B. R.* it was said *per Curiam,* That special Verdicts may be amended by the Notes, but the Notes cannot be amended or enlarged by any Averment or *Affidavit,* for that were to find a Verdict by the Court. Yet in that Case, where the Notes were, That the Judgment, *&c.* was vacated *prout per Rule,* the Verdict was amended, vacated *per Curiam prout per Rule ;* for so much is implied in the Notes. *Notes. See Keb.* 1 Part 504, 907.

See a Verdict amended by the Notes after Judgment, and Error brought. 1 *Roll. Rep.* 82.

If the Matter and Substance of the Issue be found, it is sufficient, for precise Forms are not required by Law in special Verdicts, (which are the finding of Laymen) as in Pleadings which are made by Men learned in the Law, and therefore Intendment in many Cases shall help a special Verdict, as much as a Testament, Arbitrament, *&c.* And therefore though he which makes a Deputy ought to do it by *Escript ;* yet when the Jury find generally, that *A.* was Deputy to *B.* all necessary Incidents are found by this ; and upon the Matter they find, that he was made Deputy by Deed, because it doth tantamount. *Lib.* 9. 51. And in the fifth Report, *Goodal's* Case, it was resolved, That no Matters in a special Verdict shall be intended and supplied, but only that which the Jury refer to the Consideration of the Court. *Form. Hob.* 54.

In all Cases where the Jury find the Matter committed to their Charge at large, and over-more conclude against Law, the Verdict is good,

and

Ill Conclufion. and the Conclufion ill. *Lib.* 4. 42. And the
Moor 105, Judges of the Law will give Judgment upon the
269. fpecial Matter according to the Law, without
Litt. Rep. having Regard to the Conclufion of the Jury,
135, 94, 106. who ought not to take upon them Judgment of
the Law. *Lib.* 10. 11.

Upon every *General Iſſue,* if the Jury are
in Doubt, they may give their Verdict at large,
and leave the Matter to the Difcretion of the
Court ; but it is otherwife on a *Special Iſſue.*

Though the Jury may take upon them the
Knowledge of the Law, and give a *general
Verdict,* yet it is not prudent for them fo to do ;
for if they miftake the Law, they run into the
Danger of an Attaint ; 'tis therefore the fafeft
Way, where the Cafe is doubtful, for them to
find the *fpecial Matter.*

A fpecial Verdict cannot be given in any
Action but where the Iſſue is joined upon the
General Iſſue, and not where it is joined on the
fpecial Matter with an *abſque hoc, &c.* Yet *Coke,*
1 *Inſt.* 227. *b.* tells us a fpecial Verdict, or a
Verdict at large, may be given in *any Action,*
and *upon any Iſſue,* whether general or fpecial,
and that the Law is now fettled in this Point.
Vin. Trial, 399.

A Verdict may be taken by *reaſonable Intendment* where it ftands upright and nothing in the
Verdict to impugn it ; but where they find a
meer Matter of Fact, as Livery at fuch a Day,
this fhall not be taken by Intendment one way
or the other.

After a Verdict the Court will admit any Intendment to make the Cafe good, and all Sur-
plufage will be rejected, and no Prejudice admitted. See 2 Ld. *Raym.* 860, 865.

In

In a ſpecial Verdict, whereby any Man is to be charged or hurt, or convicted, though the Jury find *Matter of Evidence* enough for them to find the Fact, and give a Verdict againſt him; yet, if they do not find the Fact, *ſuch* Matter, though pregnant Evidence, will not warrant the Judge to *intend* the Fact or convict the Party.

After a Verdict it may be *intended*, That no Damages were given for Matter *inſenſible*; but of *ſenſible* Matter it cannot be ſo intended, tho' it may be inſufficient in Law. *Ibm.* 405, 406, 407.

Whereſoever a Jury begins with a *ſpecial Matter*, with a *general* Concluſion upon it, *contrary* to what the Law and Court judge upon the *ſpecial* finding; or, when they begin with a direct Verdict, and after deduce *ſpecial Matter, contrary* to their direct Verdict, and cloſe with ſubmitting the whole to the Court; in either Caſe, the *ſpecial Matter* makes the Verdict and over-rules the *general*. *Ibm.* 413.

Where the Declaration in Treſpaſs is, *Cum aliquibus avertis*, of a Number uncertain, and the Verdict is as general as the Declaration, *Cum aliquibus averiis*, there the verdict is good. *Cro.* 2 Part 662. ^{As general as the Nar.}

In *Ejectione firmæ*, where the Plaintiff declared of a Meſſuage and three hundred Acres of Paſture in *D. per Nomina* of the Manor of *Monkhal*, and five Cloſes *per Nomina*, &c. Upon Not guilty, the Jury gave a ſpecial Verdict, *viz. Quoad* four Cloſes of Paſture, containing by Eſtimation two thouſand Acres of Paſture, that the Defendant was not guilty, *Quoad reſiduum* they found Matter in Law. And it was moved by *Yelverton*, that this Verdict ^{Quoad reſiduum, incertain.}

Verdict was imperfect in all: For when the
Jury find that the Defendant was not guilty
of four Closes of Pasture, containing by Esti-
mation two thousand Acres of Pasture, it is
incertain, and doth not appear of how much
they acquit him. And then, when they find
Quoad residuum the special Matter, it is uncertain what the Residue is, so there cannot
be any Judgment given; and of that Opinion
was all the Court, wherefore they awarded a
Venire facias de novo, to try that Issue. *Cro.*
2 Part 113.

Quoad resi-
duum.

Ejectione firmæ of thirty Acres of Land in
D. and *S.* The Defendant was found guilty of
ten Acres, and *Quoad residuum* Not guilty;
and it was moved in Arrest of Judgment, that
it is uncertain in which of the Vills this Land
lay, and therefore no Judgment can be given:
Sed non allocatur; and it was adjudged for
the Plaintiff, for the Sheriff shall take his Information from the Party, for what ten Acres
the Verdict was. *Cro.* last Part 465. *diversitas*
apparet.

Circumstan-
ces.

Where the Jury find Circumstances upon an
Evidence given, to incite them to find Fraud,
&c. yet the same is not sufficient Matter upon
which the Court can judge the same to be
Fraud, *&c. Brownlow's* 2 Part 187. Yet in
many Cases the Jury may find Circumstances
and Presumptions, upon which the Court ought
to judge. As to find that the Husband deli-

Moor 192.
Cart. Rep.
16.

vered Goods devised by the Wife. Upon this
the Court adjudged that the Husband assented
to the Devise at first.

Postea amend-
ed, how.

Where a Verdict is certainly given at the
Trial, and uncertainly returned by the Clerk
of the Assizes, *&c.* The *Postea* may be amended,

ed, upon the Judge's certifying the Truth how the verdict was given. 1 *Cro.* 338. See *Keb.* 2 Part 875. Where the Court would not compel the bringing in the *Postea.* 1 Part 346.

In many Cases a Verdict may make an ill Plea or Issue good. As in an Action for Words *Thou wast perjured, and hast much to answer for it before God.* Exception after Verdict for the Plaintiff, in Arrest of Judgment: For that it is not laid in the Declaration, that he spake the Words *auditu quamplurimorum,* or of any one, according to the usual Form: *Sed non allocatur;* for being found by the Verdict that he spake them, it is not material, although he doth not say *in auditu plurimorum;* whereupon it was adjudged for the Plaintiff. *Cro.* 1 Part 199. So want of a Day in the Nar. made good by Verdict. *Keb.* 2 Part 354.

Ill Plea made good by Verdict.
2 Keb. 362.

See *Cro.* last Part 116. where the Bar was ill, because no Place of Payment was alledged, yet the Payment being found by Verdict, it was adjudged well enough, for a Payment in one Place, is a Payment in all Places. *Keb.* 1 Part 662, 771, 786, 793. *Sid.* 306, 290, 341, 342, 379. *Litt. Rep.* 184, 200, &c. *Mod. Rep.* 42, 43. *Hard. Rep.* 42, 43.

In an Action of the Case for Continuance of a Wall, by which the Plaintiff's Lights were stopped in an ancient House. *Per Cur':* The Plaintiff ought to shew the Wall was new, and is not helped by Verdict. *Keb.* 1 Part 584.

Not guilty is a good Plea after Verdict in *Assumpsit;* so on *Non Assumpsit* the Jury may find the Defendant guilty. *Keb.* 1 Part 795.

In

In an Action *sur Assumpsit,* laid twenty Years
since, *&* *non cul. infra sex annos, & replic. in-*
fra sex annos, which is a Departure, yet the
Verdict helps it. *Keb.* 1 Part 566.

In pleading *Riens avoit Jour del brief,* and
said not *Ne unque puis,* and the Jury find it, it
is helped by the Verdict.

But *Drake* said, the same after Verdict was
helped by the Statute of *Jeofails.*

The like 22 *E.* 4. 46. *Que le Baron ne fuit*
seisie que Dower Jour del Espousal, &c.

So if an Executor plead *Riens enter mains*
jour del brief, &c. and omit *Ne unque puis.*
5 *H.* 7. 14.

Debt *versus* Heir. Debt brought upon a Bond against an Heir
in the *Detinet* only, and upon *Riens per Discent*
there was a Verdict for the Plaintiff; it is naught
upon a Demurrer, but after Verdict is aided by
the Statute 16 *&* 17 *Car.* 2. *cap.* 8. which is
(after several Matters of Substance) thereby
enacted to be amended after Verdict, and other
Matters of like Nature, not being against the
Right of the Matter in Suit, *&c.* shall not stay
Judgment. *Sid.* 342. *Keb.* 1 Part 259, 278,
309, 470. 1 Part 662, 771.

An Indictment of Extortion against a Bailiff,
quod. colore officii extorsive & injuriose he took
Money, and sheweth not the Particulars; good
per Curiam, especially after Verdict. *Keb.* 1
Part 357.

A Repleader was denied. Keb. 1 Part 498, 829,

Way. In an information for not repairing a High-
way in their Parish. Upon *Non debent re-*
parare, the Verdict found so, for the Defendant. The Court held the Issue ill, because
'tis contrary to Law; the Way being in their
own Parish, they ought to have shewed who
ought to repair; and if the Verdict had found
that

that the Defendant ought to repair, it had been well enough ; however after Verdict the Court gave Judgment, that the Defendant should be acquitted.

Trespass by Baron and Feme *de clauso fracto* of the Baron's, and for the Battery of the Feme, *ad dampnum ipsorum.* The Defendant *Quoad* the *clausum fregit* pleaded Not guilty, *Quoad* the Battery justifies. And for the first Issue, it was found for the Defendant ; and for the second, for the Plaintiff, and now moved in Arrest of Judgment, That the Declaration is not good, because the Baron joins the Feme with him in Trespass *de clauso fracto* of the Baron, which ought not to be ; but for the Battery of the Feme they may join, whereto all the Court agreed ; but it was moved, That in Regard it was found against the Plaintiffs for this Issue, in which they ought not to join, and the Defendant is thereof acquitted, and the Issue is found against the Defendant, for that Part wherein they ought to join ; this Verdict has discharged the Declaration for that Part which is ill, and is good for the Residue.   As in 9 *E.* 4. 51. Trespass by Baron and Feme, for the Battery of both : The Defendant pleaded Not guilty, and found Guilty, and Damages assessed for the Battery of the Baron, by itself, and for the Battery of the Feme, by itself ; and Judgment was given for the Damages for the Battery of the Feme ; and the Writ abated for the Residue.   And of that opinion was *Lea*, Chief Justice, and *Dodridge*, but *Houghton* and *Chamberlaine contra.*   For the Declaration being ill in itself in Substance, the Verdict shall never make it good. Adjourned. 2 *Cro.* 655.

Baron and Feme. Vide Keb. 1 Part 944. Count against Baron and Feme, of Trespass done *cum averiis suis,* after Verdict allowed good. 946.

Reccel

Rochel and his Wife against Steel.

Rochel and his Wife brought an Action of Trespass and Assault in the *Exchequer*, *Hill.* 1659. against *Steel* and others, for beating the Husband and Wife; who pleaded Not guilty, and the Verdict found *Steel* Guilty of the Battery of the Wife, but found nothing concerning the Husband; wherefore Judgment was stayed; but the Barons held, That if the Jury had found the Defendant Not guilty, as to the Husband, then the Verdict had helped the Declaration, and the Plaintiff should have had Judgment for the Damages for the Battery of the Wife. *Hardress* 166.

Horton and his Wife declared in Trespass for beating the Wife, *ad dampnum ipsorum,* and good. *Siderfin* 387.

Of what a Verdict may be. Plo. Com. 411.

The Jury may find any Thing that may be given in Evidence to them, as Records, either Patent, Statute, or Judgment, Things done in another County or Country; for which see Evidence before, *Hob.* 227. And of those Things they ought to have Conusance; they

Incidents.

are to have Conusance also of all Incidents and Dependants thereupon; for an Incident is a Thing necessarily depending upon another. *Co. Lit.* 227. *b.*

How construed.

If the Verdict may any ways be construed good, a construction to destroy it ought not to be made. *Carter*'s Rep. 80, 94.

Outlaw.

If one of the Jury be outlawed when the Verdict is found, the Verdict is not good, but may be reversed by Error.

In a special Verdict, the Case in Fact must be found clear to a common Intent, without Equivocation. *Vaughan*'s Rep. 78.

If

If the Jury collect the Contents of a Deed, and also find the Deed *in hæc verba*, the Court is not to judge upon their Collection, but upon the Deed itself. The Jury may find the Contents of a Deed or Will proved by Witnesses. *Ibid.* Contents of a Deed.

Trespass for disturbing him of his Common belonging to an hundred Acres, and the Jury find Common for fifty, this is for the Plaintiff; otherwife upon an *Avowry*, or *Quod permittat*, which are founded upon the Right, but the *Trespass* is for Damages. *Palmer's* Rep. 289. Common.
Vide apres.

If the Matter and Subftance of the Iffue be found it is fufficient, though it be againft the *Letter* of the Iffue. As in the firft *Inftitutes*, *fol.* 114. *b.* A *Modus decimandi* was alledged by Prefcription Time out of Mind, for Tithes of Lambs, and thereupon Iffue joined. And the Jury found, that before twenty Years then laft paft, there was fuch a Prefcription, and that for thefe twenty Years, he had paid Tithe-Lamb in Specie. And it was objected firft, That the Iffue was found againft the Plaintiff, for that the Prefcription was general for all the Time of the Prefcription, and twenty Years fail thereof. Secondly, That the Party, by Payment of Tithes in Specie, had waved the Prefcription or Cuftom. But it was adjudged for the Plaintiff; for albeit the *Modus decimandi* had not been paid by the Space of twenty Years, yet the Prefcription being found, the Subftance of the Iffue is found for the Plaintiff. The Verdict may be againft the Letter of the Iffue, fo the Subftance is found.

Prefcription.

In an Affife of *Darrein Prefentment*, if the Plaintiff alledge the Avoidance of the Church, by Privation, and the Jury find the Voidance Avoidance.

by Death, the Plaintiff fhall have Judgment ; for the *Manner* of Voidance is not the Title of the Plaintiff, but the Voidance is the *Matter.* 1 *Inft.* 282.

Deprivation.

If a Guardian of an Hofpital bring an Affife againft the Ordinary, he pleadeth that in his Vifitation he deprived him as Ordinary ; whereupon Iffue is taken, and it is found that he deprived him as Patron ; the Ordinary fhall have Judgment, for the Deprivation is the Subftance of the Matter. *Ibid.*

Breach of 20 Trees cut down for 10.

The Leffee covenants with the Leffor not to cut down any Trees, &c. and binds himfelf in a Bond of forty Pounds for the Performance of Covenants. The Leffee cut down ten Trees, the Leffor bringeth an Action of Debt upon the Bond, and affigneth a Breach, That the Leffee cut down twenty Trees ; whereupon Iffue is joined, and the Jury find that the Leffee cut down ten : Judgment fhall be given for the Plaintiff, for fufficient Matter of Iffue is found for the Plaintiff to forfeit the Bond. *Ibid.*

Indictment of Murder, and Verdict finds Manflaughter. Sid. 325.

And this Rule holds in Criminal Caufes : For if *A.* be appealed or indicted of Murder, *viz.* that he of Malice prepenfed killed *J. A.* and pleads that he is Not guilty *modo & forma,* yet the Jury may find the Defendant Guilty of Manflaughter without Malice prepenfed, becaufe the Killing of *J. A.* is the Matter, and Malice prepenfed is but a Circumftance. *Plo. Com.* 101. 1 *Inft.* 282.

Modo & forma.

And generally where *modo & forma* are not of the *Subftance* of the Iffue, but Words of *Form,* there it fufficeth, though the Verdict doth not find the precife Iffue.

As

As if a Man bring a Writ of Entry *in casu proviso*, of the Alienation made by the Tenant in Dower to his Disinheritance, and counteth of the Alienation made in Fee ; and the Te- Alienation. nant saith, That he did not alien in manner as the Demandant hath declared ; and upon this they are at Issue, and it is found by Verdict, that the Tenant aliened in Tail, or for Term of another Man's Life.   The Demandant shall recover, yet the Alienation was not in Manner as the Demandant hath declared. *Littleton*, *Sect*. 483.

Also if there be Lord and Tenant, and the Tenant hold of the Lord by Fealty only, and the Lord distrain the Tenant for Rent, and the Tenant bringeth a Writ of Trespass against his Tre*s*pass by Lord, for his Cattle so taken, and the Lord the Tenant plead that the Tenant holds of him by Fealty against the and certain Rent, and for that Rent behind he Lord. came to distrain, *&c.* and demands Judgment of the Writ brought against him, *Quare vi & armis*, *&c.*   And the other saith, That he doth not hold of him in Manner as he supposed ; and upon this they are at Issue.   And it is found by Verdict, that he holdeth of him by Fealty only ; in this Case the Writ shall abate, and yet he doth not hold of him, in Manner as the Lord hath said ; for the Matter of the Issue is, Whether the Tenant holdeth of him or no ; for if he holdeth of him, although that the Lord distrain the Tenant for other Services which he ought not to have, yet such Writ of Trespass, *Quare vi & armis*, *&c.* doth not lie against the Lord, but shall abate. *Littleton*, *Sect*. 484.

Also

The Verdict may find the Defendant guilty of the Trespass at another Day or Place.

Also in a Writ of Trespass for Battery, or for Goods carried away, if the Defendant plead Not guilty in Manner as the Plaintiff supposeth, and it is found that the Defendant is guilty in another Town, or at another Day, than the Plaintiff supposes, yet he shall recover. *Ibid. Sect.* 485.

Conspiracy.

So the Jury may find the Conspiracy at another Day, for the Day is but Form.

Battery.

In Battery, if the Defendant justify at another Day with a Traverse, *Devant & apres,* he may be found guilty at another Day.

Son assault demesn.

If the Defendant by his Plea agree with the Plaintiff in the Day, Year and Place, and the Plaintiff reply *de son tort demesn sans tiel cause,* and the Defendant prove an Assault by the Plaintiff, the Plaintiff shall not give in Evidence a Battery at another Day. *Roll.* Tit. *Trial* 687. *Vide devant, cap.* 11.

And so in many other Cases these Words, *scil. In Manner as the Demandant or the Plaintiff supposed,* do not make any Matter of Substance of the Issue. *Littleton, Sect.* 485.

Modo & forma when Words of Form, *Siderfin* 357.

And 'tis a Rule, That where the Issue taken goeth to the Point of the Writ or Action, there *modo & forma* are but Words of Form, as in the Cases aforesaid. *Ibid.*

When of Substance, and must be found by the Verdict.

But when a collateral Point in Pleading is traversed, as if a Feoffment be alledged by two, and this is traversed *modo & forma,* and 'tis found the Feoffment of one, there *modo & forma* is material; so if a Feoffment be pleaded by Deed, and it is traversed *Absque hoc, quod feoffavit modo & forma,* upon this collateral Is-

So in *non Assumpsit modo & forma,* upon an *Indebitatus Assumpsit,* there *modo & forma* were not material. *Secus* when the Action is upon a Collateral Promise.

sue,

fue, *modo & forma* are fo effential, as the Jury cannot find a Feoffment without Deed. *Co. Littleton* 282.

But here is a Diverfity to be obferv'd, That albeit the Iffue be upon a collateral Point, yet if by the finding of Part of the Iffue, it fhall appear to the Court, that no fuch Action lieth for the Plaintiff, no more than if the whole had been found, there *modo & forma* are but Words of Form, as in the aforefaid Cafe of the Lord and Tenant, in *Littleton*, *Sect.* 484. it plainly appears; for it was all one, whether the Tenant held by Fealty only, or by Fealty and Rent, becaufe if either was true, the Tenant could have no Trefpafs, *Quare vi & armis*, againft the Lord in that Cafe, by the Statute of *Marlbridge, cap.* 3. 1 *Inft.* 281. *b.* *{Trefpafs Quare vi & armis lies not againft the Lord for diftraining his Tenant, without Caufe.}*

After the Verdict recorded, the Jury cannot vary from it, but before it is recorded they may vary from the firft Offer of their Verdict. And that Verdict which is recorded fhall ftand. 1 *Inft.* 227. *Plo. Com.* 212. *{Jury cannot vary from their Verdict when it is recorded.}*

There is alfo a Verdict given in open Court, and a privy Verdict given out of Court, before any of the Judges of the Court; fo called, becaufe it ought to be kept fecret and privy from each of the Parties, before it be affirmed in Court. *Plowd.* 211. *{Open Verdict and privy Verdict.}*

Becaufe the Jury may vary from their private Verdict; as if that find for the Plaintiff, the open Verdict may be for the Defendant, and this fhall ftand, and the private Verdict fhall not be deemed a Verdict; for the Jury are charged openly in Court, and in Court their Verdict ought to be received, and this which they pronounce openly in Court, fhall be adjudged their Verdict. *Plowd.* 211. *b.* *{The Jury may vary from a private Verdict.}*

And although it is ufual to take the Verdict fecretly, when the Jurors are agreed, yet this is not of the Neceffity of Law, but of the Curtefy of the Law, for the Eafe of the Jurors; and in this Cafe, their Saying fhall not be their Verdict till it is openly pronounced in the Court; for when they come in the Court, the Plaintiff fhall be demanded, and then may be nonfuited: But when they give their Verdict fecretly, the Plaintiff is not demandable, nor can be then nonfuited; but he may be nonfuited, when the Verdict of Right ought to be rendred; *ergo* the Force is in the giving of the Verdict in the Court, and not elfewhere. *Plowd.* 211. *b.*

Bro. *Tit.* Verdict, 12.

And alfo in the Court itfelf, if they pronounce their Verdict, they may change it, if they be miftaken, or if it be not full in Law, or for fome other reafonable Caufe immediately perceived; therefore if they may vary and contradict their firft Verdict given in open Court; *a fortiori* upon better Advifement they may do fo, when their firft Verdict was given out of Court, and they not difcharged; for they be in the Cuftody of the Bailiff, till they be difcharged in Court. *Plo. Com.* 211. *Moor* 33.

Jury fhall give but one Verdict in the fame Caufe.

The Jury having once given their Verdict, although it be imperfect, fhall never be fworn again upon the fame Iffue (unlefs it be in Cafe of Affize, when the Party is to recover by View of the Jurors.) But there muft be a *Venire facias de novo. Cro.* 2 Part 210.

Verdict good in Part.

If a Verdict be good in Part, and naught in another Part, it fhall ftand in Part, and a new Inqueft fhall be for the reft. *Bro.* Tit. *Verdict,* 89.

For

For the Jury's Direction in their Verdict, greater Liberty is permitted in pleading a Matter doubtful in Law; for a Traverse (for this Reason) may be omitted: As in Debt against an Executor, it is a good Plea to say, Administration was committed to him, and therefore he should be named Administrator, and not Executor, without traversing that he is not Executor; for the Lay-People know no Difference between one administring as Executor, and one administring as Administrator. 9 *E.* 4. 33.

What permitted in Pleading for the Jury's Direction in their Verdict.

For this Reason likewise the Special Matter may be pleaded together with the General Issue, &c. As that the Obligation put in Suit was sealed by him and delivered to *A.* to keep till certain Indentures were made between the Plaintiff and him, before which Indentures made, the Plaintiff took the Obligation out of the Possession of *A.* so is not his Deed. This is good, and yet by this general Conclusion, the Matter precedent shall not be waved, for it were perilous to put the Special Matter in the Mouth of Lay-People.   9 *H.* 6. 38.

A special Non est factum.

* So likewise in Trespass, if a Release be pleaded in a foreign County, and tried there for the Plaintiff, there also shall Damages be assessed by the same Jury. For where the Principal is tried, there also shall the Accessary and Incidents be inquired of. I need use no other Instances to illustrate this, than the Case abovesaid. *Roll. Trial,* 687. *L. pl.* 1.

* Where the Issue upon a collateral Matter is tried in a foreign County, Hundred, &c. where the Principal, there the Accessary shall be tried. 21 *Ass.* 14.

They may find a Condition to defeat a Freehold of Land, although it be not pleaded; but of Things in Grant, they must also find the

What Things the Jury must find.

X 4

the Deed of the Condition. *Ibid.* 690. *P. pl.* 1.

Modo & forma. Upon a Traverse of a Lease *Modo & forma,* the Jury may find a Lease of another Date, although the Date be miftaken in the Pleading, but not a Lease made by another, than from whom it was pleaded ; for this is out of the Iffue in Matter and Form. *Ibid. pl.* 6. *Hob.* 272.

Rent. In an Affize of Rent, the Jury may find that the Rent was granted with an Attornment, although no Specialty be fhewed. *Ibid.* 691. *pl.* 8.

Matter of Record. A Fine or Recovery may be found by the Jury without fhewing of it under Seal. The Jury cannot find againft what is admitted by the Record. *Siderfin* 271. *Roll. Trial,* 691. *Q. pl.* 3.

Record. If the Verdict be contrary to a Matter of Record, it may be fet afide as nought.

Infpection. If a Party be found by Infpection to be within Age, the Verdict that finds him of Age fhall be holden for none.

Jeofail. A Verdict finding Matter againft the Record is a Jeofail.   11 *H.* 6. 42.

Divorce. They may find a Divorce, which is a Record in the Spiritual Court, but not by our Law. *Roll. Trial,* 691. *Q. pl.* 4.

Attainder. The Verdict found an Attainder of Felony not pleaded, nor given in Evidence *fub pede figilli,* 26 *Aff.* 2. and the Court took it ill.

So if a Fine and Recovery were found, not pleaded, nor given in Evidence *fub pede figilli,* 26 *Aff.* 5. *Ibid. pl.* 2, 3.

The Jury is not to inquire of that which is agreed by the Parties. *Ibid. R. pl.* 1.

Dower. As in Dower, if the Tenant fays he has been always ready to render Dower, and the Iffue be

if

if the Husband died seised, the Jury is not to inquire if the Estate was dowable, for this is confessed. *Ibid. pl.* 2.

If the Defendant doth not deny the Waste, but pleads another Matter, *scilicet, nul tiel vill lou, &c.* The Jury is not to inquiry of the Waste, but give Damages although no Waste be made. *Ibid. pl.* 3. Waste.

In Debt upon a Bond, with a Condition to perform an Award, and the Defendant plead *nullum fecit Arbitrium*, and the Plaintiff reply, *fecit Arbitrium*, and sets it forth, and the Defendant rejoin *Nul tiel Award*, the Jury cannot find any Matter *Dehors* to make the Award void in Law, which doth not appear within the Award pleaded ; as that the Release awarded would discharge the Bond of the Submission ; for nothing is in Issue, but whether such an Award was made *in fait*, as is alledged ; neither could this Matter be alledged by any Rejoinder ; for it would have been a Departure from the Plea, and a Jury cannot find that which would have been a Departure, because out of their Issue. But in this Case, if the Defendant would have took Advantage of it, he ought to have pleaded all this Matter in his Bar, and not have said *nullum fecit Arbitrium* ; for 'tis a Departure in the Rejoinder, to acknowledge an Award which was denied in the Plea. *Ibid.* 692. *pl.* 10. Award.

In Debt for twenty Shillings, and the Issue be *solvit ad diem*, and the Verdict be *quod debet* the twenty Shillings, this is not good, because it is not direct but by Argument. *Ibid.* 693. *pl.* 4. How the Jury ought to find their Verdict, and what shall be intended.

In Debt upon an Obligation, if the Defendant say, That he is a Lay-Man, not lettered

3   and

Nient lettered. and 'twas read as an Acquittance, *& issint nient son fait,* if the Jury find he knew what he did, and that it was a Bond, and he was willing to be bound, this is no good Verdict, because they ought precisely to find if it was his Deed or not. *Ibid. pl.* 4.

If the Issue be, whether where a Copyhold is granted to three for the Lives of two, if he

Custom.   which died seised, *&c.* ought by Custom to pay an Heriot or not, and the Jury find that there was never any such Estate granted in the Manor, this is not good for the Reasons aforesaid. *Roll. Trial,* 693. *S. pl.* 1.

So if the issue be, if by Custom an Estate Tail may be granted, and the Jury find that it may be granted in Fee, which is greater, yet 'tis not good. *Ibid. pl.* 3.

Trespass.   In Trespass for taking and cutting his Leather, if the Defendant justify as a Searcher; and cut it for the better Search *More Scrutatorum,* without any other Damage; and the Plaintiff reply, *De injuria sua propria, absque hoc,* that he cut it *More Scrutatorum,* upon which Traverse Issue is joined, and the Jury find that the Defendant cut it as the Plaintiff has alledged; this is no good Verdict, because 'tis not any Answer to the Issue but by Argument. *Ibid.* 694. *pl.* 4.

Battery.   In Trespass and Battery in *A.* to find Not guilty in *A.* is not good; for it ought to be generally Not guilty.   *Ibid. V. pl.* 1.

In Debt on Bond against an Heir who pleads *Riens per Discent,* upon this Plea, if the Plaintiff reply, That he hath divers Lands in *D. per Descent,* and the Jury find he had divers Lands by *Descent,* this is good, without finding what; for 'tis not material, in regard upon this false

Plea

Plea a general Judgment is to be given without having respect to the Assets. *Ibid. pl.* 4.

In an *Ejectione firmæ* of five Acres, if they find the Defendant guilty in eight Pieces *de terra parcel' tenementorum prædict'*, 'tis a void Verdict because uncertain, and no Execution can be made of Pieces. *Ibid. pl.* 5.

In Ejectment of a Manor, on *Non culp.* the Verdict was for the Plaintiff for the Manor, and *Quoad servitia Non culp.* 'Twas objected, That the Verdict was not for the Plaintiff for the Manor, because as to the Services 'twas for the Defendant; but 'twas answered the last Part as to the Services was void and Surplusage. *Siderfin* 232. *Keb.* 1 Part 810. **Ejectment. Manor.**

In Case upon *Non Assumpsit* pleaded, if the Jury find that the Defendant *Non assumpsit*; yet if two Witnesses say true, then we find that he did assume. The first shall stand for the Defendant, and the last Words are void; and Surplusage shall not vitiate. *Roll. Trial,* 695. *pl.* 2. *Dyer* 372 **Verdict special. Surplusage.**

If in an Ejectment upon a Lease of twenty Acres, and the Jury find *quod dimisit* ten Acres *tantum*, and the Conclusion of the Verdict is, *Et si super totam materiam Curiæ videbitur quod Defendens dimisit* twenty Acres, then they find for the Plaintiff; and if not, then for the Defendant; this is repugnant, and so the Verdict is void in all. *Ibid. pl.* 4. **Ejectment.**

In Ejectione firmæ de 7 *Messuagiis sive Tenementis,* and Verdict *pro Querente.* 'Tis ill for the Incertainty, and the Verdict doth not help it; and *Hale* refused to let the Jury find for the Plaintiff, for the Messuages, and *Non Culp.* for the Tenements. But by *Twisden,* if it had been *de uno Messuagio sive Tenemento, vocato*

cato the *Black Swan*, it had been good, because the last Part makes it certain. *Siderfin* 295. *Keb.* 2 Part 80. *Cro.* 3 Part 186.

Certain.

To affess Damages incertainly, is void ; as to say we affess forty Pounds, if we must by Law ; if not, then but three Pounds, this is void. *Roll. Trial,* 695. *pl.* 6.

Damages.

Indebitatus affumpfit, to affess Damages *occafione debiti prædicti,* is good, although it ought to be *occafione non performationis, &c. Ibid.* 696. *pl.* 8.

Information.

In an Information upon the Statute 39 *Eliz. cap.* 11. for dying with Logwood, by which he lost twenty Pounds for every Offence ; upon Not guilty, if the Jury find him guilty for ufing this against the Statute for forty Days, by which he lost   this is not good, becaufe he forfeits twenty Pounds for every Time, and the Number of Times do not appear. *Ibid. pl.* 7.

If the Jury find the Words in the Will, and yet do not find the Will, the Verdict is not good. *Ibid.* 695. *pl.* 1.

If they first find the Special Matter, and then find the Iffue generally, the Special Matter is hereby waved. *Ibid.* 696. *X. pl.* 1.

Where a fpecial Verdict fhall be good by Intendment.

If the Jury find that *J. S.* was feifed in Fee, and devifed the Land to *J. D.* although they do not find that the Land was held in Socage, yet this is good, for this fhall be intended, this being a collateral Thing, and this being the moft common Tenure. *Ibid.* 697. *pl.* 4.

Devaftavit.

Verdict of Eloinment and Converfion to his own Ufes proves a *Devaftavit. Keb.* 2 Part 488.

Will.
Roll. Trial,
697. *pl.* 5.

If they find that he was feifed and made his Will *in hac verba, &c.* although they do not

find

find that he devised the Land as in the former; yet this is good by Intendment.

But if a Thing is left out, and cannot be intended, the Verdict is not good.

If the Issue be, whether the Sheriff took *J. S.* and kept him in Prison in Execution for certain Debt and Damages by Force of a *Capias ad satisfaciendum,* and the Jury find that he took him by Force of an *Alias Capias ad satisfaciendum, &c.* although they do not find that he kept him in Execution for the Debt and Damages aforesaid, according to the Issue; yet this is a good Special Verdict; for it shall be intended; for the consequence is necessary from this which is found, for he could not take him, but that he must be in Execution; *Vide* several Instances of this, *Roll.* Tit. *Trial,* 697. *T. pl.* 2.

If the Jury find that *J. S.* was seised in Fee, Will. and made his Will *in hæc verba,* and that he afterwards died; although they do not find that he died seised, yet it shall be intended that he died seised, and so good. *Ibid. pl.* 6.

If they find that *A.* did bargain and sell, Bargain and *&c.* although they do not find any Conside-Sale. ration, yet this shall be intended. *Ibid.* 699. *pl.* 6.

So if they find that such Persons *Authorizati* Letters Pa-*virtute literarum patentium Dominæ Elizabethæ,* tent. *&c.* and do not find that the Letters Patent were under the Great Seal, yet this shall be intended. *Ibid. pl.* 9.

Verdicts of Laymen shall be taken according Intent. to their Intent, and need not so precise a Form as in Pleadings. *Lib.* 4 65. *Hob.* 76. *Sid.* 27, 75. *Lit. Rep.* 133, *&c.*

Therefore

Therefore if the Jury find a Recognizance in Nature of a Statute Staple in this Manner, That the Conusor came before *R. O.* Recorder of *London*, and *T. O.* Mayor of the Staple, *& recognovit se debere* to *B.* for 200 *l.* and do not say, *secundum formam Statuti, &c.* nor *per Scriptum Obligatorium, &c.* although the Statute of 23 *H.* 8. provide, That it shall be by Bill Obligatory, sealed with three Seals ; and here it does not appear that there was any Bond or Seal, nor that it was according to the Statute ; yet these Things shall be intended, they having found a Recognizance before the Mayor and Recorder. *Roll. Trial,* 700. *pl.* 14.

Notes.

A Special Verdict may be amended by the Notes. *Keb.* 1 Part 907. see a Coroner's Inquisition amended by his Notes.

Where a Special Conclusion of a Special Verdict shall aid the Imperfections of it.

If the Jury find a special Verdict, and refer the Law upon that special Matter to the Court, although they do not find any Title for the Defendant, which is a collateral Thing to the Point which they refer to the Court, yet the Verdict is good enough, for all other Things shall be intended, except this which is referred to the Court. *Lib.* 5. 97. *Lit. Rep.* 135, *&c. Keb.* 2 Part 362, 412.

In Ejectment, if the Plaintiff declare upon a Lease made by *A.* and the Jury find a Special Verdict and Matter in Law upon a Power of Revocation of Uses by an Indenture, and Limitation of new Uses, and then a Lease for Years made to the Plaintiff by the Lessor in the Declaration, and another in which there is an apparent Variance ; but they conclude the Verdict, and refer to the Court, whether the Grant of a new Estate found in the Verdict be a Revocation

vocation of the first Indenture, or not: The Special Conclusion shall aid the Verdict, so that the Court cannot take Notice of the Variance between the Lease in the Declaration and Verdict, because the Doubt touching the Revocation, is only referred to the Court. And although they refer to the Court, whether this be a Revocation of the first Indenture, and not of the former Uses, and Limitation of new Uses, as it ought to be; yet in a Verdict this is good, for their Intention appears. *Roll. Trial,* 701. *pl.* 1.

So *Note* a Difference between a *special* Conclusion and Reference to the Court, and a *general* Conclusion and Reference to the the Court; *vide hic Postea.*

In Debt for forty Shillings for a Horse sold, and the Jury find forty Shillings Debt for two Horses sold; this is found against the Plaintiff, for this is not the same Contract.

For whom the Verdict shall be said to be found. Roll. Trial, 702. C. *pl.* 1.

So in Debt, for twenty Pounds, if the Jury find forty Pounds Debt, this is against the Plaintiff. *Ibid. pl.* 3.

In Debt for twenty Pounds for Wood sold, and the Jury find the Bargain was for twenty Marks; the Plaintiff shall not have Judgment for this Variance. *Ibid. pl.* 5.

So in Debt for Rent upon a Demise of two Acres, and the Jury find it upon the Demise of one Acre, the Plaintiff shall not have Judgment. *Ibid. pl.* 6.

But in Debt for twenty-four Pounds eight Shillings, received for the Plaintiff's Use, if the Jury find the Defendant owes twenty-four Pounds, but not the eight Shillings, the Plaintiff shall have Judgment; for perhaps he had paid the eight Shillings. *Ibid. pl.* 7.

I 1

In an Action upon the Case againſt *A.* if the Plaintiff declares, That by Cuſtom, *&c.* amongſt Merchants, *&c.* if two are found in Arrearages upon Account, and they aſſume to pay this at certain Days, that any one of them may be charged for the whole by himſelf, and then ſhews the Account of *A.* and *B.* who are found in Arrear in ſo much, *&c.* And promiſed to pay this at certain Days, but paid it not; and now he brings his Action againſt *A.* although upon *Non Aſſumpſit* pleaded, it be found that the Days of Payment are miſtaken, yet the Days being paſt the Action lies, becauſe the Law makes the Promiſe upon the Account, and the Days are no Part of the Conſideration. *Ibid. pl.* 8.

In Debt upon a Leaſe of twenty Acres, the Defendant pleaded the Leaſe was of twenty-four Acres, *ſans ceo que il demiſe les* 20 *Acres tantum.* The Verdict found the Demiſe of twenty one Acres only; 'twas looked upon as a *Jeofail,* and found for neither Plaintiff nor Defendant. *Dyer* 32.

If the Iſſue be Aſſets in *Sale,* and the Verdict be Aſſets in *Dale,* 'tis a good Verdict, for the Place is not material. *Keb.* 1 Part 662.

So of an Account before *A.* and *B.* an Account before *A. tantum* is good.

In Eſcape of Baron and Feme, and the Jury find of the Baron only, 'tis good, and ſo in other Actions grounded upon a *Tort* to find Part. But upon a Contract, the Verdict ought to purſue the Declaration, otherwiſe in Debt upon a Leaſe for Years, for Rent. *Sid.* 5, 6. *Keb.* 1 Part 371.

Iſſue whether Money was paid for *Blackacre.* Verdict, that it was paid for *Blackacre* and *Whitacre,*

Whitacre, good: So *per Twisden*, whether a Common was from *Lady-day* to *Michaelmas*, and the Verdict find from *Christmas* to *Michaelmas-day*, 'tis good. *Keb.* 1 Part 192.

Indictment of forcible Entry and Detainer, a Verdict of peaceable Entry and forcible Detainer, is sufficient to grant Restitution upon. *Keb.* 1 Part 419.

Barwel prayed a Bill of forcible Entry and Detainer; found *Ignoramus* as to the Detainer, and *Billa Vera* as to the Entry; might be quashed; which was done; for the Offence as charged being intire, the Grand Jury cannot apportion their Verdict as the Petit Jury on Indictment may. *Keb.* 1 Part 931.

Where all is to be given in Damages, the Jury are Chancellors, and may give so much as the Case requires in Equity.   *Damages.*

In Detinue of a Bond of 100 *l.* if the Jury find that he received a Bond of a greater or less Sum, the Verdict is for the Defendant.   *Detinue. Roll. Trial, 703. pl. 11.*

So in a Promise to do two Things, if the Jury find but one of them, 'tis for the Defendant. *Ibid. pl.* 12.   *Promise.*

Otherwise in Ejectment upon a Demise of ten Acres, if the Jury find a Demise of less, the Plaintiff shall have Judgment. *Ibid. pl.* 13.   *Ejectment.*

If the Issue be upon a Prescription for Common belonging to a Mesuage, and two hundred Acres of Land, fifty of Meadow, and fifty of Pasture; if the Jury find Common belonging to the House, twenty Acres of Meadow, and twenty of Pasture in two of the Vills, and not in the rest, the Prescription is not found. *Ibid. pl.* 14. *Hob.* 209.   *Prescription, Vid. devant.*

If Part of the Trespass, or Wrong, be found, it is sufficient in Trespass, or an Action of the   *Trespass.*

Case. Case upon a *Tort* ; as by a Commoner, for put-ring and depasturing Cattle in the Common. *Ibid.* 704. *pl.* 16, 17.   9 *Coke* 112.

Inductive Conclusion. If the Issue be, whether all the Lands in Execution were the Estate of the Father in Tail, or in Fee, and Part is found in Tail, and Part in Fee ; Judgment shall be given for the Defendant, who pleaded the Seisin in Fee. *Ibid.* *pl.* 18.

Ejectment. If the Plaintiff in Ejectment declares upon a Demise made the first of *May*, to commence at *Michaelmas* next, if the Jury find a Lease made at any other Day before the Feast, it is found for the Plaintiff ; for the Day of making is not material. *Ibid. pl.* 10.

Otherwise of a Lease of Years in Possession ; as of a Lease made the 5th of *May*, *Habend.* for three Years from *Lady-day* before ; and the Jury find a Lease made the 15th Day of *May*, for three Years from the same *Lady-day* ; for this is a Lease in Possession. *Ibid. pl.* 21.

Imprisonment. In false Imprisonment in *Middlesex*, and the Defendant justifies in *London*, to which the Plaintiff saith, the Defendant took him in *Middlesex de son Tort demesn* ; and Issue upon this, and the Jury find the Defendant took him in *Middlesex* lawfully, upon a Writ, yet this is for the Plaintiff ; for the Issue is upon the Place, and not upon the *Tort*, for that is confessed by the Pleading, if the Taking was in *Middlesex*. *Ibid.* 705. *pl.* 31.

Debt. *Ibid. 705. pl. 32.* In Debt for twenty Pounds, and the Jury find forty Pounds, the Plaintiff shall not have Judgment ; the Reason seems to be, because it cannot be the same Debt, which is intire ; but upon another Contract which is mis-laid.

If the Issue be Payment after Execution, and *Audita Que-* the Jury find Payment before, yet the issue is *rela.* proved; for Payment before is Payment after. *Ibid. pl.* 34.

In Debt upon a Bond, bearing Date the 25th *Obligation.* of *June,* upon *Non est factum,* if the Jury find it his Deed, but that it was delivered eight Days after the Date, this is found for the Plaintiff. *Ibid. pl.* 35.

If the Issue be, that two made the Feoffment, *Joint and se-* or two were Church-wardens, *&c.* and the Jury *veral.* find but one, *&c.* the Issue is not found. *Ibid. pl.* 36, 37.

If the Breach of Covenant or Waste be as- *Obligation.* signed in cutting twenty Trees, and the Jury *Covenant.* find but ten, yet the Plaintiff shall have Judg- *Waste.* ment. *Ibid. pl.* 40.

If in *Replevin, &c.* the Jury find that Part *Totum &* of the Cattle were Levant and Couchant, and *pars.* Part not, and the Issue is upon all, the Issue is not found. *Ibid. pl.* 41.

In Debt, *tam quam,* on the Statute 1 *Jac. cap.* 22. for cutting Oaks unseasonably; on Not guilty, and Verdict for the Plaintiff, it was excepted in Arrest of Judgment, That the Jury found the Value of each Tree, six Shillings eight Pence, but do not cast up the Sum. *Sed per Curiam,* In this Issue it is needless; but had the Issue been *Nil debet,* they must cast it up, and not leave it to the Court. *Keb.* 1 Part 835.

Keiynge excepted to an Indictment of Assault, *Indictment.* Battery and Wounding. The Jury find him only guilty *de transgres. & insult. præd. Sed per Cur',* 'Tis well enough, and comprehends the whole; *contra* if it had been *de insult. præd'* only. And the Presentment, Traverse and

Trial was all at the same Day and Sessions, *ex assensu,* being a Favour to the Party. *Keb.* 1 Part 879.

Ejectment.
Void in Part. In Ejectment of fourteen Acres, the Defendant pleaded Not guilty, the Jury find him Guilty of twenty, the Plaintiff shall have Judgment for the fourteen, and the Verdict is void for the Residue. *Roll. Trial,* 707. *pl.* 42.

Information.
Usury. In an Information upon an Usurious Contract by two, it is not sufficient to find a Contract by one. Otherwise where the *Tort* and Offence is several, as against two upon the Statute 4 *E.* 6. *Pro emptione butiri,* and selling it by Retail, *&c.* and so in an Action upon the Case in Nature of Conspiracy, and for Words laid twice in **Modo & forma.** one Declaration. This will put in Issue the Manner as well as the Matter where the Manner is Material, as the Time of the Fact and other Circumstances. *Ibid. pl.* 49, 50.

Replevin.
Lease. In Replevin the Defendant avows as a Commoner; the Plaintiff replies, that *W.* made a Lease to him 30 *Martii, Habend.* from *Lady-day* last, and Issue *Modo & forma;* and the Jury find a Lease made 25 *Martii, Habendum extunc* for a Year; this is good, although the Time of making and Commencement of the Lease is mistaken, in as much as *extunc* includes the Feast. Yet because a sufficient Title and Lease is found for the Plaintiff to put in his Cattle, this is sufficient; this being the Substance, and the *Modo & forma* shall not put the Circumstances in Issue. *Roll. Trial,* 707. *pl.* 44, 54.

Ibid. 708. *pl.* 55. So in Trespass, if the Defendant justify the putting in his Cattle for Common, which he claims from *Pentecost,* to a certain Time every Year, which is traversed *Modo & forma,* and

the

the Jury find that he had Common *in vigilia Pentecostes in festo*, this is found for the Defendant.

But otherwise in these Cases, in an Assize of Common, because there he ought to recover his Title. *Ibid. pl. 56.*

In Debt for Rent, if the Defendant plead an Entry by the plaintiff, before the Rent was due, *scilicet* such a Day, which was after, and Issue upon the Entry *Modo & forma*, and the Jury find for the Defendant, he shall have Judgment; for the *Scilicet* is void, and the *Modo & forma* go to the Matter. See after. *Ibid.* 709. *pl.* 59.

In Debt upon a Bond, and the Defendant plead *Non est factum*, and the Jury find the Bond made jointly by another with the Defendant, the Plaintiff shall have Judgment; for the Defendant should have pleaded this. *Ibid. pl.* 60. *5 Coke* 119. *Non est factum.*

If a Devise be pleaded absolute, if the Jury find a Devise upon a Condition precedent, it is not good. *Ibid. pl.* 61. *Devise.*

In Debt against *A.* as Daughter and Heir to *B.* and the Defendant plead *Riens per Discent*, of *B.* and the Jury find that *B.* was seised in Fee, and died, having Issue the Defendant his Daughter, and his Wife with Child of a Boy, who was afterwards born alive, and died one Hour after; this Issue is found against the Plaintiff, because the Defendant had the Land as Heir to her Brother, who was last seised, and not to the Father, and so the Defendant had not the Land by Discent from the Father, but from the Brother; yet this is Assets in her Hands, if it had been specially pleaded. *Ibid. pl.* 62. *Riens per Discent.*

Y 3

In

Error.   In a Writ of Error brought by him in Remainder in Tail to reverſe a Fine, if the Defendant plead in Bar of the writ of Error, a Common Recovery by the Tenant in Tail ; to which the Plaintiff replies, That at the Time of the Recovery ſuffered, he himſelf was Tenant to the *Præcipe*, and ſo the Recovery void, upon which Iſſue is joined, and the Jury find that he was Tenant of Part, but not of other Part.

Part.   This Iſſue is partly found for the Plaintiff, and partly for the Defendant, ſo the Court ſhall proceed to the Examination of the Error, for that whereof he is found no Tenant ; but it is a good Bar of the Writ of Error, for that whereof he is found Tenant to the *Præcipe*. *Ibid.* 711. *pl.* 4.

Promiſe.   In *Aſſumpſit* to pay Money upon Requeſt, and Iſſue upon this, if the Jury find the Plaintiff promiſed to pay the Money, but do not ſay upon Requeſt, nor *Modo & forma*, it is not found for the Plaintiff. *Ibid. pl.* 5.

If the Subſtance of the Iſſue be found it is ſufficient. Manor.   In Ejectment of a Manor, if the Jury find that there were no Freeholders, and ſo it is no Manor in Law, yet being a Manor by Reputation, and ſo the Tenements paſs by the Leaſe ; therefore this Verdict is found for him who pleads the Leaſe of the Manor, for the Subſtance is, Whether any Thing was demiſed or not ? *Ibid.* 712. *pl.* 1.

Gaol.   In an Information of Extortion againſt the Gaoler of the Gaol, or Priſon of the Caſtle of *Maidſtone* ; the Jury found there was no Caſtle, but that there was a Gaol ; this was for the Plaintiff, becauſe Gaol is the Subſtance. *Ibid.* 711. *pl.* 6.

Account.   If the Iſſue be, Whether the Defendant had accounted before *R.* and *W.* Auditors aſſigned

signed by the Plaintiff, and the Jury find an
Account before *R.* only, the Issue is found
for the Defendant; for the Account is the
Effect of the Issue. *Vide Roll.* Tit. *Trial*, 707.
pl. 46.

If Eleven agree, and the Twelfth will not, Jury agree.
the Verdict of the Eleven cannot be taken, but *Ibid.* 712. *pl.*
the Court may carry the Jurors with them in 9.
Carts until they are agreed. 41 *Aff.* 11.

A privy Verdict may be altered in open Verdict al-
Court. *Ibid. pl.* 1. tered.

In an *Extendi fac.* upon a Statute, if the Jury deliver their Verdict in Writing, they may
afterwards make it more formal, but they cannot alter it in Substance, for it is a compleat
Verdict by the Delivery. So of Presentments,
&c. Ibid. pl. 2.

A Fine pleaded in Bar, and that after the Fine and
Death of *A. scil.* 1 *August* 3 *Car.* B. Father of Non claim.
the Plaintiff was alive, *& in plena vita, & remansit infra hoc regnum infra quatuor Maria,
&c. apud* W. *in Com.* D. and no Entry or
Claim within five Years after; and the Plaintiff
replies, and takes Issue, *Que il non fuit & remansit infra hoc regnum Angliæ modo et forma,
&c.* And the Jury find *Quod non fuit & remansit infra hoc Regnum Angliæ* 1 *August*
3 *Car.* but that he was there 1 *Maii* 4 *Car.*
and remained there a Month, and refer to
the Court, *An fuit & remansit infra hoc
Regnum modo & forma, &c.* This Issue is *Modo & for-*
found for the Defendant, for the Matter and *ma.*
Substance of the Plea is, whether he was within the Realm after the Death of *A.* and five
Years before Entry or Claim *per* him or the
Plaintiff, and *modo & forma* shall not make
Y 4 the

the Day material. *Roll.* Tit. *Trial,* 713. *F. pl.* 1.

Judgment, arrested, at what Time.

Judgment upon a Demurrer, and a Writ of Inquiry executed at the Return; the Party may shew any Thing in Arrest of Judgment; for Judgment is not compleat until the last Judgment. The first is but an Award: A Man may plead any Thing in Arrest of Judgment after Verdict, which will make Error if the Judgment be given. *Roll. Trial,* 716. *H.* 1. *I.* 1.

In Debt upon a simple Contract against an Executor, if he will not plead in Abatement, but other Matter which is found against him, he shall not afterwards alledge that he is not chargeable in Arrest of Judgment. *Ibid. pl.* 2.

So in Debt against Executors upon Arrearages of Account, where they are not chargeable. *Ibid. pl.* 3.

What may be alledged.

That which appears ill upon the same Record, may be alledged in Arrest of Judgment; but not a Matter of Fact, which doth not appear upon the Record, because the Parties cannot try the Issue. As that a Juror was challenged, and yet served on the *Tales,* for this cannot appear without alledging Matter of Fact. Nor that the Defendant's Attorney had no Warrant. But if there be any irregular or foul Practice, this may be offered to set aside a Judgment. *Ibid. K. pl.* 1, 2, 3, 4.

Visne.

In Error upon Judgment in *Durham,* in Debt upon Bond to pay twenty Pounds; the Defendant pleaded *solvit ad diem,* not saying where; a Verdict thereupon is void, because there is no *Visne,* and so no Trial. *Keb.* 2 Part 620.

If

If any Thing be omitted in the Declaration, or if more is put in the Declaration than is found by the Jury, if it makes a material Variance betwixt the Nar and the Verdict, the Action shall abate. Variance between the Verdict and the Declaration.

These following are adjudged material Variances. *Roll. Trial,* 717, 718.

If the Declaration be for these Words, *Thou procuredst eight or ten of thy Neighbours to perjure themselves,* and the Jury find that he said, *Thou hast caused eight or Ten, &c.* for it might be a remote cause, *scilicet* with out Procurement. Nar. *He is a Bankrupt.* Ver. *He will be a Bankrupt within two Days.* Nar. *He is a Thief.* Ver. *He stole a Horse.* Nar. *Thou art a Murderer.* Ver. *He is, &c.* Nar. *I know him to be a Thief.* Ver. *I think him to be a Thief.* Words.

So it is material Variance, if a special Promise be laid to be upon Request, and the Verdict find it without Request. So if the Declaration be upon a Lease made by two, or by Baron and Feme, and the Jury find that one of them had nothing in the Land, or that the Baron only made the Lease, or that the two were Tenants in Common, and so several Leases; otherwise if they were Copartners. Promise. *Ibid.* 719. *pl.* 17, 22, 23, 24, 25, 26.

So in Case, that the Testator was indebted to the Plaintiff in fifty-five Pounds, and the Defendant being Administrator *in consideratione, &c.* promised to pay this; upon *Non Assumpsit,* if the Verdict find the Promise to be to pay thirty Pounds, Part of the fifty-five Pounds. *Ibid. pl.* 27.

So in Ejectment, if the Nar. be of a Lease of three Acres, a Lease of a Moiety will not maintain the Nar. *Ibid.* 720. *pl.* 29. Ejectment.

So

Waste.

So in Waste, for cutting Trees, and the Verdict find that he eradicated the Trees, but did not cut them. *Ibid. pl.* 28.

Prescription.

A Prescription *in modo decimandi,* That every one who hath seven Lambs, or under seven, shall pay to the Parson *ob.* for every Lamb, and the Jury find that; and farther, That if he had more than seven Lambs, he should pay a Lamb; and that the Parson should pay the Parishioner *ob.* This is not the same Prescription, but makes a Variance. *Ibid. pl.* 30.

Variance.

But if there be a Variance between the Verdict and the Nar. either by Way of Surplus or Defect; yet if this Matter of Variance be not material in the Extenuation of the Action or Damages, the Action shall lie notwithstanding the Variance. *Ibid.* 717. *pl.* 5.

These ensuing are adjudged not to be material.

Nar. *Strong Thief.* Verdict *Thief.* Nar. *I say, &c.* Ver. *I affirm, or I doubt not.* Nar. *The Plaintiff will do such a Thing.* Ver. *I think in my Conscience he will, &c.* Nar. Of a Lease by a Parson for five Years; if he *tam diu* should be Parson, *& tam diu viveret.* And the Ver. find the Lease to be for five Years, if he *tam diu viveret,* without the Words, *and shall continue Parson;* for the Law implieth, that if he be deprived or resign, that the Lease determines. Nar. *He is a Murderer.* Ver. *He was a Murderer;* for when he says, *He is a Murderer,* it is not intended, that he did the Act *in præsenti,* but before. So in Trespasses or Actions upon *Torts* and Wrongs which are several, if the Verdict find Part, it is no material

rial Variance; and the Plaintiff in these Cases
shall have Judgment. *Roll.* Tit. *Trial,* 717.
pl. 6, 7, 10, 12, 20, 21.

A Jury of *Middlesex* was demanded in the Inquest by
Common Pleas, the first Day of the Term, and Default.
some appeared, and some not, so that there was
not a full Jury, and neither the Defendant nor
his Attorney did appear; and therefore the
Plaintiff prayed that the Inquest might be a-
warded by Default; and by the Opinion of
Welsh and *Dyer,* his Prayer shall be granted,
and the *Custos Brevium,* and all the Prothonotaries said the Course was so, for the Parties
are demandable before the Jury; and if the
Plaintiff make Default, he shall be nonsuited;
and if the Defendant make Default, the Jury
shall be awarded by Default, whether they appear or not. *Dyer* 265.

Where an Inquest is taken by Default, the What the De-
Defendant shall lose his Challenges, and by fendant loses
28 *Ass. p.* 42. Tit. *Enquest* in *Fitz.* he shall by his De-
lose his Evidences also. *Bro. Enquest* 10. *quod* fault.
non est lex.

Det. The Defendant pleaded a Release, and When the
the Plaintiff replied *Non est factum,* and at the Defendant
Day of the *Venire facias* the Defendant made may be con-
Default, and the Inquest was taken upon his Default, and
Default, and found for the Defendant, for which when an In-
the Plaintiff took nothing by his Bill; and yet quest must be
if the Plaintiff had prayed it, he might have taken upon
had the Defendant condemned by his Default the Default.
before the taking of the Verdict. *Et sic vide*
fully in le Plaintiff, Bro. Ibid. 5. But upon such
Release and Default in Trespass, the Inquest
shall be taken by Default, and the Defendant
shall not be condemned by Default, though the
                                    Plaintiff

Plaintiff pray it; and the Reafon is, becaufe the Debt is certain, and the Damages are incertain in Trefpafs. *Bro. Ibid.* 3.

And *Finch, fol.* 409. hath well collected out of *Brook,* That always in an Action of Trefpafs, whatfoever the iffue be, Releafe, Juftification, *&c.* and alfo in Debt, Detinue, Account, and the reft which are for Things in Certainty, if the Iffue be taken upon a Matter in *fait* only, as Payment, or that an Acquittance pleaded in Bar by the Defendant was made by *Dures, &c.* The Inqueft fhall be taken by Default, if the Defendant makes Default; but in the laft recited Actions of Debt, *&c.* if the Iffue be upon the Acquittance itfelf, Releafe, or other Matter in Writing, the Plaintiff may pray Judgment upon the Defendant's Default, if he will; but if he do not pray it, the Jury fhall be taken by Default, as in an Action of Trefpafs.

Verdict with-
out or againft
Teftimony.
The Jury may give a Verdict without Teftimony, or againft Teftimony, when they themfelves have Conufance of the Fact. *Plo. Com.* 86.

The Jury are to find Cofts and Damages in Debt, Trefpafs, Ejectment, Nufance, Covenant, *&c.* in Debt for Tithes, treble Value of the Tithes, and no Cofts nor Damages.

In *Audita Querela fur Statute,* the Iffue and Value of the Land.

In Wafte, Treble Damages.

In *Quare Impedit.* 1. Whether the Church was void by the Death of the Incumbent?
2. Whether it be now full, or not? If it be full, at whofe Prefentation? And if fix Months
be

be past since the last Avoidance? And of what Value it is by the Year? And what Costs and Damages?·

The Verdict. In Dower, *Inquiratur si vir obierit seizitus de Tenementis prædict. in dominico suo ut de feodo, aut de feodo talliat. Et si ita invenerint, tunc quantum tenementa illa valent per annum in omnibus exitibus ultra reprisas, juxta verum valorem eorund. & quantum tempus dilabitur a tempore mortis præd. viri, & quæ dampna petens sustinet tam occasione detentionis dotis quam præmissorum.*

En Dower, Nota, The Jury finding the Dying seised, they must assess Costs and Damages; but if they find the Husband was seised, but did not die so, then no Costs nor Damages, but only the Value of the Land.

In Detinue. *Si pro quer. de valore rei detent. & custag. & dampna.*

In *Replevin,* Damages for both Parties, and Costs.

In Account, no Damages nor Costs.

In placito terræ. Nulla dampna nec custag. Warrantia Chartæ Consimile.

Assise Consimile.

Prohibition. *Si pro quer. tunc inquir. de exitibus & non plus.*

Partitione facienda. Si pro quer. tunc de exitibus & non plus.

En brief de Entry en le Per. Custag. & dampna.

In all real Actions, generally no more than the Issue.

In *Replevin,* if the Plaintiff be called, and do not appear, the Court takes the Verdict for the Defendant, and the Jury assess Damages and Costs. But *Nota,* That a Verdict is

4   not

not ufually taken in other Actions after the
Plaintiff is nonfuit. *Sid.* 2 Part 155.

Affident dam-
na, well in a
Verdicts.

Redwood verfus *Coward, Hill.* 8 *W.* 3. *B. R.*
Intr. Trin. 8 *W.* 3. *Rot.* 645. A Verdict was
entred *affident damna* for *affidunt,* and on a Writ
of Error, this was affigned for Error, and infifted was future. *Sed non allocatur* ; for it
may be the prefent Tenfe of the Word *Affideo* ;
however, in Verdicts the fame exactnefs of Expreffion is not required as in Pleading, for they
are the Words of a Lay Jury, and though it
may not be proper *Latin,* yet it is fo common
that it is now made good by Prefcription. *Vide
Plo.* 347. 3 *Cro.* 647. 4 *Co.* 7. And the Court
faid, it was not like *Conceffum* inftead of *Confi-
deratum eft* in a Judgment, for that thefe Words
were of different Import, and the Law requires
that Judicial Acts fhould appear to be done upon Confideration. *Salk.* 328.

Copyhold
Eftate laid
without fay-
ing *ad volun-
tatem domini,*
and held well
after Verdict,
becaufe the
Lands alledg-
ed to be Par-
cel of the
Manor.

Crouther verfus *Oldfield, Hill.* 4 *Ann. B. R.*
The Plaintiff declared ' Quod cum feifitus fu-
' iffet de uno Meffuagio & decem acris terræ
' in N. parcell. Manerii de W. ac tent. per
' copiam rotulor. Cur. Manerii illius ut tenens
' cuftumarius in feodo fimplici fecund. con-
' fuetudinem Manerii ; cumque ipfe præfat.
' quer. habeat & habere debeat, ipfeque &
' omnes tenentes cuftumarii Manerii prædict.
' per confuetud. infra Manerium ill. a tempore
' cujus, &c. habuer. & habere debuerunt &
' confueverunt communiam Pafturæ in quo-
' dam loco vocat. Waimles Moor parcell.
' dicti Manerii pro omnibus averiis commu-
' nicalibus fuper tenementa fua cuftumaria le-
' van. & cuban. tanquam ad tenementa fua
' prædict fpectan. & pertinen. prædict. tamen
' defendens,' to deprive him of his faid Com-

mon,

mon, had inclofed, *per quod, &c.* Upon Not guilty pleaded, the Plaintiff had a Verdict; but upon Motion in the *Common Pleas*, Judgment was arrefted. Upon this the Plaintiff brought a Writ of Error in *B. R.* and that Judgment was reverfed: 1ft, It was agreed in this Cafe, that a Man cannot be a Copyholder, nor an Eftate be a Copyhold Eftate, tho' it be held *per Copiam Rotulorum & fecundum confuetudinem Manerii*, unlefs it be alfo *ad voluntatem Domini*; and the Chief Juftice faid, the great Difference between Copyholds and cuftomary Freeholds which pafs by Surrender is, that the Copyholder is in by Demife from the Lord; but in the Cafe of cuftomary Freeholds, the Lord is only an Inftrument; and that in pleading a Title to a Copyhold Eftate, it is fufficient to fhew a Grant from the Lord; but in the other Cafe it is not enough to fhew, that the Lord granted it, or that *A.* furrendered to the Lord, and he granted, but it muft be fhewn that the Surrenderor was feifed in Fee and furrendered to the Lord, and he granted, *&c.* 2dly, It was agreed, That if this Eftate muft be taken to be Freehold, the Judgment of the *Common Pleas* was rightly given: For then the Plaintiff being feifed of a Freehold Eftate, to make a Title to the Common, fhould have prefcribed, that he and all thofe whofe Eftate he had, have Time out of Mind had, *&c.* and cannot make a Title by Cuftom, according to 1 *Cro.* 418. And here the Court admitted the Cafe of *Dorne* and *Cafhford*, and faid, That though the Plaintiff in Poffeffory Actions may declare upon his Poffeffion without fetting out a Title; yet if he undertakes to fet out a Title, and fhews a bad one, the Verdict

In pleading Copyhold it is fufficient to fhew the Grant of the Lord; in cuftomary Freeholds the Eftate of the Surrenderor muft be fhewn.

Verdict will not aid a bad Title when fhewn, tho' it need not have been fhewn.

Verdict cannot cure that. *Vide* 1 *Cro.* 418.
2 *Cro.* 315.   2 *Saund.* 136, 186. 1 *Mod.* 294.
But the Court held, That now after Verdict,
this Estate of the Plaintiff must be taken to be
a Copyhold Estate, and not a Freehold Estate,
because it is both laid and found, that the
Tenements were Parcel of the Manor, and that
by Custom, the Plaintiff *ut tenens custumar.* has
Common ; all which is utterly impossible, unless the Tenement was Copyhold, and therefore must be supposed such, though the Words
ad voluntatem Domini were omitted, comparing it to the Case of Debt for Rent by an
Assignee of a Reversion, who shews no Attornment, and has a Verdict, and the Case in
1 *Sid.* 218.   Upon this Foot the whole Court
held, That though a Title, which could not be
good, could never be aided by a Verdict ; yet
a Title in a Declaration which was only im-
perfectly set forth, and where the Want of
somewhat omitted might be supplied by Intendment, was cured by Verdict : And hereupon, supposing this to be a Copyhold Estate,

Verdict aids a Title defectively set forth, not a bad one. there arose these Objections: 1st, That the
Custom was not allecged expresly, *quod infra
manerium praedict. talis habetur & a tempore,
&c.* but *quod cum ipse per consuetudinem habere debeat,* which does not affirm a Custom,
but suppose it. *Vide* 4 *Co.* 31. *b. Vaug.* 251,
253. 2 *Cro.* 185. *Co. Ent.* 123. *b. Rast.* 627.
2dly, That they ought not to claim Common
tanquam ad tenementa sua spectan. & pertinent.
for it is annexed to the Estate and not to the
Land ; the Reason is because the Estate grew
by Custom, and so did the Common as Part
thereof, or rather a Privilege annexed thereto.
Vide 2 *Cro.* 253.   2 *Brownl. Entr.* 96. If a
                                                    Copyholder

Copyholder purchase the Freehold of his Copyhold, his Common is gone. As to the first Objection the Court held, that it was but a defective Title, and there was Room enough to induce a Proof of the Custom; and it was only an Informality of laying the Custom, which is cured by the Verdict. As to the second Objection the Chief Justice took this Difference, *viz.* Where a Copyholder claims Common in the Wastes of a Manor, it properly and strictly belongs to his Estate; and if he enfranchise his Copyhold, in that Case his Common is lost; but where he claims it out of the Manor, it belongs to the Land, and not to the Estate; and if he enfranchise the Estate, the Common continues: But all the Precedents of Common are, *tanquam ad tenementa sua spectan'.* 9 *Co.* 113. *Co. Ent.* 9. *Dyer* 363. *b.* 1 *Saund.* 349. 2 *Saund.* 321. *Co. Ent.* 574. *Winch Ent.* 931, 1026, 1027, 1111. *Hern.* 81. *Brown'. Red.* 428, 430. And the Chief Justice thought, that since the Pleadings were so, the Common might be said to belong to the Copyhold Tenement, since it belonged to the Copyhold Estate; for that which belongs to the Estate belongs to the Tenement, and the Judgment was reversed after great Deliberation. *V.* 1 *Lut.* 126. the Report of the Judgment of the *Common Pleas. Salk.* 364.

[margin: Diversity between Common belonging to the Estate, and to the Land.]

Upon a Writ of Enquiry, either on Demurrer or Judgment by Default, executed the last Day of a Term, the Plaintiff may enter Judgment the 5th Day after, and not before: So where there is a Verdict, there must be four Days between the Verdict and the Judgment; not that in all Cases there can be a Motion in Arrest, as in the principal Case, where the Verdict or Inquest is the last Day of the Term; but still there may be a Writ of Error, and this

[margin: There must be four Days between the Verdict and the Judgment; and between the executing a Writ of Enquiry and entring the Judgment]

Time is allowed for thefe Purpofes; and there-fore, after Verdict or Writ of Enquiry, the Courfe is for the Plaintiff to give a Rule to enable h'm to enter his Judgment *Nifi caufa oftenfa fit in contrarium infra quatuor dies;* and in the Principal Cafe, Execution was fet afide, becaufe it was fued out the 4th Day after the Term, the Writ of Enquiry being executed and returned the laft Day. *Clerk* v. *Rowland, T. 5 W. & M. B. R. Salkeld* 399.

Want of A-verment aided by Verdict. Trefpafs, the Defendant juftified by reafon of Common in the Place where, for Cattle Levant and Couchant, and did not aver that the Beafts were Levant and Couchant; but this was held to be aided by the Verdict. *Anon. T.* 21 *Car.* 2. *B. R.* 1 *Vent.* 34.

Intendment. After Verdict the Court fhall admit any Intendment to make the Cafe good. *Per* Ch. J. in the Cafe of *Pollexfen* and *Afhford* v. *Crifpin,* 23 *C.* 2. in *B. R.* and *Twifden* cited a Cafe which was in Trefpafs; *Quare Phafianos fuos cepit,* and the Plaintiff had Judgment after Verdict; for it fhall be intended they were dead Pheafants. 1 *Ventris* 123.

Privy Verdict in an Information, but not in Cafe of Treafon or Felony. *The King* verfus *Ledgingham, Mich.* 22 *Car.* 2. *B. R.* In an Information againft him for the King, the Court took a privy Verdict, and fo as was faid was the ufual Courfe at the Affizes, but it cannot be fo in Cafes of Felony or Treafon, as is faid in 1 *Inft.* 227. *b.* In

Verdict may be given out of the County. Cafes of Life and Member, if the Jury cannot agree before the Judges depart, they are to be carried in Carts after them; fo that they may give their Verdict out of the County. 1 *Ventris* 97.

Verdict a-mended by Notes. *The King* verfus *Kent, Hill.* 8 & 9 *W.* 3. *B. R.* A Verdict General or Special may be amended by the Notes of the Clerk of Affize; but this is in Civil, not in Criminal Cafes. *Vide* 1 *Ro. Rep.* 82. *Salkeld* 47.   Bifhop

Bishop of *Worcester*'s Case, *Mich.* 8 *W.* 3. *Ejectment versus 7 Defendants, and all join in the common Rule, and the Issue was right in the Plea roll, &c. but the Nisi prius Roll was versus 5 only; and after Verdict pro Quer. this was amended by adding the other two Defendants.*
B. R. Ejectment against seven Defendants, who enter into the common Rule for confessing Lease, Entry and Ouster, and plead to Issue: The Plea-roll was right, so was the *Venire, Distringas,* and the *Jurata;* but the Issue in the *Nisi prius* Roll was between the Plaintiff and five Defendants only, which was tried, and Verdict *pro Quer.* and an Amendment being moved for, it was opposed, because it was to alter the Verdict, to subject the Jury to an Attaint, to make another Issue, and to make two Defendants guilty who were not tried: But it was amended; for nothing could be inquired of but the Title of the Lessor, and the Issue depended on his Title, which is not altered by this Amendment.   And it must be considered that all seven entred into the common Rule, and that the Plea-roll, &c. are all Right; and this cannot be intended other than the same Issue, and the Amendment is only to rectify a plain Mistake, and make that the Issue which was apparently intended to be so. *Salkeld* 48.

Child versus *Harvey, Mich.* 11 *W.* 3. B. R. *In the Distringas the Day of Nisi prius was appointed after the Day in Bank, and after Verdict held not amendable by the Plea roll, because the Judges Authority was confined to that Day.*
A *Scire facias* on a Recognizance; upon Issue *Non solvit* it was found for the Plaintiff: Mr. *Northey* moved to set aside the Verdict, because in the *Distringas* and *Jurata* the Return was *a die Sanctæ Trin. in tres Sept. nisi Johannes Holt, Mil.* 27 *die Junii prius venerit,* the twenty-seventh Day of *June* being the Morrow after *tres Trin.* But the Plea-roll was right, for the Award there was *tres Mich.* It was agreed on all sides, that the Trial must be set aside unless the Mistake could be amended, because it appeared the Judge had no Authority to try the Issue; and the Court held it could not be amended. The Court agreed, That

where

Where the Nisi prius Roll may be amended by the Plea roll, and where not.

where the *Distringas* or *Jurata* are right, and the Amendment does not alter the Point in Issue, the *Nisi prius* Roll may be amended by the Plea-roll. So it was in the Bishop of *Worcester's* Case, and there the *Distringas* and *Jurata* were right. 2 *Cro.* 353. *Dyer* 260. *Hut.* 81. 1 *Cro.* 596. But here neither *Distringas* nor *Jurata* are right. The Day appointed for the *Nisi prius* is impossible; and the Judge's Authority is confined to the Day. And where a Judge's Authority is confined to a Day, his Trial at another Day must be without Authority. *Salkeld* 48, 49.

Insufficient Return of Devastavit aided by the Verdict.

Brook versus *Ellis, Pas. 5 W. & M. B. R.* Upon a *Devastavit* suggested against both Executors, *viz. A.* and *B.* the Writ was to the Sheriff to inquire of a Wasting by both; the Sheriff returned a *Devastavit* as to *A.* but said nothing as to *B.* This being assigned for Error, after Judgment upon a Verdict, was held to be aided by the Verdict, being but an insufficient Return or Misreturn, by reason of the Omission; otherwise if no Return at all. *V.* 3 *Cro.* 587. 3 *Co.* 81. *Noy* 72. *Cro. Car.* 295, 312. *Salkeld* 363.

Court must judge according to the Verdict.

When a Verdict is found there can be nothing added to it, or taken from it; but as it is found, so the Court must judge of it, and whatever is found in a Verdict, whereupon the Court can give any Judgment, must be positively found, not ambiguously; for if the Jury doubt, the Court can never resolve the Matter of Fact: And *Shower* held, That if the Jury do find positively the Matter of Argument, and do not make the Conclusion *de facto,* the Court shall reject the Matter of Argument, and give Judgment to the contrary: And for this cited *Cro. Car.* 549. *Crisp* and *Pratt's* Case, where Issue being joined upon a Fraud, it was

adjudged

adjudged there, That though there be never ſo many Circumſtances of a Fraud found, unleſs the Jury find it to be a Fraud, the Court ſhall adjudge it to be none. *Shower* 539.

Peachy verſus *Harriſon, Trin.* 9 *W.* 3. *C. B.* It is not a good Exception in Arreſt of Judgment, that there is no Warrant of Attorney filed, tho' that be Matter of Record, and may be aſſigned for Error. The Reaſon is, becauſe tho' it be a Matter of Record, yet it is not of that Record before the Court, but of another. *Salk.* 77.

What Matter of Record may be taken Advantage of in Arreſt of Judgment, and what not.

Anonymus, Paſ. 11 *W.* 3. *B. R.* Indictment in *B. R.* for a Miſdemeanor, was tried three Days before the End of the Term, and Judgment was entered the ſame Term ; ſo that the Defendant had not four Days to move in Arreſt of Judgment. And the Queſtion was, Whether this Entry of the Judgment was regular, and whether it ſhould not have been ſtayed till the Term following? *Et per Holt,* C. J. If there be four Days and more between the Trial and the End of the Term, Judgment ought not to be entered within the four Days; but if the *Diſtringas* be returnable within the Term, and the Party is tried within two or three Days before the End of the Term, the Judgment ſhall be entered that Term, tho' there be not four Days to move in Arreſt of Judgment ; ſo it was ſettled in the Caſe of *Knox* and *Levarr,* upon a Conference between *Scrogs* C. J. and Sir *William Jones* Attorney General, contrary to the Report of Sir *Samuel Aſtrey.*

If the Diſtringas be returnable within Term, and there happen not to be four Days between the Trial and the End of the Term, yet Judgment ſhall be entered that Term.

' Arreſt of Judgment is either for Matter
' intrinſick, that is, ſuch as appears by the
' Record itſelf, which will render the Judgment
' erroneous, and reverſible ; or extrinſick, *i. e.*
' ſome foreign Matter ſuggeſted to the Court,
' which proves the Writ is abated, for it is
                                            ' not

Two Ways of taking Advantage in Arreſt of Judgment.

' not enough that it proves the Writ is only a-
' bateable: The old Course of taking Advan-
' tage in Arreft of Judgment was thus: The
' Party after a general Verdict, having a Day
' in Court, (for fo he has as to Matters of
' Law, tho' not of Fact) did affign his Excep-
' tions in Arreft of Judgment by Way of Plea;
' and it was called Pleading in Arreft of Judg-
' ment. This differed from moving in Ar-
' reft of Judgment, which was done by one as
' *Amicus Curiæ,* where the Party was out of
' Court. *Vide Co. Entr.* 295. *b.* the Manner of
' doing it'. *Vide* 2 *Ro.* 716. 9 *E.* 11. *a.* 4 *H.*
7. 9. 5 *H.* 7. 23. *Raft.* 107. *Salkeld.* 77, 78.

The Courfe of moving in Arreft of Judgment. It is againft the antient Courfe of the Court to make a Rule to ftay Judgment, unlefs the *Poftea* be brought in; but the Court, if there be probable Caufe fhewn, will order the *Poftea* to be brought in. *Et per Cur',* If one moves in Arreft of Judgment, he ought to give Notice to the Clerk in Court of the other Side; but the better Way is to give a Rule upon the *Poftea* for bringing it into Court, for that is a Notice of itfelf. *Wood* verfus *Shephard, T.* 2 *Ann. B. R. Salkeld* 78.

Where a Divorce fhall be intended after Verdict. *Deerly* verfus the Dutchefs of *Mazarine, Hill.* 8 *W.* 3. *B. R. Affumpfit* for Wages and Money lent; on *Non Affumpfit,* the Defendant proved fhe was married, and her Hufband alive in *France:* The Jury found for the Plaintiff; upon which, as a Verdict againft Evidence, fhe moved for a new Trial; but it was denied; for it fhall be intended fhe was divorced. *Salk.* 116.

Want of Averment aided by the Verdict. Indorfee declared on a Bill of Exchange againft the Drawer; and the Bill was, *Pray pay this my firft Bill of Exchange, my fecond and third not being paid*; and the Indorfement was fet out in this Manner, that the Drawee *indorfavit* *dorsavit super billam illam, content. billæ illius solvend.* to the Plaintiff, without shewing that it was subscribed. On *Non Assumpsit,* and Verdict *pro Quer.* It was objected in Arrest of Judgment, that there was no Averment, that the second and third Bill was not paid, which is a Condition precedent: *Sed non allocatur. Et per Cur',* That must be intended, for the Plaintiff could not otherwise have had a Verdict: And for the same Reason also, the Indorsement, which was likewise excepted against as set forth in the Declaration, was held good, being aided by the Verdict; the Court comparing it to an Action of Debt by an Assignee of a Reversion, without shewing an Attornment, which on *Non debet* is aided by Verdict; for if the Indorsement be necessary to transfer the Bill, so is the Attornment to pass the Reversion. *Ergo,* as the Attornment shall be supplied by the Jury's finding *Debet,* so shall the Indorsement by their finding *Assumpsit. East* v. *Essington,* M. 1. *Ann.* B. R. *Salkeld* 130.

Action on a promissory Note against the second Indorsor, and the Plaintiff declared without any Averment, that the Money was demanded of the Drawer, or the first Indorsor. And this was held good upon Motion in Arrest of Judgment; for the Indorsor charges himself in the same Manner as if he had originally drawn the Bill. *Harry* versus *Petit,* T. 9 *Ann.* B. R. *Salkeld* 133.

Want of Averment, that the Money was demanded of the Drawer, no Cause for arresting Judgment.

The Defendant was indicted before Justices of the Peace, and pleaded Not guilty; and after the Jury were gone out to consider of their Verdict, he deliver'd in a *Certiorari*; and the Justices return'd the Verdict; and it was held well; for it cannot be delivered after the Jury is sworn. *Rex* versus *North,* H. 8 W. 3. B. R.

Certiorari not to be served after the Jury sworn.

B. R. Salkeld 144. See 1 *Sid.* 317. 2 *Keb.* 138. 141, *&c.* 6 *Mod.* 17, 61, 62. 1 *Sid.* 296. 1 *Mod.* 41.

Difcontinuance by Leave of the Court may be after fpecial Verdict, not after general.

Price verfus *Parker, Paf.* 8 *W.* 3. *B. R.* Upon a Motion to difcontinue upon Payment of Cofts, the Court held, That after a general Verdict there can be no Leave given to difcontinue; but that after a Special Verdict there may, becaufe that is not compleat and final; but in that Cafe it is a great Favour. The fame Point was fo ruled, *inter Reeve* and *Gelding, Paf.* 5 *& 6 W. & M. B. R. Salkeld* 178. See 1 *Lev* 48, 227, 298. 2 *Lev.* 118, 124. 1 *Sid.* 60, 84, 306. 1 *Mod.* 13, 41. 2 *Danv.* 156. 1 *Saund.* 23, 339. 2 *Saund.* 73. *Far.* 5.

Two Counts in Nar. for Things of the fame Kind, not averred to be different: Helped by the Verdict.

Weft verfus *Troles, Mic.* 9 *W.* 3. *B. R.* The Plaintiff declared, That whereas the Defendant 6 *Maii* 1695, for 120 Weeks Diet then paft, had promifed to pay him 7 *s. per* Week, and that the Plaintiff *poftea, fcil.* 6 *Maii* 1695, having found the Defendant Diet 120 Weeks then paft, the Defendant promifed to pay the Worth, and that it was worth 7 *s. per* Week: Upon *Non Affumpfit* and Verdict *pro quer.* it was now moved in Arreft of Judgment, that the Weeks in the *Quantum meruit* are not faid to be *aliæ* than thofe laid in the fpecial Promife, fo that the Defendant is twice charged for the fame Thing. *Sed non allocatur;* for they do not appear neceffarily to be the fame, and without Neceffity the Court will not intend them fo. *Salkeld* 213. See *Far.* 149.

The End of the Firft Volume.